Differentiating Instruction for Learners with Special Needs

Differentiating Instruction for Learners with Special Needs

An Anthology

First Edition

Edited by Barry W. Birnbaum
Western Illinois University

cognella®
SAN DIEGO

Bassim Hamadeh, CEO and Publisher

Angela Schultz, Senior Field Acquisitions Editor

Michelle Piehl, Senior Project Editor

Celeste Paed, Associate Production Editor

Emely Villavicencio, Senior Graphic Designer

Greg Isales, Licensing Associate

Natalie Piccotti, Director of Marketing

Kassie Graves, Senior Vice President of Editorial

Jamie Giganti, Director of Academic Publishing

Cover image copyright © 2011 Depositphotos/monkeybusiness.

Printed in the United States of America.

3970 Sorrento Valley Blvd., Ste. 500, San Diego, CA 92121

Contents

Introduction   vii

Part 1   Special Education and the Law   1

Reading 1.1   Introduction: Making the Case for Special Education Legal Literacy   3
Kevin P. Brady, Charles J. Russo, Cynthia A. Dieterich, Allan G. Osborne, Jr., and Nicole D. Snyder

Reading 1.2   Historical Development of Laws Impacting Students with Disabilities   33
Kevin P. Brady, Charles J. Russo, Cynthia A. Dieterich, Allan G. Osborne, Jr., and Nicole D. Snyder

Reading 1.3   The Emergence of Special and Inclusive Educatio: USA   60
Sally Tomlinson

Reading 1.4   IQ, Ability, and Eugenics   76
Sally Tomlinson

Topics for Further Discussion   99

Part 2   Differentiated Instruction   101

Reading 2.1   Differentiated Instruction: An Integration of Theory and Practice   102
Carol Ann Tomlinson, Marcia B. Imbeau

Reading 2.2   Role-Playing in an Inclusive Classroom: Using Realistic Simulation to Explore Differentiated Instruction   137
Peter Clyde Martin

Reading 2.3   Technology as a Differentiated Instruction Tool   150
Ann M. De Lay

Reading 2.4   Classroom Routines, Motivation, and Effective Learning   156
Rhonda Bondie and Akane Zusho

Reading 2.5   Peer Mediation: A Means of Differentiating Classroom Instruction   183
Douglas Fuchs, Lynn S. Fuchs, Adina Shamir, Eric Dion, Laura M. Saenz, and Kristen L. McMaster

Reading 2.6   The Changing Extremes in Our Classrooms   207
Rhonda Bondie and Akane Zusho

Reading 2.7   Differentiated Instruction   225
John P. W. Hudson

Reading 2.8   Selections from Using Differentiated Classroom Assessment to Enhance Student
Learning   233
Tonya R. Moon, Catherine M. Brighton, and Carol A. Tomlinson

Topics for Further Discussion   265

Part 3   Universal Design for Learning   267

Reading 3.1   Expert Classroom Instruction for Students with Reading Disabilities: Explicit,
Intense, Targeted ... and Flexible   268
Ruth Wharton-McDonald

Reading 3.2   The Three-Block Model of Universal Design for Learning (UDL): Engaging
Students in Inclusive Education   285
Jennifer Katz

Reading 3.3   Addressing Learner Variability on Campus Through Universal Design for Learning   313
Shannon Haley-Mize

Reading 3.4   Developing Literacy in English Language Learners: Findings from a Review of the
Experimental Research   327
Diane August, Peggy McCardle, and Timothy Shanahan

Topics for Further Discussion   341

In Closing   343

Introduction

AS YOU BEGIN YOUR JOURNEY IN special education, I want to share with you some important details about this text. For some of you, this is a new experience, while others may have had the opportunity to work with this type of material before. This is not your standard textbook but one that focuses on the course content in a more organized manner. Each of the readings you will find here demonstrates an understanding of the course material and expectations. The articles and content are organized by topic and will follow the pattern of the course presentation. The material you read will be supplemented by course slides and other matter. This should help you as you learn about the laws that govern special education, differentiated instruction, and Universal Design for Learning. These are the three main components of the course, and this text should help you focus on these approaches.

Additionally, the readings are current and appropriate for the study of various disabilities that will be covered during the semester. Your goals are to understand how to work with children who are exceptional in the general classroom and to apply strategies for teaching them in that inclusive environment. The law states that all children with disabilities are provided an opportunity to learn with their nondisabled peers. This inclusive approach means that you will have students in your class who might struggle but can be given every opportunity to learn and be engaged. It is your responsibility to differentiate your lessons to accommodate these individuals so that they can participate and learn like everyone else.

Look for relationships between the text and the observations you have made during your visits to classes. Review the slides to see what similarities there are and how these can help you become a more effective teacher and mentor. Working with all children takes a special talent and requires that you are patient and willing to work with all children, regardless of ability.

I hope you find this text to be interesting and informative. It should provide you with opinions on topics that you can apply in your teaching. I encourage you to take advantage of the material and outline those points that you find helpful in the classroom. Look for strategies that will engage all learners in the process of gaining mastery of the topics you present. Be sure that you both provide equal opportunities for learning and demonstrate an understanding of the theories and practices you will learn in this course.

Part I

Special Education and the Law

Special education is governed by federal law. Since the 1970s, students with disabilities have been taught in the least restrictive environment (LRE) and have received a free, appropriate public education (FAPE). The law has evolved to the present time, in which all children are taught in the general education classroom along with their nondisabled peers. This is known as inclusion and is the law of the land. Every student is provided an opportunity to learn, regardless of ability, and is included in all aspects of classroom management.

The law provides specific expectations for teaching, and the classroom teacher works with the team to ensure that appropriate instruction is being provided. Collaboration is expected, and all members of the Child Study Team work together to form a meaningful learning process for students with disabilities. Many court cases have been decided based on these laws, which are driven by inclusive practices. When a student is determined to be eligible for services in special education, an Individualized Education Plan (IEP) is developed by the entire team. You will be involved in this process of writing goals and objectives for the student.

The person with whom you will work most closely is the special education teacher. You will work together to find ways to modify the curriculum so that the student with special needs can learn. This collaborative effort is essential to student success, and your input is valued, as you will be driving the instruction. There are many ways you can teach that will reach all students, and you will have the opportunity to watch them grow and mature.

The laws are written to protect the students, and you will be expected to understand the concepts as they apply to teaching all learners. You will be expected to provide adaptations and accommodations where necessary. You might find that some of these approaches work well for other students in your classroom. As the law continues to evolve, be ready to apply these changes to support instruction for all learners.

Guided Questions

1. Why is it important to understand how the law impacts educators working with students with disabilities?
2. What legal obligations must be met when working with students with disabilities?
3. How do the laws that govern special education impact the quality of the teaching that students with disabilities receive?
4. How can you best be certain that the instruction you are implementing meets the requirements and implications of the law?
5. What are some advantages of using the Child Study Team to enhance and improve instruction for students with disabilities?

Reading 1.1

Introduction

Making the Case for Special Education Legal Literacy

Kevin P. Brady, Charles J. Russo, Cynthia A. Dieterich, Allan G. Osborne, Jr., and Nicole D. Snyder

Key Concepts and Terms in This Chapter

- Ignorance of the law is not always an excuse to liability
- Special education legal literacy
- Case-based learning (CBL) model
- Exhaustion of administrative remedies rule

Ignorantia Juris Non Excusat

The Latin maxim "ignorantia juris non excusat" is roughly translated to "ignorance of the law is no excuse" and represents a fairly long-standing U.S. legal tradition that individuals claiming they are unaware of a particular law(s) or principle(s) may not escape legal liability by simply indicating that they are either unaware or not knowledgeable of the law's content (Ballentine, 1916). According to Littleton (2008), the increasing "legalization of the educational environment" combined with educators' overall lack of knowledge related to legal concerns and issues taking place in schools is a major problem that needs to be addressed (p. 76). Presently, considerable research evidence suggests that today's educators and school administrators are either improperly prepared or not trained at all to effectively handle a majority of the legal situations they encounter on a regular basis in school environments (Bull & McCarthy, 1995; Imber, 2008; McCarthy, 2008; Pazey & Cole, 2013; Zirkel, 2006). One potential benefit of the "ignorantia juris non excusat" principle is that it provides an incentive and opportunity for individuals to educate themselves and become more knowledgeable about the law. As stated by Davies (1998)

Citizens are compelled either to know the law or to proceed in ignorance at their own peril. While sometimes harsh, the gains secured by the maxim—a better educated and more law-abiding citizenry, and the avoidance of pervasive mistake of law claims—are thought to outweigh any individual injustice resulting from its application.

(p. 343)

Given the ongoing, worldwide expansion, reliance, and accessibility to online sources for our daily information, it is often much easier and less costly today for people to better educate themselves about the law and its implications. Significant technological developments in the ability to access online, digitalized legal information, including legal information related to children and youth with disabilities has the real possibility to "dramatically change the nature of legal information from an economy of scarcity to one that is abundant with information and accessible to a wide audience" (Brady & Bathon, 2012, p. 589). As will be discussed in more detail in Chapter 3, there is a current, ongoing movement to make online digitalized legal information, including legal cases, documents, and specialized legal commentary related to education much more accessible to everyone for viewing and sharing with others at little to no cost (Brady & Bathon, 2012). A clear social justice and equity-centered benefit of improved online access to special education legal information is increased access, especially to those individuals, groups/organizations, or school systems without the appropriate financial resources to pay for accurate, quality, computer-assisted legal information and research (Pazey & Cole, 2013). Thus, improving and maintaining one's special education legal literacy through an awareness of available online special education-related legal resources is "likely to find a sizable receptive audience in the diverse education law community" (Brady & Bathon, 2012, p. 596). As will become apparent quite quickly, special education law uses many acronyms. Table 1.1.1 depicts many of the most common acronyms used in special education law.

TABLE 1.1.1 Common Acronyms Used in Special Education Law, Practices, and Procedures

Acronym	Term
AAC	Augmentative and Alternative Communication
ADA	Americans with Disabilities Act
ADD	Attention Deficit Disorder
ADHD	Attention Deficit Hyperactivity Disorder
ASD	Autism Spectrum Disorder
AT	Assistive Technology
BD	Behavior Disorder
BIP	Behavior Intervention Plan
CAP	Corrective Action Plan

Acronym	Term
CCEIS	Comprehensive Coordinated Early Intervening Services
C.F.R.	Code of Federal Regulations
DD	Developmental Disabilities; Developmental Delay
EC	Early Childhood
ED	Emotional Disturbance
EDGAR	Education Department General Administrative Regulations
EIS	Early Intervening Services
ESA	Educational Service Agency
ESY	Extended School Year
FAPE	Free Appropriate Public Education
FBA	Functional Behavioral Assessment
FERPA	Family Educational Rights and Privacy Act
FR	Federal Register
IAES	Interim Alternative Educational Setting
ID	Intellectual Disability
IDEA	Individuals with Disabilities Education Act
IEE	Independent Educational Evaluation
IEP	Individualized Education Program
IFSP	Individualized Family Services Plan
ILC	Independent Living Center
ISP	Individualized Service Plan
LD	Learning Disability
LEA	Local Educational Agency (e.g., school district)
LEP	Limited English Proficiency
LRE	Least Restrictive Environment
MDR	Manifestation Determination Review
MTSS	Multi-Tiered System of Support
NCLB	No Child Left Behind
OCR	Office of Civil Rights, U.S. Department of Education
OHI	Other Health Impairment
OSEP	Office of Special Education Programs, U.S. Department of Education
OSERS	Office of Special Education and Rehabilitative Services, U.S. Department of Education
OT	Occupational Therapy
PBS	Positive Behavioral Supports
PWN	Prior Written Notice
SEA	State Educational Agency

(Continued)

TABLE 1.1.1 *(Continued)*

Acronym	Term
Section 504	Section 504 of the Rehabilitation Act of 1973
SPP	State Performance Plan
TA	Technical Assistance
U.S.C.	United States Code
VI	Visual Impairment

Current State of Special Education Legal Illiteracy in Our Schools

Based on a review of the research literature, legal and educational researchers stress the need to improve the current state of legal literacy among today's educators and building and district-level administrators, as well as the many individuals employed within school settings (Decker & Brady, 2016; Davidson & Algozzine, 2002; DiPaola & Walther-Thomas, 2003; Pazey & Cole, 2013; Painter, 2001; Powell, 2010; Osterman & Hafner, 2009; Zirkel & Lupini, 2003). The current state of insufficient legal awareness and knowledge among educators, school and district-level leadership, and school employees appears to be particularly acute in the area of special education (Bineham, 2014; Davidson & Algozzine, 2002; Decker & Pazey, 2017; Herbst, 2004; Militello, Schimmel, & Eberwein, 2009; Painter, 2001; Powell, 2010; Wagner & Katsiyannis, 2010; Yell, 2019). Despite nearly a half century of increased legal protections at both the federal and state levels assisting students with disabilities, many of the individuals who work closely with today's students with disabilities remain either uninformed or unaware of the legal rights and policies designed to protect students with disabilities (Umpstead, Decker, Brady, Schimmel, & Militello, 2015). Unfortunately, this lack of legal literacy is not without negative implications, including the unequal treatment, discrimination, and even abuse of students with disabilities in schools (Umpstead, Decker, Brady, Schimmel, & Militello, 2015). This introductory chapter begins with the premise that actively addressing and maintaining one's special education legal literacy can more effectively serve the interests and needs of children and youth with disabilities enrolled in schools. While the significance and overall impact of the law in contemporary schools is increasing nationwide, the research evidence suggests that today's educators and the variety of other school employees who work closely with students are often either ill-informed or completely unaware of critical legal knowledge directly related to their jobs (McCarthy, 2016; Decker, 2014; Gullat & Tollet, 1997). The direct and applicable benefits to educators and school employees of a having a better knowledge and understanding of the law as it impacts schools are significant, including the ability to "recognize the extent and limits of their discretion, to exercise leadership, to use the law to advance policy objectives, to avoid unnecessary litigation, and to make optimal use of limited resources" (Heubert, 1997, p. 566).

A lack of legal knowledge among contemporary school leaders, educators, parents, and other school employees is particularly evident as it relates to legal issues, policies, and practices involving students with disabilities (Umpstead, Decker, Brady, Schimmel, & Militello, 2015). Legal scholars maintain that special education legal compliance is one of the leading and "most contentious" topics involving the myriad of legal issues impacting schools (Eckes, 2008, pp. 8–9). Based on recent statistics, it is evident that the number of students receiving special education and related services is steadily rising. During the 2015–16 school year, for example, the number of eligible students ages three through twenty-one receiving special education services was calculated at approximately 6.7 million, or 13 percent of all enrolled public-school students in the U.S. (McFarland et al., 2018). It is a misconception to conclude that legal concerns of students with disabilities are restricted to special education teachers with classes comprised exclusively of students with disabilities. Instead, it is estimated that more than half of students identified with disabilities are enrolled in today's general education classrooms across the country (Institute of Education Sciences, 2010). While today's students with disabilities in the U.S. are afforded numerous legal entitlements and protections, a combination of confusion, misinformation, and general lack of legal knowledge has negatively impacted the delivery of legally mandated special education and related services to eligible students with disabilities. As a result, special education-related lawsuits are increasingly becoming a more common area of legal action initiated by parents against schools (Karanxha & Zirkel, 2014; Katsiyannis & Herbst, 2004).

While many of today's educational organizations recognize legal information and knowledge as an essential professional competency for today's educators, few states actually mandate training specifically targeting legal issues that impact schools as part of their pre-service or ongoing professional development for either educators or school administrators (Militello, Schimmel, & Eberwein, 2009). For over a half century, researchers have recommended that teachers and administrators receive additional and specialized legal training (McCarthy, 2008; Reglin, 1992). An increasing number of studies reveal a significant correlation between legal training and increased legal knowledge (Bull & McCarthy, 1995; Eberwein, 2008). Relatedly, other national surveys indicate that a majority of educators report not feeling legally prepared to properly handle legal issues arising in their own schools (Militello, Schimmel, & Eberwein, 2009). Despite real perceptions of feeling unprepared to handle legal concerns in schools, the research shows that surveyed school leaders and educators indicate a genuine desire to want more specialized training in legal issues, specifically the myriad of legal issues involving special education (Davidson & Algozzine, 2002).

Additionally, existing research reveals the need for substantially greater legal training for today's pre-service and in-service educators (Fischer, Schimmel, & Stellman, 2007; Gullatt & Tollett, 1997). For example, Gajda (2008) found that only one state currently requires its pre-service teachers to complete a single course in school law or a related course. In order to make better and more informed legal decisions involving students with disabilities, today's school administrators and educators must do more than simply learn the fundamentals of special education law (Decker & Pazey, 2017). Instead, the expectation should be that all school employees who work directly with students with disabilities and their families are taught the relevant skills of applying the law to the specific situations they encounter. In other words, school officials must not only be legally knowledgeable, but they must also be legally literate. Decker and Brady (2016) have defined legal literacy as:

> the legal knowledge, understanding, and skills that enable educators to apply relevant legal rules to their everyday practice. Those who are legally literate are able to spot legal issues, identify applicable laws or legal standards, and apply the relevant legal rules to solve legal dilemmas.
>
> (p. 231)

The research literature has identified the need to significantly increase the special education legal literacy of today's school communities (Decker & Brady, 2016; Katsiyannis & Herbst, 2004; Pazey & Cole, 2013; Wagner & Katsiyannis, 2010). More specifically, research evidence supports that an overwhelming majority of today's educators and school administrators receive little to no specialized training in legal issues involving special education (Eberwein, 2009; Militello & Schimmel, 2008). For instance, the overwhelming majority of college and university-level school administrator preparation programs in the U.S. currently do not require aspiring school principals to complete any formal coursework in legal aspects of special education (Bineham, 2014; Pazey & Cole, 2013; Powell, 2010). Decker and Brady (2016) argue that special education legal literacy must be prioritized in today's schools based on four primary justifications, including

1. Students with disabilities are already guaranteed a unique set of both federal and state-level legal protections and entitlements;
2. Existing research provides compelling evidence that a majority of today's educators as well as school-level administrators educators are significantly underprepared to competently handle special education-related legal situations;
3. Most schools are experiencing increases in legal challenges involving students with disabilities; and
4. Many of these special education-related legal challenges could be properly addressed with more effective and specialized training in special education legal concepts and principles.

Inadequate Professional Development and Specialized Legal Training

Administrators, educators, and pre-service teachers are not adequately trained in special education law despite the unique legal protections given to student with disabilities. According to Schimmel and Militello (2008), school principals rarely realize that they are "the chief teachers of law in their schools" (p. 54). In fact, the advice principals provide is "a mixture of accurate, inaccurate, and ambiguous" information that may confuse and misinform educators (Militello, Schimmel, & Eberwein, 2009, p. 39). It is especially problematic that today's school-level leadership lack requisite legal knowledge considering that one of their professional and ethical responsibilities is to ensure that all school employees comply with existing special education laws and practices serving eligible students with disabilities enrolled in their schools.

To date, for example, only two large-scale, multistate studies measuring educators' legal knowledge exist. In the first study, Schimmel and Militello (2007) surveyed 1,317 elementary though secondary public-school teachers across 17 states and concluded that approximately half of those educators who were surveyed were either uninformed or misinformed about the law. The authors of the study determined that "teachers' primary source of information and misinformation about school law was from other teachers who were often similarly uninformed" (p. 257). Eighty-five percent of the surveyed teachers indicated that they had not taken a school law-related course during their teacher preparation program while only 9 percent had previously taken a school law course since they started teaching. Schimmel and Militello's study reiterated previous concerns that teachers lacked legal literacy and offered new, additional research-based findings concerning the primary sources of teachers' legal information as well as direct implications involving the relationship between a teacher's legal literacy level(s) and how it impacts their professional practice as educators.

In addition to the legal literacy studies measuring principals' and teachers' legal knowledge, a few studies have examined whether pre-service teachers have received adequate legal training and professional development (Bruner & Bartlett, 2008). In a second study of pre-service teachers, Gullatt and Tollett (1997) discovered that only two states required pre-service teachers to complete an education law-related course. Specifically, this study also identified that over two-thirds of the 480 Louisiana teachers surveyed did not complete a postsecondary-level course in education law, and consequently, many reported feeling "under-prepared in all legal areas of education" (Gullatt & Tollett, p. 133).

Furthermore, traditional public schools are not the only schools facing legal illiteracy. Evidence also suggests today's charter schools are experiencing significant challenges in addressing special education-related legal issues within their school environments (Garda, 2011; Drame, 2011; Estes, 2009). For instance, students with disabilities have been sometimes illegally counseled away from enrolling in charter schools and school officials have admitted to feeling unprepared to serve students with disabilities in charter school environments (Drame, 2011).

The Use of Case-Based Learning (CBL) to Address the Special Education Legal Literacy Gap

A review of existing research suggests that the adoption of a case-based learning, commonly referred to as CBL, can be an effective method for teaching the law to various members of today's educational community, especially instruction pertaining to relevant legal principles and strategies drawn from actual legal cases involving students (Decker & Pazey, 2017). In a review of the literature, Williams (2005) describes how CBL adopts collaborative learning, facilitates the integration of learning, develops students' intrinsic and extrinsic motivation to learn, encourages learner self-reflection and critical reflection, allows for scientific inquiry, integrates knowledge and practice, and supports the development of a variety of learning skills. If used appropriately, the case method instructional model can be effectively used to facilitate training and professional development initiatives for educators and school employees (Leko, Brownell, Sindelar, & Murphy, 2012; McNergney, Ducharme, & Ducharme, 1999a). For example, a case-based instructional model affords educators the opportunity to examine specific details associated with an individual legal case as well as analyze a legally viable course of action grounded on legal principles and precedent discussed in the legal case (McNergney, Ducharme, & Ducharme, 1999b). Additionally, reading school-level legal cases actually exposes educators to alternative perspectives and potentially conflicting ethical and legal considerations, as well as the unique subtleties of a particular legal situation in a specific school environment. Moreover, all of these discussions allow the "learner" the unique opportunity to contemplate their own personal reactions and decision-making process in a "simulated and safe environment" but that also reflects situations and dilemmas that closely replicate what they can expect to encounter in their own school environments (Rodriguez, Gentilucci, & Sims, 2006).

Established legal case-based method of instruction as used extensively in legal education for over a century can be successfully transferred from a traditional legal education context to develop effective, contextualized learning environments for educators (Decker & Pazey, 2017; Lasky & Karge, 2006; Williams, 1992). Since the late nineteenth century, the dominant teaching method adopted by U.S. law schools across the country is the legal case method, which is often characterized by teacher-led, group-based discussions (Williams, 1992). The creation of the case method has been credited to Christopher Langdell, who became the dean of Harvard Law School in 1870. Presently, legal case-based instruction is used extensively at almost every accredited law school nationwide and provides law students with a useful structure for organizing legal knowledge that can be applied in professional practice. A major assumption of the legal case method instructional process is that it will assist individuals to learn and recognize important legal concepts and principles though the reading of actual situations that have already taken place. The authors of this book maintain that the legal case-based learning model holds significant potential for improving the special education legal literacy levels of those persons who work closely with children and youth with disabilities in educational settings.

The use of case-based learning requires learners to not only to acquire legal knowledge but simultaneously develop the necessary analytical thinking required for improving and maintaining their legal literacy, which for the purposes of this book is defined as "the legal knowledge, understanding, and skills enabling educators to apply relevant legal rules to their everyday practice" (Decker & Brady, 2016, p. 231). As illustrated in Figure 1.1.1, case-based learning (CBL) can be used as a conceptual learning model for improving a person's special education legal literacy, especially for those in the education profession. The following seven steps can be applied to someone using the legal cases in this book as a means to learn more about important special education legal concepts and principles. These seven steps in a CBL–based model approach to improving special education legal literacy include:

1. Legal case is established
2. Legal case is analyzed in groups
3. Brainstorming occurs among group members

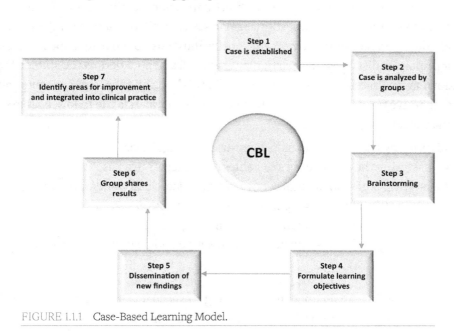

FIGURE 1.1.1   Case-Based Learning Model.

4. Formulate learning objectives surrounding the legal case
5. Dissemination of new findings
6. Group share results
7. Identify areas for improvement and integrate into clinical, or professional practice

Case-Based Learning (CBL) in Practice: Special Education Law in Practice

As a review of the existing research literature supports, today's schools are faced with the problem of a sizable gap in educators' and other school employees' lack of appropriate training and professional development addressing the unique legal protections and entitlements for eligible students with disabilities (Miles, 2011; MacNaughton, Hall, & Maccini, 2001; Merseth, 1990). The authors of this book believe that including specific, school-level legal cases combined with appropriate discussion of relevant legal concepts and principles as they impact eligible students with disabilities is an effective method to inform professional practitioners in education about the law and thus improve their overall special education legal literacy.

As seen with other landmark legal decisions involving education, including the seminal *Brown v. Board of Education* (1954) as well as numerous other cases, a single legal case and its impact has the potential to change the course of American schools. With this in mind, many of the chapters in this book include carefully selected and edited excerpts from specific legal cases involving students with disabilities, which contain important legal concepts and principles that are useful and directly applicable to educators as well as other practitioners who work closely with students with disabilities in school settings. At the end of certain chapters, one or more special education legal cases is profiled in a section the authors call "Special Education Law in Practice," which helps illustrate to the reader specific legal concepts or principles discussed in a particular chapter. Table 1.1.2 details the sixteen "Special Education Law in Practice" legal cases profiled in this book and the legal concepts and principles that derive from these cases. Sudzina (1999) recommends the following five steps in analyzing a legal case, including:

1. Identifying the issues and facts in a particular legal case
2. Considering the perspectives or values of the actors in a case
3. Identifying professional knowledge from practice, theory, and/or research that might be relevant in developing a particular course of action
4. Projecting actions that might be taken in a legal case
5. Forecasting likely consequences, both positive and negative, of particular actions

(p. 19)

By actively reading, analyzing, and discussing the actual legal language used by judges from various legal jurisdictions, including the U.S. Supreme Court, federal and state-level

TABLE 1.1.2 Profiled "Special Education Law in Practice" Legal Cases

Case #	Case Name/Citation	Chapter	Legal Concept/Principle
No. 1	*Fry v. Napoleon Community Schools* 137 S. Ct. 743 (2017)	1	IDEA's "Exhaustion of Administrative Remedies" Rule
No. 2	*Watson v. City of Cambridge* 157 Mass. 561 (1893)	2	Sanctioned Exclusion of Students with Disabilities From Public Schools
No. 3	*Pennsylvania Association for Retarded Children (PARC) v. Commonwealth of Pennsylvania* 343 F. Supp. 279 (1972)	2	Rights of Students With Disabilities to a Public Education
No. 4	*Mills v. Board of Education of the District of Columbia* 348 F. Supp. 866 (1972)	2	Establishment of Due Process Rights for Students With Disabilities
No. 5	*Timothy W. v. Rochester, New Hampshire School District* 875 F. 2d 954 (1989)	5	IDEA's Zero Reject/Child Find Principle
No. 6	*J.D. v. Pawlet School District* 224 F. 3d 60 (2000)	5	IDEA Eligibility Requires That the Student's Disability(ies) "Adversely Impacts" the Student's Educational Performance
No. 7	*D.D. Ex. Rel. V.D. v. New York City Department of Education* 465 F. 3d 503 (2006)	6	Right to a Free Appropriate Public Education Requires That Individualized Education Programs Be Implemented as Soon as Possible
No. 8	*Board of Education of the Hendrick Hudson Central School District v. Rowley* 458 U.S. 176 (1982)	7	Definition of Free Appropriate Public Education (FAPE)
No. 9	*Endrew F. v. Douglas County School District RE-1* 137 S. Ct. 988 (2017)	7	Clarified Existing FAPE Standard. A Student's IEP Must Be "Reasonably Calculated to Enable a Child to Make Progress in Light of the Child's Circumstance."
No. 10	*Gibson v. Forest Hills School District* 655 Fed. Appx. 423 (6th Cir. 2016)	8	Postsecondary Transition Needs of a Student With Multiple Disabilities
No. 11	*Honig v. Doe* 484 U.S. 305 (1988)	9	IDEA's Stay-Put Provisions Involving Disciplinary Proceedings
No. 12	*Schaffer ex. Rel. Schaffer v. Weast* 546 U.S. 49 (2005)	10	Burden of Proof at Due Process Hearings

(Continued)

TABLE 1.1.2 *(Continued)*

Case #	Case Name/Citation	Chapter	Legal Concept/Principle
No. 13	*Florence County School District Four v. Carter* 510 U.S. 7 (1993)	11	Unilateral Placements in Private Schools If Free Appropriate Public Education Is Not Provided in Public Schools
No. 14	*Doug C. v. Hawaii Department of Education* 720 F. 3d 1038 (2013)	12	Right of Non-Attorney Parents to Proceed *Pro Se* in IDEA Lawsuits
No. 15	*Doug C. v. Hawaii Department of Education* 720 F. 3d 1038 (2013)	12	Importance of Parental Participation in the IEP Process in the Change of Current Educational Placement
No. 16	*School Board of Nassau Country, Florida v. Arline* 480 U.S. 273 (1987)	13	Legal Defenses Under Section 504

courts, as well as lower court opinions, readers develop an improved and more detailed understanding of the impact of judicial opinions on their own professional practice of working and serving the best interests of students with disabilities within their own school environments. The authors are keenly aware of the complexity associated with special education law, including the myriad of federal and state statutes, regulations, and multitude of legal cases spanning different legal jurisdictions that special education-related legal disputes between parents and/or legal guardians and schools have generated. Please note that it is a common practice not to reference the full names of students in the legal case names. This explains why the names of minor students are often abbreviated in the legal cases.

IDEA's Exhaustion of Administrative Remedies

As reflected in a legal case from New Mexico, "[t]he IDEA favors prompt resolution of disputes" (*Sanders v. Santa Fe Public Schools*, 2004, p. 1311) involving the education of students with disabilities because Congress acknowledged the need to help children with disabilities who may be at formative stages in their development. As such, the IDEA requires parties (parents or school officials) to exhaust administrative remedies before filing suits unless it clearly is futile to do so. The first legal case involving a student with disabilities to be profiled in the "Special Education Law in Practice" section of this book is *Fry v. Napoleon Community Schools* (2017), a fairly recent case decided by the nation's highest court, the U.S. Supreme Court, meaning that this legal case ruling has implications on schools nationwide regardless of which state you currently reside. Under the Individuals with Disabilities Education Act, or IDEA, Congress created a detailed system of procedures and rules whereby schools are strongly encouraged to collaboratively work with families to resolve special education-related legal disputes in a non-adversarial manner, and if parents and school officials cannot successfully resolve their dispute, at some point the parents can file a lawsuit in either a state or federal-level court. The leading federal law impacting students with disabilities, the Individuals with Disabilities Education Act (hereafter referred to as IDEA 2004) has a specific rule governing legal enforcement under the IDEA 2004, Section 504 of the Rehabilitation Act (hereafter Section 504), and the Americans with Disabilities Act (hereafter the ADA) called the "IDEA exhaustion rule," meaning that any person filing a legal action under the IDEA 2004 must "exhaust" all those administrative remedies before pursuing legal relief under either Section 504 or the ADA (Colker, 2018). If a parent or legal guardian believes that their child is not receiving a free and appropriate public education, or FAPE, which is legally required under the IDEA 2004, they must seek legal relief from a state-level hearing officer prior to filing a formal legal complaint in either a state or federal-level court (Colker, 2018). The parents must "exhaust" their administrative remedies by formally requesting a special education due process hearing officer before going directly to the court system and filing legal action. One of the important practical considerations of the *Fry* ruling is that if a case does not expressly involve the discrimination of a student with disabilities, then the parent(s) or legal guardian is not legally required to exhaust IDEA procedures. The relevant part on the statute detailing the IDEA exhaustion rule states:

> Nothing in this chapter shall be construed to restrict or limit the rights, procedures, and remedies available under the Constitution, [the ADA, Section 504], or other federal laws protecting the rights of children with disabilities, except that before the filing of a civil action under such laws seeking relief that it is also available under this subchapter, the procedures under subsections (f) and (g) shall be exhausted to the same extent as would be required had the action been brought under this subchapter.
>
> (20 U.S.C. § 1415(l))

The U.S. Supreme Court's ruling in *Fry v. Napoleon Community Schools* (2017) provides useful and practical legal guidance on the issue of when a parent or legal guardian can actually seek legal relief under Section 504 instead of exhausting legal remedies under the IDEA. In this case, the student, Ehlena Fry, has cerebral palsy and her local public school district provided her with an Individualized Education Plan (IEP) when she entered kindergarten at the school. The main dispute between Ehlena's parents and the school was whether she could bring a trained service dog, a goldendoodle called Wonder, to school with her. The student's service dog was trained to do tasks that included retrieving dropped items, opening and closing doors, turning lights on and off, assisting the student in taking off her coat, and helping the student go to and from the toilet (*Fry*, 2017, p. 751). Initially, the school allowed the student's service dog to accompany the student to school on a 30-day trial basis. At the end of the trial of the 30-day trial basis, however, school officials informed Ehlena's parents that the service dog was no longer allowed in the school. Ehlena's parents filed a legal complaint with the U.S. Department of Education's Office for Civil Rights (OCR) for allegedly violating two federal civil rights laws, including Section 504 and the ADA. While the Office for Civil Rights (OCR) rendered a decision in the favor of Ehlena's parents, the parents decided to place Ehlena in a new school because they believed that school officials would "make her return to school difficult" (*Fry*, 2017, p. 751). Shortly after, Ehlena's parents sued the school district in federal court alleging that school officials had violated the student's legal rights under Section 504 and the ADA based on her emotional distress and pain, embarrassment, and mental anguish (*Fry*, 2017, p. 752). After reversing a legal decision by the federal U.S. Court of Appeals for the Sixth Circuit in a unanimous 8–0 decision, the Supreme Court reversed the Court of Appeals decision and ruled in favor of the parents. The Court stated, "we hold that exhaustion is not necessary when the gravamen of the plaintiff's suit is something other than the denial of the IDEA's core guarantee—what the Act calls a 'free appropriate public education'." One possible implication of the *Fry* decision is that it allows both parents and school officials to think more broadly about education, including the use of a service dog as an integral part of a student with disability's educational process (Colker, 2018). Under the IDEA 2004, a person seeking legal relief must "exhaust administrative remedies" prior to pursuing legal action under Section 504, the Americans with Disabilities Act (ADA), or other federal antidiscrimination laws. As a result, the *Fry* ruling can potentially serve as legal justification in situations where parents can now pursue legal remedies under the Americans with Disabilities Act (ADA) or Section 504 of the Rehabilitation Act of 1973 (Section 504) without exhausting their IDEA-based remedies.

IDEA's Exhaustion of Administrative Remedies Not Required

For the most part, courts agree that parents are not required to exhaust administrative remedies under the IDEA in a variety of circumstances. Parties may not have to exhaust administrative remedies when complaints allege systemic failures.

Challenges to school board policies that could violate the IDEA may not be subject to the administrative process. As such, the Ninth Circuit was convinced that a claim that the school day for specified special education students was shorter than for children in regular education was not subject to the exhaustion requirement because it had nothing to do with individual IEPs (*Christopher S. ex rel. Rita S. v. Stanislaus County Office of Education*, 2004).

Courts have considered exhaustion to be futile when hearing officers lacked authority to grant the requested relief. The Second Circuit decided that a father's complaint about the method by which hearing officers were selected was not subject to exhaustion since a sole hearing officer lacked the authority to alter the procedure (*Heldman v. Sobol*, 1992). Federal trial courts in New York also found that exhaustion was not required when the requested relief was that a child be placed in a school that was not on the state's list of approved placements because the hearing officer could not order a student to attend classes in an unapproved facility (*Straube v. Florida Union Free School District*, 1992), or in challenging an adjudication of officials of the state education department who rejected a parental request but declined to make an exception to general procedures (*Vander Malle v. Ambach*, 1987).

Yet, since not all courts agree, exhaustion may not be necessary in class action suits where the claims of plaintiffs are systemic in nature and hearing officers would not have the authority to the requested relief. For example, the Second Circuit affirmed that exhaustion was not required when a hearing officer could not order a systemwide change to correct the alleged wrongs (*J.G. v. Board of Education of the Rochester City School District*, 1987). Exhaustion may be unnecessary in emergency situations if it would cause severe or irreparable harm to students. However, the Third Circuit held that since mere allegations of irreparable harm are insufficient to excuse exhaustion, a plaintiff must present actual evidence to support such a claim (*Komninos v. Upper Saddle River Board of Education*, 1994).

When litigation involves issues that are purely legal rather than factual, the Third Circuit was of the opinion that exhaustion may not be required (*Lester H. v. Gilhool*, 1990). Similarly, the Second Circuit determined that exhaustion may not be necessary if a state persistently fails to render expeditious decisions regarding a student's educational placement (*Frutiger v. Hamilton Central School District*, 1991).

Finally, courts have refused to apply the exhaustion requirement when students are determined to not need special education. To this end, courts agree that parents do not have to exhaust administrative remedies in cases under Section 504 if their children are not receiving services under the IDEA, even if they are disabled (*Doe v. Belleville Public School District No. 118*, 1987; *Robertson v. Granite City Community Unit School District No. 9*, 1988).

SPECIAL EDUCATION LAW IN PRACTICE

Legal Case No. 1—IDEA's "Exhaustion of Administrative Remedies" Rule

FRY V. NAPOLEON COMMUNITY SCHOOLS

137 S. CT. 743 (2017)

Justice KAGAN delivered the opinion of the Court.

The Individuals with Disabilities Education Act (IDEA or Act), 84 Stat. 175, as amended, 20 U.S.C. § 1400 *et seq.*, ensures that children with disabilities receive needed special education services. One of its provisions, § 1415(*l*), addresses the Act's relationship with other laws protecting those children. Section 1415(*l*) makes clear that nothing in the IDEA "restrict[s] or limit[s] the rights [or] remedies" that other federal laws, including antidiscrimination statutes, confer on children with disabilities. At the same time, the section states that if a suit brought under such a law "seek[s] relief that is also available under" the IDEA, the plaintiff must first exhaust the IDEA's administrative procedures. In this case, we consider the scope of that exhaustion requirement. We hold that exhaustion is not necessary when the gravamen of the plaintiff's suit is something other than the denial of the IDEA's core guarantee—what the Act calls a "free appropriate public education." § 1412(a)(1)(A).

I

A

Important as the IDEA is for children with disabilities, it is not the only federal statute protecting their interests. Of particular relevance to this case are two antidiscrimination laws—Title II of the Americans with Disabilities Act (ADA), 42 U.S.C. § 12131 *et seq.*, and § 504 of the Rehabilitation Act, 29 U.S.C. § 794—which cover both adults and children with disabilities, in both public schools and other settings. Title II forbids any "public entity" from discriminating based on disability; Section 504 applies the same prohibition to any federally funded "program or activity." 42 U.S.C. §§ 12131–12132; 29 U.S.C. § 794(a). A regulation implementing Title II requires a public entity to make "reasonable modifications" to its "policies, practices, or procedures" when necessary to avoid such discrimination. 28 C.F.R. § 35.130(b)(7) (2016); In similar vein, courts have interpreted § 504 as demanding certain "reasonable" modifications to existing practices in order to "accommodate" persons with disabilities. And both statutes authorize individuals to seek redress for violations of their substantive guarantees by bringing suits for injunctive relief or money damages. See 29 U.S.C. § 794a(a)(2); 42 U.S.C. § 12133.

This Court first considered the interaction between such laws and the IDEA in *Smith v. Robinson*, 468 U.S. 922.... The plaintiffs there sought "to secure a 'free appropriate public education' for [their] handicapped child." But instead of bringing suit under the IDEA alone, they appended "virtually identical" claims (again alleging the denial of a "free appropriate public education") under § 504 of the Rehabilitation Act and the Fourteenth Amendment's Equal Protection Clause.

Congress was quick to respond. In the Handicapped Children's Protection Act of 1986, it overturned *Smith*'s preclusion of non-IDEA claims while also adding a carefully defined exhaustion requirement. Now codified at 20 U.S.C. § 1415(*l*), the relevant provision of that statute reads:

> "Nothing in [the IDEA] shall be construed to restrict or limit the rights, pro-
> cedures, and remedies available under the Constitution, the [ADA], title V
> of the Rehabilitation Act [including § 504], or other Federal laws protecting
> the rights of children with disabilities, except that before the filing of a civil
> action under such laws seeking relief that is also available under [the IDEA],
> the [IDEA's administrative procedures] shall be exhausted to the same extent
> as would be required had the action been brought under [the IDEA]."

The first half of § 1415(*l*) (up until "except that") "reaffirm[s] the viability" of federal statutes like the ADA or Rehabilitation Act "as separate vehicles," no less integral than the IDEA, "for ensuring the rights of handicapped children." H.R.Rep. No. 99–296, p. 4 (1985). According to that opening phrase, the IDEA does not prevent a plaintiff from asserting claims under such laws even if, as in *Smith* itself, those claims allege the denial of an appropriate public education (much as an IDEA claim would). But the second half of § 1415(*l*) (from "except that" onward) imposes a limit on that "anything goes" regime, in the form of an exhaustion provision. According to that closing phrase, a plaintiff bringing suit under the ADA, the Rehabilitation Act, or similar laws must in certain circumstances—that is, when "seeking relief that is also available under" the IDEA—first exhaust the IDEA's administrative procedures. The reach of that requirement is the issue in this case.

B

Petitioner E.F. is a child with a severe form of cerebral palsy, which "significantly limits her motor skills and mobility." When E.F. was five years old, her parents—petitioners Stacy and Brent Fry—obtained a trained service dog for her, as recommended by her pediatrician. The dog, a goldendoodle named Wonder, "help[s E.F.] to live as independently as possible" by assisting her with various life activities. In particular, Wonder aids E.F. by "retrieving dropped items, helping her balance when she uses her walker, opening and closing doors, turning on and off lights, helping her take off her coat, [and] helping her transfer to and from the toilet."

But when the Frys sought permission for Wonder to join E.F. in kindergarten, officials at Ezra Eby Elementary School refused the request. Under E.F.'s existing IEP, a human aide provided E.F. with one-on-one support throughout the day; that two-legged assistance, the school officials thought, rendered Wonder superfluous. In the words of one administrator, Wonder should be barred from Ezra Eby because all of E.F.'s "physical and academic needs [were] being met through the services programs/accommodations" that the school had already agreed to. Later that year, the school officials briefly allowed Wonder to accompany E.F. to school on a trial basis; but even then, "the dog was required to remain in the back of the room during classes, and was forbidden from assisting [E.F.] with many tasks he had been specifically trained to do." And when the trial period concluded, the administrators again informed the Frys that Wonder was not welcome. As a result, the Frys removed E.F. from Ezra Eby and began homeschooling her.

C

The Frys then filed this suit in federal court against the local and regional school districts in which Ezra Eby is located, along with the school's principal (collectively, the school districts). The complaint alleged that the school districts violated Title II of the ADA and § 504 of the Rehabilitation Act by "denying [E.F.] equal access" to Ezra Eby and its programs, "refus[ing] to reasonably accommodate" E.F.'s use of a service animal, and otherwise "discriminat[ing] against [E.F.] as a person with disabilities." According to the complaint, E.F. suffered harm as a result of that discrimination, including "emotional distress and pain, embarrassment, [and] mental anguish." In their prayer for relief, the Frys sought a declaration that the school districts had violated Title II and § 504, along with money damages to compensate for E.F.'s injuries.

The District Court granted the school districts' motion to dismiss the suit, holding that § 1415(*l*) required the Frys to first exhaust the IDEA's administrative procedures. A divided panel of the Court of Appeals for the Sixth Circuit affirmed on the same ground. In that court's view, § 1415(*l*) applies if "the injuries [alleged in a suit] relate to the specific substantive protections of the IDEA." And that means, the court continued, that exhaustion is necessary whenever "the genesis and the manifestations" of the complained-of harms were "educational" in nature. On that understanding of § 1415(*l*), the Sixth Circuit held, the Frys' suit could not proceed: Because the harms to E.F. were generally "educational"—most notably, the court reasoned, because "Wonder's absence hurt her sense of independence and social confidence at school"—the Frys had to exhaust the IDEA's procedures. 788 F.3d, at 627. Judge

Daughtrey dissented, emphasizing that in bringing their Title II and § 504 claims, the Frys "did not allege the denial of a FAPE" or "seek to modify [E.F.'s] IEP in any way."

We granted certiorari to address confusion in the courts of appeals as to the scope of § 1415(*l*)'s exhaustion requirement. We now vacate the Sixth Circuit's decision.

II

Section 1415(*l*) requires that a plaintiff exhaust the IDEA's procedures before filing an action under the ADA, the Rehabilitation Act, or similar laws when (but only when) her suit "seek[s] relief that is also available" under the IDEA. We first hold that to meet that statutory standard, a suit must seek relief for the denial of a FAPE, because that is the only "relief" the IDEA makes "available."

A

In this Court, the parties have reached substantial agreement about what "relief" the IDEA makes "available" for children with disabilities—and about how the Sixth Circuit went wrong in addressing that question. The Frys maintain that such a child can obtain remedies under the IDEA for decisions that deprive her of a FAPE, but none for those that do not. So in the Frys' view, § 1415(*l*)'s exhaustion requirement can come into play only when a suit concerns the denial of a FAPE—and not, as the Sixth Circuit held, when it merely has some articulable connection to the education of a child with a disability. The school districts, for their part, also believe that the Sixth Circuit's exhaustion standard "goes too far" because it could mandate exhaustion when a plaintiff is "seeking relief that is *not* in substance available" under the IDEA. Brief for Respondents 30. And in particular, the school districts acknowledge that the IDEA makes remedies available only in suits that "directly implicate[ ]" a FAPE—so that only in those suits can § 1415(*l*) apply. Tr. of Oral Arg. 46. For the reasons that follow, we agree with the parties' shared view: The only relief that an IDEA officer can give—hence the thing a plaintiff must seek in order to trigger § 1415(*l*)'s exhaustion rule—is relief for the denial of a FAPE.

We begin, as always, with the statutory language at issue, which (at risk of repetition) compels exhaustion when a plaintiff seeks "relief" that is "available" under the IDEA. The ordinary meaning of "relief" in the context of a lawsuit is the "redress[ ] or benefit" that attends a favorable judgment. Black's Law Dictionary 1161 (5th ed. 1979). And such relief is "available," as we recently explained, when it is "accessible or may be obtained." (quoting Webster's Third New International Dictionary 150 (1993)). So to establish the scope of § 1415(*l*), we must identify the circumstances in which the IDEA enables a person to obtain redress (or, similarly, to access a benefit).

The IDEA's administrative procedures test whether a school has met that obligation—and so center on the Act's FAPE requirement. As noted earlier, any decision by a hearing officer on a request for substantive relief "shall" be "based on a determination of whether the child received a free appropriate public education." § 1415(f)(3)(E)(i); Suppose that a parent's complaint protests a school's failure to provide some accommodation for a child with a disability. If that accommodation is needed to fulfill the IDEA's FAPE requirement, the hearing officer must order relief. But if it is not, he cannot—even though the dispute is between a child with a disability and the school she attends.... For that reason, § 1415(*l*)'s exhaustion rule hinges on whether a lawsuit seeks relief for the denial of a free appropriate public education. Rather, that plaintiff must first submit her case to an IDEA hearing officer, experienced in addressing exactly the issues she raises. But if, in a suit brought under a different statute, the remedy sought is not for the denial of a FAPE, then exhaustion of the IDEA's procedures is not required. After all, the plaintiff could not get any relief from those procedures: A hearing officer, as just explained, would have to send her away empty-handed. And that is true even when the suit arises directly from a school's treatment of a child with a disability—and so could be said to relate in some way to her education. A school's conduct toward such a child—say, some refusal to make an accommodation—might injure her in ways unrelated to a FAPE, which are addressed in statutes other than the IDEA. A complaint seeking redress for those other harms, independent of any FAPE denial, is not subject to § 1415(*l*)'s exhaustion rule because, once again, the only "relief" the IDEA makes "available" is relief for the denial of a FAPE.

B

Still, an important question remains: How is a court to tell when a plaintiff "seeks" relief for the denial of a FAPE and when she does not? Here, too, the parties have found some common ground: By looking, they both say, to the "substance" of, rather than the labels used in, the plaintiff's complaint. And here, too, we agree with that view: What matters is the crux—or, in legal-speak, the gravamen—of the plaintiff's complaint, setting aside any attempts at artful pleading.

That inquiry makes central the plaintiff's own claims, as § 1415(*l*) explicitly requires. The statutory language asks whether a lawsuit in fact "seeks" relief available under the IDEA—not, as a stricter exhaustion statute might, whether the suit "could have sought" relief available under the IDEA (or, what is much the same, whether any remedies "are" available under that law).

But that examination should consider substance, not surface. The use (or nonuse) of particular labels and terms is not what matters. The inquiry, for example, does not ride on whether a complaint includes (or, alternatively, omits) the precise words(?) "FAPE" or "IEP."

After all, § 1415(*l*)'s premise is that the plaintiff is suing under a statute *other than* the IDEA, like the Rehabilitation Act; in such a suit, the plaintiff might see no need to use the IDEA's distinctive language—even if she is in essence contesting the adequacy of a special education program. And still more critically, a "magic words" approach would make § 1415(*l*)'s exhaustion rule too easy to bypass. It requires exhaustion when the gravamen of a complaint seeks redress for a school's failure to provide a FAPE, even if not phrased or framed in precisely that way.

In addressing whether a complaint fits that description, a court should attend to the diverse means and ends of the statutes covering persons with disabilities—the IDEA on the one hand, the ADA and Rehabilitation Act (most notably) on the other. The IDEA, of course, protects only "children" (well, really, adolescents too) and concerns only their schooling. § 1412(a)(1) (A). And as earlier noted, the statute's goal is to provide each child with meaningful access to education by offering individualized instruction and related services appropriate to her "unique needs." § 1401(29); by contrast, Title II of the ADA and § 504 of the Rehabilitation Act cover people with disabilities of all ages, and do so both inside and outside schools. And those statutes aim to root out disability-based discrimination, enabling each covered person (sometimes by means of reasonable accommodations) to participate equally to all others in public facilities and federally funded programs. In short, the IDEA guarantees individually tailored educational services, while Title II and § 504 promise non-discriminatory access to public institutions. That is not to deny some overlap in coverage: The same conduct might violate all three statutes—which is why, as in *Smith*, a plaintiff might seek relief for the denial of a FAPE under Title II and § 504 as well as the IDEA. But still, the statutory differences just discussed mean that a complaint brought under Title II and § 504 might instead seek relief for simple discrimination, irrespective of the IDEA's FAPE obligation.

One clue to whether the gravamen of a complaint against a school concerns the denial of a FAPE, or instead addresses disability-based discrimination, can come from asking a pair of hypothetical questions. First, could the plaintiff have brought essentially the same claim if the alleged conduct had occurred at a public facility that was *not* a school—say, a public theater or library? And second, could an *adult* at the school—say, an employee or visitor—have pressed essentially the same grievance? When the answer to those questions is yes, a complaint that does not expressly allege the denial of a FAPE is also unlikely to be truly about that subject; after all, in those other situations there is no FAPE obligation and yet the same basic suit could go forward. But when the answer is no, then the complaint probably does concern a FAPE, even if it does not explicitly say so; for the FAPE requirement is all that explains why only a child in the school setting (not an adult in that setting or a child in some other) has a viable claim.

Take two contrasting examples. Suppose first that a wheelchair-bound child sues his school for discrimination under Title II (again, without mentioning the denial of a FAPE) because the building lacks access ramps. In some sense, that architectural feature has educational consequences, and a different lawsuit might have alleged that it violates the IDEA: After all, if the child cannot get inside the school, he cannot receive instruction there; and if he must be carried inside, he may not achieve the sense of independence conducive to academic (or later to real-world) success. But is the denial of a FAPE really the gravamen of the plaintiff's Title II complaint? Consider that the child could file the same basic complaint if a municipal library or theater had no ramps. And similarly, an employee or visitor could bring a mostly identical complaint against the school. That the claim can stay the same in those alternative scenarios suggests that its essence is equality of access to public facilities, not adequacy of special education.

But suppose next that a student with a learning disability sues his school under Title II for failing to provide remedial tutoring in mathematics. That suit, too, might be cast as one for disability-based discrimination, grounded on the school's refusal to make a reasonable accommodation; the complaint might make no reference at all to a FAPE or an IEP. But can anyone imagine the student making the same claim against a public theater or library? Or, similarly, imagine an adult visitor or employee suing the school to obtain a math tutorial? The difficulty of transplanting the complaint to those other contexts suggests that its essence—even though not its wording—is the provision of a FAPE, thus bringing § 1415(*l*) into play.

A further sign that the gravamen of a suit is the denial of a FAPE can emerge from the history of the proceedings. In particular, a court may consider that a plaintiff has previously invoked the IDEA's formal procedures to handle the dispute—thus starting to exhaust the Act's remedies before switching midstream. Recall that a parent dissatisfied with her child's education initiates those administrative procedures by filing a complaint, which triggers a preliminary meeting (or possibly mediation) and then a due process hearing. A plaintiff's initial choice to pursue that process may suggest that she is indeed seeking relief for the denial of a FAPE—with the shift to judicial proceedings prior to full exhaustion reflecting only strategic calculations about how to maximize the prospects of such a remedy. Whether that is so depends on the facts; a court may conclude, for example, that the move to a courtroom came from a late-acquired awareness that the school had fulfilled its FAPE obligation and that the grievance involves something else entirely But prior pursuit of the IDEA's administrative remedies will often provide strong evidence that the substance of a plaintiff's claim concerns the denial of a FAPE, even if the complaint never explicitly uses that term.

III

The Court of Appeals did not undertake the analysis we have just set forward. As noted above, it asked whether E.F.'s injuries were, broadly speaking, "educational" in nature That is not the same as asking whether the gravamen of E.F.'s complaint charges, and seeks relief for, the denial of a FAPE. And that difference in standard may have led to a difference in result in this case. Understood correctly, § 1415(*l*) might not require exhaustion of the Frys' claim. We lack some important information on that score, however, and so we remand the issue to the court below.

The Frys' complaint alleges only disability-based discrimination, without making any reference to the adequacy of the special education services E.F.'s school provided. The school districts' "refusal to allow Wonder to act as a service dog," the complaint states, "discriminated against [E.F.] as a person with disabilities ... by denying her equal access" to public facilities. The complaint contains no allegation about the denial of a FAPE or about any deficiency in E.F.'s IEP. More, it does not accuse the school even in general terms of refusing to provide the educational instruction and services. As the Frys explained in this Court: The school district "have said all along that because they gave [E.F.] a one-on-one [human] aide, that all of her ... educational needs were satisfied." The Frys instead maintained, just as OCR had earlier found, that the school districts infringed E.F.'s right to equal access— even if their actions complied in full with the IDEA's requirements.

And nothing in the nature of the Frys' suit suggests any implicit focus on the adequacy of E.F.'s education. Consider, as suggested above, that the Frys could have filed essentially the same complaint if a public library or theater had refused admittance to Wonder. Or similarly, consider that an adult visitor to the school could have leveled much the same charges if prevented from entering with his service dog. In each case, the plaintiff would challenge a public facility's policy of precluding service dogs (just as a blind person might challenge a policy of barring guide dogs, see *supra*, at 751) as violating Title II's and § 504's equal access requirements. The suit would have nothing to do with the provision of educational services. From all that we know now, that is exactly the kind of action the Frys have brought.

But we do not foreclose the possibility that the history of these proceedings might suggest something different. As earlier discussed, a plaintiff's initial pursuit of the IDEA's administrative remedies can serve as evidence that the gravamen of her later suit is the denial of a FAPE, even though that does not appear on the face of her complaint. The Frys may or may not have sought those remedies before filing this case: None of the parties here have addressed that issue, and the record is cloudy as to the relevant facts. Accordingly, on remand, the court below should establish whether (or to what extent) the Frys invoked the IDEA's dispute resolution process before bringing this suit. And if the Frys started down that road, the court should decide whether their actions reveal that the gravamen of their complaint is indeed the denial of a FAPE, thus necessitating further exhaustion.

With these instructions and for the reasons stated, we vacate the judgment of the Court of Appeals and remand the case for further proceedings consistent with this opinion.

It is so ordered.

Justice Alito, with whom Justice Thomas joins, concurring in part and concurring in the judgment.

The Court first instructs the lower courts to inquire whether the plaintiff could have brought "essentially the same claim if the alleged conduct had occurred at a public facility that was *not* a school—say, a public theater or library." Next, the Court says, a court should ask whether "an *adult* at the school—say, an employee or visitor—[could] have pressed essentially the same grievance." These clues make sense only if there is no overlap between the relief available under the following two sets of claims: (1) the relief provided by the Individuals with Disabilities Education Act (IDEA), and (2) the relief provided by other federal laws (including the Constitution, the Americans with Disabilities Act of 1990 (ADA), and the Rehabilitation Act of 1973). The Court does not show or even claim that there is no such overlap—to the contrary, it observes that "[t]he same conduct might violate" the ADA, the Rehabilitation Act and the IDEA. *Ibid.* And since these clues work only in the absence of overlap, I would not suggest them.

The Court provides another false clue by suggesting that lower courts take into account whether parents, before filing suit under the ADA or the Rehabilitation Act, began to pursue but then abandoned the IDEA's formal procedures. This clue also seems to me to be ill-advised. It is easy to imagine circumstances under which parents might start down the IDEA road and then change course and file an action under the ADA or the Rehabilitation Act that seeks relief that the IDEA cannot provide. The parents might be advised by their attorney that the relief they were seeking under the IDEA is not available under that law but is available under another. Or the parents might change their minds about the relief that they want, give up on the relief that the IDEA can provide, and turn to another statute.

Although the Court provides these clues for the purpose of assisting the lower courts, I am afraid that they may have the opposite effect. They are likely to confuse and lead courts astray.

Questions for Discussion

1. Do you think the 2017 Supreme Court's *Fry* ruling will encourage increased litigation of parents seeking monetary damages against school districts refusing to accommodate the requests of students with disabilities?

2. One of the goals of the Individuals with Disabilities Education Act (IDEA) is to encourage students with disabilities to "lead productive and independent adult lives"

(See 20 U.S.C. § 1400(c)(5)(A)(ii)). Do you think certain student accommodations, such as a service dog, can be successful at improving the educational progression of students with disabilities?

3. As mandated under the IDEA's "exhaustion of administrative remedies rule", public school districts sued by parents under the Americans with Disabilities Act (ADA), Section 504 of the Rehabilitation Act, as well as other federal antidiscrimination statutes should evaluate the substance and validity of their legal claim(s) to determine whether the legal relief sought really is for a failure to provide a free appropriate public education (FAPE). If so, the parents of students with disabilities are required to exhaust IDEA's administrative remedies, and a failure to do so would likely result in dismissal of the case. Do you agree or disagree with the *Fry* case's interpretation of the IDEA's "exhaustion of administrative remedies" rule? Why or why not?

Summary of Important Legal Policies, Principles, and Practices

This chapter starts with the premise that "ignorantia juris non excusat" or "ignorance of the law is no excuse," a long-standing U.S. legal tradition that if individuals claim they are unaware of a particular law(s) or principle(s), they may not escape legal liability by simply responding they are either unaware or not knowledgeable of the law's content. The main concepts and principles of this chapter include:

1. Despite nationwide increases in the number of eligible students with disabilities enrolled in schools, a review of the research literature demonstrates that many educators and others who work closely with students with disabilities are either poorly informed or uninformed concerning their knowledge in special education law. As a result, today's school administrators, educators, and pre-service teachers are not adequately trained in special education law despite the unique federal and state-level legal protections afforded student with disabilities.

2. For the purposes of this book, special education legal literacy is defined as "the legal knowledge, understanding, and skills that enable educators to apply relevant legal rules to their everyday practice" (Decker & Brady, 2016, p. 231). Those individuals, who are legally literate in special education are better able to spot legal issues, identify applicable laws or legal standards, and apply the relevant legal rules to solve legal dilemmas.

3. The use of case-based learning, or CBL has been shown to be an effective method for teaching the law and legal principles to members of the educational community, especially instruction involving relevant legal principles and strategies drawn from actual legal cases involving students with disabilities. The legal case-based learning model has significant potential for improving the special education legal literacy levels of those persons who work closely with children and youth with disabilities in educational settings.

4. This chapter's *Special Education Law in Practice* legal case, *Fry v. Napoleon Community Schools* (2017) was decided by the U.S. Supreme Court and explains the IDEA's "exhaustion of administrative remedies" rule preferring alternative dispute resolution measures, including mediation and due process hearings over litigation proceedings in our nation's courts. In *Fry*, the Supreme Court developed a test for determining when students with disabilities are legally obligated to exhaust claims under the IDEA. The IDEA's exhaustion requirement actively encourages alternative dispute resolution alternatives to formal litigation actions in federal or state-level courts. If the nature of the alleged legal complaint by a parent or legal guardian pertains to or arises based on a student with disability's education, then administrative relief as opposed to litigation in the court system remains the preferred remedy to settle IDEA-based legal disputes.

Useful Online Resources

Poorvu Center for Teaching and Learning at Yale University: Case-Based Learning (CBL)

Case-based learning (CBL) is an established approach used across disciplines where individuals apply their knowledge to real-world scenarios, promoting higher levels of cognition. CBL has a long history of successful implementation in medical, law, and business schools, and is increasingly used within undergraduate education, particularly within pre-professional majors and the sciences, including education. https://poorvucenter.yale.edu/faculty-resources/strategies-teaching/case-based-learning

Recommended Reading

Bateman, D., & Cline, J. (2019). *Special education law case studies: A review from practitioners*. Lanham, MD: Rowman & Littlefield.

Bateman, D., & Yell, M. L. (2019). *Current trends and legal issues in special education*. Thousand Oaks, CA: Corwin.

Weishaar, M. K. (2007). *Case studies in special education law: No Child Left Behind and Individuals with Disabilities Education Improvement Act*. Upper Saddle River, NJ: Pearson.

References

Ballentine, J. A. (1916). *Ballentine's Law Dictionary*. Indianapolis, IN: Bobbs-Merrill Company.

Bineham, S. C. (2014). *Knowledge and skills essential for secondary campus-base administrators to appropriately serve students with special needs* (unpublished doctoral dissertation), University of Texas at Austin, Austin.

Brady, K. P., & Bathon, J. (2012). Education law in a digital age: The growing impact of the open access legal movement. *Education Law Reporter, 227*, 589.

Brown v. Board of Education, 347 U.S. 483 (1954).

Bruner, D. Y., & Bartlett, M. J. (2008). Effective methods and materials for teaching law to preservice teachers. *Action in Teacher Education, 30* (2), 36–45.

Bull, B., & McCarthy, M. (1995). Reflections on the knowledge base in law and ethics for educational leaders. *Education Administration Quarterly, 31* (4), 613–631.

Christopher S. ex rel. Rita S. v. Stanislaus County Office of Education, 384 F.3d 1205 (9th Cir. 2004).

Christopher W. v. Portsmouth School Committee, 877 F.2d 1089 (1st Cir. 1989).

Colker, R. (2018). *Special education law in a nutshell*. St. Paul, MN: West Academic.

Davidson, D. N., & Algozzine, B. (2002). Administrators' perceptions of special education law. *Journal of Special Education Leadership, 15* (2), 43–48.

Davies, S. (1998). The jurisprudence of willfulness: An evolving theory of excusable ignorance, *Duke Law Journal, 48* (3), 341–427.

Decker, J. R. (2014). Legal literacy in education: An ideal time to increase research, advocacy, and action. *Education Law Reporter, 304* (1), 679–696.

Decker, J. R., & Brady, K. (2016). Increasing school employees' special education legal literacy. *Journal of School Public Relations, 36* (3), 231–259.

Decker, J. R., & Pazey, B. L. (2017). Case-based instruction to teach educators about the legal parameters surrounding the discipline of students with disabilities. *Action in Teacher Education, 39* (3), 255–273.

DiPaola, M., & Walther-Thomas, C. (2003). *Principals and special education: The critical role of school leaders* (COPSSE Document No. IB-7E). Gainesville, FL: University of Florida.

Doe v. Belleville Public School District No. 118, 672 F. Supp. 342 (S.D. Ill. 1987).

Drame, E. (2011, January/February). An analysis of the capacity of charter schools to address the needs of SWDs in Wisconsin. *Remedial and Special Education, 32* (1), 55–63.

Eberwein, H. J. (2008). *Raising legal literacy in public schools, a call for principal leadership: A national study of secondary principals' knowledge of public school law* (Unpublished doctoral dissertation), University of Massachusetts, Amherst.

Eckes, E. (2008, Summer). Significant issues for inclusion in pre-service teacher preparation. *Action in Teacher Education, 30* (2), 25–35.

Estes, M. (2009). Charter schools and students with disabilities: How far have we come? *Remedial and Special Education, 30* (4), 216–224.

Fischer, L., Schimmel, D., & Stellman, L. (2007). *Teachers and the law* (7th ed.). Boston: Allyn & Bacon.

Fry v. Napoleon Community Schools, 137 S. Ct. 743 (2017).

Gajda, R. (2008). States' expectations for teachers' knowledge about school law. *Action in Teacher Education, 30* (2), 15–24.

Garda, R. (2011). Culture clash: Special education in charter schools. *North Carolina Law Review, 90* (3), 655–718.

Gullatt, D., & Tollett, J. (1997). Educational law: A requisite course for preservice and inservice teacher education programs. *Journal of Teacher Education, 48* (2), 129–135.

Heldman v. Sobol, 962 F.2d 148 (2d Cir. 1992).

Heubert, J. (1997). The more we get together: Improving collaboration between educators and their lawyers. *Harvard Educational Review, 67* (3), 531–583.

Imber, M. (2008). Pervasive myths in teacher beliefs about education law. *Action in Teacher Education, 30* (2), 88–97.

Institute for Educational Sciences (IES). (2010, July). Do states have certification requirements for preparing general education teachers to teach students with disabilities (SWDs)? *Institute for Educational Sciences, 90.* Retrieved from http://eric.ed.gov/?id=ED511104

J.G. v. Board of Education of the Rochester City School District, 830 F.2d 444 (2d Cir. 1987).

Karanxha, Z., & Zirkel, P. (2014). Longitudinal trends in special education case law: Frequencies and outcomes of published court decisions. *Journal of Special Education Leadership, 27,* 55.

Katsiyannis, A., & Herbst, M. (2004). 20 Ways to minimize litigation in special education. *Intervention in School & Clinic, 40,* 106–110.

Komninos v. Upper Saddle River Board of Education, 13 F.3d 775 (1994).

Lasky, B., & Karge, B. (2006). Meeting the needs of students with disabilities: Experience and confidence of principals. *NASSP Bulletin, 90,* 19–36.

Leko, M. M., Brownell, M. T., Sindelar, P. T., & Murphy, K. (2012). Promoting special education preservice teacher expertise. *Focus on Exceptional Children, 44* (7), 1–16.

Lester H. v. Gilhool, 916 F.2d 865 (3d Cir. 1990).

Littleton, M. (2008). Teachers' knowledge of education law. *Action in Teacher Education, 30* (2), 71–78.

MacNaughton, D., Hall, T. E., & Maccini, P. (2001). Case-based instruction in special education teacher preparation. *Teacher Education and Special Education, 24* (2), 84–94.

McCarthy, M. (2008, Summer). One model to infuse the law in teacher education. *Action in Teacher Education, 30* (2), 59–70.

McCarthy, M. (2016). The marginalization of school law knowledge and research: Missed opportunities for educators. *Education Law Reporter, 331,* 565–584.

McFarland, J., Hussar, B., Wang, X., Zhang, J., Wang, K., Rathbun, A., et al. (2018). *The condition of education 2018 (NCES 2018-144).* U.S. Department of Education. Washington, DC: National Center for Education Statistics. Retrieved from https://nces.ed.gov/pubsearch/pubsinfo. asp?pubid=2018144.

McNergney, R. F., Ducharme, E. R., & Ducharme, M. K. (Eds.). (1999a). *Educating for democracy: Case method teaching and learning.* Mahwah, NJ: Lawrence Erlbaum.

McNergney, R. F., Ducharme, E. R., & Ducharme, M. K. (1999b). Teaching democracy through cases. In R. F. McNergney, E. R. Ducharme, & M. K. Ducharme (Eds.), *Educating for democracy: Case method teaching and learning* (pp. 3–13). Mahwah, NJ: Lawrence Erlbaum.

Merseth, K. K. (1990). Case methodology in the study and practice of teacher education. *Teacher Education Quarterly, 17* (1), 53–62.

Miles, A. D. (2011). Bridging the gap between theory and application: Using the Harvard case study method to develop higher order thinking skills with college students. *Teaching and Learning Journal, 1* (1), 1–22.

Militello, M., & Schimmel, D. (2008). Toward universal legal literacy in American schools. *Action in Teacher Education, 30* (2), 98–106.

Militello, M., Schimmel, D., & Eberwein, H. J. (2009). If they knew, they would change: How legal knowledge impacts principals' practice. *NASSP Bulletin, 93* (1), 27–52.

Osterman, K. F., & Hafner, M. (2009). Curriculum in leadership preparation programs. In M. Young, G. M. Crow, J. Murphy, & R. T. Ogawa (Eds.), *Handbook of research on the education of school leaders* (pp. 269–318). New York, NY: Routledge.

Painter, S. (2001). Improving the teaching of school law: A call for dialogue. *Brigham Young University Education and Law Journal, 2001* (2), 213–230.

Pazey, B. L., & Cole, H. (2013). The role of special education training in the development of socially just leaders: Building an equity consciousness in educational leadership programs. *Educational Administration Quarterly, 49* (2), 243–271.

Powell, P. R. (2010). *An exploratory study of the presentation of special education law in administrative preparation programs for aspiring administrators* (doctoral dissertation). Retrieved from Dissertation Abstracts International (Order No. AAI3390580).

Reglin, G. (1992). Public school educators' knowledge of selected Supreme Court decisions affecting daily public school operations. *Journal of Education Administration, 30* (2), 26–32.

Robertson v. Granite City Community Unit School District No. 9, 684 F. Supp. 1002 (S.D. Ill. 1988).

Rodriguez, M. A., Gentilucci, J., & Sims, P. G. (2006, November). *Preparing school leaders to effectively support special education programs: Using modules in educational leadership.* Paper presented at the University Council for Educational Administration, San Antonio, TX.

Sanders v. Santa Fe Public Schools, 383 F. Supp.2d 1305 (D.N.M. 2004).

Schimmel, D., & Militello, M. (2007). Legal literacy for teachers: A neglected responsibility. *Harvard Educational Review, 77* (3), 257–284.

Schimmel, D., & Militello, M. (2008, December). Legal literacy for teachers. *Principal Leadership, 9* (4), 54–58.

Straube v. Florida Union Free School District, 801 F. Supp. 1164 (S.D.N.Y. 1992).

Sudzina, M. R. (1999). Organizing instruction for case-based teaching. In R. F. McNergney, E. R. Ducharme, & M. K. Ducharme (Eds.), *Educating for democracy: Case method teaching and learning* (pp. 15–28). Mahwah, NJ: Lawrence Erlbaum.

Umpstead, R., Decker, J., Brady, K., Schimmel, D., & Militello, M. (2015). *How to prevent special education litigation: Eight legal lesson plans.* New York, NY: Teachers College Press.

Vander Malle v. Ambach, 667 F. Supp. 1015 (S.D.N.Y. 1987).

Wagner, J. Y., & Katsiyannis, A. (2010). Special education litigation update: Implications for school administrators. *NASSP Bulletin, 94* (1), 40–52.

Williams, B. (2005). Case-based learning: A review of the literature: Is there scope for this educational paradigm in prehospital education? *Emerging Medicine, 22,* 577–581.

Williams, S. M. (1992). Putting case-based instruction into context: Examples from legal and medical education. *The Journal of the Learning Sciences, 2* (4), 367–427.

Yell, M. L. (2019). *Law and special education* (5th ed.). Upper Saddle River, NJ: Pearson.

Zirkel, P. A. (2006). The effect of law on education: The common ungoodness of paralyzing fear? *Journal of Law and Education, 35* (4), 461–495.

Zirkel, P. A., & Lupini, W. H. (2003). An outcomes analysis of education litigation. *Educational Policy, 17* (2), 257–279.

Reading 1.2

Historical Development of Laws Impacting Students with Disabilities

Kevin P. Brady, Charles J. Russo, Cynthia A. Dieterich, Allan G. Osborne, Jr., and Nicole D. Snyder

Key Concepts and Terms in This Chapter

- Historical development of special educational laws

- Introduction to Individuals with Disabilities Education Act (IDEA 2004)

- Introduction to Section 504 of the Rehabilitation Act of 1973 (Section 504)

- Introduction to the Americans with Disabilities Act (ADA)

The primary purpose of this chapter is to provide readers with an overview of the historical development of laws relating to the inclusion of students with disabilities in the nation's public elementary through secondary schools. Next, the chapter reviews significant historical events and efforts to obtain equal educational opportunities for school-aged children and youth with disabilities. Specifically, this chapter highlights several landmark legal decisions that have led to federal legislation mandating a free appropriate public education, often referred to as FAPE in the least restrictive environment, commonly called LRE for students with disabilities. Readers who might be unfamiliar with certain legal terminology should consult the glossary found towards the back of this book for definitions of various legal terms used in this chapter as well as throughout the book.

When non-tuition, public schools in the U.S. emerged beginning in the 1820s, classrooms were largely unavailable to students with disabilities. In fact, the exclusion of students with disabilities was often legally sanctioned by the courts. In one of the earliest reported legal cases involving a child or youth with disabilities attempting to gain access to a public school, the Supreme Judicial Court of Massachusetts in 1893 upheld a public school committee's exclusion of a student who was considered "too weak-minded to derive profit from instruction," made "uncouth noises," and was "unable to take ordinary decent physical care of himself" (*Watson v. City of Cambridge*, 1893, p. 32) (for more details of this case, *see* Special Education Law in Practice: *Case 2*). In the court's legal decision, they indicated that by law the school committee (as school boards in Massachusetts are known) had general charge of the public schools and refused to interfere with its judgment. Furthermore, the court explained that if acts of disorder by a student interfered with the operation of the schools, whether committed voluntarily or based on the student's intellectual ability, the school committee should have been able to exclude a student with disabilities without being overruled by a jury that lacked expertise in educational matters.

Compulsory Education and the Exclusion of Students with Disabilities

The historical development of the laws and legislation allowing children and youth with disabilities to attend U.S. public schools was achieved through the combined efforts of many individuals, groups, and governmental entities, including the parents of students with disabilities, advocacy groups for individuals with disabilities, Congress, and individual state legislatures (Yell, 2019). As will be discussed in Chapter 3, it is important to realize that public education is not directly mentioned in the U.S. Constitution. According to the U.S. Constitution, the Tenth Amendment specifies that any authority or powers not expressly granted to the federal government are reserved to the states (Turnbull, Stowe, & Huerta, 2007). While the majority of states had passed compulsory education laws by 1918 requiring that students attend schools until a certain age, children and youth with disabilities were a group of students initially excluded from state compulsory education laws. Prior to 1975, no federal statute legally obligated states to provide comprehensive special education programming or individualized services for students with disabilities. Initially, some states enacted legislation offering limited special education services to students with disabilities, but these state jurisdictions were in the distinct minority (Yell, 2019). For example, in 1911, New Jersey became the first state to legally allow the education of students with disabilities in its public schools followed closely by New York in 1917 and Massachusetts in 1920 (Colker, 2018). Unfortunately, however, the actual enforcement of these state laws was largely ineffective. Prior to the enactment of state compulsory education laws, as discussed at the outset of this chapter, local public schools routinely excluded students with disabilities.

In a second legal case involving whether to permit a student with disabilities access to a public school, the Supreme Court of Wisconsin, in 1919, upheld the exclusion of a student with a form of paralysis (*State ex rel. Beattie v. Board of Education of Antigo*, 1919). The student was determined to have normal intelligence, but his medical condition caused him to drool and make facial contortions. The student attended public schools through the fifth grade but was excluded from advancing to the next grade level since school officials claimed his physical appearance nauseated teachers and other students, his disability required an undue amount of his teacher's time, and the student had a negative impact on the discipline and progress of the school. School officials suggested that the student attend a day school for students with hearing impairments and defective speech, but the student refused and was supported by his parents. When the local school board refused to reinstate the student, the court affirmed its decision, maintaining that the student's right to attend the public schools was not absolute when his presence at the school was harmful to the best interests of others. The court went so far as to suggest that as the student's presence was not in the best interest of the school, the local school board had a legal obligation to exclude the student. Despite the fact that the state of Wisconsin at the time had a compulsory education law requiring a free public education "to all children between the ages of four and twenty years," the court ruled "the right of a child of school age to attend the public schools of this state cannot be insisted upon when its presence therein is harmful to the best interest of the school" (*State ex rel. Beattie v. Board of Education of Antigo*, 1919, p. 154).

The Legal Significance of the Civil Rights Movement

The greatest historical legal advancements in special education have occurred since World War II. The impetus for ensuring equal educational opportunities for all American children can be traced back to the United States Supreme Court's landmark 1954 *Brown v. Board of Education* decision, a school desegregation case ruling that public schools that were segregated based on race are "inherently unequal." Although equal access to public education was addressed in the context of racial school desegregation as a result of the *Brown* ruling, a unanimous Supreme Court set the tone for later legal developments, including those leading to increased constitutional protections as well as access to public education for students with disabilities, in asserting that "education is perhaps the most important function of state and local governments." Unfortunately, immediately following the Supreme Court's 1954 *Brown* ruling, the legal rights of individuals with disabilities continued to be overlooked. Throughout the 1950s, for example, more than half of the states still had laws calling for the sterilization of individuals with disabilities, while other state jurisdictions limited the basic rights of persons with disabilities, including voting, marrying, and obtaining drivers' licenses (Russo, 2018). By the 1960s, the percentage of children with disabilities who were served in public schools began to rise. While 12 percent of the students in public schools in 1948 had disabilities, the number of students with disabilities increased to 21 percent by 1963 and to 38 percent by 1968 (Zerrel & Ballard, 1982). While advancements in the legal rights of students with disabilities attempting to gain access to the country's public schools did not come easily, these legal rights advanced gradually with improved professional research and knowledge about individuals with disabilities, social advancements, and legal mandates initiated by concerned parents, educators, politicians, and advocates.

More specifically, the legal movement to advance the equal educational opportunities for students with disabilities gained sizable momentum during the late 1960s and early 1970s when parent activists filed legal suits on behalf of their children attempting to advance educational equality for the poor, language minorities, and racial minorities. Much of the legal language emerging from some of these judicial opinions had direct implications influencing the legal cause of students with disabilities. In a 1967 groundbreaking federal lawsuit in Washington D.C., Judge Skelly Wright declared that the tracking system used by the District of Columbia School District to assign students to various classes purportedly based on academic ability and achievement was discriminatory (*Hobson v. Hansen*, 1967). As part of this student tracking system, students were placed in tracks, or curriculum levels, as early as elementary school based on an academic ability assessment that relied heavily on nationally normed standardized aptitude tests. Once placed, it was difficult for students to ever move out of their assigned tracks. The court ordered school board officials to abolish the tracking system after hearing testimony suggesting that the tests produced inaccurate and misleading results when used with populations other than white middle-class students. The court found that using these tests with poor minority students, especially African-American students often resulted in the students being placed according to environmental and psychological factors rather than academic ability.

The court saw that since the school board lacked the ability to render scores that accurately reflected the innate learning abilities of a majority of its students, the students' placements in lower tracks was not justified. The federal court concluded that the local school district unconstitutionally used the tracking system to place racial minorities, especially African-American students in segregated and academically inferior classrooms (Colker, 2018). Moreover, school officials denied students placed in the lower academic tracks equal educational opportunities by failing to provide these students with compensatory educational services that would have helped to bring them back into the mainstream of public education.

At least two courts disallowed school systems from placing students in segregated educational programs on the basis of culturally biased assessments. In the first case, a student who was Spanish-speaking was placed in a class with students with intellectual and developmental disabilities on the basis of an intelligence quotient, or IQ test administered in English (*Diana v. State Board of Education*, 1970, 1973). The legal issue was similar in the second legal case, except that the student was African-American (*Larry P. v. Riles*, 1972, 1974, 1979, 1984). In the latter case, the court ruled that standardized student IQ tests were inappropriate because they were not validated for the class of students on whom they were used. This resulted in the students being placed disproportionately in special education classes. In both instances, the courts ordered the respective local school boards to develop nondiscriminatory procedures for placing students in special education classes. However, in a separate case, another federal trial court commented that standardized IQ tests commonly used in schools were not culturally or racially biased (*Parents in Action on Special Education v. Hannon*, 1980).

In 1974, the U.S. Supreme Court ruled that the failure to provide remedial English language instruction to non-English-speaking students violated Section 601 of the Civil Rights Act of 1974 (*Lau v. Nichols*, 1974). Plaintiffs filed a class action suit on behalf of Chinese students in the San Francisco school system who did not speak English and who had not been provided with English language instruction. The Court found that the board's denying the students the chance to receive remedial instruction denied them of meaningful opportunities to participate in public education. The Court contended that, as a recipient of federal funds, the school board was bound by Title VI of the Civil Rights Act of 1964 and a Department of Health, Education, and Welfare regulation that required it to take affirmative steps to rectify language deficiencies.

The growing legal success that advocates for students with disabilities enjoyed in mostly lower court cases initially are considered landmark opinions despite their limited precedential legal value since they provided the impetus for Congress to pass sweeping federal legislation mandating a free appropriate public education for students with disabilities, regardless of the severity or nature of their disabilities. These legal cases, which are listed by their conceptually related holdings, rather than chronologically, occurred in less than a decade of each other and are important because they helped establish many of the legal principles that shaped the far-reaching federal legislation that is now known as the Individuals with Disabilities Education Act (IDEA).

Legal Entitlement to an Appropriate Education for Students with Disabilities

One of the first legal cases that shifted the tide in favor of students with disabilities, *Wolf v. State of Utah* (1969), was filed in a state court on behalf of two children with mental retardation (now referred to as intellectual disability) who were denied admission to public schools. As a result, the parents of these children enrolled them in a private daycare center at their own expense. As background to the dispute, the parents, through their lawyer, pointed out that according to Utah's state constitution, the public school system should have been open to all children, a provision that the state supreme court interpreted broadly; other state statutes stipulated that all children between the ages of six and twenty-one who had not completed high school were entitled to public education at taxpayers' expense. In light of these provisions, the *Wolf* court, in language that was remarkably similar to portions of *Brown*, declared that children who had an intellectual disability were entitled to a free appropriate public education under the state constitution.

Two Landmark Federal Court Cases: The Legal Significance of PARC and Mills

Two federal class action suits combined to have a profound impact on the education of students with disabilities. The first case, *Pennsylvania Association for Retarded Children v. Commonwealth of Pennsylvania (PARC)* (1972), was initiated on behalf of a class of individuals between the ages of six and twenty-one with intellectual disabilities who were excluded from public schools. School officials justified the exclusions on the basis of four statutes that relieved them of any obligation to educate children who were certified, in the terminology used at that time, as uneducable and untrainable by school psychologists, allowed officials to postpone the admission to any children who had not attained the mental age of five years, excused children who were found unable to profit from education from compulsory attendance, and defined compulsory school age as eight to seventeen while excluding children who were mentally not between those ages.

PARC was resolved by means of a consent agreement between the parties that was endorsed by a federal trial court. In language that preceded the IDEA, the stipulations maintained that no "mentally retarded" child, or child thought to be "mentally retarded," could be assigned to a special education program or be excluded from the public schools without due process. The consent agreement added that school systems in Pennsylvania had the obligation to provide all children with intellectual disabilities a free appropriate public education and training programs appropriate to their capacities. Even though *PARC* was a consent decree, thereby arguably limiting its legal value to the parties, there can be no doubt that it helped to usher in significant positive change with regard to protecting the educational rights of students. *PARC* helped to establish that students who were "mentally retarded" (now referred to as an "intellectual disability") were entitled to receive a free appropriate public education, or FAPE.

The second legal case, *Mills v. Board of Education of the District of Columbia (Mills)* (1972), extended the same legal right to other classes of students with disabilities, establishing the principle that a lack of funds was an insufficient basis for denying children with disabilities services. Moreover, *Mills* provided much of the due process language that was later incorporated into the IDEA and other federal legislation. The *Mills* case similar to *PARC*, was a class action lawsuit brought on behalf of children who were excluded from the public schools in the District of Columbia after they were classified as being behavior problems, mentally retarded, emotionally disturbed, and hyperactive. In fact, in an egregious oversight, the plaintiffs estimated that approximately 18,000 out of 22,000 students with disabilities in the school district were not receiving special education services. The plaintiff class sought a declaration of rights and an order directing the school board to provide a publicly supported education to all students with disabilities either within its system of public schools or at alternative programs at public expense. School officials responded that while the board had the responsibility to provide a publicly supported education to meet the needs of all children within its boundaries and that it had failed to do so, it was impossible to afford the plaintiff class the relief it sought due to a lack of funds. Additionally, school personnel admitted that they had not provided the plaintiffs with due process procedures prior to their exclusion.

Entering a judgment on the merits in favor of the plaintiffs, meaning that it went beyond the consent decree in *PARC*, the federal trial court pointed out that the United States Constitution, the District of Columbia Code, and its own regulations required the board to provide a publicly supported education to all children, including those with disabilities. The court explained that the board had to expend its available funds equitably so that all students would receive a publicly funded education consistent with their needs and abilities. If sufficient funds were not available, the court asserted that existing funds would have to be distributed in such a manner that no child was entirely excluded and the inadequacies could not be allowed to bear more heavily on one class of students. In so ruling, the court directed the board to provide due process safeguards before any children were excluded from the public schools, reassigned, or had their special education services terminated. At the same time, as part of its opinion, the court outlined elaborate due process procedures that it expected the school board to follow. These procedures later formed the foundation for the due process safeguards that were mandated in the federal special education statute.

Major Legislative Initiatives

With the prospect of additional litigation, Congress, along with select state legislatures, passed new laws expanding the rights of students with disabilities to receive an appropriate education. In so doing, the legislatures incorporated many of the legal principles that emerged from the legal cases discussed previously. Table 1.2.1 chronologically depicts the foundational legal cases and federal legislation that helped secure the access of students with disabilities in the nation's public schools.

TABLE 1.2.1 Case Law and Legislation That Influenced the Education of Students with Disabilities

Date	Case Law or Legislation	Description
1954	*Brown v. Board of Education*	• Legally prohibited segregation in public schools on the basis of race
1965	Elementary and Secondary Education Act (ESEA) (P.L. 89–10)	• Provided federal funding to assist states in educating students as part of the war on poverty
1966	Amendments to the ESEA, Title VI (P.L. 89–750)	• Provided federal funding to assist states to expand programs for children with disabilities
1970	Education of the Handicapped Act (P.L. 91–230)	• Expanded state grant programs for children with disabilities • Provided grants to institutions of higher education to train special education teachers • Created regional resource centers
1972	*PARC v. Commonwealth of Pennsylvania*	• Required the state of Pennsylvania to provide students with "mental retardation" with a free appropriate education
1972	*Mills v. Board of Education of the District of Columbia*	• Ruled that since segregation in public schools by race is illegal, it would be unconstitutional for the District of Columbia Board of Education to deprive students with disabilities from receiving an education
1973	Section 504 of the Rehabilitation Act (P.L. 93–112)	• Prohibits discrimination against otherwise qualified individuals with disabilities in programs that receive federal funding
1974	Education Amendments (P.L. 93–380)	• Incorporated the rights from the legal cases from *PARC* and *Mills* into federal law
1975	Education for All Handicapped Children (P.L. 94–142)	• Provided federal funding to states that agree to educate eligible students with disabilities as required in the EAHCA • Established the rights of eligible students with disabilities to a free appropriate public education in the least restrictive environment • Required public school to develop an Individualized Education Plan (IEP) for each eligible student with disabilities • Established procedural safeguards
1986	The Handicapped Children's Protection Act (P.L. 99–372)	• Allowed parents to recover attorney's fees if they prevail in a due process hearing or court case
1986	Education of the Handicapped Amendments (P.L. 99–457)	• Created federal financial incentives to educate infants (birth through age two) using early intervention strategies • Extended the EAHCA's Part B programs to 3-to-5-year olds in participating states

Date	Case Law or Legislation	Description
1990	Individuals with Disabilities Education Act (P.L. 101–476)	• Renamed the EAHCA to IDEA • Added traumatic brain injury and autism as new disability categories under the IDEA • Added a transition requirement to the IEP for students age sixteen or older • Added language that states that were not immune from lawsuits under the 11th Amendment for violations of the IDEA • Changed to "people first" language
1997	Individuals with Disabilities Education Act Amendments (P.L. 105–17)	• Added new IEP content and changed the IEP team composition • Added new disciplinary provisions • Required states to offer mediation to parents prior to due process hearings • Reorganized the structure of the IDEA
2004	Individuals with Disabilities Education Improvement Act (P.L. 108–446)	• Defined "highly qualified" special education teacher • Removed the short-term objectives requirement from IEPs, except for students with severe disabilities • Prohibited states from requiring school districts to use a discrepancy formula for determining eligibility of students with learning disabilities

Source: Yell, M.L. (2019). *The law and special education (5th Ed.)*. New York, NY: Pearson.

The Standards-Based Reform Movement and Students With Disabilities

Beginning in the 1980s, the U.S. educational system experienced a standards-based reform movement. In 1983, the National Commission on Excellence in Education published an influential report, *A Nation at Risk*, highlighting the fact that U.S. students were lagging behind academically when compared with other students in other countries. In order to address this educational deficit, state and local school systems began to develop and implement educational reforms supporting the use of national academic standards promoting improvements in academic performance. As a way to incentivize the implementation of these education reforms, levels of federal funding were contingent on individual states demonstrating improvement in the academic performance of students.

Approximately a decade after the beginning of the standards-based education reform movement, the 1997 reauthorization of the Individuals with Disabilities Education Act (IDEA) included an expectation for encouraging high academic expectations for students with disabilities. Despite continued low overall student academic performance in U.S. schools throughout the 1990s, Congress passed the No Child Left Behind Act of 2001, often referred to as NCLB. President George W. Bush signed this bill into law on January 8, 2002. NCLB expanded the existing standards-based reforms of the 1990s and developed a comprehensive system of enforcement measures requiring the regular testing of students. Individual student test results were compared to specific state-defined standards of academic achievement. The regular testing of students mandated under NCLB included the reporting of traditionally underperforming subgroups of students, including students with disabilities. Prior to the passage of NCLB, many students with disabilities either did not participate or their test scores were withdrawn from state academic testing assessments. Under NCLB, schools were required to demonstrate through specific data assessment measures, a steady and measured increase in student achievement levels in order to satisfy NCLB's designated adequate yearly progress, or AYP goals. If schools were repeatedly unable to satisfy these designated AYP targets, there would be penalties imposed by the federal government, including the withholding of federal funds. Students with disabilities were one of the identified student subgroups under NCLB. As such, the academic performance of students with disabilities became an integral part of the NCLB student accountability system, which became a central theme of the 2004 IDEA reauthorization process. A primary focus of the most recent 2004 IDEA reauthorization was linking NCLB's objective of holding all schools accountable for the academic progress of its students, including students with disabilities as well as maintaining the IDEA's existing goal of providing eligible students with disabilities a free and appropriate public education (FAPE) in the least restrictive environment (LRE). Congress struggled to find a balance between NCLB demands for increased school accountability with the need to legally safeguard existing IDEA entitlements and protections for students with disabilities.

Today, special education in the U.S. is governed primarily by three federal laws as well as individual state laws. The three federal laws are the Individuals with Disabilities Education Act (IDEA), Section 504 of the Rehabilitation Act (Section 504), and the Americans with Disabilities Act (ADA). While the IDEA receives considerably more attention in this book, both Section 504 and the ADA are federal antidiscrimination statutes assisting students with disabilities achieve improved access in schools nationwide. These two federal statutes are discussed in more detail in Chapter 12.

Individuals with Disabilities Education Act (IDEA)

In 1975, Congress passed Public Law (P.L.) 94–142, which at that time was known as the Education for All Handicapped Children Act. In a 1990 amendment, this landmark statute was given its current title, the Individuals with Disabilities Education Act (IDEA). P.L. 94–142, signifying that it was the 142nd piece of legislation introduced during the Ninety-Fourth Congress, was not an independent act. Instead, the IDEA was an amendment to previous legislation that provided funds to the states for educating students with disabilities.

The important aspect of the IDEA is that it is permanent legislation, while previous laws expired unless they were reauthorized.

The IDEA mandates a free appropriate public education (FAPE) in the least restrictive environment (LRE) for all students with disabilities between the ages of three and twenty-one based on the contents of their Individualized Education Programs (IEPs). Educators must develop IEPs in conferences with students' parents for any children who require special education and related services. The IDEA specifies how IEPs are to be developed and what they must contain. Additionally, the IDEA includes elaborate due process safeguards to protect the rights of students and ensure that its provisions are enforced. As part of the IDEA's funding formula that allows all school districts to qualify for funds, boards receiving funds are subject to fairly rigid auditing and management requirements.

The IDEA has been periodically amended, or reauthorized, since its original enactment in 1975. The Handicapped Children's Protection Act (1986), an important modification, added a clause that allows parents who prevail in litigation against their school boards to recover legal expenses. Another amendment, the Education of the Handicapped Amendments of 1986, provided grants to states that wish to provide services to children with disabilities from birth to age two. The 1990 amendments, mentioned previously, changed the statute's name and abrogated the states' Eleventh Amendment immunity to litigation.

Another important reauthorization, the Individuals with Disabilities Education Act Amendments of 1997, which was passed after a great deal of debate, incorporated disciplinary provisions into the IDEA. The most recent amendments, the Individuals with Disabilities Education Improvement Act of 2004, now codified as the IDEA, modified the 1997 disciplinary provisions and brought the IDEA in alignment with other federal legislation. More specifically, the most recent IDEA 2004 represents Congress' efforts to incorporate increased school and student accountability requirements of NCLB with the existing statutory structure of providing special education and related services to eligible students with disabilities. The most recent IDEA 2004 has altered and adjusted many provisions in the federal law compared to its predecessors, including requiring state educational agencies (SEAs) and local educational agencies (LEAs) to do the following:

1. Increase accountability and improve the educational performance for students with disabilities
2. Reduce the administrative burden on today's special education teachers and administrators
3. Reduce the over-identification or misidentification of nondisabled children and youth, including minority children and youth
4. Increase the flexibility of educational programs offered to students with disabilities

5. Improve the overall safety of school environments as they impact students with disabilities
6. Reduce the litigation of special education-related legal disputes
7. Support both general education and special education teachers
8. Improve early intervention strategies for students with disabilities

Section 504, the Rehabilitation Act of 1973

According to Section 504 of the Rehabilitation Act of 1973:

> No otherwise qualified individual with a disability in the United States ... shall, solely by reason of her or his disability, be excluded from the participation in, be denied the benefits of, or be subjected to discrimination under any program or activity receiving Federal financial assistance or under any program or activity conducted by any Executive agency or by the United States Postal Service.

Section 504 was the first federal civil rights legislation that specifically guaranteed the rights of disabled persons, even though it relies on the broader term "impairment" in offering its protections to qualified individuals. Section 504's provisions that prohibit discrimination against individuals with disabilities in programs receiving federal funds are similar to those found in Titles VI (2005) and VII of the Civil Rights Act of 1964 (2005), which forbids employment discrimination in programs that receive federal financial assistance on the basis of race, color, religion, sex, or national origin. Section 504 effectively prohibits discrimination by any recipient of federal funds in the provision of services or employment. Individuals are covered by Section 504 if they have physical or mental impairments that substantially limit one or more of life's major life activities, have a record of such impairments, or are regarded as having impairments (29 U.S.C. § 706(7) (B)). Major life activities are "functions such as caring for oneself, performing manual tasks, walking, seeing, hearing, speaking, breathing, learning, and working" (28 C.F.R. § 41.31).

Americans with Disabilities Act (ADA)

The Americans with Disabilities Act (ADA), passed in 1990, prohibits discrimination against individuals with disabilities in the private sector. The ADA's preamble explains its purpose as acting "to provide a clear and comprehensive national mandate for the elimination of discrimination against individuals with disabilities" (42 U.S.C. § 12101). Basically, the intent of the ADA is to extend the protections afforded by Section 504 to programs and activities that are not covered by Section 504 because they do not receive federal funds. While the

ADA is aimed primarily at the private sector, public agencies are not immune to its provisions. Compliance with Section 504 does not automatically translate to compliance with the ADA. The legislative history of the ADA indicates that it also addresses what the judiciary had perceived as shortcomings or loopholes in Section 504 (Marczely, 1993).

State Statutes

Since public education is a function of the states, rather than the federal government, special education is governed by state laws in addition to the federal statutes discussed earlier. While state special education laws must be consistent with federal laws, to the extent that they cannot do less than the federal statutes require, states can provide greater legal protection(s) for children with disabilities if they wish to do so. To this end, while most states have laws that are similar in scope and language to the federal IDEA statute, several jurisdictions include provisions in their legislation that exceed the federal IDEA's requirements. For example, some states have higher standards of what constitutes a free appropriate education for a student with disabilities. Other states have stricter procedural requirements designed to protect students with disabilities as well as their parents. Most states have established procedures for special education program implementation that are either not covered by federal law or have been left to the discretion of individual states to determine. If a conflict develops between provisions of the IDEA or other federal statutes and state laws, federal law is almost always considered to be supreme under Article VI of the United States Constitution.

A comprehensive discussion of the laws of each of the fifty states, the District of Columbia, and various American possessions and territories is beyond the scope of this book. Each of these governmental entities has its own terminology, laws, regulations, funding schemes, and legal systems. Indeed, entire books could be written on the special education laws of each state. The primary purpose of this book is to improve the special education legal literacy of persons who work closely with students with disabilities by providing comprehensive information on the federal mandate, the laws encompassing the entire nation. As such, readers are cautioned that they cannot acquire a complete understanding of special education law if they are not familiar with their existing state's law relating to students with disabilities. Thus, readers are advised to seek out sources of information involving the pertinent laws of their states to supplement this book.

SPECIAL EDUCATION LAW IN PRACTICE

Legal Case No. 2—Sanctioned Exclusion of Students with Disabilities From Public Schools

WATSON V. CITY OF CAMBRIDGE

157 Mass. 561 (1893)

OPINION

KNOWLTON, J.

The records of the school committee of the defendant city set forth that the plaintiff in 1885 was excluded from the schools "because he was too weak-minded to derive profit from instruction." He was afterwards taken again on trial for two weeks, and at the end of that time again excluded. The records further recite that "it appears from the statements of teachers who observed him, and from certificates of physicians, that he is so weak in mind as not to derive any marked benefit from instruction, and, further, that he is troublesome to other children, making unusual noises, pinching others, etc. He is also found unable to take ordinary, decent, physical care of himself." The evidence at the trial tended strongly to show that the matters set out in the records were true.

The defendant requested the court to rule that if the facts are true which are set forth in the records of the committee, as to the cause of the exclusion of the plaintiff from the public schools, the determination of the school committee thereon, acting in good faith, was final, and not subject to revision in the courts. The court refused so to rule, and submitted to the jury the question whether the facts stated, if proved, showed that the plaintiff's presence in school "was a serious disturbance to the good order and discipline of the school."

The exceptions present the question whether the decision of the school committee of a city or town, acting in good faith in the management of the schools, upon matters of fact directly affecting the good order and discipline of the schools, is final, so far as it relates to the rights of pupils to enjoy the privileges of the school, or is subject to revision by a court. In *Hodgkins v. Rockport*, it appeared that the school committee, acting in good faith, excluded the plaintiff from school on account "of his general persistence in disobeying the rules of the school, to the injury of the school." Of the plaintiff's acts of misconduct, it is said, in the opinion in that case, that "whether they had such an effect upon the welfare of the school as to require his expulsion was a question within the discretion of the committee, and upon which their action is conclusive." The principles there laid down are decisive of the present case. It was found by the presiding justice that the alleged misconduct of the plaintiff in that case was not mutinous or gross, and did not consist of a refusal to obey the commands of the teachers, or of any outrageous proceeding, but of acts of neglect, carelessness of posture in his seat, and recitation, tricks of playfulness, inattention to study and the regulations of the school in minor matters. The only difference between the acts of disorder in that case and in this is that in this they resulted from the incapacity and mental weakness of the plaintiff, and in the other they were willful or careless,-the result in part of youthful exuberance of spirits and impatience of restraint or control. In their general effect upon the school, they were alike; and the reasons for giving the school committee, acting in good faith, the power to decide finally a question affecting so vitally the rights and interests of all the other scholars of the school, are the same in both cases.

Under the law the school committee "have the general charge and superintendence of all the public schools in the town" or city. Pub. St. c. 44, § 21. The management of the schools involves many details; and it is important that a board of public officers, dealing with these details, and having jurisdiction to regulate the internal affairs of the schools, should not be interfered with or have their conduct called in question before another tribunal, so long as they act in good faith within their jurisdiction. Whether certain acts of disorder so seriously interfere with the school that one who persists in them, either voluntarily or by reason of imbecility, should not be permitted to continue in the school, is a question which the statute makes it their duty to answer; and if they answer honestly, in an effort to do their duty, a jury composed of men of no special fitness to decide educational questions should not be permitted to say that their answer is wrong. Spear v. Cummings, 23 Pick. 224, 226. We are of opinion that the ruling requested should have been given.

Exceptions sustained.

Questions for Discussion

1. In this case, the courts indicate that ultimately local school boards have the discretion to make judgements concerning the admission of students to a school. What are your thoughts about the local school board having full legal authority to make admissions decisions on all students, especially students with disabilities?

2. The current IDEA provides parents significant procedural due process protections, including the ability to formally request a hearing to challenge a local school district's decision regarding the identification, evaluation, or educational program or placement of their child. Can you think of any modern-day practices of schools limiting the access of students with disabilities to educational programs and services?

SPECIAL EDUCATION LAW IN PRACTICE

Legal Case No. 3—Rights of Students with Disabilities to a Public Education

PENNSYLVANIA ASSOCIATION FOR RETARDED CHILDREN (PARC) V. COMMONWEALTH OF PENNSYLVANIA

343 F. Supp. 279 (1972)

OPINION, ORDER AND INJUNCTION

MASTERSON, District Judge.

This civil rights case, a class action, was brought by the Pennsylvania Association for Retarded Children and the parents of thirteen individual retarded children on behalf of all mentally retarded persons between the ages 6 and 21 whom the Commonwealth of Pennsylvania, through its local school districts and intermediate units, is presently excluding from a program of education and training in the public schools. Named as defendants are the Commonwealth of Pennsylvania, Secretary of Welfare, State Board of Education and thirteen individual school districts scattered throughout the Commonwealth. In addition, plaintiffs have joined all other school districts in the Commonwealth as class defendants of which the named districts are said to be representative.

The exclusions of retarded children complained of are based upon four State statutes: (1) ... which relieves the State Board of Education from any obligation to educate a child whom a public school psychologist certifies as uneducable and untrainable. The burden of caring for such a child then shifts to the Department of Welfare which has no obligation to provide any educational services for the child; (2) ... which allows an indefinite postponement of admission to public school of any child who has not attained a mental age of five years; (3) ... which appears to *excuse* any child from compulsory school attendance whom a psychologist finds unable to profit therefrom and (4) ... which defines compulsory school age as 8 to 17 years but has been used in practice to postpone admissions of retarded children until 8 or to eliminate them from public schools at age 17.

[T]he parties agreed upon a Stipulation which basically provides that no child who is mentally retarded or thought to be mentally retarded can be assigned initially (or re-assigned) to either a regular or special educational status, or excluded from a public education without a prior recorded hearing before a special hearing officer. At that hearing, parents have the right to representation by counsel, to examine their child's records, to compel the attendance of school officials who may have relevant evidence to offer, to cross-examine witnesses testifying on behalf of school officials and to introduce evidence of their own. ...

[T]he parties submitted a Consent Agreement to this Court which, along with the ... Stipulation, would settle the entire case. Essentially, this Agreement deals with the four state statutes in an effort to eliminate the alleged equal protection problems. As a proposed cure, the defendants agreed, that since "the Commonwealth of Pennsylvania has undertaken to provide a free public education for all of its children between the ages of six and twenty-one years" ... therefore, "it is the Commonwealth's obligation to place each mentally retarded child in a *free, public program of education and training appropriate to the child's capacity*."

The lengthy Consent Agreement concludes by stating that "[e]very retarded person between the ages of six and twenty-one shall be provided access to a free public program of education and training appropriate to his capacities as soon as possible but in no event later than *September 1, 1972*. ..." Finally, and perhaps most importantly, the Agreement states that:

"The defendants shall formulate and submit ... *a plan to be effectuated by September 1, 1972*, to commence or recommence a free public program of education and training for all mentally retarded persons ... aged between four and twenty-one years as of the date of this Order, and for all mentally retarded persons of such ages hereafter. The plan shall specify the range of programs of education and training, there [sic] kind and number, necessary to provide an appropriate program of education and training to all mentally retarded children, where they shall be conducted, arrangements for their financing, and, if additional teachers are found to be necessary, the plan shall specify recruitment, hiring, and training arrangements."

Thus, if all goes according to plan, Pennsylvania should be providing a meaningful program of education and training to every retarded child in the Commonwealth by September, 1972.

Questions for Discussion

1. Although the *PARC* legal case dealt only with the right to an education for students who suffered from intellectual difficulties (at the time, referred to as mental retardation) it is considered a landmark case involving the access of students with disabilities to an education. Why is this particular legal decision also important for students with other types of disabilities?
2. The fact that this legal dispute was settled by a stipulation and consent agreement indicates that the state of Pennsylvania accepted its legal obligation to provide appropriate *educational opportunities for its students with disabilities*. Compare this case to

the *Mills v. Board of Education of the District of Columbia* case where the District of Columbia School District claimed that it did not have the proper financial resources to appropriately educate its students with disabilities. Do you think this is a valid argument? Why or why not? Many public school districts nationwide claim they do not have the necessary financial resources to appropriately educate their population of students with disabilities. Do you think this is a valid argument for today's public school districts to make?

SPECIAL EDUCATION LAW IN PRACTICE

Legal Case No. 4—Establishment of Due Process Rights for Students with Disabilities

MILLS V. BOARD OF EDUCATION OF THE DISTRICT OF COLUMBIA

348 F. Supp. 866 (1972)

MEMORANDUM OPINION, JUDGMENT AND DECREE

WADDY, District Judge.

This is a civil action brought on behalf of seven children of school age by their next friends in which they seek a declaration of rights and to enjoin the defendants from excluding them from the District of Columbia Public Schools and/or denying them publicly supported education and to compel the defendants to provide them with immediate and adequate education and educational facilities in the public schools or alternative placement at public expense. They also seek additional and ancillary relief to effectuate the primary relief. They allege that although they can profit from an education either in regular classrooms with supportive services or in special classes adopted to their needs, they have been labeled as behavioral problems, mentally retarded, emotionally disturbed or hyperactive, and denied admission to the public schools or excluded therefrom after admission, with no provision for alternative educational placement or periodic review....

The Problem

The genesis of this case is found (1) in the failure of the District of Columbia to provide publicly supported education and training to plaintiffs and other "exceptional" children, members of their class, and (2) the excluding, suspending, expelling, reassigning, and transferring of "exceptional" children from regular public school classes without affording them due process of law.

The problem of providing special education for "exceptional" children (mentally retarded, emotionally disturbed, physically handicapped, hyperactive and other children with behavioral problems) is one of major proportions in the District of Columbia. The precise number of such children cannot be stated because the District has continuously failed to comply with Section 31–208 of the District of Columbia Code which requires a census of all children aged 3 to 18 in the District to be taken. Plaintiffs estimate that there are " ... 22,000 retarded, emotionally disturbed, blind, deaf, and speech or learning disabled children, and perhaps as many as 18,000 of these children are not being furnished with programs of specialized education." According to data prepared by the Board of Education, ... the District of Columbia provides publicly supported special education programs of various descriptions to at least 3880 school age children. However, in a 1971 report to the Department of Health, Education and Welfare, the District of Columbia Public Schools admitted that an estimated 12,340 handicapped children were not to be served in the 1971–72 school year.... Each of the minor plaintiffs in this case qualifies as an "exceptional" child. Plaintiffs allege in their complaint and defendants admit as follows:

"PETER MILLS is twelve years old, black, and a committed dependent ward of the District of Columbia resident at Junior Village. He was excluded from the Brent Elementary School on March 23, 1971, at which time he was in the fourth grade. Peter allegedly was a 'behavior problem' and was recommended and approved for exclusion by the principal. Defendants have not provided him with a full hearing or with a timely and adequate review of his status. Furthermore, Defendants have failed to provide for his reenrollment in the District of Columbia Public Schools or enrollment in private school. On information and belief, numerous other dependent children of school attendance age at Junior Village are denied a publicly-supported education. Peter remains excluded from any publicly-supported education.

- "DUANE BLACKSHEARE is thirteen years old, black, resident at Saint Elizabeth's Hospital, Washington, D. C., and a dependent committed child. He was excluded from the Giddings Elementary School in October, 1967, at which time he was in the third grade. Duane allegedly was a "behavior problem." Defendants have not provided him with a full hearing or with a timely and adequate review of his status. Despite repeated efforts by his mother, Duane remained largely excluded from all publicly-supported education until February, 1971. Education experts at the Child Study Center examined Duane and found him to be capable of returning to regular class if supportive services were provided. Following several articles in the Washington Post and Washington Star, Duane was placed in a regular seventh grade classroom on a two-hour a day basis without any catch-up assistance and without an evaluation or diagnostic interview of any kind. Duane has remained on a waiting list for a tuition grant and is now excluded from all publicly-supported education.

- "GEORGE LIDDELL, JR., is eight years old, black, resident with his mother, Daisy Liddell, at 601 Morton Street, N. W., Washington, D. C., and an AFDC recipient. George has never attended public school because of the denial of his application to the Maury Elementary School on the ground that he required a special class. George allegedly was retarded. Defendants have not provided him with a full hearing or with a timely and adequate review of his status. George remains excluded from all publicly-supported education, despite a medical opinion that he is capable of profiting from schooling, and despite his mother's efforts to secure a tuition grant from Defendants.

- "STEVEN GASTON is eight years old, black, resident with his mother, Ina Gaston, at 714 9th Street, N. E., Washington, D. C. and unable to afford private instruction. He has been excluded from the Taylor Elementary School since September, 1969, at which time he was in the first grade. Steven allegedly was slightly brain-damaged and hyperactive, and was excluded because he wandered around the classroom. Defendants have not provided him with a full hearing or with a timely and adequate review of his status. Steven was accepted in the Contemporary School, a private school, provided that tuition was paid in full in advance. Despite the efforts of his parents, Steven has remained on a waiting list for the requisite tuition grant from Defendant school system and excluded from all publicly-supported education.

- "MICHAEL WILLIAMS is sixteen years old, black, resident at Saint Elizabeth's Hospital, Washington, D. C., and unable to afford private instruction. Michael is epileptic and allegedly slightly retarded. He has been excluded from the Sharpe Health School since October, 1969, at which time he was temporarily hospitalized. Thereafter Michael was excluded from school because of health problems and school absences. Defendants have not provided him with a full hearing or with a timely and adequate review of his status. Despite his mother's efforts, and his attending physician's medical opinion that he could attend school, Michael has remained on a waiting list for a tuition grant and excluded from all publicly-supported education.

- "JANICE KING is thirteen years old, black, resident with her father, Andrew King, at 233 Anacostia Avenue, N. E., Washington, D. C., and unable to afford private instruction. She has been denied access to public schools since reaching compulsory school attendance age, as a result of the rejection of her application, based on the lack of an appropriate educational program. Janice is brain-damaged and retarded, with right hemiplegia, resulting from a childhood illness. Defendants have not provided her with a full hearing or with a timely and adequate review of her status. Despite repeated efforts by her parents, Janice has been excluded from all publicly-supported education.

- "JEROME JAMES is twelve years old, black, resident with his mother, Mary James, at 2512 Ontario Avenue, N. W., Washington, D. C., and an AFDC recipient. Jerome is a retarded child and has been totally excluded from public school. Defendants have not given him a full hearing or a timely and adequate review of his status. Despite his mother's efforts to secure either public school placement or a tuition grant, Jerome has remained on a waiting list for a tuition grant and excluded from all publicly supported education."

- Although all of the named minor plaintiffs are identified as Negroes the class they represent is not limited by their race. They sue on behalf of and represent all other District of Columbia residents of school age who are eligible for a free public education and who have been, or may be, excluded from such education or otherwise deprived by defendants of access to publicly supported education.

Minor plaintiffs are poor and without financial means to obtain private instruction. There has been no determination that they may not benefit from specialized instruction adapted to their needs. Prior to the beginning of the 1971–72 school year minor plaintiffs, through their representatives, sought to obtain publicly supported education and certain of them were assured by the school authorities that they would be placed in programs of publicly supported education and certain others would be recommended for special tuition grants at private schools. However, none of the plaintiff children were placed for the 1971 Fall term and they continued to be entirely excluded from all publicly supported education. After thus trying unsuccessfully to obtain relief from the Board of Education the plaintiffs filed this action on September 24, 1971.

Judgment and Decree

Plaintiffs having filed their verified complaint seeking an injunction and declaration of rights as set forth more fully in the verified complaint and the prayer for relief contained therein; and having moved this Court for summary judgment pursuant to [the rules of civil procedure], and this Court having reviewed the record of this cause ... it is hereby ordered, adjudged and decreed that summary judgment in favor of plaintiffs and against defendants be, and hereby is, granted, and judgment is entered in this action as follows:

1. That no child eligible for a publicly supported education in the District of Columbia public schools shall be excluded from a regular public school assignment by a Rule, policy, or practice of the Board of Education of the District of Columbia or its agents unless such child is provided (a) adequate alternative educational services suited to the child's needs, which may include special education or tuition grants, and (b) a constitutionally adequate prior hearing and periodic review of the child's status, progress, and the adequacy of any educational alternative.

2. The defendants, their officers, agents, servants, employees, and attorneys and all those in active concert or participation with them are hereby enjoined from maintaining, enforcing or otherwise continuing in effect any and all rules, policies and practices which exclude plaintiffs and the members of the class they represent from a regular public school assignment without providing them at public expense (a) adequate and immediate alternative education or tuition grants, consistent with their

needs, and (b) a constitutionally adequate prior hearing and periodic review of their status, progress and the adequacy of any educational alternatives; and it is further ORDERED that:

3. The District of Columbia shall provide to each child of school age a free and suitable publicly-supported education regardless of the degree of the child's mental, physical or emotional disability or impairment. Furthermore, defendants shall not exclude any child resident in the District of Columbia from such publicly-supported education on the basis of a claim of insufficient resources….

13. Hearing Procedures.

a. Each member of the plaintiff class is to be provided with a publicly-supported educational program suited to his needs, within the context of a presumption that among the alternative programs of education, placement in a regular public school class with appropriate ancillary services is preferable to placement in a special school class.

b. Before placing a member of the class in such a program, defendants shall notify his parent or guardian of the proposed educational placement, the reasons therefor, and the right to a hearing before a Hearing Officer if there is an objection to the placement proposed. Any such hearing shall be held in accordance with the provisions of Paragraph 13.e., below.

c. Hereinafter, children who are residents of the District of Columbia and are thought by any of the defendants, or by officials, parents or guardians, to be in need of a program of special education, shall neither be placed in, transferred from or to, nor denied placement in such a program unless defendants shall have first notified their parents or guardians of such proposed placement, transfer or denial, the reasons therefor, and of the right to a hearing before a Hearing Officer if there is an objection to the placement, transfer or denial of placement. Any such hearings shall be held in accordance with the provisions of Paragraph 13.e., below.

d. Defendants shall not, on grounds of discipline, cause the exclusion, suspension, expulsion, postponement, interschool transfer, or any other denial of access to regular instruction in the public schools to any child for more than two days without first notifying the child's parent or guardian of such proposed action, the reasons therefor, and of the hearing before a Hearing Officer in accordance with the provisions of Paragraph 13.f., below.

e. Whenever defendants take action regarding a child's placement, denial of placement, or transfer, as described in Paragraphs 13.b. or 13.c., above, the following procedures shall be followed.

....

(15) Pending a determination by the Hearing Officer, defendants shall take no action described in Paragraphs 13.b or 13.c, above, if the child's parent or guardian objects to such action. Such objection must be in writing and postmarked within five (5) days of the date of receipt of notification herein above described.

Questions for Discussion

1. The plaintiffs in *Mills* estimated that as many as 18,000 of the District of Columbia's 22,000 students with disabilities were not receiving specialized educational services. In today's world that would be unconscionable, but sadly, in 1972 it was not that unusual.

2. The **local** board of education in *Mills* basically claimed that it could not afford to provide the required services to give the plaintiffs the relief they sought. The court responded that the available funds needed to be expended equitably so that students with disabilities would not be disproportionately deprived of an equal educational opportunity. How does this decision compare with other equal educational opportunity opinions?

3. Many legal commentators have expressed the view that *Mills* laid the groundwork for the elaborate due process provisions that are included in the IDEA. Compare the due process procedures outlined in this decision with those currently included in § 1415 of the IDEA. What are the similarities and differences?

Summary of Important Legal Policies, Principles, and Practices

This chapter provides a brief overview of major historical developments impacting the axis of students with disabilities to public schools. Prior to the mid-1970s, there was considerable exclusion of children and youth with disabilities from the nation's schools. The legal rights afforded children and youth with disabilities were gained through the efforts of many individuals. Some historical highlights in the development of influential case law and legislation impacting children and youth with disabilities and their access to schooling include

1. Despite compulsory education laws in many states by the 1900s, children and youth with disabilities were largely excluded from public schools and this exclusion was sanctioned by both the federal and state courts across the country.

2. The Civil Rights Movement, especially the U.S. Supreme Court's *Brown v. Board of Education* (1954) decision was a catalyst for subsequent litigation and legislation related to providing students with disabilities the right to a free appropriate public education (FAPE).

3. Two seminal legal cases, *PARC v. Pennsylvania* (1972) and *Mills v. Board of Education* (1972) became precursors to federal legislative efforts to improve the education of students with disabilities. These early major pieces of legislation were Section 504 of the Rehabilitation Act of 1973 (Section 504) and the Education for All Handicapped Children Act of 1975 (EAHCA).

4. More recent federal efforts to improve the educational rights of students with disabilities include the Individuals with Disabilities Education Act and the Americans with Disabilities Act (ADA).

5. Beginning with the passage of the No Child Left Behind Act of 2001(NCLB), increased nationwide school accountability efforts led to increased monitoring efforts of the academic progress of students with disabilities in conjunction with maintaining legal entitlements and protections already provided under the IDEA.

Useful Online Resources

Celebrating the 40th Anniversary of IDEA

This YouTube video provides an excellent 10-minute overview on the history and impact of the Individuals with Disabilities Education Act (IDEA). www.youtube.com/watch?v=Oj4b9d4XAdY

Recommended Reading

Ballard, J., Ramirez, B., & Weintraub, F. (Eds.). (1982). *Special education in America: Its legal and governmental foundations*. Reston, VA: Council for Exceptional Children.

Katsiyannis, A., Yell, M. L., & Bradley, R. (2001). Reflections on the 25th anniversary of the Individuals with Disabilities Act. *Remedial and Special Education, 22*, 324–334.

Martin, E. W. (2013). *Breakthrough: Special education legislation 1965–1981*. Sarasota, FL: Bardolf & Company.

Winzer, M. A. (1993). *History of special education from isolation to integration*. Washington, DC: Gallaudet Press.

Yell, M. L., Rogers, D., & Rogers, E. L. (1998, July/August). The legal history of special education: What a long, strange trip it's been! *Remedial and Special Education, 19* (4), 219–228.

References

Americans with Disabilities Act, 42 U.S.C. §§ 12101–12213 (1990).

Brown v. Board of Education, 347 U.S. 483 (1954).

Civil Rights Act of 1964, Title VI, 42 U.S.C. §§ 2000 *et seq.* (2005).

Colker, R. (2018). *Special education law in a nutshell*. St. Paul, MN: West Academic Publishing.

Diana v. State Board of Education, Civ. No. C-70-37 RFP (N.D. Cal. 1970 & 1973).

Education for All Handicapped Children Act, 20 U.S.C. § 1400 *et seq.* (1975).

Education of the Handicapped Amendments of 1986, P.L. 99–457, 100 Stat. 1145 (1986).

Hobson v. Hansen, 269 F. Supp. 401 (D.D.C. 1967).

Individuals with Disabilities Education Act Amendments of 1997, P.L. 105–17, 11 Stat. 37 (1997).

Individuals with Disabilities Education Improvement Act of 2004, P.L. 108–446, 118 Stat. 2647 (2004).

Larry P. v. Riles, 343 F. Supp. 1306 (N.D. Cal. 1972), *aff'd*, 502 F.2d 963 (9th Cir. 1974), *further action*, 495 F. Supp. 926 (N.D. Cal. 1979), *aff'd*, 793 F.2d 969 (9th Cir. 1984).

Lau v. Nichols, 414 U.S. 563 (1974).

Marczely, B. (1993). The Americans with Disabilities Act: Confronting the shortcomings of Section 504 in public education. *Education Law Reporter, 78*, 199–207.

Mills v. Board of Education of the District of Columbia, 348 F. Supp. 866 (D.D.C. 1972).

Parents in Action on Special Education v. Hannon, 506 F. Supp. 831 (N.D. Ill. 1980).

Pennsylvania Association for Retarded Children v. Commonwealth of Pennsylvania, 334 F. Supp. 1257 (E.D. Pa. 1971), 343 F. Supp. 279 (E.D. Pa. 1972).

Russo, C. J. (2018). *Russo's law of public education* (9th ed.). New York: Foundation Press.

State ex rel. Beattie v. Board of Education of Antigo, 169 Wis. 231 (Wis. 1919).

Turnbull, H. R., Stowe, M. J., & Huerta, N. E. (2007). *Free appropriate public education: The law and children with disabilities*. Denver, CO: Love.

Watson v. City of Cambridge, 157 Mass. 561 (Mass. 1893).

Wolf v. State of Utah, Civ. No. 182646 (Utah Dist. Ct. 1969).

Yell, M. L. (2019). *The law and special education* (5th ed.). New York: Pearson.

Zerrel, J. J., & Ballard, J. (1982). The Education for All Handicapped Children Act of 1975 (P.L. 94–142). Its history, origins, and concepts. In J. Ballard, B. Ramirez, & F. Weintraub (Eds.), *Special education in America: Its legal and governmental foundations* (pp. 11–22). Reston, VA. Council for Exceptional Children.

Reading 1.3

The Emergence of Special and Inclusive Education

USA

Sally Tomlinson

> Special education is the dark side of public education, the institutional practice
> that emerged in twentieth century industrial democracies to conceal the failure
> to educate all citizens to full political, economic and cultural participation in
> a democracy.
>
> (Skrtic 1991b: preface)

Although education systems differ between countries in terms of their histories, values and practices, there are many similarities between England and the USA as to how they have elaborated their systems to incorporate the special and lower attainers. A major difference between the education systems is that while the English system is now heavily centralised, in the USA a Federal government sets an agenda within which the 50 states function. The educational control is delegated to states, school districts and school boards. A major similarity is that both countries have embraced neo-liberal policies in education, with a competitive ethos between individuals and schools, marked by constant central exhortations to raise standards for all students, and a heavy emphasis on the likely deficiencies of students, families, schools and teachers, if there is failure to achieve higher standards.

The history, policies and practices that emerged as education for the disabled, disruptive, less able and special, have been documented more thoroughly in the USA than England, as from the nineteenth century the country used education more extensively as a means to create a nation from disparate groups inhabiting wide geographical areas (Sarason and Doris 1979; Chambers and Hartman 1983; Richardson 1999; Osgood 2009; Danforth 2009; Powell 2011). Legislators and educators aim was to create a common school out of disparate migrant groups and social classes, while retaining a white middle class norm of what constituted acceptable social and cultural behaviour (Tulkin 1972). When states from the later nineteenth century began to enact compulsory attendance laws, the enforcement of these laws "threw a new burden on public schools. Not only have the truant and incorrigible been brought into schools, but also many suffering from physical and mental defects as well as those of low mentality" (Wallin 1924: introduction). An influential special education profession emerged earlier than in England and the plethora of literature on emerging policies and practices continues to be marked by antagonisms between those supporting special education as a sub-system in its own right and proponents of inclusion. As Osgood noted "stakeholders in special education have become more vocal about the issues, with their views reaching a much wider and more attentive audience than ever before" (Osgood 2009:126). As in the previous chapter, this chapter briefly covers the origins and emergence of special and inclusive education in the USA over 150 years, in the light of prevailing social, economic, political and administrative interests.

In contrast to England, there was less stress on ideologies of benevolence and more punitive concern about the problems troublesome children caused to a developing public schooling system. There was also more overt concern with the future careers of the young people, either vocational training and low paid jobs, or reformatories and prisons (Richardson et al. 2017). In one of the few commentaries comparing 'British' special education with the USA Kirp (1983), took the view that special education in the UK had been largely left to medical and psychological professionals, with minimal government interference, whereas in the USA there was more bureaucratic concern for control and legislative accountability, and special education was placed in a wider political and legal framework. The history of special education, disability and inclusion is related to a racialised history of education. In the USA, at all levels of education beliefs, policies and practices are bound up with the early exclusion and then the negative incorporation of African-American, Latino and Native American students in particular, in public education systems. Kirp noted that the major English report on special education in the 1970s (DES 1978) had no non-white person on its committee, or lawyer who might voice concerns about the disproportionate number of non-white children identified then as educationally subnormal or maladjusted (Kirp 1983:90).

Public and Private Troubles

Through the nineteenth century the USA went through massive social and economic changes. While slavery, exploitation and indentured labour had fuelled early population numbers, the immigration of millions of people from Europe, Mexico, Caribbean countries, East Asia and other parts of the world ensured a massively expanded population. Movement from rural to urban areas contributed to urbanisation, and as in England, large cities quickly developed slum areas and exploitative factory conditions for men, women and children. Child labour, youth vagrancy, and poverty were common and the need to use education to improve economic progress, and some charitable concern led to public laws on child labour and compulsory education. The state of Massachusetts established the first Board of Education in 1837 and passed compulsory education laws in 1852. Massachusetts was also the home of social reformer Samuel Gridley Howe, who convinced the state to support the first schools for the blind, deaf and 'feeble-minded', while from France Edward Seguin brought methods for teaching mentally deficient children. Once public elementary and secondary education schooling developed and became more bureaucratic and regimented, children who were troublesome in intellectual, physical and behavioural ways needed attention. The city of Boston had created Schools for Special Instruction as early as 1838, mainly for non-English speaking immigrants. These filled quickly up with children regarded as problems for teachers in the developing mainstream schools.

By 1900 schools and classes for intellectually backward, recalcitrant, incorrigibles, truants and low achievers, were set up in other East Coast states (Tropea 1987), and as in England, children who impeded the progress of others, were candidates for removal. Upper class parents with defective children made private provision, while children of the poor and immigrants were public responsibility in the expanded public school system. By 1915 over 19.7 million children were enrolled, class sizes increased, and as Lazerson noted, elaborate and hierarchical modes of operating while attempting to keep costs down, meant the rapid creation of classes for the retarded, rebellious and deviant children (Lazerson 1983:23). Many of the 'defects' discovered by schools boards such as dirty unkempt children with speech defects, hearing and sight problems and inability to adjust to the behaviours required in schools, were problems of poverty and slum living, and the insults heaped on the children and families were numerous. Wallin wrote that

> in regular grades, the feeble-minded and sub-normal represent as it were, an unassiminable accumulation of human clinkers, ballast, driftwood or derelicts which seriously retards the progress of the entire class, and which constitutes a positive irritant to the teachers and other pupils.

> (Wallin 1924:94)

Sarason and Doris noted the economic arguments presented to the taxpaying public that the presence of defective children interfered with the education of the more capable (Sarason and Doris 1979:263). Unlike England, there were no aristocrats to chair Commissions and Committees and policy was influenced more directly by state legislators and administrators, by medical and psychological interests, school heads, directors of other institutions, religious bodies and charitable reforming groups. As in England, economic arguments were always present in the US systems, with early arguments that the rate of return by employing the specially educated might be worth the outlay on some education.

Compulsory Ignorance

The developing special education system in the USA had its share of individuals with sufficient power and authority to influence its development as a mechanism for social control of potential deviants who might 'pollute' the society. Henry Goddard, Director of the Vineland School for the Feeble-minded in New Jersey was the first to use the newly created intelligence tests to separate out the mentally defective, having also claimed in his book on the Kallikak family (Goddard 1912) that mental deficiency was a hereditary characteristic, and the public needed protection from this social menace. Lewis Terman, revising the first Binet scales for separating out children in need of special education (see Chapter 4 for details on early testing and eugenic influence), was also convinced that feeble-mindedness was

> a serious social menace to the social economic and moral welfare of the state.... It is responsible for one fourth of the commitments to state penitentiaries and reform schools and for the majority of cases of pauperism, alcoholism, prostitution and venereal disease.
>
> (Terman 1917:161)

Goddard set out the case for a science of "mental levels" by associating lower mental levels with manual work and asked "how can there be such a thing as social equality with this wide range of mental capacity?" (Goddard 1920:99)—an argument that resonates to the present day. He further added that workers, especially (low paid) coal miners, had only themselves to blame if they did not spend and save wisely. Robert Yerkes, chair of a committee on the inheritance of mental traits in the Eugenic Research Society, also thought that psychological tests were of great value in placing less able people in suitable low level occupations, again a view that still resonates. As Powell has noted, when special educators elaborated their profession, they drew on test statistics and psychometrically derived definitions of abnormality and intelligence (Powell 2011:5). While beliefs in normal versus not normal supported the exclusion of troublesome children from mainstream schools—thus creating levels of ignorance—there were even worse fates for some whose defects were regarded as hereditary. Michigan introduced a castration bill into its legislature in 1898, and although the Bill was not passed, "twenty-four male children were castrated because of epilepsy, imbecility, masturbation and weakness of mind" (Floud 1898).

By the 1930s special education with its separate classes had become, according to a report on Chicago public schools, places that cast a stigma on anyone associated with them, and Lazerson documented the comments from officials in other cities that "special classes were dumping ground for children who are trouble-makers in their regular classes" and "cripples do not belong in our schools" (Lazerson 1983:39–40). However, by the 1960s while the system of special education was larger than it had ever been it was subjected to more criticism. A well-known article by Dunn in the journal *Educational Researcher* (Dunn 1968) questioned the numbers of children, especially minorities, labelled as educably mentally retarded, and in 1973 Jane Mercer's influential book (Mercer 1973) also criticised the development of this EMR category. The attempts to create common public schooling which were from the outset dependent on the exclusion into separate classes and schools of disparate groups of trouble-some children were now being questioned by human and civil rights groups, by academics and by parental groups, especially African American parents. For government though, as Sarason and Doris noted, "it seemed reasonable not to make any fundamental changes in the school system, but to build an auxiliary system—the special education programmes designed for the defective or incapable child" (1979:334) and they were clear that this was mainly about the removal of the large number of children regarded as mentally retarded[1] the "schooling for kids no-one wants" (ibid:376) and the elimination of these young people from the possibility of a mainstream curriculum. Where they remained in mainstream, the Federal government had early on encouraged state school systems to include vocational education, rather than provide a separate vocational system, and it became the norm for lower attaining and minority children to be tracked into vocational programmes (Weiss 1990).

Compulsory Racial Ignorance

Historians of public education in the USA are generally agreed that from the first it was built on "a system of compulsory ignorance for black children" (Weinberg 1977:11) and deliberate attempts at "darkening the mind" (Crummell 1898:11). Ignorance was a primary instrument in enslavement in America, despite the fact that West Africa, where most slaves were seized, had existing kinds of formal education. Early in the nineteenth century states passed laws outlawing gatherings of Black people for educational purposes and schools for Black children established in northern states were often attacked and burnt by white groups. In 1846 an article in the Boston newspaper *Liberator* asserted in an editorial that "the physical, mental and moral structure of the black child requires an educational treatment different from that of white children" (*Liberator* 1846). After the Second World War racial discrimination and segregation persisted in education, employment, and other institutions, although by this time the NAACP [2] and its lawyers led national demands for equal treatment, a classic case being

McLaurin (1950) when a Black student was admitted to an all-white university but forced to sit outside the lecture rooms. In May 1954 the US Supreme Court made the unanimous decision in the case of *Brown versus the Board of Education of Topeka* that "in the field of public education the doctrine of separate but equal has no place. Separate educational facilities are inherently unequal" (Brown 1954:1). Despite this, desegregation proceeded slowly and with much white violence against Black families and children. The passing of the Civil Rights Act in 1964 resulted in slow desegregation with often reluctant administrative enforcement of legislation and the decision to bus children around cities to end segregated schools became a major point of opposition to desegregation. As Blanchett (2010) pointed out the sorting practices in schools were in any case intentionally designed to prevent the integration of Black and white children, and special education practices became a way to ensure they were not in the same classrooms. Ferri and Connor also described ways in which the Brown judgement had been subverted over the years, to ensure that segregation persisted (Ferri and Connor 2004).

A US Commission on Civil Rights 1969–72 found that, as with Black children, those of Mexican–American origin were also subject to high levels of segregation with low academic achievement and poor English language teaching (Weinberg 1977). A 1970 court decision *Diana v the State Board of Education*, decided that as 'intelligence' tests were being given in English to Spanish speaking Mexican–American children, they could not be assigned to classes for the educationally mentally retarded. While it might have been reasonable to assume that the long-term denial of education and a grudging acceptance of shared educational institutions might lead to Black and minority children getting equal treatment in schools, a report commissioned by the Federal government in 1966 (Coleman et al. 1966) reinforced what became an orthodox belief—that it was deficiencies in families and children, embedded in their lower socio-economic status, that created failure in schools—a social determinism that continues to resonate in both the USA and England. This led to continuing assumptions that it was acceptable for disproportionate numbers of lower class and racial minorities to be relegated to special education classes and low achievement groups, although this was not without continual opposition. In 1972 in the case of *Larry P v Riles* the California court ruled that African–American children could not be classed as EMR as the tests given were based on middle class cultural assumptions and the case *Mills v the Board of Education* decided that the exclusion of students for behavioural and emotional problems, and mental retardation was unlawful as the students had a right to an 'appropriate education'.

Integration for Disability

A legal high point appeared to be reached in 1975 when the Senate approved the *Education for All Handicapped Children Act* (PL 94-142) preceded by a 1973 Act outlawing discrimination against handicapped people. At this time around 8 million young people were estimated to have a disability or handicap that prevented them receiving 'appropriate education'. The Act, taking effect in 1978, was intended to integrate as many students as possible in mainstream education, with zero reject—no child to be excluded because of handicap, non-discriminatory evaluation with culture fair test materials, appropriately designed education programmes with an IEP (individual education programme) for every child, education to be given in the least restrictive environment and all to be subject to due process of law. At this time the categories of handicap included 32 per cent of students in the developing category of learning disabled, shortened to LD, 22 per cent in the category of Educationally Mentally Handicapped, 22 per cent in the speech impaired category, 30 per cent described as emotionally disturbed, 8 per cent deaf or hard of hearing, 2 per cent visually handicapped, 1 per cent visually impaired and 3 per cent in another health impaired category.

Long before England had developed the idea of Alternative Education, mainly for the disruptive, in the USA there were numerous alternative schools for disruptive or non-conforming students, faith and ethnic schools, career schools, performing arts schools, community schools, skill-training schools and many others (Ysseldyke and Algozzine 1982). Ysseldyke and Algozzine documented the subsequent ways in which state agencies and schools coped with troublesome students. These included denying that students were not being served, exclusion of the disruptive, ability grouping in regular schools, and more special education classes for the dull and retarded (Ysseldyke and Algozzine 1982:36–44). They also made a study of the 'testing industry' that developed over the years with the professional interests of psychologists in mind. Of the tests developed to that time by joint committees of the American Psychological Association and the American Educational Research Association they identified 24 tests with inadequately constructed norms. These included the famous Stanford-Binet Intelligence Scale, 13 tests with inadequate reliability date, some 50 tests used that had questionable reliability, and 15 with questionable validity (ibid: 139–145). Nevertheless, testing children remained the major method of ensuring that some children were consigned to what in effect was levels of inability, and an education deemed 'appropriate' for them. By 1990, the Education for All Handicapped Children was amended to become an Individuals with Disabilities Education Act (IDEA). Autism and brain injury were added to categories of disability and more services were mandated. An interesting judgement was given in 1993 in *Oberti v the Board of Education Clementon* that a disruptive child with mental retardation could be placed in a regular class as a child did not have to earn such a place, it was a right rather than a privilege, which could be regarded as a victory for social justice.

Subsuming Race

The pressure to recognise the rights of the disabled and all those in special education followed the Brown decision, civil rights legislation and the IDEA. But it soon became evident that there had been a shift from race to disability to undermine minority gains. Using a discourse of low ability greatly affected racial groups The disproportionate identification of minority students as disabled or 'special' meant that racial discrimination was easily transposed into disability discrimination. As Beraton pointed out (2008:349), discrimination against disabled people is scrutinised far less than racial discrimination, and acceptance of disability legislation enables the acceptance of otherwise illegal racial discrimination, as many academics and practitioners since the 1990s have noted. Artiles (2011) described how those with a variety of disabilities benefited from the civil rights legislation racial groups had demanded, but which worked for the greater benefit of the disabled through the IDEA. The historical connections of race and disability created the paradox that a victory for one group—the disabled—became a potential source of inequality for racial groups, despite a shared history of struggles for rights. His view was that in the early moves towards an inclusive education there had been no attention paid to the issue of the over-representation of minorities, 41 states reporting in 2009 that there was no change in their disproportionate racial identifications for special education and 31 reporting no change in identification in disability categories (Artiles 2011:439).

While for years African-American children and other minorities had predominantly been labelled as educationally mentally retarded or emotionally disturbed, the category of Learning Disability gradually became the label most frequently applied to minority students, although ironically, as Sleeter pointed out, it was white middle class children who populated the LD programmes over the first years of the recognition of the category (Sleeter 1986, 1987). An Action for Excellence Task force, reporting on ways to raise achievement in American schools in 1963, described children unable to achieve required literacy standards as Learning Disabled. In 1969 legislation provided funds for research into the causes of Learning Disability, as this was now an official handicapping condition whose growth has been exponential. In the first year of the label existing over a million children had been identified as LD. Sleeter examined the construction of this category dating it back to the early nineteenth century when medical research suggested links between brain damage and slow learning. Subsequent psychological and neurological studies suggested a notion of minimal brain dysfunction, but the children were regarded as coming from "normal" (white) families (Strauss and Lehtinen 1963). As Sleeter pointed out, failures of poor and minority students were regarded due to their low IQ, social and cultural maladjustment, inner city living, and poverty while "white middle class parents and educators who saw their failing children as different from poor or minority students pressed for the creation and use of this category" (Sleeter 1987:50).

The situation did not appear to improve over the years. Losen and Orfield, in a third edition of their book, which first appeared in 2002, wrote that

> Evidence suggests that black over representation (in special education) is substantial in state after state. The studies reveal wide differences in disability identification between blacks and Hispanics and between black boys and girls that cannot be explained in terms of their social background or measured ability.
>
> (Losen and Orfield 2010:xvii)

From the 1990s a developing Disability Studies movement attempted to explain the intersections of race, class, disability and gender more clearly and the persistence of inequalities in education that led students of colour into special education programmes, low achievement and a school to prison pipeline. Linking Disability Studies to the field of Critical Race Theory, writers (who were also practitioners) were developing an area that further attempted to explain the legacy in which historical beliefs about race and ability are still present in both policy and practice, resulting in minority students' experience of disability and learning difficulty being very different from those of white students (Gillborn 2012; Connor et al. 2016). Some academics, however, persisted in attempts to demonstrate that there was no over-representation of minorities in various categories of special education (Morgan et al. 2015), a view that was difficult to substantiate.

Initiatives and Resistances

After the 1975 legislation via the EHA numbers of educators and academics encouraged by what appeared to be Presidential support for organisational and curriculum reform in schooling, proposed a Regular Education Initiative (REI) which might address social and racial issues in really extending rights and resources to all students and including them in regular classrooms. By 1991, as Skrtic documented, there were over 4.5 million children classed as needing special education services, and two-thirds of these were labelled as Learning Disabled, emotionally disturbed or mentally retarded, with the familiar associations with lower class and minority status. In an influential article in the *Harvard Educational Review* (Skrtic 1991a) he described the clash between the proponents of the REI, who supported an end to separate classes and more assistance in mainstream classes for a majority of students, and the opposition to these proposals. He proposed that in a post-industrial era, educational equity was a pre-condition for educational excellence, and segregation, ability groupings and tracking had no place in excellent schooling. Among critics of reform James Kauffman emerged as one of the most vocal and consistent critics of the REI, and of subsequent initiatives to include students in regular classrooms (Kauffman 1989; Kauffmann and Hallaghan 1995). Kauffman argued that special educators did not believe the REI would work, and that a whole profession of special educators (who had vested interests in continuing their practices) were against changes. From this point continuing arguments over mainstreaming, integration, and inclusion have continued on political, administrative, organisational and educational levels, often, as noted, becoming acrimonious. Ballard, for example, documented the way in which his support for inclusive education in New Zealand in the 1990s, earned him labels of zealot, biased, and ideological, with others supporting inclusion being labelled as politically correct bullies who demonised special schooling! (Ballard 2004). Ellen Brantlinger took up the claim that those supporting inclusion were ideological, demonstrating the ways in which supporters of traditional special education "are quick to see ideology in others but do not turn the gaze inwards and recognise it in their own practice" (Brantlinger 1997:448). She pointed out that special education was infused with a bureaucratic belief in ideologies of professionalism and expertism that the 'experts' believed should not be criticised (see Chapter 6).

An expansion of candidates for special education provision was ensured by the curiously named *No Child Left Behind* Act (NCLB) signed into law by President Bush early in 2002. The Act was a result of pressure from policymakers and private corporate influence, who wanted standardised testing of all children, in order to hold teachers more accountable for low performance and further an agenda of marketisation in schooling. All states were to carry out standardised tests, in reading and maths, later in science. Schools had to make 'adequate yearly progress' (AYP) in tests scores or be taken over as privately administered charter schools. The Secretary of State for Education claimed that in particular

> We have an educational emergency in the USA. Nationally blacks score lower on reading and maths tests than their white peers ... we have to make sure that African-American parents understand how this historic new education law can specifically help them and their children.
>
> (quoted in Hursh 2005:610)

The arguments for increased testing were similar to those made in England, that more testing, and blaming schools if more children did not pass tests, would somehow close achievement gaps between poor and minority children. The resulting educational efficiency would increase national economic competitiveness. Ladson-Billings (2005) commenting on this 'achievement gap' that always seemed to exist between poor and minority students and their more advantaged peers, suggested that in the light of the poor quality education offered to these disadvantaged groups, the gap should be renamed the 'educational debt'. Ending the denigration and deficit assumptions about these groups and actually offering good quality education might do much to close achievement gaps. The results of high stakes testing, while opening up elements of a marketisation of education, did not reduce differences in educational achievements between advantaged and disadvantaged students, whether minority or not, and encouraged cheating strategies in states in order to claim that indeed no child was being left behind (Hursh 2005). Teacher student relations were not improved as Valli and Buese (2007) documented, when students in low-performing schools were shuffled through the school day between remedial programmes and interventions in attempts to increase their test scores.

Further initiatives included a Response to Intervention (RTI) whereby, in an echo of the English 2001 three levels of support, students moved between two Tiers depending on their responses to more intensive teaching intervention, ending up in Tier 3—special education, which, as Artiles noted led to some schools "referring students to RTI" (Artiles 2011:438). A policy initiated by President Obama in 2009, was a 'Race to the Top' programme that offered financial incentives to states to further judge teachers' performance if their students did not perform well in tests, and in a Common Core of Standards students were expected to achieve in academic subjects, all of which led to more young people designated as failing in schools. While Obama's Secretary of State Arne Duncan in 2016 was recorded as regretting blaming teachers and wishing he had advocated paying them more, he also made the admission that the $4 billion spent on Race to the Top had not improved standards any more in states that did take the money, than those that did not (Duncan 2016).

As continuing pressure to raise standards persisted, many parents, especially more vocal middle class parents, became increasingly anxious that their children with various learning difficulties, might not achieve the standards required and pressed for more special education resources and services, with a consequent expansion of a 'SEN industry'. There was an expansion of claims via old and new categories of disability: ADHD, dyslexia, autism and autistic spectrum disorder being the most common. An example of this was provided in 2012 by the Division of Education in the Los Angeles Unified District, which served some 680,000 students, with around 80,000 students (12 per cent) assessed as having special educational needs, plus those classed as delinquent, at-risk, homeless or teenage pregnancy. The Unified District in 2012 spent around $1.3 million on special education services and a large proportion of this money went on litigation instigated by parents demanding and defending placements and services. The administrators noted with some amusement that autism in one district "nearly bankrupted us" (Tomlinson 2013:81). Although California, with Transitional Services and a Department of Rehabilitation worked hard to help all those with "physical and mental impairments" find vocational training and employment, middle class parents, as in England, were reluctant to have their children placed on vocational courses. The District was concerned that "there is no let-up in testing and assessment ... and the punitive strategies on schools and teachers" (ibid:81) and the demand for special educational services was an inevitable consequence of policies to raise standards and pressure schools into credentialing more children at ever higher levels.

Comparing Countries

In both England and the USA, as public school systems were developing to meet the needs of employers in an industrial revolution, and reinforce social order, schooling was organised as factories on mass production principles with products meeting uniform standards or being rejected. The current focus in both countries on raising standards is premised on making the systems more efficient and accountable. In the twentieth century public education worked for many, but many suffered in what Skrtic called 'the dark side' of this mass bureaucratic sub system in which school failure was deemed pathological, whereas an unchanged school system was taken as rational (Skrtic 1991b). In the USA regular (mainstream education), with its pathological extensions of testing and accountability was and is taken as normal, even though, as in the UK, this manifestly does not prepare all young people for political, economic and social participation in what notionally is a democratic society. Federal, state and local governments and policy-makers analyse the failings of public education as individual and schools failures, which bolsters the perpetuation of a separate administrative and organisational system of special education, in which practices claimed as inclusion becomes "inclusive service delivery models" (Menzies and Falvey 2008:92). Special education practices continue to treat the disabled, difficult and troublesome differently and the aim of the whole system is not to produce democratic citizens but to enhance test scores.

The ideology behind policy is adherence to an economic model that links higher test scores to economic competitiveness on a global level. On international comparisons this does not appear to be working well for the USA or the UK. At the end of Chapter 8 in this book some graphs are reproduced to illustrate that countries that have wide income inequalities also have students who overall do not achieve well in basic education. The graphs are from an OECD survey (OECD 2015) showing overall the skills of students aged 16–24 in maths, literacy and problem solving in 17 developed economies. The USA now has the greatest level of income inequality in the developed world, and in maths, the country comes bottom of the league table, with the UK second from the bottom. Japan and Finland, countries with the least income inequality and more egalitarian and inclusive school systems, come top. In literacy levels, the USA and UK are second and third from the bottom and in problem solving both are at the bottom of the table. This might suggest that both countries could do well to examine their whole education systems rather than developing sub-systems and practices that actually sustain failure. The following chapter documents the history and current beliefs in the ongoing attempts to present large numbers of children and young people as having less ability, 'intelligence' (as measured by IQ scores) and capabilities, rather than examining the capabilities of the whole education system.

Notes

1. Sarason and Doris pointed out that in a society like the USA where a high value is placed on 'intelligence' those who are considered to have less of it (whatever it is) are devalued. As soon as a child was diagnosed as 'mentally retarded' the social, educational and productive worth of the child was seen as minimal, even less so than children given labels of emotionally disturbed or 'learning disabled' (Sarason and Doris 1979:277; Sleeter 1986).

2. The National Association for the Advancement of Coloured People (NAACP) is an African-American civil rights organisation set up in 1909 to work for the social, political, economic and legal rights of all ethnic minority groups. It has a headquarters in Baltimore, with regional organisations and an annual conference.

References

Artiles, A. J. (2011) "Towards an interdisciplinary understanding of equity and difference: the case of the racialisation of ability" *Educational Researcher* 40/9: 431–445 (The Wallace Foundation Distinguished Lecture).

Ballard, K. (2004) "Ideology and the origin of inclusion: a case study" in (ed.) Ware, L. *Ideology and the Politics of (in) Exclusion*. New York. Peter Lang.

Beraton, G. (2008) "The song remains the same: the disproportionate representation of minority students in special education" *Race Ethnicity and Education* 11/4: 337–354.

Blanchett, W. J. (2010) "Telling it like it is: the role of race, class and culture in the perpetuation of learning disability as a privileged category for the white middle class" *Disability Studies Quarterly* 32/2: 1–11.

Brantlinger, E. (1997) "Using ideology: Cases on non-recognition of the politics of research and practice in special education" *Review of Educational Research* 67/4: 425–459.

Brown vs. the Board of Education of Topeka (1954) Washington DC.

Chambers, J. G. and Harman, W. T. (1983) *Special Education Policies: their history, implantation and finances*. Philadelphia PA. Temple University Press.

Coleman, J. S., Cambell, E., Hobson, C. J., McPartland, J., Mood, A. M., Weinfeld, F. D. and York, R. L. (1966) *Equality of Educational Opportunity*. Washington DC. US Department of Health, Education and Welfare.

Connor, D. J., Ferri, B. A. and Annamma, S. A. (2016) *DisCrit: disability studies and critical race theory in education*. New York. Teachers College Press.

Crummell, A. (1898) "The attitude of the American mind toward the negro intellect" The American Negro Academy Occasional Papers. No 3. Washington DC.

Danforth, S. (2009) *The Incomplete Child: an intellectual history of learning disabilities*. New Jersey. Lang.

DES (1978) *Special Educational Needs*. London. HMSO.

Duncan, A. (2016) "A great teacher should make $150,000, absolutely" *Times Educational Supplement* 15 April: 32–34.

Dunn, L. (1968) "Special education for the mentally retarded: is much of it justifiable?" *Educational Researcher* 7: 5–22.

Ferri, B. and Connor, D. J. (2004) "Special education and the subverting of Brown" *Journal of Gender, Race and Justice* 81/1: 57–74.

Floud, E. (1898) "Notes on the castration of idiot children" *American Journal of Psychology* 10: 299.

Gillborn, D. (2012) "Intersectionality and the primacy of racism: race, class, gender and disability in education" Paper to Conference on Critical Race Studies in Education. New York. Teachers College, Columbia University. May.

Goddard, H. H. (1912) *The Kallikak Family: a study in the heredity of feeble-mindedness*. New York. Macmillan.

Goddard, H. H. (1920) *Human Efficiency and Levels of Intelligence*. Princeton NJ. Princeton University Press.

Hursh, D. (2005) "The growth of high stakes testing in the USA: accountability, markets, and the decline in educational equality" *British Educational Research Journal* 31/5: 605–622.

Kauffman, J. M. (1989) "The regular education initiative as Reagan-Bush educational policy: a trickle-down theory of education for the hard-to-teach" *Journal of Special Education* 23/3: 256–278.

Kauffman, J. M. and Hallaghan, D. P. (1995) (eds) *The Illusion of Full Inclusion: a comprehensive critique of a current special education bandwagon*. Austin TX. Pro-Ed.

Kirp, D. (1983) "Professionalization as policy choice: British special education in comparative perspective" in (eds) Chambers, J. G. and Hartman, W. T. *Special Education Policies: their history, implementation and finance*. Philadelphia PA. Temple University Press.

Ladson-Billings, G. (2005) "From the under-achievment gap to the educational debt" Speech to AERA conference. San Francisco CA. April.

Lazerson, M. (1983) "The origins of special education" in (eds) Chambers J. G. and Hartman, W. T. *Special Education Policies*. Philadelphia PA. Temple University Press.

Liberator (1846) Editorial. Boston. 12 August.

Losen, D. J. and Orfield, G. (2010) *Racial Inequality in Special Education* (3rd ed.). Cambridge MA. Harvard Education Press.

Menzies, H. and Falvey, M. A. (2008) "Inclusion of students with disabilities in general education" in (eds) Jimenez, T. C. and Graf, V. L. *Education for All: critical issues in the education of children and youth with disabilities*. San Francisco CA. Jossey-Bass.

Mercer, J. R. (1973) *Labelling the mentally retarded: clinical and social perspectives on mental retardation*. Berkeley CA. University of California Press.

Morgan, P. L., Farkas, G., Hillemeier, M. M., Mattison, R., Maczug, S., Li, H. and Cook, M. (2015) "Minorities are disproportionately underrepresented in special education: longitudinal evidence across five disability conditions" *Educational Researcher* Online June 2015.

OECD (2013) Skills Outlook. Source: Survey of Adult Skills (PIACC) Reprinted in Stotesbury N. and Dorling, D. (2015) *Understanding income inequality and its implications; why better statistics are needed*. Statistics Views 21 October. www.ststisticsviews.com/details/features 8493411/.

Osgood, R. L. (2009) *The History of Special Education: a struggle for equality in American public schools*. Westport CT. Praeger.

Powell, J. W. (2011) *Barriers to Inclusion: special education in the United States and Germany*. Boulder CO. Paradigm Publishers.

Richardson, J. G. (1999) *Common, Delinquent and Special: the institutional shape of special education*. New York. Falmer Press.

Richardson, J. G., Wu, J. and Judge, D. (2017) *The Global Convergence of Vocational and Special Education*. London. Routledge.

Sarason, S. B. and Doris, J. (1979) *Educational Handicap, Public Policy and Social History*. New York. The Free Press.

Skrtic, T. M. (1991a) "The special education paradox: equity as a way to excellence" *Harvard Educational Review* 61/2: 148–206.

Skrtic, T. M. (1991b) *Behind Special Education: a critical analysis of professional culture and school organisation*. Denver CO. Love Publishing.

Sleeter, C. E. (1986) "Learning disabilities: the social construction of a special education category" *Exceptional Children* 53: 46–54.

Sleeter, C. (1987) "Why is there learning disabilities? A critical analysis of the birth of the category in its social context" in (ed.) Popkewitz, T. *The Formation of School Subjects: the struggle for creating an American institution*. New York. Falmer.

Strauss, A. A. and Lehtinen, L. E. (1963) *Psychology and the Education of the Brain-injured Child*. New York. Grune and Stratton.

Terman, L. M. (1917) "Feeble-minded children in public schools in California" *School and Society* 5: 165.

Tomlinson, S. (2013) *Ignorant Yobs? Low attainers in a global knowledge economy.* London. Routledge.

Tropea, J. L. (1987) "Bureaucratic order and special children in urban schools" *History of Education Quarterly* 27. Spring: 20–32.

Tulkin, S. R. (1972) "An analysis of the concept of cultural deprivation" *Developmental Psychology* 6/2: 326–339.

Valli, I. and Buese, D. (2007) "The changing role of teachers in an era of high stakes accountability" *American Education Research Journal* 44: 519–558.

Wallin, J. E. W. (1924) *The Education of Handicapped Children.* Boston. Houghton Mifflin.

Weinberg, M. (1977) *A Chance to Learn: the history of race and education in the United States.* Cambridge. Cambridge University Press.

Weiss, L. (1990) *Working Class Without Work.* New York. Routledge.

Ysseldyke, J. E. and Algozzine, B. (1982) *Critical Issues in Special and Remedial Education.* Boston. Houghton-Mifflin.

Reading 1.4

IQ, Ability, and Eugenics

Sally Tomlinson

> While all of you are brothers, we will say in our tale, God in fashioning those who are fit to rule mingled gold in their generation, for this reason they are most precious, but in the helpers are silver, and iron and brass in farmers and Scraftsmen. You are all kin, but for the most part you will breed according to your kind.
>
> (Plato: *Republic bk3*:415a)

> Genes, intelligence and education: a heady brew of issues. Add class, race and gender, as has happened many times over the past 100 years and you have a simmering mixture ready to boil over at any moment.
>
> (Stephen Rose 2014:27)

Plato's views sounded like the perfect justification for an harmonious society, in which everyone happily knew their place, apart from slaves and women who did not get a mention. But even Socrates called this myth of the metals a 'noble lie'. It was a political legitimation for an inequitable society and it is unfortunate that the idea that people differ from each other as much as metals has resonated down the centuries, providing an ideological justification for class, race, gender and disability divisions, for imperial conquests and subjugation of whole populations. It is a myth still resonating in schools and classrooms today, that children are born with the potential to be very able, less able, unable or disabled. Behind the current mantra from all political parties that children should be educated to reach their 'potential' lies the myth of some kind of fixed ability, defect or disability. A major task in the sociology of education has been to demonstrate the ways in which inequalities in education and life chances—particularly by social class, race, gender and disability, have been created and recreated by policies and policy-makers rather than defective populations. Inequalities are underpinned by ideological beliefs in the different abilities and potential of different groups.

From the mid nineteenth century, the long-term justification for the treatment of those designated as defective has had a profound effect on education systems globally. Rationalisations for the treatment of those regarded as low attainers, under-achievers, special, or 'not normal' was provided by eugenics. Views of genetic inherited difference, combined with psychometric theories of measurable intelligence contributed to the denigration of these groups. It is a difficult task to turn a century-old set of beliefs around and ask why it became so important to rank children and adults by their mental worth and use biological determinism to treat people unequally.

The completion of the human genome project, advances in genomics, behavioural genetics and the neurosciences have led to some researchers, who still use 'intelligence' as measured by IQ tests, to search for 'intelligence genes', and to argue that there are groups of genes underpinning 'intelligence' but so far there is a failure to find them—the 'missing heritability' position (Joseph 2015). In addition, the English Economic and Social Research Council (ESRC) has developed a framework to enable biosocial research linking the Biotechnology and Biological Sciences Research Council with the social sciences. A strategic advisor to the ESRC programmes has written enthusiastically about the ability to demonstrate that negative life experiences, such as poverty and bad parenting, can lead to lasting epigenetic changes, and lasting links between environmental experiences and brain development (Hobcraft 2016). While genomic and neuroscience research can claim to enhance understanding, the history of eugenics and assumptions of the inferior genetic inheritance of some social and racial groups raises concerns that it may all continue to provide legitimation for unequal treatment of these groups.

It was not accidental that early industrialising countries, notably the USA and UK, needed to rationalise the unequal treatment of urban slum, immigrant, and potentially economically 'useless' populations, and these were the countries that initially developed and popularised notions of genetic inherited differences between social and racial groups. Indeed it was not accidental that as soon as the development of secular mass education for the working classes became a possibility, that the upper classes found ways of denigrating the educational possibilities of the minds of the lower classes and minorities. If, as Ann Morning wrote in the journal *Ethnic and Racial Studies* "you thought we had moved beyond all that" (Morning 2014:1676), the belief that differences in 'ability' is largely due to genetic inheritance, again appears to be influencing policies supporting selection and separation of young people in schooling. Some behavioural geneticists have claimed that "the ability to learn from teachers is, we know, more influenced by genes than experience" (Asbury and Plomin 2014:7). Herrnstein and Murray's thesis that "the twenty-first century will open on a world where cognitive ability is the decisive dividing force" (Herrnstein and Murray 1994:25), seems to be a belief embraced by many governments committed to improving the achievements of their populations and searching for 'better brains'. The rationale for this seems to be to enhance national economic competitiveness, although it could be claimed that the supposed high cognitive ability of politicians, and their advisors, financiers, bankers, global business leaders and others, has not been conspicuously demonstrated so far in the twenty-first century. While for over a hundred years there has been a plethora of writing on ability, intelligence, mental measurement and eugenic influences, this chapter reviews the history and development of the science, pseudo-science, and political and educational implications of past and current developments.

Eugenics and Mental Measurement

It was Francis Galton, second cousin to Charles Darwin, who set himself the task of providing a 'scientific' base for selective breeding to improve the genetic inheritance of the human race, worried that the lower classes with their ineducable minds were overbreeding and producing defective people who were a danger to the (British) race. In his books on *Hereditary Genius* (1869) and *Inquiries into Human Faculty* (1883) he advocated selective reproduction and used the term eugenics—derived from the Greek eugenes 'a person hereditarily endowed with noble qualities' as a science that would preserve the best inborn qualities of the population. He argued, as did other medical and political interests at the time, that just as genius and talent were inborn, and confined largely to privileged families, so low abilities, mental defects, delinquency, crime, prostitution, illegitimacy and even unemployment were the product of inherited tendencies in the lower classes. Eugenic theories were taken up by the political left and right[1] and an Eugenics Education Society was founded in 1907 (later simply the Eugenics Society). The Society became an influential pressure group, concerned to promote the fitness of the Anglo-Saxon race and worried that mass education was indicating the presence of large numbers of defective, feeble-minded, delinquent and subnormal children. Similar claims are being made in the present day, one economist suggesting that "in the case of England, some groups are so elite, that it would take 25 generations for them to become average" especially as elites marrying other elite members would pass on their genetic traits conferring high status and that "it's a dismal discovery that genetics could actually influence what people's outcomes will be" (Clark 2016: 95). As no one has data on 25 generations it is safe to say Clark did not discover this, he assumed it, on the same basis that the early eugenicists made assumptions about genetic inheritance between the privileged and paupers.

Galton was credited with the introduction of correlation, and one of his protégés (and later biographer) was Karl Pearson. As a mathematician Pearson produced numerous statistical techniques, multiple correlations, biserial correlations, chi-squared tests, goodness-of-fit tests, techniques that were adopted by the developing science of psychology, followed by other techniques, notably Spearman's use of factor analysis in developing a measurement of general intelligence (Spearman 1904). To understand the persistence of links between eugenics, psychology and its mental measuring techniques and the persistent denigration of lower social classes and their possible dangers, the views of these influential men (hardly any women) must be studied.[2] Although their beliefs have to be viewed as historical expressions of their time, the outcomes and persistence of the views over the twentieth century and into the twenty-first century are less excusable. Pearson had strong views on 'degenerates' affecting what was commonly termed a 'race'. "No degenerates or feeble-minded stock can ever be converted into healthy and sound stock by the accumulated efforts of education, general laws or sanitation" (Pearson 1892:32), and he believed with other Social Darwinists, that life was "a struggle of race by race for the survival of the physically and mentally fitter race" (ibid.).

Pearson was interested in statistical probability and in the 1890s collected data on the geographical distribution of paupers (those receiving basic poverty 'outdoor' relief) and actually drew a graph (Figure 1.4.1 as redrawn by Dorling 2015:117) implying that the distribution of paupers around the country followed some natural distribution, purporting to show by a bell-shaped curve this distribution.

He inferred that some areas had more paupers because of genetically inferior people clustering there and reproducing. Dorling (2015:116) has pointed out that, apart from other explanations for areas of poverty the data for this graph were almost certainly fabricated. It was Pearson who first referred to this bell-shaped curve as a normal distribution,[3] and this is crucial to understanding the now century-old assumptions of a 'normal' bell-shaped curve

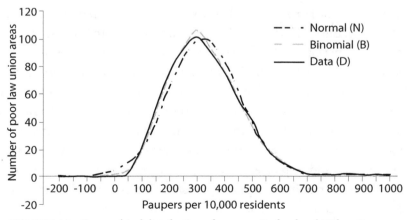

FIGURE 1.4.1   Geographical distribution of paupers, England and Wales, 1891.

of the spread of human abilities. Pearson was one of the founders of the Eugenics society, and eugenics as Dorling has noted "had become almost a religion by the 1920s, it being an article of faith that some were more able than others and that the differences were strongly influenced by some form of inherited acumen" (Dorling 2015:121). The pioneers of mental measurement, a group of like-minded privileged men working mainly in London and Oxford, but with visits to German universities, thus combined eugenic beliefs with the development of those tests of mental measurement. Intelligence tests, purporting to assess levels of cognitive ability, have continued to be relied on as 'scientific measurements' to correlate with individual and group performance in schooling, and eventually to predict not only individual futures but futures for whole societies. This allows for example, some economists to claim that studies in labour economics find that one IQ point raised for the whole population corresponds to an increase in wages to the order of 1 per cent (Zax and Rees 2002) and there are even those studying the possibility of genetically interfering with human embryos who claim that an "individual increase in earnings from a genetic intervention can be assessed in the same fashion as pre-natal care and similar environmental intervention" (Shulman and Bostrom 2014:86).

Uses and Abuses of Mental Measurement

In 1905 the French Minister of Public Instruction asked Alfred Binet to produce a test to help find children of low ability who should be placed in special schools. He obligingly did this but never believed that "the intelligence of individuals is a fixed quantity, we must react against this brutal pessimism" (Binet 1913:40). In England there were no such reservations, and in 1905 a committee of the Anthropological section of the British Association, which was originally chaired by Galton, set up a sub-committee to gather psychological measurements of the British population. Oxford Professor William McDougall recruited several of his students, which included Cyril Burt, to assist him in constructing tests. In keeping with a prevailing view that the level of national intelligence was decaying due to high levels of reproduction of the 'genetically unfit' (Heron 1906) in 1907 the Board of Education[4] approved the observation and testing of children, and tests duly showed a difference in performance between pupils in elementary schools and those in private preparatory schools with suggestions that this was innate (Hearnshaw 1979:26). In 1911 William Stern coined the term IQ as an index of general intelligence with an assumption that a normal distribution of this intelligence as measured by tests could be plotted via a bell curve graph, with 100 being the mean and standard deviations of 15 points purporting to show levels of intelligence. Subsequently, many thousands of psychologists, educationalists and the general public became acquainted with a graph showing the very dull (initially labelled as idiots and imbeciles) with an IQ below 70–75, dull between 75 and 90, normal between 90 and 110, bright between 110 and 125 and very bright up to 150 (see Herrnstein and Murray 1994:120–121 for this graph, which they equated with social class) and people also became acquainted with the notion of fixed intelligence, which the points on the graph showed. The persistence of beliefs in the fixed points of an IQ scale were illustrated in 2016 by the eminent evolutionist Richard Dawkins who used a tweet to assert that "living in a university it is easy to forget that the mean IQ of the population is 100, and 50% of them are in the bottom half" (Dawkins 2016). Indeed the persistence of what was called the nature–nurture debate, the relative contribution of genetic inheritance or environmental conditions, appears to be a permanent fixture in economically unequal societies. As Liam Hudson pointed out much of the debate centres on a single technical device—the IQ test—and the use of IQ tests has taken on many of the qualities of a mystic rite, "to have a low IQ is seen as the equivalent of having a low caste" (Hudson 1972:14–15). As IQ testing is the major rationale for the profession of educational psychology, further discussion of this is found in Chapter 6.

The obsession with the assumed innate inferior qualities of the poor, as previous chapters have noted, has been well documented by historians. Hurt (1988) wrote that beliefs in the hereditary nature of defects or deviance from what was regarded as acceptable social and economic behaviour reached a peak by the time of the First World War. One report, noted in Chapter 2, illustrated the anxiety of governing groups that there were large numbers of a dull and defective population who should be discovered and dealt with. This was the Commission on the Care and Control of the Feeble-Minded, set up in 1904 and reporting in 1908 (RCCCFM 1908, 8 vols). Chaired by an aristocrat, it included one woman among its members, and all were strongly of the hereditarian view that mental defects and attendant ills were caused by defect in the parents and near ancestors. Echoes of current twenty-first century views of the poor were contained in the introduction, which asserted that

> the mass of facts we have collected compels the conclusion that there are large numbers of defective persons over whom no sufficient control is exercised and whose wayward and irresponsible lives are productive of crime and misery ... causing much expenditure wasteful to the community.
>
> (ibid. 1908, vol 1:1)

The committee assiduously sought to count numbers of defectives over the whole of England, seeking them out in existing special schools, Poor Law institutions, reformatories, asylums, prisons, homes for inebriates and other places. One commissioner, a Dr Potts (sent to the Potteries area in Staffordshire), actually put a notice in the local paper asking people to nominate any defectives they knew, which yielded a number of names! Potts was the member quoted in the introduction to this book who thought as did the other commissioners that women giving birth to degenerate children was the major problem, give or take tea, alcohol and lazy men (RCCCFM 1908, vol 8). One of his recommendations, which chimed with widely held views, was that the solution to the problem was segregation in institutions or 'colonies', sterilisation of women, and finally 'the lethal chamber' (i.e. killing people).

A visit made by committee members to America also led to the view of women as the main danger to the well-being of the nation, although some states had already passed laws permitting sterilisation and even castration of male 'idiots', and noted that segregation, prohibiting marriage and turning troublesome immigrant children out of schools might solve problems of deviant behaviour (RCCCFM 1908, vol 2). In the USA dismal conclusions to studies of defective families (Dugdale 1877; Goddard 1912) reinforced notions of the danger of defectives 'breeding' and in England fear of delinquent girls becoming slaves to their 'animal spirits' and giving birth to illegitimate children led to their segregation to prevent them 'producing other lives' (Hurt 1988:128). Young women continued to be presented as a moral danger and economic concern by sexual activity. In the 1930s a 'colony' for defectives in the north of England incarcerated feeble-minded women who were "a source of moral corruption for men as there is a danger that men will gratify themselves upon them" (Langley 1988: 36). There was no record of the offending males being removed from the community.

The abuses by those who believed in biological determinism and the dangers of defective populations were commonplace in the early twentieth century. In England, Winston Churchill, Home Secretary in 1912, believed that segregation in labour camps, sterilisation and even euthanasia were suitable ways of dealing with defectives, although by 1932 a report of a Departmental Committee on Sterilization, while conceding that the 'selective mating' of poor with poor might lead to defect, took the view that social and economic conditions might have something to do with the problem and came out against the practice. Eugenics operated, as Barker (1983) noted, with the clear assumption about the relationship between social class and eugenic worth. Advocates were convinced of the innate inferiority of the lower working classes. An influential woman from the 1920s was Marie Stopes, well known for advocating contraception. Less well known is that she too believed fervently in curtailing the reproduction of the working classes, setting up her family planning clinics in areas of poverty, and leaving a large amount of money to the Galton Society.

In the State of Victoria, Australia, a eugenics society continued to lobby in the 1930s for sterilisation of the unfit (Lewis 1987) and in Sweden and the USA the sterilisation of women usually without their consent, continued into the 1970s and beyond. It took the practices of the Nazis from the 1920s to the 1940s to bring about a general revulsion to practices of incarcerating, killing or sterilising anyone considered defective and a danger to an 'Aryan race', although Lowe (1980) has commented that the concentration on the Nazi regime has drawn attention away from other countries' practices. The Holocaust Education and Archive Research team have documented the systemic killing of the disabled, Sinti and Roma (gypsies), Black people and Jews as 'racial inferiors', with trials of gas to kill the disabled, and persecution of gypsies preceding the full Nazi regime of killing Jews. Robert Ritter, a German psychiatrist who had attempted to find links between heredity and criminality, was largely responsible, with two women anthropologists, for the elimination of large numbers of gypsies from all over Europe. One woman, Eva Justin, studied gypsy children raised apart from their families. At the end of the study she had the children deported to Auschwitz and killed. Both Ritter and these two women were employed after 1947 in the Frankfurt Health Office in West Germany (HEART 2010), although the employment of former Nazis was not unusual post-war. The company who marketed the drug thalidomide, which caused birth defects and deformities, was run by Hermann Wirth—a former Nazi.[5]

The Eternal Influence of Cyril Burt

The work and influence of those who Jay Gould called the "Great Men" who combined eugenic beliefs with mental measurement have been well documented and critiqued (see especially Kamin 1974; Hearnshaw 1979; Gould 1981; Rose et al. 1984; Montague 1999; Chitty 2007; Gillborn 2008, 2016 and others), with often enraged replies and defence from those who continue to believe in the 'truths' of inferior and superior human differences produced by these men. Cyril Burt is an especially important figure in England as from 1920 he was advocating a treble track system of secondary education and an annual examination taken at 11 by every child in the country to determine their schooling, the 'most able' of the working class to progress via a scholarship to grammar schools (Burt 1920 and see Chapter 2). The shadow of the 11+ examination, used in the formalised tripartite system of schooling after 1945, has blighted the lives of hundreds of thousands of people into adulthood, who were told they had 'failed the 11+' and thus could not attend the academic grammar school. Versions of the 11+ are still in use in 2016 in some 36 local authorities in England that retain grammar schools, with an extension of such schooling looked on favourably by the current Conservative government.

By 1913 Burt was influencing legislation via a Mental Deficiency Act which excluded children with 'mental defect' from elementary schools after testing and in 1937 when he wrote his influential book on *The Backward Child* he was concerned to separate out the mental and moral 'subnormals' likely to be found in London's elementary schools, almost all coming from lower working class homes. He was influenced by a woman, Mary Dendy, who having given evidence to the 1904 Royal Commission on the evil of feeble-mindedness, suggested a category of 'moral imbecile' in the 1913 Act. This was primarily young women who had illegitimate children. Burt agreed with her that the feeble-minded and moral imbeciles should not be taught to read and write as they might write letters to each other while segregated! Burt's interest in delinquent children overlapped with his interest in mental and moral subnormality, and his book on *The Young Delinquent* (1925) led to the opening of the first London Child Guidance clinic. Although he was aware of poverty and environmental handicaps he could still refer to "the slum child's (facial) profile as a Negroid or almost simian outline" (Burt 1937:186). Later, he chaired a working party on 'maladjusted' children that reported to the Underwood Committee (1955) from which sprang subsequent descriptions of maladjusted, disruptive, emotionally and behaviourally disturbed and other labels for young people who would not subscribe to prescribed social behaviour. Delinquency and subnormality, as Richardson et al. (2017) have observed, were officially joined early on.

Burt was brought up in the village of Snitterfield near Stratford on Avon, and his father, the local doctor, introduced him as a boy to the aging Galton, who lived nearby, and influenced him in his life-long belief in the influence of heredity on intelligence. At Oxford, Burt studied classics, philosophy and the emerging 'science' of psychology, which included visits to German universities. In Wurzburg his landlady apparently fed him well and even ironed his trousers (Hearnshaw 1979:13)! Burt's career included a lectureship at Liverpool University, 20 years as the official psychologist at the London County Council, a prestigious Chair in Psychology at University College, London and a long retirement during which he continued to assert the links between heredity and intelligence via his studies of twins. As editor of the Statistical Section of the *British Journal of Psychology* he published 63 articles in 17 years under his own name and several under pseudonyms or with two co-workers who may or may not have existed (see Hearnshaw 1979:190). His views on the inheritance of intelligence never wavered throughout his career. He buttressed his views with studies of identical twins reared apart and eventually claimed 53 pairs of twins studied, the numbers increasing in subsequent publications, but all claiming a high heritability as shown by high correlations of IQ scores of identical twins. His data were first questioned as fraudulent by Kamin (1974), and despite accusations that it was 'left-wing environmentalists' trying to discredit Burt, his official and careful biographer, Hearnshaw, concluded that his post-war data on twins were invented and "nearly all Burt's work during his period of retirement was mainly of a defensive kind, designed to uphold the Galtonian standpoint against environmentalists" (Hearnshaw 1979:241). In 1976 the medical correspondent of *The Sunday Times* repeated the charge that much of Burt's data was faked arguing that this was a matter for political and public interest, given the influence Burt had had on the establishment of secondary education (Gillie 1976). Many psychologists sprang to Burt's defence, among them J. Phillipe Rushton, a Professor at the University of Western Ontario, who argued in support of his correlations. Rushton was himself a strong supporter of inherent racial differences, who did much research comparing not only IQ scores between 'Mongoloids, Caucasoids, and Negroids' but also compared the size of their genitalia and frequency of intercourse, asserting that mothers of identical twins had a greater frequency of coitus (Rushton 1990).[6]

Do We Take Eysenck Seriously?

Hans Eysenck, a student and later colleague of Burt's at University College, was a fervent supporter of Burt against his critics, despite Burt's sometimes cursory and devious treatment of him. He, too, was a life-long believer in heredity being the major influence on intelligence as measured by mental tests asserting that "there is no doubt that a close relationship exists between high IQ and success in schooling. Pupils with high IQs tend to gain high marks and stay longer at school, those with poor IQs tend to do poorly in their class work and drop out early" (Eysenck v Kamin 1981:29). He believed that the average IQ of members of different occupations could be assessed, accountants and lawyers with an IQ of 128, farmhands and miners down to 91, but there are occasions when this congruence breaks down, and "there are groups of people whose earnings bears no relation to their intelligence, actors, tennis players, prostitutes, TV personalities, royalty, gigolos and golfers" being among these for-tunates! (Eysenck ibid.:36). There are also more high and low IQs among males and here environmental causes are noted. Women have to undertake child-bearing and traditional female tasks, which impedes their pursuit of scientific or artistic pursuits, although "men-tally defective women may have been able, *if at all attractive*, to escape institutionalisation by marrying" (Eysenck ibid.:42).

Eysenck's views of race and intelligence were especially important in England as he was writing at a time when immigration from former colonial countries was at its height, bringing not only necessary workers, but also a reassertion of imperial views of the biological inferi-ority and cultural deficiencies in 'other races', especially those from slave ancestry. He wrote a paper in a series of Black Papers produced by traditionalists in which he criticised com-prehensive education and a supposed reduction in standards (Eysenck in Cox and Boyson 1977). Then in 1971, surprising for one who was himself a refugee from Nazi Germany, pro-duced a book that reproduced a now familiar bell curve purporting to show that 'Negroes' always scored 15 points below white children in IQ tests. He also lamented the low scores of a white lower class in Britain, concluding that "a considerable proportion of this difference is genetic in origin", and that environmental differences failed to explain the better scores of 'Orientals' as he termed Chinese, Japanese and other Asian children". He did, however, suggest that social and economic pressures on Black people "make it highly likely that their gene pools differ in some genetically conditioned characteristics" including intelligence (Eysenck 1971:20). He concluded with the astonishing comment that as compensatory edu-cation had failed, and Black Power in the 1970s was on the rise, "a solution is only possible in terms of the general abolition of the proletariat—both black and white" (ibid.:151), although he thought that politicians, rather than psychologists, ought to undertake this task!

Enduring Racial Views in the USA

Gould has suggested that "The hereditarian interpretation of IQ arose in America largely through the proselytization of the three psychologists, Goddard, Terman and Yerkes" (Gould 1997:29). In the first edition of his book in 1981 Gould had noted that while there was a resurgence of biological determinism and its racial assumptions every few years, "the Great Men quickly become forgotten.... the hot topics of 1981 becoming legless history" (ibid.:23). He was right in that biological determinism and a seeming determination to prove the inferiority, in particular, of African Americans endures, but wrong that the influence of men regarded, and who regard themselves, as producing 'scientific truth' disappears. In 2007 Nobel-Prize winning geneticist James Watson claimed in a lecture that "all testing shows that African intelligence is not the same as ours ... and people who have to deal with black employees" find this the case (Hunt-Grubbe 2007). His subsequent forced 'retirement' from his academic post, and 'retirement' of another academic who took the view that "today's immigrants are not as intelligent on average as white natives" (Richwine 2009) led to a long debate in the prestigious journal *Nature* as to whether scientists should study race and IQ (*Nature* vol 457 Feb 2009). It also led to a spirited defence by Charles Murray that Watson had only made a factually accurate remark about low IQ scores among African Blacks. From around 2000 a whole new 'scholarship' developed asserting that in the light of new findings in human genetics and widened genomic knowledge, the search for biological underpinnings in race and class should continue (Shiao et al. 2012; Wade 2014).

The story of the pioneers of eugenic thinking and IQ testing, while producing much literature, was particularly well documented by Kamin (1974). He noted that Lewis Terman at Stanford, Henry Goddard, whose own book on the degenerate Kallikak family had photographs altered to produce an appearance of evil or stupidity (see Gould 1981:202), and Robert Yerkes at Harvard were the main pioneers in mental testing. These were all men who, no doubt as a product of their times, held elitist and racist sociopolitical views. Terman, who standardised Binet's tests to produce the much used Stanford-Binet tests in 1916, thought that

> in the near future intelligence tests will bring tens of thousands of high-grade defectives under the surveillance and protection of society. This will result in the curtailing of reproduction of feeble-mindedness and the elimination of an enormous amount of crime, pauperism and industrial inefficiency.
>
> (Terman 1916:6)

He also thought that "low-level IQ deficiency was common among Spanish-Indian, Mexicans and Negroes … whose dullness appears to be racial … the whole question of racial differences in mental traits will have to be taken up anew" (ibid.:91–2). Furthermore, he wrote that children of this group should be segregated in special classes as "they cannot master abstractions, but can often be made efficient workers". Terman, like Eysenck later, was evenhanded in that the poor of all colours were a problem, and there was a need to prevent the reproduction of mental degenerates "thus curtailing the increasing spawn of degeneracy" (Terman 1916:92). Terman, whose own PhD was a study of seven bright and seven stupid boys, began a study in the early 1900s of 1,500 supposedly highly gifted children, following those who did not drop out from the study, through their lives (Terman and Oden 1947). These fortunate people had successful lives and professions. It later transpired that the sample were white middle class children chosen initially by teachers as gifted! This spurious study continues to be quoted (see Herrnstein and Murray 1994:57, and see below by Cummings 2013).

Robert Yerkes, President of the American Psychological Society when the US joined World War I, suggested that all soldiers should be given mental assessment tests to determine their classification. The Army tests included Alpha tests and Beta tests for illiterates, and for non-English speakers test instructions were to be given 'in pantomime'. The mental age of white draftees turned out to be 13, and Black soldiers scored much lower. Post-war, Yerkes and his associates formed a Galton Society, whose purpose was to provide scientific advice to government agencies (Kamin 1974:35) and a committee on the Scientific Problems of Human Migration was formed under Yerkes. The committee supported the research of Carl Brigham, whose influential book *A Study of American Intelligence* had been published in 1923. This book reanalysed the army data on immigrant groups and calculated the amount of different immigrant intelligence. At this point, Poles, Italians and Russians scored below the Negro average but later he blamed a decline of American intelligence levels on "incorporating Negroes into our racial stock" (Brigham 1923:210). Further research work apparently proved the intellectual inferiority of immigrants by country and by blood type (Hirsch 1930). Dr Hirsch also undertook a study of twins which led him to conclude that "heredity is five times as potent as environment" (ibid.:148).

As noted, suggestions of mental inferiority between groups died down somewhat after World War II, as the appalling consequences of these beliefs became apparent and the United Nations, through UNESCO, commissioned biologists and social scientists to study the concept of race and group distinctions made on the basis of phenotypical and cultural characteristics (see Rex 1986). The 1960s onwards saw a resurgence of often bitter debate about race, class and intelligence. Arthur Jensen, a former research colleague of Eysenck, was the protagonist with a 123-page article in the *Harvard Education Review* initially complaining that compensatory education programmes designed to alleviate poverty and narrow achievement gaps between minority and majority children had failed through not being able to overcome innate factors, although he ended with a plea for schools to find ways of "utilizing other strengths in children whose major strength is not of the cognitive variety" (Jensen 1969:202; Jensen 1973). Jensen was a fervent admirer of Cyril Burt, corresponding with him and dedicating a book to him. He and Eysenck vigorously defended Burt against the accusations of fraud. Jensen argued that very severe mental retardation was caused by gene defects, and that higher grade defectives were at the lower end of a normal curve of IQ distribution. He stated that the upper classes rarely had children with low IQ scores, apart from the occasional pathological defect; it was lower class parents who had children at the lower end of normal variation. As Kamin commented, "The upper class child stands a better chance of having his stupidity attributed to his asthma or diabetes rather than to his genes" (Kamin 1974:185).

Jensen's work caused some bitter dispute[7] and even more dispute followed the publication in 1994 of *The Bell Curve* (Herrnstein and Murray 1994). This book of 845 pages was "about differences in intellectual capacities among people and groups and what these differences mean for America's future" (ibid.:xxi). The book meticulously documented almost every study carried out over the century on the mental measurement of populations and groups, and although noting that IQ testing had become a controversial product of science denied that "no-one of any stature was trying to use the results to promote discriminatory, let alone eugenic laws" (ibid.:7). It was unfortunate that major conclusions to the book were so negative as regards Black Americans, lower socio-economic groups, and women. Writing that an emerging white underclass was developing as "the dry tinder for the formation of an underclass community is the large number of births to single women of low intelligence concentrated in a spatial area" (ibid.:520) and linking Black single parentage, welfare payments, and Black crime statistics to low intelligence was not likely to endear the authors to many Americans, however wrapped up in disclaimers. Although those eager to apportion blame for lower attainments to lower class and Black groups found the ideas appealing. *The Bell Curve*'s conclusion was that public policy assuming that interventions can overcome both genetic and environmental disadvantage was "overly optimistic" and that "cognitive partitioning will continue" as "inequality of endowments, including intelligence, is a reality". The suggestion that "it is time for Americans once again to try living with inequality" (ibid.:551–2) rings somewhat hollow in 2016, as the USA is already one of the most unequal societies in terms of income distribution. The book had ardent supporters. Professor Linda Gottfredson wrote an article in the *Wall Street Journal* supporting the notion that the IQ of Black people always worked out 15 points below whites, and that *The Bell Curve* conclusions were congruent with mainstream views on IQ and intelligence. Fifty-two other professors signed in support of her article, among them Plomin (see below). Jensen never moderated his views. Giving an interview in 1999, aged 77, he again reiterated his beliefs in the predominance of hereditary factors in learning and the failure of compensatory education, and in 2005 collaborated with J. Phillipe Rushton (Rushton and Jensen 2005).

A New Eugenics?

As Gould and Stephen Rose had forecast, there is again a resurgence of biological determinism and an emergence of more (mainly) men deemed to be important in the field of genetics. From the turn of the century and the completion of the mapping of the 23,000 human genes in the human genome project, a new 'scholarship' has developed asserting that in the light of new findings in human genetics and widened genomic knowledge, work on the biological underpinnings of groups differences, especially by 'race' should continue (Shiao et al. 2012; Wade 2014). Although contemporary work using genome wide studies makes no claims that genetic make-up significantly determines the educational or social destiny of children, belief in the inherent ability of children is again being reinforced and is underpinning the selection and separation of young people in schooling. It appears that the early twentieth century popularity of eugenic theories and resulting nature-nurture debates, are now being resurrected via advances in human genetics to support notions of the bright and the dull, the academic and the practical mind, and in England the grammar school, the secondary modern and the special needs student.

Since both England and the USA already have well-segregated education systems as regards race and class, questions must be asked as to why there is a resurgence of eugenic explanation for educational achievements. These questions are not merely 'academic'. Influential political elite thinking in England was demonstrated by the then Mayor of London and an MP who aspired to be Prime Minister. In the third annual Margaret Thatcher memorial lecture in November 2013 Boris Johnson claimed that "human beings are already very far apart in raw ability... as many as 16% of our species have an IQ below 85 while about 2% have an IQ above 130". He also claimed in this lecture that "greed is a valuable spur to economic activity" (Johnson 2013). One reason for such biological determinism may be a search for legitimation of increasing economic inequality, especially in the UK and USA, which both now have grossly unequal labour markets that give rise to very high (often obscene) levels of remuneration to a few, and low wages or unemployment to the many. Low educational performance followed by low wages can be falsely legitimated by claims of intrinsic ability when economic inequalities are high. Eugenics was last at its height of popularity when countries were as unequal economically as at present. It seems that one project of neo-liberal governments and its elites has for the past 35 years attempted to denigrate social-democratic attempts to value the capabilities of all citizens.

The 'long revolution' described by Raymond Williams (1961) of the attempts from the industrial revolution onwards to gain opportunity, voice and justice for ordinary people who were constantly regarded as inferior members of the society was, according to one commentator "halted or in ruins" by 2012 (T. Clark 2012). Major tools in the structuring of inferiority have been the propagation of beliefs that there are such strong differences in the educational potential of children, often passed on to students on teacher education courses and their training schools, by continued IQ and other assessments, and currently by a new eugenics movement and as in the past, those with lower abilities turn out to be racial minorities, the manual working classes and, in particular, people living in poverty.

Into the twenty-first century debates have been infused with new life by the completion of the first stage of the human genome project, the creation of massive DNA biobanks and an expansion in behavioural genetics and the neurosciences. While eminent geneticist Steve Jones has noted that "the hubris which accompanied the Human Genome project has stalled" and "what genes can activate depends on the environment in which they find themselves" (Jones 2013:109) there are, in addition to the geneticists, numbers of sociologists, political scientists, labour economists and others, who are enthused again for study of 'race' and class differences, cognitive enhancement for better brains, or linking raised IQ scores to improve the economy. The question of 'who owns the human genetic code?' caused much debate from 2000, and although there were some attempts to ensure that genetic information did not impinge negatively on minority groups a Human Diversity Project in the USA targeting specific indigenous groups led to accusations of racism and 'genetic colonisation' (Ammons 2000). Heritability studies in criminology expanded, with dubious attempts to separate out genetic and environmental effects, complex social questions being reduced to simple numbers. Indeed, some criminologists have called for an end to these studies, which once again target poor and minority groups negatively (Burt and Simons 2014).

Influence on Education Policy

No such qualms have yet affected the education scene and currently in England some research appear to be influencing government education policy. Robert Plomin, an American behavioural geneticist currently working at King's College London, and as noted above, a supporter of the *Bell Curve* thesis, was closely connected to former Minister of Education Michael Gove. Plomin has gained millions of pounds of research money to carry out his long-term twin studies (James 2016). Although post-Burt twin studies, purporting to measure the respective influence of genetic heritability and environment had a bad press, Plomin's twin project had been described as "leading an international research effort" (Geake 2009:88).

His work was given prominence in late 2013 when an adviser to Gove produced a 237-page paper for his Minister claiming on the first page that

> the education of the majority even in rich countries is between awful to mediocre ... in England, less that 10% per year leave school with formal training in basics such as exponential function, normal distribution (the bell curve) and conditional probability.
>
> (Cummings 2013)

Oxford educated Cummings had never taught, although his mother was a special needs teacher. Cummings claimed that Plomin had shown that the largest factor accounting for variation in children's school performance was accounted for by genes, scores in national curriculum tests showing 60–70 per cent dependence on heritability. Cummings also quoted Lewis Terman's spurious "high ability studies" in defence of his thesis and echoing Jensen, claimed that money spent on programmes such as Sure Start, were useless. Plomin and his colleague Katherine Asbury, had just published their book *G is for Genes* (Asbury and Plomin 2014), which made some sweeping claims such as "the technology will soon be available to use DNA 'chips' to predict strengths and weaknesses of individual pupils and use this information to put personalized strategies in place for them" (ibid.:12), and recommended that teachers use IQ tests and other assessments to check whether pupils are making progress towards fulfilling a potential fixed by their genes. They also suggested that horse-riding should be encouraged as a school activity in case a child turns out to "have the potential to be a jockey" (p. 172). The horse fraternity actually know that a major genetic component necessary for becoming a jockey is height! However, Plomin was invited to meet Government Ministers and in December 2013 gave evidence to the Education Select Committee in the House of Commons on the 'under-achievement' of working class children.

While a mild media furore surrounded Cummings paper (Helm 2013), Plomin, who has never disavowed his support for Herrnstein and Murray's book, claimed that he preferred to 'keep his head down' and take a 'softly softly approach' to racial issues (Gillborn 2016). Dorling, reviewing the Asbury and Plomin book, commented that "it may serve as a source of many examples of why modern day geneticism is often little more advanced than its precursor eugenics" (Dorling 2014:4). Nevertheless, Plomin continues to be newsworthy. An interview with him published in the *Times Educational Supplement*, a paper widely read by teachers, claimed that his research shows that "IQ—a flawed but handy measure of general intelligence—is around 70% heritable" (Arney 2016:27). The conclusions seem to be reasonable—that more money should be spent on the disadvantaged, as these will be the children whose genetic deficiencies show up most and need help so that their "brains can flourish and develop and they can express their full genetic potential" (ibid.:29). Spending money to overcome the plight of disadvantaged genes may be kinder than the historical treatment of the defective, but the eugenic messages are still present.

The Flynn Effect

While much of the more recent work reported above was in progress, the academic world was treated to the publication of James Flynn's work indicating that from the 1930s in each decade, there had been an increase in scores in traditional IQ tests (Flynn 1987, 2009). This led to such questions as "Are you smarter than your granny" and even "Are you smarter than Aristotle?" The spate of publications discussing and attempting to explain this often appeared to run parallel to the heritability debates reported above, although neuroscientists figured prominently in explanations for 'better brains'. Explanations varied from suggestions that children were better trained to pass tests, and thus had better test-taking skills, improved health and nutrition, smaller families, more stimulating environments, and improved schooling. Geake (2009) checked the tests given and concluded that it was abstract problem solving that had improved, and not general intelligence. He put this down to technical developments in ITC and computing, which had apparently improved the part of the brain (parietal cortices) that was responsible for memory and mathematics and spatial organisation (ibid.:92).

This chapter has reviewed major writings and debates over a hundred or more years, which purport to claim scientific backing for differences in the educational capabilities of lower class and ethnic minorities, especially Black people. IQ is still the 'mismeasure of man' and old and new versions of eugenicism continue to have influence, although currently much is coded and inexplicit. Genetic heritability is claimed once more to take precedence over environment, despite claims that the IQ of whole populations is improving. Although there are few politicians who unlike Johnson would claim in public their beliefs in the natural stupidity of some groups, whose 'potential' is unfortunately less than others, this ideology is currently shaping education policy via moves to more high stakes testing, and separation of the 'bright' and the less able. Underlying current beliefs and polices though, there is also a fear that the stupid may not be as dull as supposed. This is taken up in the next chapter, which takes on the story of English developments in special and inclusive education, and notes the strategies that attempt to manufacture inability.

Notes

1. Members of the Eugenics Society included poets T. S. Eliot and W. B. Yeats, writers Aldous Huxley, George Bernard Shaw and H. G. Wells, and psychologist Raymond

Cattell who in 1933 congratulated the Hitler government for passing laws enforcing the sterilisation of the unfit. Writer D. H. Lawrence was also a supporter, admiring the philosopher Freidrich Nietzsche who wrote that education should remain a privilege for 'higher beings'. Lawrence was in favour of working class boys only attending craft and gymnastics classes and girls only being taught domestic studies.

2. Liam Hudson pointed out the research on human intelligence had long been dominated by 'men of statistical flair', which meant that many people felt they were not qualified to intervene (cited in Kamin 1977:11). This is similar to the present day when those not expert in genetics feel they are not qualified to debate genetic propositions. Yet as the mental testers and their beliefs that tests accurately measured intellectual capacity have given so much ammunition to racists and political reactionaries (especially in the USA supporting racist immigration policies), mental testing and arguments over genetic heritability must be entered into.

3. Pearson was apparently trying to end an argument over whether this curve should be called Gaussian or Laplacian by calling it a 'normal' curve, thus influencing generations of psychologists and educationalists in an assertion, not a 'truth'.

4. The Secretary of the Board of Education from 1902 to 1911 was Sir Robert Morant, an elitist who wrote of "the need of submitting the many ignorant to the guidance and control of the few wise...." (Allen 1934:125) and in his Board of Education report of 1906 wrote that "the majority of children must be educated to be efficient members of the class to which they belong". He also had a distain for technical and vocational education.

5. Grunenthal, later bought by the firm Distillers, was the firm that marketed thalidomide and other employees included Otto Ambrose, credited with developing the nerve gas Sarin used in the war. He ran a work camp at Auschwitz and served some time in prison before his employment. The drug, never trialled, was marketed for morning sickness and some 20,000 babies with deformities were born to women who took it.

6. Rushton (1995) claimed a gene-based evolutionary theory of differences between 'races'—Mongoloids, Orientals, Caucasoids, Negroids—with the last at the end of the spectrum. Brain size, intelligence, reproductive behaviour, family stability and law-abidingness were some of the attributes of different races. He drew on an analysis of the Kinsey study of sexual behaviour (Kinsey et al. 1948) to make claims about differences in genitalia, menstruation and sexual behaviour. He was sanctioned by his university for some of his research methods.

7. Peter Medawar, distinguished geneticist, wrote that "Jensenism grows naturally out of...the phoney science of IQ with psychologists who maintain that 'intelligence' can be measured by a simple scalar ratio and that by applying certain formulas from a

science-genetics—which they do not understand—it is possible to attribute a certain percentage of intellectual prowess to the effects of nature, and the balance to nurture" (Medawar 1977:13).

References

Allen, B. M. (1934) *Sir Robert Morant.* London. Macmillan.

Ammons, B. (2000) "Who owns the human genetic code?" in *Annotated Bibliography.* Washington DC. The Human Genome program, Office of Biological and Environmental Research, Department of Energy.

Arney, K. (2016) "Unleashing the power of potential" *Times Educational Supplement* 22 January.

Asbury, K. and Plomin, R. (2014) *G is for Genes.* Chichester. Wiley.

Barker, D. (1983) "How to curb the fertility of the unfit: the feeble-minded in Edwardian Britain" *Oxford Review of Education* 9/3: 197–211.

Binet, A. (1913) *Les idées modernes sur les enfants.* Paris. Flammarion.

Brigham, C. C. (1923) *A Study of American Intelligence.* Princeton NJ. Princeton University Press.

Burt, C. *The Backward Child.* London. University of London Press.

Burt, C. H. and Simons, R. D. L. (2014) "Pulling back the curtains on heritability studies: biosocial criminology in the postgenomic era" *Criminology* 52/2: 223–262.

Burt, C. L. (1920) *Report of an Investigation upon Backward Children in Birmingham.* Birmingham. Birmingham Education Committee.

Burt, C. L. (1925) *The Young Delinquent.* London. London University Press

Chitty, C. (2007) *Eugenics, Race and Intelligence in Education.* London. Continuum.

Clark, G. (2016) "Gregory Clark on names" in (eds) Edmonds, D. and Warburton, N. *Big Ideas in Social Science.* London. Sage.

Clark, T. (2012) "For a left with no future" *New Left Review* 74 March/April.

Cummings, D. (2013) *Some Thoughts on Education and Political Priority.* Paper presented to the Secretary of State for Education. October 2013.

Dorling, D. (2014) "G is for genes: book review" *International Journal of Epidemiology* 44/1: 374–378.

Dorling, D. (2015) *Injustice: why social inequality still persists* (2nd ed.). Bristol. Policy Press.

Dugdale, D. (1877) *The Jukes: a study in crime, pauperism and disease.* New York. Putnam.

Eysenck, H. J. (1971) *Race, Intelligence and Education.* London. Temple-Smith.

Eysenck, H. J. (1977) "When is discrimination?" in (eds) Cox, C. B. and Boyson, R. *Black Paper 1977.* London. Temple-Smith.

Eysenck, H. J. v. Kamin, L. (1981) *Intelligence: the battle for the mind.* London. Pan Books.

Dawkins, R. (2016) tweet@axleranges, 31 January.

Flynn, J. R. (1987) "Massive IQ gains in 14 nations: what IQ tests really measure" *Psychological Bulletin* 101: 171–191.

Flynn, J. R. (2009) *What is Intelligence? Beyond the Flynn effect.* Cambridge. Cambridge University Press.

Galton, F. (1869) *Hereditary Genius.* London. Macmillan.

Galton, F. (1883) *Inquiries into Human Faculty and Development.* London. Macmillan.

Geake, J. (2009) *The Brain at School: educational neuro-science in the classroom.* Maidenhead. Open University Press/McGraw-Hill.

Gillborn, D. (2008) *Racism and Education: coincidence or conspiracy.* London. Routledge.

Gillborn, D. (2016) "Softly, softly: genetics, intelligence and the hidden racism of the new geneism" *Journal of Education Policy* 31/4: 365–388.

Gillie, O. (1976) "Crucial data faked by eminent psychologist" *The Sunday Times* 24 October.

Goddard, H. H. (1912) *The Kallikak Family.* New York. Macmillan.

Gould, S. J. (1981) *The Mismeasure of Man.* London. Penguin Books.

Gould, S. J. (1997) *The Mismeasure of Man* (rev. ed.). London. Penguin Books.

Hearnshaw, L. (1979) *Cyril Burt: psychologist.* London. Hodder and Stoughton.

HEART (2010) *Sinti and Roma, the Gypsies.* Berlin. Holocaust Education and Archive Team.

Helm, T. (2013) "Gove urged to reject 'chilling views' of his special adviser" *The Observer* 13 October.

Heron, D. (1906) *On the Relation of Fertility in Man to Social Status, and on the Changes in this Relation that have Taken Place during the Last Fifty years.* London. Dulau.

Herrnstein, R. J. and Murray, C. (1994) *The Bell Curve.* New York. The Free Press.

Hirsch, N. D. (1930) *Twins: heredity and environment.* Cambridge MA. Harvard University Press.

Hobcraft, J. (2016) "ABCDE of biosocial science" *Society Now* Spring edition: 18–19.

Hudson, L. (1972) "The context of the debate" in (eds) Richardson, K., Spears, D. and Richmond, M. *Race, Culture and Intelligence.* Harmondsworth. Penguin.

Hunt-Grubbe, C. (2007) "The elementary DNA of Dr Watson" *Sunday Times* 14 October.

Hurt, J. S. (1988) *Out of the Mainstream.* London. Batsford.

James, O. (2016) *Not in Your Genes.* London. Vermillion.

Jensen, A. R. (1969) "How much can we boost IQ and scholastic ability?" *Harvard Educational Review* 33: 1–123.

Jensen, A. R. (1973) *Educability and Group Differences.* London. Methuen.

Johnson, B. (2013) *The 2013 Annual Margaret Thatcher Lecture.* London. Centre for Policy Studies. 27 November.

Jones, S. (2013) *The Serpent's Promise.* London. Little Brown.

Joseph, J. (2015) *The Trouble with Twin Studies: a reassessment of twin research in the social and behavioural sciences.* New York. Routledge.

Kamin, L. J. (1974) *The Science and Politics of IQ.* New York. Lawrence Erlbaum and Associates. Reprinted 1977. Harmondsworth. Penguin.

Kinsey, A. C., Pomeroy, W. B. and Martin, C. E. (1948) *Sexual Behaviour in the Human Male*. Philadelphia PA. Saunders.

Langley, K. (1988) *From Morality to Management*. M. Phil dissertation. Lancaster. University of Lancaster.

Lewis, J. (1987) "So much grit in the educational machine" in (ed.) Bessant, B. *Mother State and her Little Ones: children and youth in Australia 1860–1930*. Melbourne. PIT.

Lowe, R. (1980) "Eugenics and education: a note on the origins of intelligence testing in England" *Educational Studies* 6/1: 1–8.

Medawar, P. B. (1977) "Unnatural science" *New York Review of Books* 3: 13–18.

Montague, S. (1999) *Race and IQ*. New York. Oxford University Press.

Morning, S. (2014) "And you thought we had moved beyond all that: biological race returns to the social sciences" *Ethnic and Racial Studies* 37/10: 1676–1687.

Nature (2009) vol 457, Commentary: Should scientists study race and IQ. pp 786–789, and editorial p. 763.

Pearson, K. (1892) *The Grammar of Science*. London. Walter Scott.

Plato (c 500 BCE) *The Republic*. Book 3. Trans. Jowett, B. London. Project Gutenberg.

RCCCFM (1908) *Report of the Royal Commission on the Care and Control of the Feeble-minded* (8 vols). London. HMSO.

Rex, J. (1986) *Race and Ethnicity*. Milton Keynes. Open University Press.

Richardson, J. G., Wu, J. J. and Judge, D. (2017) *The Global Convergence of Vocational and Special Education*. London. Routledge.

Richwine, J. (2009) *IQ and Immigration Policy* (unpublished PhD study). Cambridge MA. Harvard University.

Rose, S. (2014) "Is genius in the genes?" *Times Educational Supplement* 24 January: 27–29.

Rose, S., Kamin, L. J. and Lewontin, R. C. (1984) *Not in Our Genes: biology, ideology and human nature*. London. Pelican Books.

Rushton, J. P. (1990) "Race differences, r/K theory and a reply to Flynn" *The Psychologist* 5: 195–198.

Rushton, J. P. (1995) *Race, Evolution and Behaviour: a life history perspective*. New Brunswick NJ. Transaction Books.

Rushton, J. P. and Jensen, A. R. (2005) "Thirty years of research on race differences in cognitive ability" *Psychology, Public Policy and Law* 11/2: 235–294.

Shiao, J. L., Bode, T., Beyer, A. and Selvig, D. (2012) "The genomic challenge to the social construction of race" *Sociological Theory* 30/2: 67–88.

Shulman, C. and Bostrom, N. (2014) "Embryo selection for cognitive enhancement: curiosity or game-changer" *Global Policy* 5/1: 85–92.

Spearman, C. E. (1904) "General intelligence: objectively measured and determined" *American Journal of Psychology* XV: 201–299.

Terman, L. M. (1916) *The Measurement of Intelligence.* Boston MA. Houghton Mifflin.

Terman, L. M. and Oden, M. H. (1947) *The Gifted Child Grows Up. Twenty-five years follow-up of a superior group.* Genetic Studies of Genius vol 4. Stanford CA. Stanford University Press.

Underwood Report (1955) *Report of the Committee on Maladjusted Children.* London. HMSO.

Wade, N. (2014) *A Troublesome Inheritance: genes, race and human history.* New York. Penguin Books.

Williams, R. (1961) *The Long Revolution.* Harmondsworth. Penguin.

Zax, J. S and Rees, D. I. (2002) "IQ, academic performance, environment and earnings" *Review of Economics and Statistics* 84/4: 600–616.

Part I Special Education and the Law

Topics for Further Discussion

1. How do you think we can prepare teachers in training to work with students with special needs? What do you recommend as ways to provide services to all children so that they all have the opportunity to learn?
2. What aspects of inclusion do you think work? What changes would you suggest for improving the quality of instruction students with disabilities receive?
3. What aspects of Response to Intervention (RTI) do you think are appropriate when evaluating students with disabilities? How would you go about making sure that the interventions you provide are based in research and are appropriate?
4. What are some of the key elements of special education teacher quality? What aspects do the foundations of teaching play in developing effective teachers?
5. How do you see the law as a key player in developing teaching strategies for students with disabilities? How has the law influenced the way we provide services to students with disabilities?

Part II

Differentiated Instruction

Differentiated Instruction (DI) is a technique that is used most widely when teaching students with disabilities. It involves accommodating and modifying the instruction for these pupils in order to develop an approach that helps them learn. DI requires that all students in the classroom learn the same material but in different ways. Your close association with the special education teacher will help you learn how to differentiate the instruction so that students with disabilities will learn. These techniques are based on sound, research-based theories and approaches to learning and can be demonstrated by another member of the team.

DI involves all subject matter—reading, math, physical education, and art, just to name a few. It involves all learners and groups of students and can be supported by ability level or social context. What is most important is that DI should be reasonable and appropriate for the student involved. The expectation is that students will meet the outcomes of the lesson and master the material. Student success is the key to effective DI. The process prepares the student for passing the class and is helpful in getting students to focus.

Guided Questions

1. How does DI help students with disabilities be successful in the classroom?
2. What are some strategies you can use to ensure that DI is being implemented?
3. What are some ways to modify goals and objectives to better teach students with disabilities?
4. What strategies can you use to team with the special education teacher to teach and use DI?
5. How can you help students focus when approaching a lesson that uses DI?

Differentiated Instruction

An Integration of Theory and Practice

Carol Ann Tomlinson
University of Virginia

Marcia B. Imbeau
University of Arkansas

D IFFERENTIATED INSTRUCTION IS A MODEL STEMMING from theory, research, and classroom practice and designed to guide planning for teaching and learning. The three-part premise of the model is an ancient one: (a) people differ as learners, (b) those differences matter in learning, and (c) teachers are more effective when they seek to understand those differences and plan with them in mind.

The idea of differentiation, or addressing individual variance in teaching, is a very old one. Its underlying tenet is found in the writings of Confucius, in the texts of Judaism, and in the ancient writings of Islam. More recently, a form of what we have come to call "differentiated instruction" was accepted practice in many of the one-room schoolhouses commonly found in the United States, Canada, the United Kingdom, Australia, New Zealand, Spain, and Ireland in the late nineteenth and early twentieth centuries. They are still used in some developing nations and in remote areas in many countries.

The model of differentiation referenced in this chapter was developed as a classroom practice during the 1970s and 80s by Carol Tomlinson and some of her colleagues in the Fauquier County (Virginia) Public Schools. From its inception, the model has been informed both by research findings and by current and evolving theories in psychology, pedagogy, and, more recently, the emerging field of neuroscience. The evolution of the model will be discussed in greater detail later in the chapter.

The current model of differentiation is a synthesis model in that it draws and distills practices from a variety of educational specialties such as reading, special education, multicultural education, and gifted education, as well as from curriculum and instruction, psychology, and child development. It unifies insights and practices from multiple fields for coherent and ready access for practitioners.

Description of the Model

This model of differentiation envisions the classroom elements as a system of interdependent parts, with each element affected by and affecting the others. Those key elements are: learning environment, curriculum, assessment, instruction, and management of routines. While differentiated instruction is, at its core, an instructional approach, it addresses all of the classroom elements based on the proposition that attending to one of the elements without attention to all of them and to their interaction diminishes learning for most students. Figure 2.1.1 depicts the principle-driven model which reflects that proposition.

The model proposes that:

- Differentiating instruction is a process that evolves over time in teacher development. It is not a particular act or event. Rather, it is a way of thinking about teaching and learning.

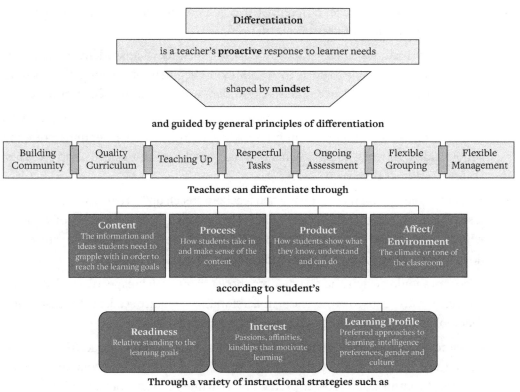

FIGURE 2.1.1   A flowchart of the elements of differentiated instruction.

- The process begins when a teacher reaches out in some way to address the needs of particular students which, at the time, appear somewhat different from the needs of others in the class.

- The teacher's capacity to attend to learner variance is shaped by the teacher's "mindset" (Dweck, 2000)—or beliefs about the malleability of human potential. A teacher's mindset impacts students' mindsets.

- The most effective differentiation is likely to be proactively planned rather than reactive or improvisational. Although improvisation plays a role in understanding and attending to learner needs, solely or largely improvisational differentiation is not powerful enough to address the learning needs of many students.

- Developing the classroom as a community of learners in which students support one another's growth makes the environment safe for students to risk learning and helps students achieve a sense of belonging or affiliation.

- The power of what a teacher differentiates (quality of curriculum) impacts the power of the differentiation (quality of instruction).

- Quality curriculum includes: (a) clarity about precisely what students must know, understand, and be able to do as the result of any segment of learning, (b) a plan to engage students, (c) and an emphasis on student understanding of content.

- Persistent use of preassessment and ongoing assessment that are tightly aligned with essential knowledge, understanding, and skill should inform teacher understanding about student learning needs, teacher planning to address those needs, and students' ability to address their own success.

- Student outcomes are most robust when teachers "teach up"—that is, when they plan tasks that require students to work at high levels and scaffold the success of students who are not yet able to function independently at those levels rather than "teaching down" or diluting goals and opportunities for those students.

- Teachers should design and all students should work with "respectful tasks"—that is tasks that are focused on essential understandings, require students to reason, and that look equally interesting and appealing to students.

- Classrooms that facilitate attention to student variance balance structure and flexibility. In such classrooms, students understand the reason for and contribute to the success of routines that provide predictability while allowing for variability.

- Teachers can modify content (what students learn or how they access what they learn), process (how students make sense of or come to "own" content), products (how students demonstrate what they have learned at summative points in a unit of study), affect/learning environment (the physical environment in the classroom as well as how students feel about or respond to learning and the classroom environment),

- There are many instructional strategies that facilitate attending to students' varied learning needs. No specific set of strategies is required for differentiation. Rather teachers should develop and draw from an extensive repertoire of strategies suited to the nature and needs of the students and content requirements of the subjects they teach.

Original Development and Iterations of the Model

"Differentiated instruction" was born of a practical need. During the early part of her 20-plus year teaching career, Tomlinson was hired in Warrenton, Virginia to develop and teach in a middle school language arts program. A typical class of 35–40 students included 10–15 students who read 4 to 6 years below grade level and 15–18 students who read 4–5 years above grade level. In most classes, students working at or near grade level numbered no more than five or six. It was immediately apparent that selecting a single "target" group of students as the focus of instructional planning was ineffective. With that approach it was not only impossible to move the diverse learners ahead academically, but also very difficult to maintain their engagement with course content. Tomlinson and colleagues, therefore, developed classroom routines that allowed students to work together on common tasks at some points, while working independently or working in small groups with either common or differentiated tasks at other times. Simultaneously, the teachers used formative assessment of student proficiency with specified learning goals to learn how to target instruction for varied learner needs.

From the outset of their work with this approach (which would only receive the name "differentiated instruction" some 2 years later), Tomlinson and her colleagues also emphasized high engagement curriculum that focused on student understanding and on developing a community of learners that functioned like a team in shared responsibility for supporting one another's academic growth and for establishing and executing flexible classroom processes and routines.

Also part of the original iteration of the model, of course, was the use of a broad range of instructional strategies that facilitated attention to a range of learning needs. Many of these were drawn from the field of reading, which Tomlinson studied at the masters and doctoral levels as she taught in public school. Use of flexible versus stable instructional groupings of students was also an important feature of the model in its early stages of development in order to help establish a cohesive community of learners rather than classes in which readiness or economic background became the predictor of student instructional or work groups and thus became divisive.

During the early years of implementing differentiation in the classroom, Tomlinson and her colleagues were awarded funds from the Virginia Department of Education to test and ultimately disseminate the principles and practices of their classes, called Communications Core, within and beyond their school district. A part of the grant called for measuring impacts of their approach on students. For 3 years, Communications Core students served as a treatment group and seventh graders in peer schools without Communications Core served as a control group in assessing student growth in reading comprehension, vocabulary, spelling, and attitude about English. In every instance, communications core students performed significantly better than students in the control group in every category measured.

Based on those findings, communications core ultimately provided both the curriculum and pedagogical approach for all seventh grade language arts classes in the school district for the next 2 decades. "differentiation" was also used in other middle school English classes in the district. During that time, Communications Core teachers met regularly to ensure a shared understanding of the curriculum and the instructional approach they shared. Throughout that time they refined and extended their practices and assessed its impacts on both student growth and their own work.

In the early 1990s, Tomlinson joined the faculty at the University of Virginia. It was not her intent to further develop or share the approach to teaching she and her colleagues had developed. In working with teachers in the field, however, she found two common themes. First, teachers saw a clear need to plan differently for different students—for example, students with reading problems, learning disabilities, advanced levels of performance, and so on. Second, they had difficulty envisioning how the class would function in terms of curriculum, instruction, and management if they attempted to address more than one set of student needs at a time. Hearing about a framework for academically responsive instruction appeared both interesting and helpful to the teachers with whom she often worked and it therefore seemed worthwhile to develop the framework further.

At the same time, she was engaged in research projects with university colleagues. In designing one of the early research projects, Tomlinson named the instructional approach she had used in the classroom and developed the first graphic depiction of the model. Over time, a number of these projects provided an opportunity for the research group to extend their understanding of differentiation as both a theory and a practice. Tomlinson's work in the field informed the direction of her research interests and her research findings informed her work with practitioners. In combination, these two venues contributed to an evolving conception of differentiation.

The following key publications reflect some key steps and stages in informing the model's iterations between 1990 and 2011.

- *Deciding to Differentiate Instruction in Middle School: One School's Journey* (Tomlinson, 1995) is a case study of the understanding and application of differentiation in a middle school in the Midwest. It is a first look at how educators understand and misunderstand the concept of differentiation, how teachers' beliefs impact their practice regarding students' learning differences, and the origin of the concept of proactive versus reactive differentiation.

- *How to Differentiate Instruction* in *Mixed Ability Classrooms* (1st ed.) (Tomlinson, 1995) delineates and defines the model of differentiation for practitioners for the first time.

- *The Differentiated Classroom: Responding to the Needs of All Learners* (Tomlinson, 1999) elaborated on the framework of differentiation and provides additional examples of differentiated instruction in K-12 classrooms with particular emphasis on teacher rationales for differentiating content, process, and product based on students' readiness levels, interests, and learning profiles.

- *Leadership for Schoolwide Differentiation* (Tomlinson & Allan, 2000) begins to explore the role of school leaders in developing teacher attitudes and practices that are more responsive to academically diverse student populations.

- *Fulfilling the Promise of the Differentiated Classroom* (Tomlinson, 2003) introduces the affective underpinnings of differentiation as well as providing extended examples of classroom differentiation.

- *Differentiation in Practice: A Resource Guide for Differentiating Curriculum* is a three-volume set for K-5 (Tomlinson & Eidson, 2003), 5-9 (2003), and 9-12 (Tomlinson & Strickland, 2005) that provides examples of fully developed, differentiated units of study in the core content areas of math, science, language arts, and history/social studies. Teachers who designed the units annotate their work with the thinking behind the units' design.

- *Integrating Differentiated Instruction and Understanding by Design: Connecting Content and Kids* (Tomlinson & McTighe, 2006) details important connections between curriculum quality and differentiation, delineating ways in which curriculum and instruction work in tandem to connect a wide range of students with meaningful content.

- *The Differentiated School: Making Revolutionary Changes in Teaching and Learning* (Tomlinson, Brimijoin, & Narvaez, 2008) documents the work of an elementary principal, a high school principal, and their faculties in moving to differentiation throughout the schools. The book synthesizes literature related to the nature of school leaders whose work results in extensive change as a means of analyzing the work of the two principals. It also includes student outcome data during the period of the study.

- *Leading and Managing a Differentiated Classroom* (Tomlinson & Imbeau, 2010) for the first time expands on the philosophy or rationale for differentiation. It also provides specific guidance for teachers who seek to work with their students in establishing classroom communities of learning built around that philosophy and in which teacher and students work together to support the academic growth of all students in the classroom.

- *Differentiation and the Brain: How Neuroscience Supports the Learner-Friendly Classroom* (Sousa & Tomlinson, 2011) examines how an emerging knowledge of the brain relates to the key principles of differentiated instruction and provides support beyond the fields of education and psychology for those principles.

The progression of writing on differentiation as an instructional model demonstrates an intent to present the model as a whole as well as exploring each of its key elements in greater detail. Writings also reflect an intent to update the model and its components based on emerging research on relevant aspects of learning and pedagogy.

Generalizability of the Theory

The model of differentiated instruction discussed in this chapter was developed to attend to student variance of any kind in a classroom, including variance related to gender, culture, ethnicity, and economic status. A primary aim of the model is to support equity of access to excellent instruction for the broadest possible range of learners. The model is heuristic or principle-driven rather than algorithmic or recipe-like. Its principles apply to varied cultures, economic groups, ethnicities, and genders while making room for differences that exist within groups as well.

The culture of a classroom may or may not align with the cultural, economic, or gender perspectives of a given learner. When there is a mismatch between what any student brings to class in terms of skills and expectations, it is likely that student achievement suffers. That is particularly problematic if the school or classroom is centered in the patterns of a dominant culture while some students in the classroom are more comfortable with the patterns and expectations of other cultures.

While differentiation cautions that generalizing *across* cultures or ethnicities in terms of instructional design and implementation is unwise, it does not generalize *within* a culture, gender, or economic group either. In other words, while it points to some differences in learning that can exist between males and females, for example, it cautions educators against assuming that all males will learn alike or that all females will approach learning in the same way. Likewise, it cautions against generalizing within ethnic, cultural, ethnic, and economic groups as well. Differentiation encourages and supports teachers in learning about students' backgrounds and learning preferences in order to provide a range of approaches to learning and to help students develop awareness of conditions that facilitate their learning.

In terms of culture, ethnicity, and economic status, experts in the area of multicultural education note particular concern for students from nondominant groups and students from any group that is judged by peers to be of low status. Figure 2.1.1 lists, according to classroom elements, some conditions that can impede achievement of students from nondominant groups and low status students (Cohen & Lotan, 2004; Knapp & Woolverton, 2004). Table 2.1.1 also notes principles and practices of differentiation that address those concerns.

TABLE 2.1.1 Experts' Concerns for Students From Nondominant Groups and Low Status Students From Any Group in Classrooms

Classroom Element	Concerns for Students From Nondominant Groups and Low Status Students	Principles and Practices From Differentiation That Address the Concerns
View of ability	In schools and classrooms, ability is often viewed from the perspective of the dominant culture. Students from other groups are then viewed as deficient if they display abilities other than those expected for success.	Differentiation emphasizes the dignity and worth of each student. It approaches ability from a growth mindset perspective, proposing that most students can learn most things if they work hard and are supported by teachers and peers in their work and notes the impact of mindset on teacher effectiveness and student outcomes.
Grouping students for instruction	Students are often tracked and labeled based on perceptions of their ability. This transmits negative messages about perceptions of and expectations for students in low tracks.	Differentiation strongly advocates maximum feasible heterogeneity and minimum student labeling. The raison d'etre of the model is to facilitate equity of access to high quality curriculum and instruction in heterogeneous settings.
Nature of the learning environment	In low track classes, the environment is often teacher-focused and controlling, displays few positive student-teacher connections, and isolates students from one another.	Differentiation supports teachers in developing environments in which each student experiences affirmation, affiliation, challenge, and support. Teachers make decisions based on knowledge of and concern for students as individually and as a group.

(Continued)

TABLE 2.1.1 *(Continued)*

Classroom Element	Concerns for Students From Nondominant Groups and Low Status Students	Principles and Practices From Differentiation That Address the Concerns
Quality of curriculum	Within and across classes, curriculum for students from nondominant groups and low status students tends to be low level, low relevance, and less preparatory for future options than for other students.	Two key principles of differentiation are teaching up (planning for advanced learners and differentiating to support access of all students to that level of challenge) and respectful tasks (ensuring that all student work is equally engaging, requires complex thought, and focuses on understanding).
Instructional arrangements	Students from nondominant groups and low status students often move around less in class, participate less, work with a narrow range of peers, and are cast in dependent roles in the classroom.	Instructional environments include movement in the classroom, student decision-making.
Management of the classroom	Management in low track classes is often rigid, authoritarian, and conveys to students a lack of adult trust in their ability to guide their own learning and behave responsibly.	Differentiation advocates classroom management in which teachers guide students to work as a community of learners and in partnership with the teacher to create and implement classroom routines and procedures that support learning success for each member of the community.

Use and Application of the Theory

Differentiation is an instructional model intended for use in a broad range of classroom settings. It is currently used in classrooms from preschool through the university level, including general education, special education, gifted education, English language learning, and teacher education in the United States. However, when used with fidelity to the model, differentiation enables educators to drastically reduce the need for tracked and ability grouped classes by attending to learners' varied needs in heterogeneous settings. That the books on differentiation noted in the previous section are available in 13 languages suggests broad international use of the theories as well. However, it is not possible to determine with precision either the pervasiveness of the model's use or, more saliently, the degree of fidelity of its implementation.

Use of the principles of differentiation (generically, vs. a particular model of differentiation) is advocated by the National Association for the Education of Young Children, *Turning*

Points 2000 (a Carnegie Foundation document focusing on effective teaching in the middle grades), *This We Believe: Successful Schools for Young Adolescents*, a 2003 position paper of the National Middle School Association; *Breaking Ranks II* (a high school reform agenda produced by the National Association of Secondary School Principals in 2004); the core standards of the National Board for Professional Teaching Standards; and a 1997 document prepared by the American Psychological Association called *Learner-Centered Psychological Principles: A Framework For School Reform And Re-design*.

Critiques of the Theory

One criticism of the theory is that this model of differentiation is complex—in other words, that it asks teachers to attend to a variety of elements simultaneously. In fact, the model discussed here *is* a multifaceted model intended to help teachers grow in understanding of the interconnectedness of classroom environment, curriculum, assessment, instruction, and classroom management.

For many teachers, learning to differentiate instruction requires second order or pervasive change rather than first order or incremental change. Making such change requires time, intelligent support, leaders that understands the both the change initiative and the change process, leaders who are effective in guiding teachers to understand the importance of the change, and diligent use of formative assessment to inform the change process. *The Differentiated School: Making Revolutionary Changes in Teaching and Learning* documents the work of two schools in which leaders exemplified those attributes (Tomlinson, Brimijoin, & Narvaez, 2008). Failure to understand the complexity of second order change and failure of leaders to provide the degree of support necessary enact second order change often results in the downfall of the change (Marzano, Waters, & McNulty, 2005). The following study demonstrates negative impacts and outcomes of an ill-informed and ill-supported attempt to implement differentiation in a large school district.

- Valli, L. and Buese, D. (2007). *The Changing Roles Of Teachers in an Era of High-stakes Accountability.*

This multiyear, mixed-method study of fourth and fifth grade reading and math teachers from a large urban school district found that the teachers' use of a differentiated instruction was overwhelming within the climate of pressure on teachers to ensure that students met AYP (adequately yearly progress) on mandated standardized tests while they were simultaneously asked to implement newly mandated reading and math curricula as well as differentiated instruction. The authors noted that learning to differentiate instruction while also adhering to what was teachers perceived to be district mandates for strict adherence to new curriculum caused the sample of teachers to use less cognitively complex instruction and to maintain or increase assignments that placed little cognitive demand on students. In addition, teachers' relationships with students were negatively impacted by the press to prepare the students for the end of grade test, resulting in tension for many teachers between caring for students and focusing on mandates. A result was debilitating stress for teachers, causing them to feel that they had too many expectations to address in too short a period of time. The authors concluded that there were so many changes thrust upon teachers in a brief time without ample support to achieve them that it was difficult for teachers to feel any ownership in the initiatives they were expected to accept. Additionally, teachers did not have ample time and support to achieve a level of skill with the initiatives to make implementation feasible.

In recent years, some experts in psychology, neuroscience, and sociology have been critical of both the concept and use of "learning styles" in classrooms, one element in the model of differentiation. While few, if any, experts assert that all students learn in the same ways, they are sharply critical of several aspects of teacher use of learning styles. Chief among criticisms are that: (1) the concept of learning style is poorly defined—with over 70 major learning styles models that frequently conflict in terms of the meaning of the concept, (2) most instruments used to determine students' learning styles lack reliability and validity, (3) much research that has been done on application learning styles in the classroom is weak and therefore fails to provide robust evidence of its effectiveness in supporting student learning, (4) suggesting that a student only learns in a specific way is unwarranted, and (5) labeling students by learning style is potentially limiting to individual students and may result in stereotyping of groups of students (Coffield, Moseley, Hall, & Ecclestone, 2004; Pashler, McDaniel, Rohrer, & Bjork, 2008).

Some key researchers and authors on this topic note that: (1) there is widespread face validity to the idea of learning preferences, (2) not all research supporting the concept has been found lacking, (3) there is a need for additional research to be conducted with sound methodology to explore the topic further, (5) there is some evidence to support a visual-auditory-kinesthetic model of learning, and (6) it is likely that it is beneficial for students to experience multimodal learning in order to improve retention of content and storage in long-term memory (Lisle, 2006; Pashler, McDaniel, Rohrer, & Bjork, 2008; Willis, 2006, 2007).

Based on current knowledge, it would appear that judicious application of "learning styles" in the classroom would exclude use of surveys to determine a student's learning style, categorizing students by learning style, and assignment of students to tasks based on their perceived learning style. Appropriate attention to students' varied approaches to learning would likely include teachers presenting information in a variety of ways, offering students options for taking in, exploring, and demonstrating key content, planning for multi-modal student learning, and helping students become more self-aware in determining which approaches to learning work for them in specific contexts and understanding how to adjust their approach to learning when the approach does not seem to be facilitating their learning.

Studies Using the Theory as a Framework

Among studies using the model of differentiation discussed in this chapter as a theoretical framework are the following dissertations and a provincial-level study from Canada.

- Doubet, K. (2007). *Teacher Fidelity and Student Response to a Model of Differentiation as implemented in One High School.*

(This qualitative study investigated how faculty in one high school implemented differentiated instruction as a result of a school wide detracking and differentiation initiative, as well as examining the degree of fidelity with which teachers used the model. The study also examined how students in the high school responded to differentiated instruction as enacted by their teachers. Qualitative research methods of observation, interview, and document analysis were used to investigate (1) how teachers of various grades and subjects ($n = 29$) thought about and implemented differentiation; (2) how teachers ($n = 29$) and administrators ($n = 7$) perceived that students responded to differentiation; and (3) how high school students of all grade levels ($n = 80$) thought about and responded to differentiated instruction. Study findings included evidence of the interdependence of the elements in the model of differentiation and emphasized the importance of effective use of all the model's elements for maximum benefit. Formative assessment emerged as centrally important in the model, driving all other elements.

- Hockett, J. (2010). *The Influence of Lesson Study on How Teachers Plan for, Implement, and Understand Differentiated Instruction.*

A qualitative study using grounded theory methodology, this dissertation examined the influence of Lesson Study on one group of fourth grade math teachers understanding of, planning for, and implementation of differentiation in four elementary classrooms. Findings indicated that Lesson Study enhanced the flexibility of teachers' planning and instructional frameworks, use of new instructional strategies, and proactive management of differentiation in their classrooms. The teachers' conceptions of differentiation also grew more sophisticated over the course of the Lesson Study cycle. Among factors that appeared to influence teacher growth were the lesson study team's willingness to engage in conflict throughout the process, the nature of the interaction of the Lesson Study team's cofacilitators with the group, and pre- and post-Lesson Study cycle observations and interviews.)

- Maeng, J. (2011). *Differentiating Science Instruction: Success Stories of High School Science Teachers.*

Using intensive observation and teacher interviews, this qualitative case study researched the experiences of seven high school science teachers who sought to differentiate instruction in their classrooms. Each classroom observation was scored using a validated differentiated instruction implementation matrix-modified [DIIM-M]. One teacher was selected for more in-depth study based on the results from the DIIM-M. Results indicated that all teachers could use some low-prep differentiation learning profile strategies with the in-depth case study participant using more complex strategies for learning profile and fewer strategies for student readiness and interest.

- Quarrie, L. M., and McRae, P. (2010). *A Provincial Perspective on Differentiated Instruction: The Alberta Initiative for School Improvement (AISI).*

This article reviews site-based research project reports determined by Alberta Education's School Improvement Branch (SIB) to have had "significant impacts on student learning" (p. 4) based on calculated effect sizes. This article was based on data obtained from 25 schools and/or districts in Alberta, Canada that demonstrated positive impact on student learning and sought to address challenges posed by increasing learner diversity in the classroom utilizing DI practices. The schools had worked for a 3-year period with over 70,000 students representing various school settings and all school divisions in the province. Over 60% of the projects involved implementation of differentiated instruction in inclusive classrooms, while the remaining projects focused on differentiation for specific groups of learners (e.g., special education students, English language learners, etc.). The two major findings from this review are that (1) effective pedagogies and learning supports and (2) effective project supports accounted for the positive results. Using assessment data to monitor student progress, determine student interests and learning preferences, and to have students self-evaluate the degree to which personal learning goals had been reached was noted at a factor in positive outcomes. Use of technology to aid in the instruction and monitoring of student learning and small group instruction targeted to learners who were more at risk were additional examples of effective pedagogies. Support from district leaders (both formal and informal) was noted as an important component in both beginning and continuing the differentiation initiative.

- Rasmussen, F. (2006). *Differentiated instruction as a means for improving achievement as measured by the American College Testing (ACT).*

A dissertation submitted to the School of Education, Loyola University of Chicago, Chicago, IL. (This quantitative study examined the frequency of use of differentiation by teachers in a Chicago high school and the ACT achievement scores of 226 high school students in the classes of those teachers. Students receiving more instruction from a differentiated instructional methodology outperformed students receiving less instruction from a differentiated methodology on ACT English, ACT Mathematics, ACT Reading, and ACT Composite by as much as .48 sigma.)

Instruments Associated With the Theory

Following are two instruments useful in understanding effective differentiated instruction. The first is a tool designed to help school leaders and instructional coaches sharpen their own understanding of differentiation as well as for use in guiding teachers to set goals for their own growth in addressing varied student needs in academically diverse classrooms. The second is an observation matrix created to assist with systematic classroom observation for a research study on teacher use of differentiation in secondary science classrooms (Maeng, 2011).

References

American Psychological Association. (1997). *Learner-centered psychological principles: A framework for school reform and redesign.* Washington, DC: The Learner-Centered Principles Workgroup of the American Psychological Association. Retrieved from http://www.apa.org/ed/governance/bea/learner-centered.pdf

>   This document provides 14 principles designed to guide educators in developing student-centered learning contexts that take into account the diversity of students in classrooms and in ways that promote learning. Among descriptors of the principles are: assisting students in becoming self-directed, developing learning goals that are engaging and motivating to learners, guiding students to construct their own understanding, creating a nurturing environment, and use of instructional approaches that account for students varied abilities and entry points. These descriptors align directly with the principles of differentiation.

Coffield, F., Moseley, D., Hall, E., & Ecclestone, K. (2004). *Should we be using learning styles; What research has to say to practice.* London: The Learning and Skills Research Centre.

>   These authors reviewed literature on learning styles to determine what was credible regarding use in classrooms. After closer examination of 13 models, the authors concluded that research on these models failed to support their use to benefit student achievement. They caution that too much is still unknown about learning styles to support use in classrooms.

Cohen, E., & Lotan, R. (2004). Equity in heterogeneous classes. In J. Banks & C. Banks (Eds.), *Handbook of research on multicultural education* (2nd ed., pp. 736–752). San Francisco, CA: Jossey-Bass.

The authors detail several factors that work together to assist all learners in heterogeneous classrooms in becoming academically successful, while also attending to needs of low status students. Research on cooperative learning tasks often carried out in small intercultural groups was found to have a positive impact on student learning and to produce "equal-status interactions" among group members.

Doubet, K. (2007). *Teacher fidelity and student response to a model of differentiation as implemented in one high school* (Unpublished doctoral dissertation). University of Virginia, Charlottesville, VA.

See text in this chapter for annotation.

Dweck, C. (2000). *Self-theories: Their role in motivation, personality, and development.* Philadelphia, PA: Psychology Press.

Dweck describes the difference between fixed and growth mindset approaches to achievement and success. She emphasizes that extraordinary accomplishments come from individuals dedicated to working hard to develop their abilities rather than relying on "being smart."

Hockett, J. (2010). *The influence of lesson study on how teachers plan for, implement, and understand differentiated instruction* (Unpublished doctoral dissertation). University of Virginia, Charlottesville, VA

See text in this chapter for annotation.

Jackson, A., & Davis, G. (2000). *Turning Points 2000: Educating adolescents in the 21st century, A report of the Carnegie Corporation.* New York, NY: Teachers College Press.

This report is a follow-up to *Turning Points: Preparing American youth for the 21st Century* which made broad recommendations for reforming education for young adolescents. Turning Points 2000 seeks to document what works to benefit learning for young adolescents and to present both guidance and a vision for high-achieving schools that are equitable and developmentally appropriate.

Knapp, M., & Woolverton, S. (2004). Social class and schooling. In J. Banks & C. Banks (Eds.), *Handbook of research on multicultural education* (2nd ed., pp. 656–681). San Francisco, CA: Jossey-Bass.

The authors argue that the relationship of social class and schooling is complex and far-reaching and continues to impact the expectations and outcomes for many students throughout their school years. The chapter explores the influence of community, student population, teachers, peers, and instruction on the school experience.

Lisle, A. M. (2006). *Cognitive neuroscience in education: Mapping neuro-cognitive processes and structures to learning styles, can it be done?* Retrieved from http://www.leeds.ac.uk/educol/documents/157290.htm

This paper presented to the British Educational Research Association examines feasibility of learning styles theory based on brain activity observed with imaging equipment. Some evidence suggests that using multi-modal instruction and visual-auditory-kinesthetic approaches may benefit learning but the author cautioned educators that limiting students to learning in a "preferred" approach can be detrimental.

Marzano, R., Waters, T., & McNulty, B. (2005). *School leadership that works: From research to results*. Alexandria, VA: ASCD.

The authors share the results of a meta-analysis of 69 studies to determine the correlation of leadership behavior of building principals and overall student achievement in those building and offer practical suggestions regarding 21 leader responsibilities.

Maeng, J. (2011). *Differentiating science instruction: Success stories of high school science teachers* (Unpublished doctoral dissertation). University of Virginia, Charlottesville, VA.

See text in this chapter for annotation.

National Association of Secondary School Principals. (2004). *Breaking ranks II: Strategies for leading high school reform*. Reston, VA: Author.

This reform document advocates seven strategies as key to improving the performance of each student in high school. Among the strategies forging teacher-student connections, personalized planning for students' high school experiences, teaching that responds to student differences, and flexible use of instructional time. These strategies align directly with the core principles of differentiation.

National Board of Professional Teaching Standards. (n.d.). *The five core propositions*. Retrieved from http://www.nbpts.org/the_standards/the_five_core_propositions

The five core standards of NBPTS frame the knowledge, skills, beliefs, and dispositions of excellent teaching. The 5 standards include the belief that every student can succeed, equitable treatment of all students, teaching with individual learning differences in mind, attending to students cultural backgrounds, use of a wide range of instructional strategies, and use of varied formative assessments to guide instructional planning. These elements align directly with the principles of differentiation.

National Middle School Association. (2003). *This we believe: Successful schools for young adolescents*. Westerville, OH: Author.

One of a sequence of position papers published by NMSA, this document briefly describes both school cultures and classrooms that are successful for young adolescents. In the latter category, the paper calls for curriculum that is relevant, integrative challenging and exploratory, multiple approaches to teaching and learning that respond to the diversity of middle grade students, and assessment and evaluation that promote learning. These areas of focus align directly with the core principles of differentiation.

Quarrie, L. M., & McRae, P. (2010). A provincial perspective on differentiated instruction: The Alberta Initiative for School Improvement (AISI). *Journal of Applied Research on Learning*, 3(4), 1–18.

See text in this chapter for annotation.

Pashler, H., McDaniel, M., Rohrer, D., & Bjork R. (2008). Learning styles: Concepts and evidence. *Psychological Science in the Public Interest, 9*(3), 106–119.

> The authors reviewed research on teaching to students' preferred learning styles and found little substantial evidence to support the approach. They note that few studies used sound research methodology and advise that while learning preferences may exist, use of instruments to determine a student's preference followed by teaching to that preference lacks research support.

Rasmussen, F. (2006). *Differentiated instruction as a means for improving achievement as measured by the American College Testing* (Unpublished doctoral dissertation). Loyola University of Chicago, Chicago, IL.

> See text in this chapter for annotation.

Sousa, D., & Tomlinson, C. (2011). *Differentiation and the brain: How neuroscience supports the learner-friendly classroom.* Indianapolis, IN: Solution Tree.

> Sousa and Tomlinson describe links between current brain research and key principles of differentiated instruction. Specifically, it explores neuroscience/differentiation connections related to teacher mindset, curriculum, assessment, instruction and classroom management in addressing the various learning needs of students in typical school settings.

Tomlinson, C. (1995). Deciding to differentiate instruction in middle school: One school's journey. *Gifted Child Quarterly, 39*(2), 77–87.

> This case study documents one school's early implemented a district's mandate for differentiating instruction, detailing factors that enhanced and hindered their progress.

Tomlinson, C. (1995). *How to differentiate instruction in mixed ability classrooms* (1st ed.). Alexandria, VA: ASCD.

> This brief book outlines what differentiated instruction is and is not, and provides a rationale for supporting the learning needs of academically diverse student groups. Practical suggestions are offered for teachers to address student readiness, interest and learning profile through attending to the curricular elements of content, process, and product.

Tomlinson, C. (1999). *The differentiated classroom: Responding to the needs of all learners.* Alexandria, VA: ASCD.

> This volume extends the rationale for differentiation by relating the teaching practice to current views of intelligence, brain research and motivation. Several sample lessons are offered illustrating *what* was differentiated, *how* it was differentiated and *why* to assist teachers who are new to differentiation understand its logic.

Tomlinson, C. (2003). *Fulfilling the promise of the differentiated classroom.* Alexandria, VA: ASCD.

> Tomlinson presents differentiation as a system of interdependent parts or "cogs" that work together to support success for a range of learners. The three "cogs" are student needs, teacher response to those needs, and curriculum as a vehicle to assist teachers in addressing student needs. The text also contains a teacher toolkit containing several examples of differentiated lessons.

Tomlinson, C., & Allan, S. (2000). *Leadership for differentiating schools and classrooms*. Alexandria, VA: ASCD.

    This text provides guideline for school leaders working for successful implementation of differentiation within a school or district. The authors caution that leaders need to understand the complexity of change in schools as they plan for differentiation. The book also presents several areas in which teachers often need support along with several implementation tools to guide school leaders in their work with differentiation.

Tomlinson, C., Brimijoin, K., & Narvaez, L. (2008). *The differentiated school: Making revolutionary changes in teaching and learning*. Alexandria, VA: ASCD.

    The authors detail the work of an elementary school and a high school moving to school wide differentiation, discussing the obstacles and successes they encountered. The book discusses the attributes of leaders who guided the successful work in the two schools.

Tomlinson, C., & Eidson, C. (Eds.). (2003). *Differentiation in practice: A resource guide for differentiating curriculum, K–5*. Alexandria, VA: ASCD.

    This edited volume contains 6 differentiated units of study including a language arts unit concerning the alphabet for young learners and the core content areas. A two column format allows the reader to see both the details of the lessons and the teachers' thinking in designing and implementing the units.

Tomlinson, C., & Eidson, C. (Eds.). (2003). *Differentiation in practice: A resource guide for differentiating curriculum, 5–9*. Alexandria, VA: ASCD.

    This edited volume contains 6 differentiated units of study in math, science, social studies, math, and language. A two column format allows the reader to see both the details of the lessons and the teachers' thinking in designing and implementing the units.

Tomlinson, C., & Imbeau, M. B. (2010). *Leading and managing a differentiated classroom*. Alexandria, VA: ASCD.

    The authors propose that leading and managing effectively differentiated classrooms first requires teachers to examine their beliefs about human learning and their impact on that learning. Part I of the book deals with elements necessary to lead a differentiated classroom. Part II discusses how to manage details such as assigning students to groups, handling noise, and designing thoughtful anchoring activities. A toolkit provides classroom examples.

Tomlinson, C., & McTighe, J. (2006). *Integrating differentiated instruction and understanding by design: Connecting content and kids*. Alexandria, VA: ASCD.

    Tomlinson and McTighe describe intersections between understanding by design, a curriculum model, and differentiated instruction, an instructional model. The authors discuss how to addressing diverse learner needs while teaching essential content for understanding.

Tomlinson, C., & Strickland, C. (Ed.). (2005). *Differentiation in practice: A resource guide for differentiating curriculum, 9–12*. Alexandria, VA: ASCD.

This edited volume contains nine differentiated units of study from math, history, literature, earth science, art and world languages for use with high school students, focusing on key principles of the disciplines. It also highlights teachers' thinking about unit design and differentiation.

Valli, L., & Buese, D. (2007). The changing roles of teachers in an era of high-stakes accountability. *American Educational Research Journal*, 44(3), 519–558.

See text of this chapter for annotation.

Willis, J. (2006). *Research-based strategies to ignite student learning: Insights from a neurologist and class-room teacher*. Alexandria, VA: ASCD.

Based on background as a neurologist and classroom teacher, Willis offers educators practical instructional strategies that support student learning and shares, in lay terms, brain function behind the suggestions.

Willis, J. (2007). *Brain-friendly strategies for the inclusion classroom*. Alexandria, VA: ASCD.

Willis offers educators several teaching strategies backed by brain-research to promote academic success for students with learning challenges. She provides specific recommendations for addressing students' diverse learning styles, teaching for meaning and understanding, using various grouping arrangements, and creating learning environments conducive to student achievement.

Look-Fors in an Effectively Differentiated Classroom
Developed by Carol Ann Tomlinson & Jessica Hockett

Background

This tool is designed to help school coaches and leaders better understand how differentiation might look when it is effectively implemented in classrooms. It is also designed to help teachers reflect on their own practice and set goals for continuing growth as they work to meet the needs of varied learners in their classrooms.

No teacher should be expected to display all of these attributes at a given time. Rather these are elements toward which strong teachers persistently work and many of which strong teachers regularly demonstrate in their teaching. Guiding questions in this document are useful in conversations with teachers as catalysts for their thinking about their work with differentiation.

Differentiated instruction is a proactively planned, **interdependent system** marked by a positive community of learners; focused, high-quality curriculum; frequent formative assessment; flexible instructional arrangements; and respectful tasks.

- Student needs are the motivation for differentiated instruction.

- Building a sense community among students and the teacher in a positive learning environment is the foundation for differentiated instruction.

- Focused, high-quality provides the compass for differentiated instruction. (High-quality differentiation is necessary for high-quality differentiation.)

- Frequent formative assessment is the primary tool for gathering information about how and why to differentiate instruction.

- Well-managed, flexible grouping provides a mechanism for differentiated instruction.

- A variety of low-prep and high-prep strategies can be used to design and deliver respectful tasks that adjust content, process, and products for students' readiness, interests, and learning profiles.

Categories, Look-Fors, Rubrics, and Guiding Questions
Look for 1: Classroom Environment
Category: The Teacher Builds a Foundation for Differentiated Instructed on a Solid Classroom Community and a Positive Learning Environment.

Indicators:

- The physical and affective characteristics of the classroom set a positive tone for learning.

- The teacher fosters respect for individual differences and preferences.
- The teacher and students share ownership of and responsibility for the classroom.

Evidence:

- The teacher communicates explicitly and implicitly to students that they are multi-faceted individuals whose needs, preferences, and strengths are dynamic.
- The teacher communicates implicitly and explicitly to students that they and their contributions are valuable and necessary in order for the classroom to function well.
- The teacher helps students get to know one another well.
- The teacher encourages creativity of thought and expression.
- The teacher structures activities so that students see one another in varied contexts and in varied roles.
- The teacher assists students in setting their own personal and class goals for learning and behavior.
- The teacher solicits student input in making decisions that will affect the whole class.
- The teacher frequently asks students for feedback on how the class is working for them, and for suggestions about how they and the teacher could work together toward improvement.
- The teacher designs and assigns roles for students to assume in making the routines and systems flow smoothly.

RUBRIC:

Classroom Environment	
Advanced 4	a. The affective and physical attributes of the classroom environment inspire students to achieve their personal best and to take initiative in learning. b. The teacher empowers students to view their and each other's differences as assets to the classroom community such that students view one another as equals. c. The teacher and students are equal partners in sharing responsibility for the classroom.
Proficient 3	a. The affective and physical attributes of the classroom environment equip students to succeed in achieving the teacher's high expectations. b. The teacher honors student differences, nurtures student strengths and preferences, and provides opportunities for students to compensate for their weaknesses. c. The teacher shares his/her roles and responsibilities with students, allowing them to control many aspects of classroom routines.

Classroom Environment

Basic 2	a. The affective and physical attributes of the classroom environment convey ambiguous messages about how the teacher views the student's role in the learning process. b. The teacher recognizes student differences, but does not build on them to foster a positive classroom environment. c. The teacher allows students to share some of his/her roles and responsibilities.

Classroom Community—Questions for Reflection

Advanced 4	Compare the way your current classroom looks and feels with how it looked and felt in your first year of teaching. How do you encourage students to apply and transfer what they learn in your classroom about student differences to the real world? What would it look like to allow students to have even more control over the classroom?
Proficient 3	How do student differences impact your decisions about the physical aspects of your classroom (e.g., how the room is set-up, the messages students see on the walls)? How do you capitalize on the strengths and maturity level of this age group to help daily routines run more smoothly?
Basic 2	How do you help students see one another as equally valuable to the classroom community? In what ways do you communicate to students that this is their classroom? How do you decide which classroom roles responsibilities to give to students, and which to keep in your control?
Below Basic 1	What are some ways that students in your class differ from one another, and from you? What are some concrete ways you communicate to them that those differences are assets to the classroom community? What are the most flexible aspects of your physical classroom space?

Look For 2: Curriculum

Category: The Teacher Uses High-Quality, Coherent Curriculum as a Compass for Differentiated Instruction.

Indicators:

- The teacher plans curriculum so that important conceptual ideas are at the forefront of a unit of study. Essential facts and skills are used to help students make sense of these ideas.

- The teacher uses the curriculum as a point of engagement, of motivation, and of access to powerful ideas.

- The teacher ensures that the curriculum is an authentic reflection of the discipline being studied.

Evidence:

- Tasks give all students access to the same clear, high-quality lesson/unit goals.

- Tasks require students to mimic or approximate the skills, thinking, habits, dispositions, or work of real-world professionals (e.g., mathematicians, biologists, writers).

- Tasks require all students to use higher-level thinking skills (e.g., analyzing, judging, defending).

- Tasks are equally appealing and engaging from the students' perspective.

- The teacher scaffolds tasks using a variety of techniques.

RUBRIC:

Respectful Tasks
Advanced 4   a. The teacher plans tasks that are focused on the same learning goals and mimic the work of an expert/professional in the discipline.   b. The teacher articulates a continuum of criteria based on student readiness and provides multiple scaffolds to ensure successful, high-quality completion of the tasks by the full range of students.   c. Side-by-side, the tasks are equally challenging and intriguing.
Proficient 3   a. The teacher plans tasks that are focused on similar learning goals and suggest the work of an expert/professional in the discipline.   b. The teacher articulates clear criteria and provides scaffolding to ensure successful, high-quality completion of the tasks.   c. Side-by-side, the tasks are comparatively challenging and intriguing.
Basic 2   a. The teacher plans tasks that are not aligned to the same learning goals and are loosely tied to the work of an expert/professional in the discipline.   b. The teacher's criteria for successful completion are confusing or incomplete. The teacher provides some scaffolding, if students compel a need for it.   c. Side-by-side, one task may be more/less challenging and intriguing than another.
Below Basic 1   a. The teacher plans tasks without considering what all students should know, understand, and be able to do, or how an expert/professional in the discipline works. Tasks may be tangential to unit content.   b. The teacher does not articulate criteria for quality or provide scaffolding for success.   c. Tasks bore or frustrate students.

Advanced 4	What steps do you take in planning differentiated tasks to make sure each student is optimally challenged? How do you involve students in the process of determining task criteria? How do you decide what supports students might need?
Proficient 3	What are the similarities between what the students are doing and what practicing professionals in the discipline (e.g., writers) do? If you have two or more versions of a task, which version do you design first? Why? How do you adjust the tasks for readiness, interest, or learning profile?
Basic 2	Describe your process for planning a task or lesson that is differentiated for student readiness. How do ensure all students produce work that is high-quality and meets your expectations? When you give a choice between differentiated tasks, how do you prevent your students from choosing an "easy" option?
Below Basic 1	What do you want all students to know, understand, and be able to do upon completing these tasks? How do you decide what makes a worthwhile task? How might students' differences in readiness, interest, and learning profile affect their capacity to complete a task successfully?

Differentiated Instruction Implementation Matrix-Modified

Developed by and Used with Permission of Jennifer Maeng (2011)

Criteria	Novice (1)	Apprentice (2)	Practitioner (3)	Expert (4)
1. Quality and clarity of the lesson objectives: What students should know, understand, and be able to do.	Objectives are not clearly articulated for the lesson.	Lesson objectives might be informed by national or state standards, but do not include big ideas meaningful to the content area.	Lesson objectives include big ideas, issues, or problems specific and meaningful to the content area. Objectives are informed by national or state standards.	Lesson objectives are informed by national or state standards and the important ideas, issues, or problems specific and meaningful to the content area. Objectives extend learning in authentic ways.

(Continued)

Criteria	Novice (1)	Apprentice (2)	Practitioner (3)	Expert (4)
2. Alignment of lesson objectives and lesson activities	The activities are mildly related to the objectives, It is not likely that students will master the objectives.	The activities of the lesson are unevenly related to the objectives. It is likely that only some students will master the objectives after successful completion of the activities.	The activities of the lesson are clearly related to the objectives. Most students are likely to master the objectives after successful completion of the activities.	The activities of the lesson are clearly and strongly related to the objectives. All students will master the objectives after successful completion of the activities.
3. Communication of learning goals and outcomes to students	Lesson objectives and desired outcomes are not communicated to the students.	Lesson objectives and desired outcomes are listed for students but not referred to during the lesson or connected to lesson components.	Lesson objectives and desired outcomes are clearly articulated to students, but the connection between the objectives, desired outcomes, and the lesson components is not evident to students.	Lesson objectives and desired outcomes are clearly articulated to students, and it is clear to students how the lesson components are related to these goals.

DOMAIN 2: Planning and Response to Learner Needs

Criteria	Novice (1)	Apprentice (2)	Practitioner (3)	Expert (4)
1. Preassessment and Proactive Preparation	The lesson demonstrates very little consideration of student needs.	The lesson demonstrates that the teacher considered various student needs when planning the lesson.	The lesson demonstrates that the teacher used preassessment data in advance of the lesson to plan for the needs of the students.	The lesson demonstrates that the teacher used multiple sources of preassessment data and student learning profiles in advance of the lesson to plan for the needs of the students.

Criteria	Novice (1)	Apprentice (2)	Practitioner (3)	Expert (4)
2. Scaffolding for Struggling Learners; Spec. Ed., ELL, reading, etc.	Struggling learners are given irrelevant tasks of poor quality that do not require higher order thinking. Struggling learners may be grouped together most of the time.	Struggling learners are given tasks of moderate quality or better quality tasks with little or no scaffolding and may not reach the lesson's learning goals, especially the big ideas and understandings of the lesson. Struggling students may be grouped together a lot of the time.	Struggling learners are given tasks of good quality and thoughtfulness with appropriate scaffolding and are expected to approximate the lesson's learning goals. Struggling learners experience may experience variety of grouping strategies.	Struggling learners are given tasks of high-quality and thoughtfulness with appropriate scaffolding to reach the same learning goals as other students. Multiple indicators are used when grouping students so that struggling learners experience a variety of grouping strategies.
3. Challenging Advanced Students	Academically advanced students are assigned more or irrelevant work. They are used to tutor less advanced students.	Advanced students may be challenged with probing questions and challenging tasks, but are sometimes assigned more work. They may be used to tutor less advanced students.	Academically advanced students are appropriately challenged at higher levels of quality, not quantity. Occasionally, they are used to academically anchor a flexible group.	Academically advanced students are appropriately challenged at higher levels of complexity and quality, not quantity. Experiences as an academic anchor in a flexible group enhance their understanding. Options are available for compacting into independent study on the topic.

Criteria	Novice (1)	Apprentice (2)	Practitioner (3)	Expert (4)
1. Lesson Organization	The lesson is unfocused and/or dis-organized. The activities do not follow a logical progression.	The lesson has an identifiable structure, although the logic of that structure may be unclear. Progression of the activities is uneven.	The lesson is organized in a sensible manner, progressing in a fairly even manner.	The lesson is organized in a coherent (organized, unified, and sensible) manner, producing a unified whole.
2. Modes of Instruction	The lesson uses a single mode of instruction that may meet the needs of some students in the class.	The lesson uses multiple modes of instruction on a limited basis, some of which may encourage active learning with the intention of providing variety for the students.	The lesson uses multiple modes of instruction that encourage active learning and match the perceived learning profiles of the students.	The lesson uses multiple modes of instruction that require active learning and the exploration of the lesson's understandings and intentionally matches the learning profiles of the students.
3. Instructional Strategies and Best Practice	The lesson may focus on one or more strategies or activities which are not based on best practices in that content area.	Some of the strategies and activities used in the lesson reflect best practices in that content area.	The strategies and activities are used during instruction to meet the learning needs of the students and to promote higher order thinking. Most strategies and activities reflect best practices in that content area.	The strategies and activities are used flexibly during instruction to meet the learning needs of the students and to promote higher order thinking for all students. The strategies and activities reflect best practices in that content area.

Criteria	Novice (1)	Apprentice (2)	Practitioner (3)	Expert (4)
4. Engagement Capacity of Activities	Lesson components are not engaging and do not connect to the students lives.	Lesson components are somewhat interesting to learners, but do not necessarily connect with students prior learning, experiences, and/or goals.	Lesson components are engaging to learners and may be linked to students prior learning or experience, and may connect with their lives and/or goals. The teacher helps students make connections between lesson content, practical applications, current events, the real world, or other aspects of the content area.	Lesson components are stimulating, motivating, and engaging to learners, linked to students' prior learning or experiences, and clearly connect to their lives and/or goals. Students explicate connections between lesson content, practical applications, current events, the real world, or other aspects of the content area.
5. Intellectual Development[1]	Activities are designed with little regard to student readiness, interest, and/or learning profile. Few students are likely to learn as a result of the activities. The lesson design does not provide work that is challenging for most of the students.	Students with a particular readiness, interest, and/or learning profile will likely learn, but other students will find it difficult or impossible to learn. The lesson design is inconsistent in its ability to challenge students at the highest level of which they are capable.	Students with varied readiness, interest, and/or learning profiles have an opportunity to learn at some point during the lesson. A few students are able to find loopholes in the lesson design which permits them to avoid completing their highest quality work.	Each student works at levels of readiness, interest, and/or learning profile that are appropriately challenging. The lesson is designed so that all students are compelled to do their best and complete high-quality work.

1. Levels of performance are paraphrased from Strickland, C. (2006). *Differentiated lesson observation rubric.* Unpublished manuscript.

Criteria	Novice (1)	Apprentice (2)	Practitioner (3)	Expert (4)
1. Flexible Grouping *Grouping practices may not be observed in every lesson. If it is not observed, it should be rated N/O not novice.	Lesson may use a grouping strategy, but groups are not differentiated in any intentional way. Student groupings, which may have been created using some student data, are not flexible, but remain static over time.	Lesson uses at least one grouping strategy that differentiates content, process, or product by readiness, interest, or learning profile. Flexibility is to accommodate variety in the lesson as opposed to matching student needs to the lesson's learning goals.	Lesson uses at least one grouping strategy that differentiates content, process, or product by readiness, interest, or learning profile. Flexibility in grouping strategies is a planned response to student needs.	Lesson uses various student groupings: individual, pairs, small groups. Students are grouped for a great variety of reasons to differentiate content, process, and/or product by readiness, interest, and/or learning profile. The lesson may combine grouping rationales (i.e. readiness and interest). Flexibility in grouping strategies is in response to a clear analysis of student needs.
2. Flexible Use of Space, Time, and Materials *Student movement should take into consideration the physical space in which the observation is occurring. In some classrooms, it may be unfeasible for great mobility in the classroom due to space constraints. This warrants a N/O, not a "novice" rating.	Students all use the same materials, resources, or technologies as designated by the teacher. Students rarely move out of their seats and where applicable, have no flexibility in product completion.	Students have some access, as permitted by the teacher, to a variety of materials, resources. Teacher has an effective strategy for distribution of materials. Students have limited flexibility to move out of their seats and where applicable, have limited flexibility in timelines for product completion.	Students have access to a variety of materials, resources, and technologies. Students are given some flexibility to move about the room and where applicable, have some flexibility in timelines for product completion.	Students have access to and are encouraged to use a variety of materials, resources, and technologies. Students move about the room as needed and where applicable, are given flexibility in the timeframes for product completion.

Criteria	Novice (1)	Apprentice (2)	Practitioner (3)	Expert (4)
3. Clear Directions for Multiple Tasks[2]	Directions and procedures are confusing to students to the point of challenging classroom management.	Directions and procedures are mildly confusing and require clarification and/or are excessively detailed.	Directions and procedures for each activity are clear to students with appropriate levels of detail. Written directions for various groups are clear.	Directions and procedures for each activity are clear to students. Anticipated student misunderstandings are planned and accounted for. Written directions for various groups are crystal clear to limit confusion.
4. Classroom Leadership and Management[3]	Students who are not directly engaged with the teacher are not productively learning. Much instructional time is lost due to poorly executed transitions and management routines. Student behavior is not monitored and attempts to respond to misbehavior are inconsistent, too severe, and/or do not respect the student's dignity.	Students working in groups are somewhat organized so that some off-task behavior is observed when the teacher is involved with another group. Movement through transitions and management routines is irregular and results in some lost instructional time. Teacher is largely aware of student behavior, but may not notice some misbehavior. Attempts to respond to misbehavior have uneven results.	Students working in groups are organized so that most students are engaged most of the time. Transitions between differentiated and nondifferentiated activities and management routines are smooth with little loss of instructional time. Teacher is aware of student behavior at all times and responds to misbehavior in a way that preserves the student's dignity.	Students working in groups are independently and productively engaged at all times with students taking responsibility for productivity. Transitions between differentiated and nondifferentiated activities and management routines are seamless. Monitoring of behavior is subtle and preventative while interventions are sensitive to student's individual needs.

2. Levels of performance are paraphrased from Danielson, C. (1996). Enhancing professional practice: A framework for teaching. Alexandria, VA: ASCD.

3. Levels of performance are paraphrased from Danielson, C. (1996). Enhancing professional practice: A framework for teaching. Alexandria, VA: ASCD.

Criteria	Novice (1)	Apprentice (2)	Practitioner (3)	Expert (4)
1. Formative Assessment	Teacher does not make use of formative assessment during or at the end of the lesson.	Teacher may use some general informal assessment during the lesson (e.g., class poll) or at the end of the lesson (e.g., quiz, exit card). The data are used to gauge understanding of the lesson objectives and/or to plan for future whole-class instruction.	Teacher uses formative assessments embedded within the body of the lesson to make minor modifications to instruction (e.g. reviewing, clarifying misconceptions, adjusting lesson pacing) and to gauge student understanding. Assessment data are used to plan whole-class instruction.	Teacher regularly uses formative assessments throughout the lesson. Data from these lessons is used to: make modifications to instruction within a lesson, to gauge student understanding, _and_ to plan future instruction for individuals and groups.
2. Existence and Quality of Rubrics and Guidelines[4]	Rubrics and guidelines have not been developed.	Rubrics and guidelines have been developed, but are not clear or are not clearly shared with students.	Rubrics and guidelines of clearly articulated assessment criteria and standards are shared with students.	Rubrics and guidelines of clearly articulated assessment criteria and standards are shared with students. Students have participated in the creation of the rubric and guidelines and are aware of how they are meeting the standards and actively plan next steps for learning.

4. Levels of performance are paraphrased from Danielson, C. (1996). Enhancing professional practice: A framework for teaching. Alexandria, VA: ASCD.

Criteria	Novice (1)	Apprentice (2)	Practitioner (3)	Expert (4)
1. Sense of Community[5]	Environment is physically and emotionally unsafe. Students recognize and comment negatively on differences. Disrespect for one another is apparent. There are no discussions about the rationale for differentiation or related concerns.	Environment is physically safe, but some students occasionally feel as though they do not belong or are not valued. Occasional negative comments about differences are heard, although the teacher attempts to address these issues when they arise and encourage respect for each other.	Environment is physically and emotionally safe. In general, students feel as they belong and are valued. Students recognize and acknowledge similarities and differences and respect one another and the teacher.	Environment is physically and emotionally safe. There are consistent affirmations of belonging, value, and respect for each other and the teacher. Students and teacher recognize, acknowledge, and celebrate similarities and differences.
2. Teacher's Role	The teacher's only role is to deliver content and/or direct student activity. Teacher takes the lead in most classroom activities.	Teacher's role is primarily deliverer of information and/or director of student activity. Teacher invites occasional student input into lesson content and activities.	Teacher plays the role of deliverer of information and/or director of student activity, but also acts as coach or facilitator of learning at some point in the lesson. Students have some input into lesson content and activities.	Teacher's overall role is primarily that of coach or facilitator in learning. Both students and teacher have consistent input into lesson content.

(Continued)

Criteria	Novice (1)	Apprentice (2)	Practitioner (3)	Expert (4)
3. Respectful Behavior Toward Students	Teacher behavior and response to students discourages participation. Students are hesitant to ask questions and are unaware of each other's strengths, successes, and contributions. Teacher does not seek to connect individually with students.	Teacher behavior and response to students does not encourage participation from a broad range of students. Some students seem hesitant to ask questions or request assistance. Teacher does not make an attempt to make students aware of each other's strengths, successes, and contributions. Teacher only connects individually with the more outgoing students. Teacher is somewhat aware of some students' learning profiles and interests.	Teacher behavior and response to students fosters participation from most students. Students are generally comfortable asking questions or requesting assistance. Teacher attempts to make students aware of each other's strengths, successes, and contributions. Teacher seeks to connect with individual students as time permits. Teacher is aware of students learning profiles and interests.	Teacher behavior and response to students fosters active participation from all students. All students are comfortable asking questions or requesting assistance. Awareness of students' strengths, successes, and contributions are cultivated and celebrated. Teacher talks with students as they enter and exit class and seeks to connect with individual students during class. Teacher is highly aware of students' learning profiles and interests.

Criteria	Novice (1)	Apprentice (2)	Practitioner (3)	Expert (4)
4. Facilitation of Learner Independence and Student Choice	The teacher sets goals and assesses student progress toward these goals. Students have no input or choice in lesson components.	The teacher sets goals and assesses student progress toward these goals, but invites limited student input in what the goals are or the progress being made. Students have an opportunity to make a choice at some point in the lesson OR Students make all the choices with no teach input.	Students take on increasing responsibility for their own learning in terms of setting goals for learning and assessing progress toward those goals. There is a balance of student and teacher choice.	Students are consistently involved in setting goals for learning and assessing progress toward those goals, taking on increasing responsibility for their own learning. There is a perfect balance of student and teacher choice.

5. Levels of performance are taken directly from Strickland, C. (2006). *Differentiated lesson observation rubric*. Unpublished manuscript.

6. Levels of performance are taken directly from Strickland, C. (2006). *Differentiated lesson observation rubric*. Unpublished manuscript.

Criteria	Novice (1)	Apprentice (2)	Practitioner (3)	Expert (4)
1. Content "The input of teaching and learning," adapting *what* is taught and modifying *how students are given access* to the information and understandings. (Tomlinson, 2001, p. 72)	Lesson is mostly about learning discrete facts and does little to address concept-based instruction. All students are working with the same materials.	Lesson is designed to be roughly a 50/50 split between concept-based instruction and learning discrete facts. There may be two options for material use that vary in readability, complexity, and/or interest. Lesson may include one of the strategies listed in the Expert column.	Lesson is concept-based, but may contain some learning of discrete facts. There are several options for material use that vary in readability, complexity, and/or interest. Lesson includes at least one or more of the strategies listed in the Expert column.	Lesson is highly concept-based and makes use of diverse materials at various levels of readability, complexity, and/or interest. Lesson includes, but is not limited to, one or more of the following strategies: multiple ways to access and organize information, learning contracts, curriculum compacting, flex-group minilessons, and varied support systems such as audio/video recorders, note-taking organizers, highlighted print materials, digests of key ideas, peer/adult mentors.

7. Descriptors and strategies are taken from Tomlinson, C.A. How to differentiate instruction in mixed-ability classrooms. Alexandria, VA: ASCD.

Reading 2.2

Role-Playing in an Inclusive Classroom
Using Realistic Simulation to Explore Differentiated Instruction

Peter Clyde Martin

Ithaca College

Introduction

Students are sitting in pairs at their desks, practicing multiplication and division, taking turns asking each other questions. The teacher is circulating among the pairs, monitoring and redirecting students, as well as clarifying and reteaching the material. Meanwhile, Lucas is sitting by himself in one corner, quietly playing with his watch. In another corner, Monica also is sitting alone, rocking back and forth in her chair while humming to herself. Both children are left unattended. I am later told that Lucas, in keeping with goals outlined in his IEP, had been expected to be tracing numbers with a paraprofessional, who happened not to be in the room at that moment. Monica was to sit by herself, as she has difficulty working with others, and practice the math operations. It is clear, however, that neither child is being taught.

One of the major hurdles in preparing preservice teachers to differentiate instruction has been that they tend not to see much differentiated instruction in actual classrooms (Benjamin, 2002; Tomlinson, 1999). There always may be a contradiction in wanting to promote change in instructional practices while, at the same time, relying on a teacher education concept that is based on modeling by established teachers. The problem is especially obvious in the area of differentiated instruction because the practice is embedded in the contextual factors and dynamics of a classroom (Lawrence-Brown, 2004). As teacher educators, we rely on students to learn how to differentiate instruction through observation, mentoring, trial-and-error, and even differentiation that is inconsistently practiced in the schools where we place them (McBride, 2004). It is an important contradiction to resolve, as there is ample evidence to suggest that differentiating instruction allows us to better address the needs of our students, especially in the context of universal standards (Anderson, 2007; McTighe & Brown, 2005; Subban, 2006).

I have repeatedly encountered the issue of inadequate modeling in local schools while teaching courses on working with exceptional children in master's programs in elementary and secondary education. Because our students spend much of their week in public school classrooms while they take their graduate classes, it is especially important for us to connect our readings and discussions to practice by pointing to actual in-school models of the approaches that we study. At the same time, when asked to describe how her mentor teacher used differentiated instruction to meet the needs of her class, one student wrote:

> We are told to differentiate so all students can learn, but my mentor teacher doesn't differentiate. In fact, none of the teachers differentiate. They just hope the special ed kids will keep quiet. Eventually the special ed teacher will come and teach them something. Or so they hope.

Another student summed up the lesson that she took away from her placement by stating, "Mostly, differentiating means ignoring."

Given the demographic trends in our public schools, our increasingly explicit focus on addressing student diversity, the strict legal mandates to properly serve students considered to have special needs, the ongoing drive toward inclusion, and efforts to hold teachers responsible for the test scores of individual children, the lesson, "mostly, differentiating means ignoring," is troubling and runs counter to everything that we want our future teachers to learn. While, as teacher educators, we may speak to our students about the need to differentiate, this is not followed up in actual instruction, which is not differentiated in the ways that we propose. Thus, the concern is what we can do to ensure a focus on differentiated instruction in practice without relying entirely on actual classroom settings.

Literature Review

Differentiation has been presented in the literature as a promising way to target various facets of students' school-based learning. A number of authors have emphasized how important it is for teachers to find ways to take advantage of each student's ability to learn as a means to facilitate their academic achievement (Anderson, 2007; Manning, Stanford, & Reeves, 2010; McTighe & Brown, 2005; Santamaria & Thousand, 2004; Subban, 2006; Tomlinson, 1999). In addition, there is evidence that differentiated instruction also can be an effective tool for teachers and school programs to address students' social-emotional learning because such instruction considers the personal situation of each individual child (Bondy, Ross, Gallingane, & Hambacher, 2007).

In keeping with the student-specific nature of the differentiation process, differentiated instruction is described in the literature not as a strategy or a formula but, rather, as a general way of approaching teaching and learning that can suggest possible methods and strategies. In a review of the research, Subban (2006) identified pressing reasons for seeking to differentiate instruction, including the need to address learning differences and the pitfalls of trying to "teach to the middle." Similarly, Anderson (2007) explained that differentiating instruction entails the recognition that every child is unique, with his or her own learning style and preferences.

For Cohen (2008), it is the very goals of education that should be reconsidered, so that we prioritize not only academic but also social, emotional, and ethical skill development. Neglecting these is, according to Cohen, a form of social injustice whereby the basic rights of the child are denied. In this regard, instruction that systematically embeds social-emotional learning into content area teaching can connect academic skills with abilities needed for success in other aspects of life (Rimm-Kaufman, Storm, Sawyer, Pianta, & LaParo, 2006). A focus on social-emotional learning helps the child to learn to regulate his or her own emotions enough to successfully establish and participate in a community (Payton et al., 2008).

There is evidence that programs in which teachers systematically differentiate social-emotional instruction have a positive effect both academically and socially (Bondy, Ross, Gallingane, & Hambacher, 2007; Payton et al., 2008). Teachers can have a significant impact on students' well-being by establishing an environment in which prosocial behaviors are consistently modeled by both peers and adults and the situation of each child is emphasized (Kidron & Fleischman, 2006).

Further, there is evidence that differentiated instruction is needed to enable all students to meet the standards around which we currently build instruction (McTighe & Brown, 2005). While classrooms have always brought together students with a range of academic levels, traditionally, not everyone's learning received the same attention or was held to the same standards (Ankrum & Bean, 2008; Patterson, Connolly, & Ritter, 2009). McTighe and Brown found, in fact, that differentiation and standards-based instruction are, in many ways, interdependent. If all students, with their differences in academic proficiency and learning styles, are to reach the same content standards, then the teacher must use different approaches for different students. At the same time, the process of differentiating for students' needs requires the guidance of a common set of standards.

The conceptualization and implementation of differentiated instruction is highly complex. Tobin (2008) presents a number of conundrums related to instructional rigor that might make it difficult for teachers to differentiate their instruction. The foundational conundrums that Tobin describes revolve around issues of rigor versus flexibility in academic content, instructional design, and assessment. They focus on providing a robust literacy program versus an activities-based program or groupings versus whole-class instruction as well as types of feedback. According to Tobin, however, these conundrums are based on false dichotomies, as providing flexibility in how academic content is planned, taught, and assessed based on the situation of individual learners helps to ensure that every student can be held to rigorous standards. To this end, a number of authors emphasize the need for individual learning plans and assessments to ensure that all students' learning is addressed through rigorous instruction (McTighe & Brown, 2005; Rock, Gregg, Ellis, & Gable, 2008; Scigliano & Hipsky, 2010).

There is little consensus on how to differentiate instruction, in general, largely because differentiation relies on an analysis of individual learners that cannot be performed outside of the specific context (Scigliano & Hipsky, 2010; Tobin & McInnes, 2008). Grouping students to work collaboratively is recommended, although how these groupings should be structured depends on the particularities of the learners and the activities (Ankrum & Bea, 2008; Patterson, et al., 2009). Additionally, scaffolds and tiered instruction, important pieces of differentiated instruction, can be designed only in context (Lawrence-Brown, 2004; Rock et al., 2008; Scigliano & Hipsky, 2010). In the literature, differentiated instruction is seen as necessary, complex, and impossible to design outside of a classroom and a group of students.

The complexities surrounding differentiation have contributed to, and have been compounded by, the inadequacy with which differentiated instruction has generally been addressed in teacher education. According to Tomlinson (1999), teacher education programs typically have not emphasized differentiated instruction in their coursework, and classes on teaching exceptional children have focused more on the characteristics of the students than on approaches to teaching them. In one survey study, preservice teachers reported that teacher educators and mentor teachers discouraged them from differentiating instruction, supposedly because doing so was too difficult (Tomlinson, 1999). Sands and Barker (2004), however, believe that both the importance and complexity of differentiated instruction should make it an area of focus in the education of preservice teachers.

Sands and Barker (2004) recommended that modeling differentiated instruction be a central task for faculty in teacher education programs. However, few professors in these programs actually differentiate, leaving them unable to provide preservice teachers with experience with differentiation before they begin their classroom practice (Gould, 2004). As a result, few novice teachers possess an understanding of what differentiated instruction actually looks like (Tomlinson, 1999).

Tomlinson (1999) believes that teacher education programs should arrange early field experiences in which preservice teachers are partnered with mentors who effectively practice differentiated instruction (Tomlinson, 1999). Such field placements also would have the benefit of exposing prospective teachers to student differences (Gould, 2004). According to Tomlinson, the few novice teachers who had been exposed to differentiated instruction during their student teaching were more likely to differentiate in their own classrooms. As such, exposure to differentiated instruction should be a central task for teacher education programs.

Context

The interventions described below have been implemented in the context of our two intensive one-year master's programs that lead to teacher certification in elementary and secondary education. For the most part, our programs serve a fairly homogeneous population in terms of age, race, and ethnicity. In the most recent cohorts, over 87% of students were White and over 75% were under 25 years old. Both cohorts of students begin their coursework at the beginning of one summer and finish in the summer of the following year. They take additional teacher certification classes, including a course on working with exceptional children, during the fall semester and student teach in two separate public school placements throughout the spring. Students also spend part of each week during the fall semester, prior to student teaching, observing, assisting, working with small groups, and engaging in a limited amount of classroom teaching in local public school classrooms. Due to the practical focus of the program, efforts are made to connect course and field work as much as possible.

The courses on working with exceptional children address notions of difference, exceptionality, and disability as well as the special education system and differentiated instruction. The program assumes that our students will eventually be working as general education teachers in inclusion settings and will therefore be expected to address the IEP goals of students with disabilities. Differentiated teaching is presented in the latter part of the course, during the final classes before student teaching, as a strategy that is needed when working with special education students and a best practice for all students. Preservice teachers are instructed in a variety of differentiation strategies.

It is believed that, by the end of the program, the combination of graduate school instruction, school observations, forays into working with children, and modeling or mentoring by veteran teachers will have provided preservice teachers with the conceptual understanding and tools to begin teaching. It is in their classroom teaching, however, where the lack of consistent models of effective differentiated instruction in public school classrooms leaves a gap.

Intervention: Objective and Description

To address differentiated instruction within the contextual reality of a classroom in a graduate school seminar, rather than in the actual public school itself, students are presented with an elaborate simulation exercise on differentiated planning and instruction. The activity has five explicit student goals:

1. To design a lesson in which the learning process, outcomes, and factors of each child are the focus;
2. To practice implementing such a lesson;
3. To experience, in a "safe"—simulated—context, teaching as a series of adjustments to often unexpected individual student behavior;
4. To undergo how individual students might experience a lesson; and
5. To reflect on and make sense of teaching and learning as differentiated processes.

To achieve these goals, each cohort is given a list of fictitious students, with basic individual characteristics, whom they are to view as a class in the grade and subject of their choice. They are also asked to identify a concept or skill area that is appropriate for this grade and, within the structure of the subject area, of fundamental importance for subsequent curricular units. They are, in other words, asked to choose lesson content that none of their students can be allowed to skip. Table 2.2.1 presents the characteristics of the fictitious students that are given as part of the assignment.

TABLE 2.2.1 Student Characteristics

Name	Characteristics
Ariana	Is strong in all subject areas, Spanish-English bilingual; is often tired
Barbara	Has a receptive language disorder, slow verbal reasoning skills, very low self-esteem, and suffers from the taunting of others; has an IEP [Language Disorder]
Chandra	Has weak basic skills and strong inference skills; has difficulties concentrating, staying on task, and organizing her work and her materials; has an IEP [Other Health Impaired for ADHD]
Dennis	Is on grade-level and attributes this to his hard work
Gabriel	Has low proficiency in English and limited literacy skills in his native Spanish; has dysgraphia; is very withdrawn; has an IEP [Specific Learning Disabilities]
Hannah	Has extremely weak reading, writing, and basic math skills; gets easily frustrated and has angry outbursts; has an IEP [Emotional Disturbance]
Jennifer	Is on grade-level; is easily bored
Marcus	Is seen as being able to do the work, but never does his homework and is frequently absent
Martha	Is strong in all subject areas, but works only when she is interested
Michael	Is strong in all subject areas, but is afraid of making mistakes
Ramaisa	Is diligent, on grade-level, Arabic-English bilingual; struggles with some of the reading due to her limited English skills
Samuel	Is strong and interested in your subject area only
Santos	Is on grade-level, Spanish-English bilingual, struggles with some of the reading due to his limited English skills

Differentiated Lesson Planning

The activity is then split into two parts. First, students are asked to write a lesson plan to address the learning situation of each child. So far in their coursework, students have planned a number of lessons for anonymous groups identified only by grade and subject matter (such as "10th grade physics" or "3rd grade reading"). For such assignments, they are asked to take into consideration what they know about the subject matter, developmental generalizations for the age group, and best educational practices. Thus, until this point, lessons had not been planned on the level of the individual child.

The object here is to specify the learning objectives of each child and to design a lesson that meets these learning objectives for students in the same classroom with one teacher. This represents a shift in focus from a whole group defined by commonality to an assortment of individuals, a focus that runs counter to the approaches to which preservice teachers have been exposed. Thus, they are asked to first submit a draft lesson plan aimed at a specified group of students. Typically, this first attempt ends up as a fairly standard lesson plan, whereby the inclusion of diverse students is an afterthought rather than the premise, and differentiation is an addendum to the plan rather than the initial approach. In response to this first draft, students then receive detailed feedback that addresses how each phase of the lesson targets each of the students on the list. Generally, the feedback steers preservice teachers' attention toward students who might be disengaged during a whole-class activity.

Students revise these initial drafts and end up with plans that, while naturally varying in quality, take into consideration each student at each point. Figure 2.2.1 presents excerpts from the draft and revised lesson plans by a preservice teacher in the elementary education

Initial (Draft) Lesson Plan	Revised Lesson Plan
OBJECTIVE: Students will be able to tell time with fluency. • The teacher introduces the vocabulary for the animals in The Grouchy Ladybug. • The teacher reads the story. She stops at each page and asks students to say what time it is. • In pairs, students practice telling the time.	• Chandra and Marcus are asked to write on the board. Spanish-speaking students are asked to say or write the words in Spanish, and Ramaisa in Arabic. They teach their classmates. • Gabriel and Barbara are asked to show the time to their classmates with their hands, following the book. Volunteers are asked questions about the story. Hannah, Chandra, and Marcus (at least) are asked to say the repeated line of the grouchy ladybug. • Pairings: Ariana-Gabriel Dennis-Marcus Martha-Hannah Michael-Barbara Jennifer-Samuel Ramaisa-Santos Chandra (on her own)

FIGURE 2.2.1   Initial and Revised Lesson Plans

program. The point of the assignment is not so much the final quality of the plan but, rather, the degree to which the plan addresses each student instructionally.

In another lesson plan, pairs of students were asked to solve math problems on individual white boards before going over them as a class. For example, after a preservice teacher received feedback that Gabriel might not be able to solve the problem quickly enough and could instead rely on his partner to do all the work, the preservice teacher reworked the activity so that Gabriel would instead be the scribe for the teacher on the large class white board. Similarly, a preservice teacher had planned a foreign language lesson during which students were to watch a video segment in French. Upon receiving feedback that Barbara and Chandra, for example, might have difficulties following and remaining attentive, the teacher devised a study guide on which all students had to circle information during the viewing. Here, scaffolding intended for some students ended up helping the entire class. Feedback also helped students to utilize grouping possibilities to address the needs of specific students. When told that a math activity could be too difficult for Gabriel, another preservice teacher modified her lesson plan so he would be paired with another Spanish-speaking student who might be able to re-explain the concept or directions.

Role Play: Implementing the Differentiated Lesson

The second part of the activity takes the form of a dual practice teaching and role-playing activity. Students are asked to teach part of their lesson to the rest of the class, who assume the roles of the children. The latter are given name tags and colored cards with which to indicate when they think that the specific child they are role-playing would be either off-task (e.g., a blue card) or disruptive (e.g., a purple card). The goal of the student teacher, while implementing their lesson plan, is to minimize the instances and length of time these colored cards are in evidence. The experience is discussed at length after each mini-lesson. If, for example, a student is playing the role of Barbara, who has a receptive language disorder, and is asked to listen to a long, unscaffolded lecture on a difficult topic, she or he may well pull out a blue "off-task" card early on. Should this happen, it is the responsibility of the student teacher to recognize Barbara's behavior and to address it in a way that would seem appropriate, given the needs of the rest of the class and other characteristics that were given for Barbara. Similarly, if the teacher overly scaffolds a particular concept for the whole class, a more advanced student such as Martha could become disruptive and show a purple card. As would be the case in an actual classroom with actual students, the teacher is never able to fully predict how a student will respond and has to accept that her or his knowledge of the students will always be incomplete.

This is in keeping with the view of Tobin and McInnes (2008) that differentiated instruction can only be designed with regard to the actual classroom context. That the student who role-plays the child gives a personal interpretation that somewhat differs from that of the student teacher only underscores the need to be watchful and adaptable during instruction. During this role-playing activity, preservice teachers are explicitly steered away from engaging in single-minded, faithful implementation of the script of their lesson plan and toward addressing the immediate needs and learning processes of individual students. After a subsequent group discussion of the instructional simulation, preservice teachers exchange roles and name tags. Then the next lesson begins.

Discussion: Student Learning

Peer Feedback

As noted, part of the purpose of the activity is to steer preservice teachers' attention away from a regard for the collective needs of a group of students and, instead, toward attention to individual learning needs, processes, and behavior, knowing that this entails an in-the-moment attentiveness to children's reactions and a readiness to address learning requirements as they manifest themselves. This is tied in to Anderson's (2007) emphasis on how instruction needs to be based on the fact that each child, and, therefore, each child's learning process, is unique. This shift in attention is reflected in the written feedback that students give each other after their lessons. Indeed, in their reflections, they emphasized the situations of individual children. Specifically, participating in and reflecting on the role-plays helped preservice teachers to focus on particular instructional issues. Thus, scaffolding was emphasized in terms of its effect on individual learning experiences, which relates to McTighe and Brown's (2005) assertion that individualized scaffolding results in effective learning. One student's feedback, for example, was, "Giving Barbara the material beforehand was good so she could follow along." However, another wrote, "The story was overwhelming for some of us. Provide extra scaffolding for Barbara while reading the story." In both cases, scaffolding as a need in a particular activity was emphasized through the personal role-playing experience of the preservice teacher.

Similarly, the importance of addressing the needs of the more advanced students, who are easily overlooked in a classroom with many students who are struggling academically, was made clear through the experiential learning approach. One student suggested to a peer, "Since you did this yesterday, as Martha, I was bored." Another stated, "There was some downtime while you were working with Barbara, and Jennifer had nothing to do." In addition to addressing students' academic needs, preservice teachers noted how the emotional situation of the child whom they were role-playing had been addressed, which served as a reminder to focus on social-emotional learning, as suggested in the literature (Payton et al., 2008). One student noted, "Gabriel is withdrawn, and calling on him as you did could be embarrassing," while another student's feedback included, "He also integrated Gabriel's Spanish into his teaching, making him feel important and smart." By playing the roles of the students, preservice teachers experienced how instruction felt and worked, given the individual characteristics that they had been assigned.

A number of themes emerged from the peer feedback, which provided an understanding of what most paid attention to during the teaching and role-playing activity and which areas of differentiated instruction were thus highlighted. Ensuring student engagement, addressing learning styles, and providing scaffolding instruction were singled out as positive features in individual lessons and, as such, as important features of instruction. This is in keeping with the literature (Anderson, 2007; McTighe & Brown, 2005; Tomlinson, 1999).

Student Reflections

This increased attentiveness to students' well-being and, consequently, the need to focus on individual learning situations and scaffold accordingly, was confirmed in students' summative reflections on their own learning. While there are no longitudinal data as of yet to determine the long-term effect of this activity on students' future teaching, these reflections confirm how these lessons changed students' outlooks. One student stated, "I simply can't plan lessons the same anymore.... Now I know what I will be working on for years to come." When asked what questions and principles they now thought should guide how instruction is implemented as a consequence of the activity, these preservice teachers emphasized social-emotional well-being and equitable academic challenge and engagement, which echoes Tomlinson's (1999) views and research on social-emotional learning (Rimm-Kaufman et al., 2006; Weismann et al., 2008). Below is a representative sample of their responses:

- "Do the students understand the main ideas that you are trying to convey and/or are you okay if there is a lot of imbalance?"

- "Is the learning environment safe for all to participate in?"

- "Are certain students regularly disengaged? How do you engage them?"

- "Is there an appropriate level of challenge for all students?"

- "If the students are engaged in the lesson, it will be easier for them to follow the teacher's directions than to be disruptive."

- "Planning the lesson carefully means that the teacher can focus on the students instead of the content of the lesson."

How students felt was mentioned by many as a concern, given that the characters that they played had just experienced instances of being included and validated or excluded and discouraged. Students also were made aware of patterns of learning and participation and, in response, understood that they needed to watch for consistent student disengagement and to focus on the inclusion of all. Student behavior was, thus, not regarded as coming entirely from the student, but also as feedback to the instruction they were given and the quality of the learning experience. Consistent with McTighe and Brown's (2008) connection between differentiation and academic rigor, students learned to see the importance of each student being equally challenged by instruction. Finally, students saw that it is the responsibility of the teacher to engage in differentiation and to include all students and that the main focus is ultimately on the learner rather than the content.

Conclusion

As Tobin (2008) noted, one of the most obvious challenges of differentiated instruction is the time and difficulty involved in planning lessons that branch into different directions. Indeed, these require careful planning for individual students and may lead to difficulties in classroom management. The activity presented here gives students opportunities to address the challenges that Tobin described. By asking preservice teachers to focus their instructional imagination and lesson planning on students within the safety of the role-play, they are able to puzzle, make attempts, reflect on, and experience for themselves what effective and ineffective instruction look like and their consequences.

Lucas and Monica, somehow overlooked in their actual classroom, would have been considered, thought about, planned for, addressed, and discussed in the context of the intervention. The instructional bar for these two children would not have been set in a school world that is still in the process of making sense of the fact that different students have different needs but, rather, by the explicit requirement that their needs be emphasized. The use of the simulation activity allowed us to place the teacher's obligation to address individual needs front-and-center and made the design of differentiation strategies an urgent pragmatic concern. In a larger sense, the activity provides a model for how we can expose future teachers to real-life needs and instructional approaches that schools are still unevenly tackling and, thus, allow teachers to be true agents of change.

References

Anderson, K. M. (2007). Differentiating instruction to include all students. *Preventing School Failure*, 51(3), 49–54.

Ankrum J. W., & Bean, R. M. (2008). Differentiating reading instruction: What and how. *Reading Horizons*, 48(2), 133–146.

Benjamin, A. (2002). *Differentiated instruction: A guide for middle & high school teachers*. Larchmont, NY: Eye on Education.

Bondy, E., Ross, D. D., Gallingane, C., & Hambacher, E. (2007). Culturally responsive classroom management and more: Creating environments of success and resilience. *Urban Education, 42,* 326–348.

Cohen, J. (2008). Promoting school and life success: Parents and teachers working, learning and teaching together. *The Parents League Review 2008: Essential Articles on Parenting and Education, 8*(2), 118–123.

Gould, H. C. (2004, December). Can novice teachers differentiate instruction? Yes, they can! *New Horizons for Learning*. Retrieved from http://www.ne-whorizons.org/strategies/differentiated/gould.htm

Kidron, Y., & Fleishman, S. (2006). Promoting adolescents' prosocial behavior. *Educational Leadership, 63*(7), 90–91.

Lawrence-Brown, D. (2004). Differentiated instruction: Inclusive strategies for standards-based learning that benefit the whole class. *American Secondary Education, 32*(3), 34–62.

Manning, S., Stanford, B., & Reeves, S. (2010). Valuing the advanced learner: Differentiating up. *The Clearing House, 83,* 145–149.

McBride, B. (2004). Data-driven instructional methods: "One-strategy-fits-all" doesn't work in real classrooms. *T.H.E. Journal, 31*(11), 38–40.

McTighe, J., & Brown, J. L. (2005). Differentiated instruction and educational standards: Is détente possible? *Theory into Practice, 44*(3), 234–244.

Patterson, J. L., Connolly, M. C., & Ritter, S. A. (2009). Restructuring the inclusion classroom to facilitate differentiated instruction. *Middle School Journal, 41*(1), 46–52.

Payton, J., Weissberg, R. P., Durlak, J. A., Dymnicki, A. B., Taylor, R. D., Schellinger, K. B., & Pachan, M. (2008). *The positive impact of social and emotional learning for kindergarten to eighth-grade students: Findings from three scientific reviews*. Chicago: Collaborative for Academic, Social, and Emotional Learning.

Rimm-Kaufman, S. E., Storm, M. D., Sawyer, B. E., Pianta, R. C., & LaParo, K. (2006). The teacher belief Q-sort: A measure of teachers' priorities and beliefs in relation to disciplinary practices, teaching practices, and beliefs about children. *Journal of School Psychology, 44,* 141–165.

Rock, M. L., Gregg, M., Ellis, E., & Gable, R. A. (2008). REACH: A framework for differentiating classroom instruction. *Preventing School Failure, 52*(2), 31–47.

Sands, D. I., & Barker, H. B. (2004). Organized chaos: Modeling differentiated instruction for preservice teachers. *Teaching and Learning, 19*(1), 26–49.

Santamaria, L., & Thousand, J. (2004). Collaboration, co-teaching, and differentiated instruction: A process-oriented approach to whole Schooling. *International Journal of Whole Schooling, 1*(1), 13–27.

Scigliano, D., & Hipsky, S. (2010, Winter). Three ring circus of differentiated instruction. *Kappa Delta Pi Record*, 82–86.

Subban, P. (2006). Differentiated instruction: A research basis. *International Education Journal, 7*(7), 935–947.

Tobin, R. (2008). Conundrums in the differentiated literacy classroom. *Reading Improvement, 45*(4), 159–169.

Tobin, R., & McInnes, A. (2008). Accommodating differences: Variations in differentiated literacy instruction in grade 2/3 classrooms. *Literacy, 42*(1), 3–9.

Tomlinson, C. A. (1999). *The differentiated classroom: Responding to the needs of all learners.* Upper Saddle River, NJ: Pearson Education.

Technology as a Differentiated Instruction Tool

Ann M. De Lay

Within the classroom, there are a myriad of learners and styles of learning present. Differentiated instruction (DI) is a teacher's acknowledgement there are many avenues for learning and sense making (Scalise, 2007). The value-added approach of DI is essential to the teacher's arsenal for successful learning outcomes. Tomlinson condensed DI into the curricular elements of content, process and product (2001). Students must have experiences with different types and formats of content, different methods for content acquisition, and they must be able to demonstrate their learning through different types of assignments and assessments. By varying the approach taken to instruct, guide and assess, teachers increase the likelihood of reaching every student.

The idea of differentiating the learning environment is at the foundation of DI. Teachers must do all they can to communicate effectively with students and provide them a platform to reciprocate. Students comprising the Millennial generation are considered to be digital natives, exhibiting an intuitive approach to digital interaction (Haynes, 2010). When technology is excluded from the curriculum, teachers fail to address this major avenue for student learning. This means the platform for communicating about new information must include the language in which students feel most comfortable; in this case, the language of technology.

Most teachers do not fall into the Millennial generation and find technology difficult to infuse into their teaching (Murphrey, Miller, & Roberts, 2009). However, inclusion of technology need not be an all or nothing approach. Integration should occur gradually, be connected with content standards, find its way into students' hands, and maintain a high level of rigor and relevance (Rubenstein, 2010). The following tools provide opportunities for teachers to work more productively with digital natives. They also let digital natives more adequately show what they know in a formative and summative capacity. Read through the descriptions while bringing up the online addresses to experience the tools. Then brainstorm ways in which each techie tool can enrich the curricula.

Techie Tools

Glogster (edu.glogster.com) There are many poster design activities included in the lessons for a typical course. Each time the activity is used, there are a number of materials teachers must compile and track. Glogster is a free, online tool for students to design posters in a multimedia format. For example, perhaps the lesson is on oxyfuel welding. The student may wish to create a poster by adding graphics illustrating the different flames the operator must be able to identify to ensure quality penetration. As there are safety considerations, students may also include audio clips of the sounds indicating when hazards like popping or hissing should be of particular concern. Dynamic features like these pique the interest of more students and cannot be accomplished in the traditional poster format.

Animoto (animoto.com)—Video is a powerful communication medium. However, creating quality videos within a single class period can be a nearly impossible task due to the level of detail work associated. Despite the challenge, video generation should not be shied away from as a form of classroom instruction and assessment. Animoto will convert photographs, text and video clips into a stylized, engaging cinematic feature set to music with unique transitions. Should state agricultural commodities be the topic at hand, students can gather images to quickly tell the story of that crop from field to table. Students can create 30 second videos for free, or schools can purchase full access for a low monthly rate.

Flip Video Cameras (http://www.theflip.com/en-us/)—Flip cameras are great sense making tools for permitting students to demonstrate their understanding of a concept. Once students settle on a topic, they can storyboard ideas for arranging the details in a sensible order then set out to capture the necessary footage. After filming, students may integrate the footage into a video editing program for stylizing. Because of their size and simplicity, portability is a cinch and students can easily capture quality audio and video given little instruction. No money in the budget to purchase flip cameras? No problem! The Flip website boasts discounted pricing for educators.

Prezi (prezi.com)—When PowerPoint was unveiled, the world cheered. Audiences finally had the benefit of visual images and text to help them follow along during presentations. Fast forward a number of decades and PowerPoint has become overused and often used improperly, leaving speakers and audience members drowning in text and praying for a reprieve. Prezi brings a fresh perspective to the category of presentation software. Presenters can design a digital presentation as if they were writing on whiteboard. Snippets of information and graphics can be added to the screen in a random fashion then linked in the order they should appear. In show mode, information is zoomed in upon from a global perspective lending movement and flow incapable with traditional presentations. Teachers may use Prezi to jazz up classroom lectures while students may use the tool to create visuals for activities like SAE project competition, discussion meet, or even for classroom presentations of their own. Prezi is free for the basic version but there are additional features which can be purchased for a yearly subscription.

SimpleDiagrams (simplediagrams.com/)—One thing LifeKnowledge made clear is students happily and readily demonstrate their learning when asked to do so through pictures. SimpleDiagrams lets students give birth to their understandings by arranging chalkboard style drawings into graphical representations of complex ideas. Things like the nitrogen cycle, blood flowing through a heart and the process by which a four-cycle engine operates can all be communicated through diagrams and flow charts. SimpleDiagrams can provide a fun, technological format for students to simplify complex content for greater retention.

Infographics Infographics are clear, concise visual representations of data designed for quick consumption by reviewers. Featured and celebrated in the *New York Times*, Infographics can be rich tools for communicating about issues in agriculture. A challenging topic like water allocation and distribution in western states can be distilled to its very essence and presented through images and brief descriptions. An example featuring water facts and consumption can be downloaded at: http://www.circleofblue.org/water-news/2009/world/infographic-tenthings-you-should-know-about-water/. Infographics may be created using tools as simple as PowerPoint and even Microsoft Word!

Jing (jingproject.com)—This online video tool enables users to develop screenshots and screen casts. In the classroom, Jing can help students create instructional how-to's based on photos or footage associated with a skills based lesson. For example, in the floriculture classroom, students can quickly create an instructional video on boutonniere construction or may even film themselves giving a speech from home and email it to their teachers for feedback. Public speaking practice can be carried out online!

Blogging (blogger.com or wordpress.com)—The pressure to meet every standard and include more writing in the classroom is felt by teachers campus-wide. Blogs provide additional instructional time and an e-format for student writing (Colombo & Colombo, 2007). Blogs can serve as a forum for students to share how they have incorporated their classroom learning into their SAEs and how those projects have enhanced their understanding of classroom concepts. Students can cite lingering questions, needs and goals they have for the growth of their SAEs. Blogging can also be used to tell the story of an agricultural biology student's agriscience fair project. Posting guiding questions, data, decisions and next steps can help students share where they are in their research and receive guidance from others who may provide their expertise through comments to their posts. Perhaps the school is located a number of hours from the university or from an appropriate mentor. A project blog can surpass the limitations of time and space, permitting mentors to provide direction without a face-to-face meeting.

VoiceThread (ed.voicethread.com)—This multimedia tool allows students to collaborate in many ways. Students may upload an image, text, video, or audio and may respond to others in a similar fashion. Comments can be made by phone, microphone, text, file upload or webcam. Perhaps the topic of sustainability is addressed throughout the horticulture curriculum. Students can create a voice thread explaining sustainability and addressing the challenges, issues and steps necessary to implement the practice. Other students in the class could post responses to their peers' voice threads to encourage dialogue. This site charges a low monthly fee or a yearly subscription may be obtained.

Tagxedo.com (www.tagxedo.com)—Similar to Wordle (www. wordle.net), Tagxedo generates word clouds based on the frequency of words used in a document. While other word cloud design sites produce indistinguishable blobs, Tagxedo allows users to select an overall shape for their word clouds. For example, the meaning of the FFA Creed is addressed in virtually every first year agriculture class. When the creed appears in a word cloud format, students can clearly extract meaning based on the major words revealed. In addition, the final word cloud can be customized to appear in a unique shape like the United States to reference the final paragraph. Teachers may also use Tagxedo as a game with students to introduce a new topic. By entering key words from the lesson or unit plan into the online program, teachers could have students anticipate the next topic of study!

Bonus Techie Tool

Although this application could be used to enhance students' experiences in the classroom its inclusion is offered primarily for program management purposes.

Picnik (www.picnik.com)—This online photo editing site lets users enhance photos absolutely free! Think of all of the awards applications, slide shows, videos, scrapbook pages, websites, newsletters, and other materials agriculture programs must generate within a given year. Each project requires a number of stunning images to tell a gripping story. Sometimes the untouched images are a bit blurry, dull or off center and falling just shy of "stunning." The simplicity and power of Picnik is such that it is easy enough for students to use and creates magic in minutes. The site also saves pictures to the computer or the online account for use as needed. For a low monthly fee, subscribe to Picnik Premium for greater access to editing tools and storage space.

There is a very real need for teachers who can differentiate their instruction (Colombo & Colombo, 2007). The stakes for teachers to ensure their students are successful on state testing are increasing all the time. Thinking outside the box to differentiate a lesson's content, process and product is a key factor to promoting a student's potential for academic achievement (Tomlinson, 2001). Additionally, teaching in such a way as to address students' various readiness, interests and learning profiles makes the classroom experience more enjoyable for students and teachers alike.

Dr. Ann M. De Lay is an Assistant Professor in the Dept of Agricultural Education & Communication, California Polytechnic State University, San Luis Obispo.

Students using a wireless slate in a high school agricultural education classroom.

References

Colombo, M. W., & Colombo, P. D. (2007). Blogging to improve instruction in differentiated science classrooms. *Phi Delta Kappan, 89*(1), 60–63.

Haynes, E. (2010). The class of 2022: How will we meet their needs and expectations? *Library Media Connection, 28*(4), 10–11.

Murphrey, T. P., Miller, K. A., & Roberts, T. G. (2009). Agricultural science and technology teachers' perceptions of iPod and MP3 technology integration into curricular and cocurricular Activities. *Journal of Agricultural Education, 50*(4), 110–119.

Rubenstein, G. (2010, April 26). Technology integration for elementary schools. *Edutopia*. Retrieved September 8, 2010, from http://www.edutopia.org/stwdifferentiated-instruction-tehnology-integration

Scalise, K. (2007). Differenitated e-learning: Five approaches through instructional technology. *International Journal of Learning Technology, 3*(2), 169–182.

Tomlinson, C. A. (2001). *How to differentiated instruction in mixed-ability classrooms* (2nd ed.). Alexandria, VA: Association for Supervision and Curriculum Development.

Reading 2.4

Classroom Routines, Motivation, and Effective Learning

Rhonda Bondie and Akane Zusho

Overview

Objective:

Why do classroom routines promote learning?

*Think: Underline the most **familiar** word in this Objective.*

Criteria:

Use the following criteria to increase the quality of your answer to the chapter question. Try to "Take It Up a Notch" or expand your answer by reading the chapter to add these details.

- Identify the meaning of
    - ABC+M
    - Motivation
    - WERMS and
    - Cognitive science on effective learning.
- Explain the connections between research and the ALL-ED framework.
- Try Classroom Routines:
    - Plan—Choose Questions and Record Student Responses.
    - Teach—*List, Write, Draw, Rumors,* or *FQA.*
    - Adjust Instruction—React to student responses.

Starting Position: List, Write, Draw

Start your thinking about motivation by reflecting on times when you felt motivated using the ALL-ED Classroom Routine, *List, Write, Draw*. Think about a time when you felt motivated. Make a list, draw a sketch, and/or write a few notes or sentences of a story to capture your thinking about a "best time" when you were totally motivated. Now think of one of the "worst times" when you could barely force yourself to do something. Brainstorm a list, draw a sketch, and/or write about one of the worst times when you were totally unmotivated. From your best and worst list, can you begin to make a few initial observations about what moves you to act? Save this list to refer to as you learn more about motivation, cognition, and durable learning in this chapter and in the Research Roots section throughout this book. (See *Before You Start*, *Learning Journal* for examples drawing from this routine.)

From the Classroom: *The Beginning of ALL-ED*

When Rhonda Bondie was a classroom teacher, like most teachers, she was inspired to reach every child in her class. She knew that her students had divergent experiences, understandings, interests, strengths, and needs. But when she tried to build on these strengths to eliminate gaps in achievement, she found that the planning took an unbelievable amount of time. The extra planning usually led to greater student engagement, but it did not always result in better learning for students, and it was hard to determine what would make learning more effective. She tried to recall research and theories that she learned while preparing to become a teacher, but she did not know how to integrate these ideas in her daily classroom practice. Sometimes she spent her weekends creating appropriate materials, only to find students still disengaged during lessons. As a result, Rhonda routinely met with students during lunch and after school to provide additional help. She felt that students on the other extreme, who needed more challenging work, remained bored or untested. She wondered, "Was daily differentiated instruction possible, and could it lead to effective learning for all students?"

After many years of attending workshops and experimenting in her classroom, Rhonda found that daily differentiated instruction was practical and effective when routines were used to promote student learning. Student autonomy and engagement increased as students relied less on teacher prompting. Even better, she was less tired at the end of the day because classroom routines saved time in planning, giving directions, and managing behavior during lessons. Rhonda was able to teach almost two additional units during the year because she spent less time reviewing and re-teaching. With routine daily differentiated instruction, she left school with so much energy that, for the first time since she began teaching, she could join a gym!

When Rhonda began to partner with Akane Zusho, a researcher of motivation and cognition, they synthesized the research on effective learning and refined her routines using the larger psychological and educational literature. This collaboration ultimately resulted in the development of the All Learners Learning Every Day (ALL-ED) framework, which came about through working with teachers from around the world in implementing the routines with their students. The ALL-ED framework combines years of practical classroom experience with the latest research on learning and cognition.

Rooted in Research: *Theoretical Bases of ALL-ED Framework*

To understand how the decision-making framework and classroom routines promote learning, we summarize the theoretical and empirical bases in Figure 2.4.1. Focus your attention on the student learning outcomes portion of the figure on the far right. You will see the important outcomes that have been linked with college and career readiness. We believe that *all* students should: (a) develop deep, durable, and flexible understandings of course content; (b) feel empowered to take academic risks; (c) put forth effort and persist in the face of academic challenges (what the social psychologist Angela Duckworth would call grit); and, of course, (d) experience academic success.

The center portion of Figure 2.4.1 represents the research base on learning, which demonstrates that both motivational and cognitive factors are strongly predictive of desired student outcomes. The collective research on achievement motivation suggests that students are more likely to put forth effort, persist, take academic risks, and achieve when they feel **a**utonomous, a sense of **b**elonging with others, and **c**ompetent, and when they perceive that what they are learning is personally **m**eaningful (Kumar, Zusho, & Bondie, submitted; Turner, 2014). We refer to this as the ABC+M of motivation.

The cognitive research, in turn, suggests that to develop deep and lasting understanding, it is important for students to overcome the limits of **w**orking memory by engaging deeper-processing, **e**laborative, and **r**etrieval-based strategies to interrupt the process of forgetting and consolidate learning, and to overcome illusions of knowing (Brown, Roedinger, & McDaniel, 2014). Research also demonstrates that **s**elf-regulated learners—students who are **m**etacognitively aware of how they think; who set appropriate goals and plan for learning; monitor progress toward goals; adjust or regulate their thinking, motivation, and study habits—are more likely to achieve academic success than those who do not (Pintrich & Zusho, 2007; Zimmerman, 1990). ALL-ED leverages what we know about working memory, elaboration, retrieval, and metacognition as well as self-regulated learning (we remember these parts of cognition with the acronym, WERMS) to create effective and efficient learning experiences, all while meeting diverse learner needs.

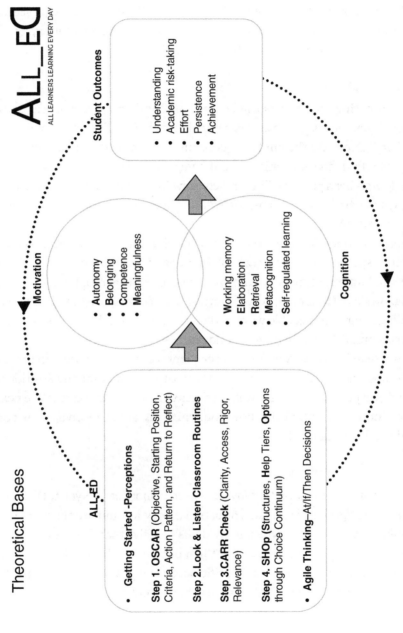

FIGURE 2.4.1   ALL-ED Framework Components, Roots in Research, and Expected Student Outcomes.

The far left of Figure 2.4.1 illustrates how the four-step ALL-ED teacher decision-making framework is rooted in motivation and cognitive sciences that lead to student outcomes. We will not discuss exactly how the specific steps of ALL-ED are linked to this literature just yet—you will find information on that in Chapters 3 to 8. First, the following section delves more deeply into the research on motivation and cognitive science that explains why the routines promote engagement and durable learning.

ABC+M of Motivation

Return to your **Starting Position** for this chapter and consider your responses to the following questions: "What moves you to act? What makes you invest time and energy in one task but not another?" These are the kinds of questions that concern motivational researchers. Researchers generally define motivation as something that influences or explains why a person will start a task, whether a person will approach or avoid a task, how much effort a person will put into a task, and whether or not a person will continue to work on the task once they start (Maehr & Zusho, 2009).

When it comes to understanding the effects on achievement, motivational factors have what researchers such as John Hattie (2009) refer to as a medium "effect size." This means that motivational interventions can improve achievement by roughly half of a standard deviation (Lazowski & Hulleman, 2016). Motivational factors have been demonstrated to enhance achievement in noticeable ways in the real world, and the effects go beyond what a teacher can accomplish in a single academic year.

Motivation researchers have identified the elements of intrinsic motivation as Autonomy, Belonging, Competence, and Meaning (ABC+M). Return to your Starting Position and identify how your description of being motivated relates to ABC+M. As you read the next section to learn more about ABC+M, notice how your thinking about motivation is confirmed, changed, and maybe challenged.

Autonomy (Perceived Independence)

Research on motivation suggests autonomy is a powerful motivator (Ryan & Deci, 2017). Ryan and Deci (2017), who developed self-determination theory, a dominant theory of motivation, define autonomy as the extent to which individuals perceive that they can accept, endorse, and regulate their own goals or behaviors. When people can decide their own destiny by shaping the environment to meet their specific needs and goals, they develop self-efficacy and competence, which is directly linked with achievement outcomes.

Belonging

Self-determination theory also suggests that humans have an innate desire to form and maintain close and secure relationships with others (Ryan & Deci, 2017). Students feel more motivated when they have a sense of connection and belonging with others, be it their friends, teachers, or caregivers. Research on motivation suggests that feelings of safety and belonging are central to the establishment of an environment that facilitates motivation (Kaplan, Sinai, & Flum, 2014; Maehr & Zusho, 2009). Such feelings of safety can be heightened when students feel that their teachers care and respect them (Wentzel, 2010), and when students are encouraged to work productively and collaboratively in groups (Roseth, Johnson, & Johnson, 2008).

Competence

A core assumption of the research on motivation is that individuals are motivated toward competence. Students are more likely to engage in tasks when they feel confident about their abilities to achieve and when people feel a sense of self-efficacy (Bandura, 1997). Research on motivation consistently finds self-efficacy to be one of the strongest predictors of academic achievement (Linnenbrink-Garcia & Patall, 2016). Research also demonstrates that when students endorse a goal of developing competence (referred to in the literature as having a mastery goal), not only are they likely to adopt a growth mindset (the understanding that abilities and intelligence can be developed (Dweck, 2006)), but they are also more likely to seek academic challenges and take risks (Maehr & Zusho, 2009).

Meaning

Theories of motivation also recognize that perceptions of competence are not always enough to spur action—students must also want to complete the task. Motivational theories largely assume that students are more likely to approach and engage in academic tasks when they have personal meaning for them. Research suggests that the quality of motivated behavior is higher when students find the task and/or subject domain important, interesting, and useful (Wigfield & Eccles, 2000). Such values are more predictive of outcomes such as choice and subsequent course enrollment. In Figure 2.4.2, we summarize Ten Facts About Motivation that are useful reminders of why students may feel motivated.

We believe that when instruction is adjusted to meet learner needs within the learning community and focused on building deep, durable, and flexible understandings, then all students will feel ABC+M every day in our lessons. Table 2.4.1 displays a summary of how the elements of motivation relate to our goals for all students in a learning community.

Ten Facts About Motivation

1. Motivation is changeable—it is not a personality trait. Altering the task or the general learning environment can change it.
2. When you are placed in a setting where you feel autonomous (or empowered), competent, and that you belong, you are more likely to feel intrinsically motivated.
3. Competence is at the core of motivation. When you feel like you can do the work, you are more likely to do it.
4. Students are more likely to be intrinsically motivated when they know what they know and do not know. There is a symbiotic relationship between motivation and self-regulated learning.
5. But … sometimes it is not enough to feel like you can do the work. You must also value it in some way—maybe it is something that interests you or something that you find useful for future goals (e.g., job, college).
6. When students perceive the task to be relevant to their lives, they are more likely to value the task.
7. The quality of behavior is generally much better when an individual feels intrinsically as opposed to extrinsically motivated. You are more likely to put in more effort, persist longer, and learn more when the source of the motivation is yourself and not others.
8. Although other people can be powerful motivators, it is generally better to decrease social comparison if you want *all* students to be motivated. Social comparison generally works as a motivator for stronger students; for weaker students, it is usually a deterrent. Do not set others as the standard; set the task as the standard (e.g., do not grade on a curve).
9. Rewards can be tricky. Simple extrinsic rewards generally do not promote lasting motivation. If you want to sustain motivation, it is much more important to find ways to get students to value the task and feel more competent about what they are working on. Rewards can backfire if they are not equitable (so everyone feels like they all have a chance to get them), if they do not make students feel competent about what they are doing, and if students do not feel in control. We recommend posting specific quality criteria to help students find value and increase feelings of competence with assigned tasks.
10. Given this research, ALL-ED classroom routines are central to fostering motivation.

FIGURE 2.4.2   Top Ten Considerations about Motivation in ALL-ED.

TABLE 2.4.1   Elements of Motivation ABC+M

All Learners Feel			
Autonomy	**Belonging**	**Competence**	**Meaning**
Empowered to take ownership of their learning.	They are valued members of a learning community.	Capable of pursuing rigorous learning.	Learning is interesting and important.

Durable Learning and WERMS

In addition to hoping students will feel motivated throughout our lessons, we also strive for all learners to develop learning that is both flexible and durable in daily lessons. When learning is flexible, students revise, expand, and even unlearn to further their learning. Students expect their learning to grow and change. When learning is durable, it sticks and is not easily forgotten. To understand durable learning, it is necessary to understand how memory works. More than half a century of research in the cognitive sciences has established that learning depends, in large part, on the interaction between two specific memory systems—working memory and long-term memory. According to Alan Baddeley, the man who coined the term, *working memory* is the "memory system that allows us to 'keep things in mind' when performing complex tasks" (Baddeley, Eysenck, & Anderson, 2014, p. 13)[1]. Long-term memory is the memory system that holds all of our knowledge. From a purely cognitive perspective, learning can be defined as a process of encoding (getting in) and retrieving (getting out) information into and out of long-term memory (Baddeley et al., 2014). Durable learning, in turn, is learning that gets consolidated in long-term memory.

Working Memory. Working memory is important because it plays a central role in the encoding process. It is also involved in most, if not all, academic tasks (Pickering, 2006). At least until students have automatized the process, reading, for example, relies heavily on working memory. To read, beginning readers have to juggle multiple things in working memory. They first recognize the letter, connect the letter to its sound, put the sounds together to form a word, put multiple words together to form a sentence, remember the meaning of each word and the sentence as a whole, and then connect the meaning of sentences. Reading is, indeed, a very complicated process.

Test your working memory using the puzzle shown in Figure 2.4.3 (to get the most out of this, do not look ahead to the answer later in the chapter). The task is one that many

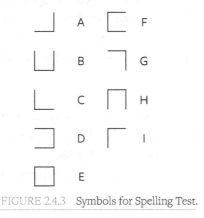

FIGURE 2.4.3   Symbols for Spelling Test.

elementary school teachers are familiar with—a spelling test but with a twist. Study the symbols associated with the letters for two minutes—you will be asked to complete a spelling test using the symbols in just a few minutes. Are you ready? Go!

Okay—two minutes are up. What strategies did you use to remember the symbols? There are, of course, many ways to memorize things—the most common is what cognitive scientists call the rehearsal strategy, which is essentially repeating things over and over again. Some of you may have attached meaning to each symbol, employing a strategy known as elaboration. Others of you may have used additional strategies to help you keep the symbols in your working memory.

Decades of research on learning and memory has established that how we encode information in working memory matters (Brown et al., 2014). For example, despite its popularity among students and teachers, research shows that repeating information over and over until it is perceived to be "burned into memory" (what researchers refer to as **massed practice**) is not a very effective way to learn, if you define learning as not just acquiring new information but also being able to apply it later—a concept known as **transfer**.

·Are you now ready for the spelling test? Using just the symbols, "spell" the words shown in Figure 2.4.4.

CEDE

DEAF

HIGH

CABBAGE

HEADACHE

FIGURE 2.4.4   Spelling Words.

How did you do? How confident are you that you spelled the words correctly? Were some words easier than others? If we asked you to repeat the spelling test at the end of the chapter, how do you think you will do? Have the symbols been stored in your long-term memory? In general, among other factors (i.e., how attentive you were to the task), research on memory would predict that your performance would depend, in large part, on what kinds of strategies you used.

Elaboration: Research on memory consistently demonstrates that *elaboration* is a much more effective strategy than rehearsal. When students give new material personal meaning by connecting it to what they already know, or organize it into a mental model or **schema**, the learning is much more durable (Brown et al., 2014). Why is this more effective? Because by attaching meaning to new information, we are far more likely to consolidate (i.e., organize and solidify) information and therefore less likely to forget it. As any student will attest, repeating information over and over may delay forgetting for a short period of time, but generally not for much longer (Baddeley, 2004). For example, the schema for the spelling test we just did is presented in Figure 2.4.5. Can you connect this figure to the symbols we gave you previously?

A	B	C
D	E	F
G	H	I

FIGURE 2.4.5   Schema for Spelling Test.

Now, if we asked you to repeat the spelling test, how well do you think you will perform? Most likely, very well—just like a student who has extensive prior knowledge (i.e., elaborate schemas) on a given topic.

Several of our routines were designed with this basic cognitive principle in mind, including *Fact, Question, Answer (FQA)*. *FQA* is a group learning routine designed to help students remember the meaning of a text by attaching the meaning of the text to a previous experience (see Figure 2.4.6). As you can see, part of the *FQA* routine involves students of mixed abilities working in groups, sharing a fact from the text, and then changing it into a how or a why question. Then, each student takes turns answering the question using their own experiences (i.e., elaborating).

ALL-ED Classroom Routine Directions: Fact, Question, Answer (FQA)

Based on the cognitive science of elaboration, *FQA* challenges students to bring personal meaning to a text. In the discussion, one at a time, each student states a fact from the text. The students choose one of the three facts to discuss. The students change the fact into a how or why question. Then each student takes turns answering the question based on their own experience, not using words from the text. The process repeats until the group has completed the routine with three different facts. Finally, students reflect on the most meaningful connection to each of the facts that was heard in the group.

Strengths of this routine:

- promotes making meaningful connections
- encourages collaboration

- provides a means for students to receive feedback on evidence or quotes selected from a text
- allows students to explore and play with a text
- invites creativity
- requires listening to and thinking about the responses of others.

Implementation Directions

Objective: To understand and remember the facts from a reading.

Starting Positions (individually and then in small groups)

Individually: Students identify facts of a text that they want to remember. Students may be asked to identify facts that support the main idea or a particular perspective; the identifying task should align to the goal of the lesson. The teacher may assign required facts that must be remembered and then students can choose two additional facts on their own.

Groups: The teacher assigns students into groups of three with a range of student reading levels in each group. The teacher designates where in the room each group of three will meet with the students sitting or standing knee to knee and eye to eye—so that it is easier to hear each student in the group.

Criteria

- *Must Haves*: Connection to personal experience must add meaning, answer/response must include the word "because."
- *Amazing*: Answer/response to the question uses vocabulary from the class word wall.

Action Pattern

The teacher identifies in the directions:

- **Roles:** Speaker and Listeners
- **Turns:** The teacher assigns one student in each group to "Go first" stating a fact from the text, and then the student who will go second and third.
- **Rules:** "Add or Repeat" students can repeat an answer from a previous student or add a new response.

- **Time:** The teacher times each round of *Fact, Question, Answer* so that all groups move through the routine at the same pace.
    1. *Fact*: One at a time, read the fact to be remembered (Rule: "Add or Repeat"—facts can be repeated or new facts added).
    2. *Question*: As a group, restate the fact into a why or how question.
    3. *Answer*: One at a time, answer the how/why question using personal experience (no quotes from the text).
    4. Reflect through an Open Discussion: As a group, discuss which personal connection is most memorable and why. Group members take turns being the recorder, who writes down the fact and the most memorable connection on an index card with the group member's names following the Open Discussion.
    5. Repeat: Repeat *Fact, Question, Answer* until at least three facts have been turned into questions and each person has provided a connection.

Reflections
1. Create a list of the most meaningful connections to each of the facts that was heard in the group. Use the Criteria to determine the most meaningful connection.
2. Answer the questions, "What is this text about? How does this text relate to our lives?"

FQA also ensures equity by offering each student opportunities to share their ideas. In addition, the "Add or Repeat" rule enables students who need to find a quote, to participate in the discussion by using a quote that another student has offered. Students use elaboration and the support of a structured collaborative discussion to encode the meaning of the text. While the students are engaged in *FQA*, the teacher is free to listen, observe, and record student thinking and vocabulary use. This enables teachers to make decisions in the moment about how to correct misunderstandings and how to tailor the next part of the lesson to further student learning. *FQA* is a great example of how ALL-ED classroom routines are rooted in research and implemented in a practical manner designed for student variability. *FQA* is also an example of practicing retrieval, our next area of focus.

Retrieval: Considering the way our memory is set up, we are far more likely to forget things than to remember them. We can at most juggle only about four bits of information in our working memory at a time, and unless we do something to keep that information active in our working memory, it is only retained for a few seconds (Baddeley, 2004). Some of you may have experienced this with the spelling activity above. We intentionally tried to interfere with your working memory by inserting text you had to read before letting you proceed to the spelling test. Considering that the window for getting information into long-term memory from working memory is quite short, the more time passes, the less likely we are to be able to do this. This is also why some students who are slow at pronunciation or counting often have difficulty with reading or doing arithmetic; by the time they are ready to work on the higher order task of reading or arithmetic, they may have already forgotten the word or the number. Learning is more about finding ways not to forget information than about remembering. Studies show that we forget about 70% of what we have just heard or read (Brown et al., 2014).

Recent cognitive research has therefore focused on finding more effective ways to counter-act this natural process of forgetting. First, studies demonstrate that having prior knowledge on the topic helps a lot. When you can tie information to a **schema**, like the schema for the spelling activity we just completed, you are much less likely to forget it because that infor-mation has meaning (APA, 2015; Mayer, 2011). Now that you know the trick to the activity, how likely is it that you would forget the symbols? Probably not very likely. In the same way, having extensive schemas on a topic helps with the processing (i.e., encoding) of informa-tion. Similarly, in the reading example, reading comprehension usually becomes easier for students as soon as they have automatized phonics, freeing up more working memory capac-ity to devote to meaning.

Apart from the research on prior knowledge and encoding, studies have also found that learning is more effective when we increase the frequency of retrieving knowledge from memory, what psychologists refer to as the **testing (or retrieval–practice) effect**. When we practice retrieving information from long-term memory, it helps us to re-remember it, and ultimately not forget it as easily. For example, *FQA* asks students to repeat factual information from the text; when students are doing this, they are essentially engaging in retrieval practice.

It is important to note that the quality of retrieval makes a difference; to be most effec-tive, studies show that retrieval must be repeated over and over again, spaced out over time, and effortful. Repetition is important for consolidating knowledge and automatizing skills, but it is also important to space out our learning to allow for some forgetting to occur so that when we try to remember information, it is not always easy. Doing the *FQA* routine once is likely to aid students' memory of the reading, but doing the *FQA* routine spaced out over time would be even better.

Metacognition and Self-regulated Learning: When we perceive a task as easy, we often fall prey to what psychologists refer to as the **illusion of knowing**—or the perception that we know more than we actually do (Brown et al., 2014). Illusions of knowing (and overconfi-dence, which often accompanies illusions of knowing) impede learning. When we think that we know something, we are less likely to take action to remediate our understanding—after all, we already know it! In most cases, we are very poor judges of our abilities. As the Nobel Laureate Kahneman (2011) notes in his book *Thinking Fast and Slow*, we have an "almost unlimited ability to ignore our ignorance" (p. 201). How many times have you encountered that flabbergasted student who was so convinced that he knew the material that he could not possibly fathom why he did so poorly on the exam?

Such students essentially lack what researchers refer to as **metacognitive awareness**, or awareness about their thinking. Metacognitive awareness is the hallmark of a self-regulated learner—a learner who, upon being given an assignment, thinks about what she knows about the topic, what she did in the past to succeed on similar assignments, and her goals for the assignment. Such a learner monitors his progress toward his goals when working on the assignment and adjusts his strategies when he finds that they are not working. A learner with metacognitive awareness reflects on her work and thinks about what she could do better next time (Zimmerman & Schunk, 2011).

Not surprisingly, research on self-regulated learning finds that such students typically perform well in school. John Hattie (2009) lists metacognition as among the top factors related to academic achievement. The use of metacognitive strategies—including planning how to approach a task, evaluating progress, and monitoring understanding—was determined to have a large effect size. Skills related to self-regulated learning have always been considered critical for academic success; however, we would argue that these skills are perhaps even more imperative now. Standards like the Common Core State Standards (CCCS) and the Next Generation Science Standards (NGSS) collectively emphasize the development of real-world, higher-order thinking skills, making training in self-regulated learning (SRL) not only important but a necessity (White & DiBenedetto, 2015). See Figure 2.4.6 for a summary of the research on cognition.

Importance of Context: Thus far, we have argued that both motivational and cognitive factors are predictors of important learning outcomes. Learning is enhanced when students feel autonomous, belonging to a learning community, competent, and find meaning in their learning (ABC+M). Research on cognition (WERMS) further suggests that self-regulated learners who use more effective encoding strategies to interrupt the process of forgetting are less likely to fall prey to biases related to overconfidence and illusions of understanding, and are more likely to ultimately achieve higher levels of learning.

What we have not said is that both motivational and cognitive processes are highly dependent upon context. Often, we hear from teachers that "my students are simply not motivated." There is a tendency for teachers to think of motivation as a personality trait—students either have it or they do not. Although it is certainly possible to identify students who appear more

> **Top Ten Considerations About Cognition (WERMS) in ALL-ED**
>
> 1. Durable learning is learning that sticks. It largely depends on the interaction between two specific memory systems—working memory and long-term memory. Working memory is involved in all academic tasks (like reading and math) that has multiple steps.
> 2. We can at most juggle only about four bits of information in our working memory at a time. Unless we do something to keep that information active in our working memory, it is only retained in working memory for a few seconds. Thus, effective learning involves learning how to overcome the limits of working memory.
> 3. One way to overcome the limits of working memory is to use deeper-processing cognitive strategies, like elaboration. The more meaning you attach to information you are trying to learn, the more likely it is that you will not forget it.
> 4. Prior knowledge (or having elaborate schemas) aids in the processing of information because it can help make the incoming information more meaningful.
> 5. You are less likely to forget information if you increase the frequency of retrieving knowledge from memory—or, what psychologists refer to as the testing (or retrieval–practice) effect. To be most effective, retrieval must be repeated over and over again, be spaced out over time, and be effortful.
> 6. Illusions of knowing (and overconfidence, which often accompanies illusions of knowing) impede learning. Students with metacognitive awareness (i.e., students who know what they know and do not know) are less likely to fall prey to illusions of knowing.
> 7. Students with metacognitive awareness are also more likely to regulate their learning. Upon given an assignment, they are more likely to think about what they know about the topic and their goals. Self-regulated learners are also more likely to monitor their progress toward goals and adjust their strategies when they find that they aren't working. Upon completion of the task, they are also more likely to reflect on their work and think about what they could do better next time.
> 8. Research on transfer further suggests that in order for learning to be flexible and durable, you need to know when and how to use that knowledge. It is not enough to know about a topic—you need to be able to do something with that knowledge. Building metacognitive awareness and self-regulation is one way to promote transfer.
> 9. Research demonstrates a positive association between motivation and cognition. Students who feel ABC+M are much more likely to use effective cognitive strategies that lead to durable learning.
> 10. Given this research, ALL-ED classroom routines are central to fostering durable learning.

FIGURE 2.4.6   Top Ten Considerations about Cognition (WERMS) in ALL-ED.

or less motivated in a classroom through their behavior, it is important to note that *motivation is NOT a personality trait. Altering the task or the general learning environment can change it.* Recall the students that appear unmotivated in your class. If you take them out of your classroom and put them in a setting where they are working on something that they love—an athletic field or their workplace—what are they like? In a different context, you may see a totally different student. Again, motivation is not a personality trait.

Similarly, research on self-regulated learning assumes that it is a teachable skill. Skills associated with self-regulated learning are learned skills that can be modified and improved, thus making it an ideal target for intervention at any age level. Research suggests that students are more likely to regulate their learning when they have adequate resources available, including time, effective and supportive teachers and peers, as well as access to supplementary learning materials. Students are more likely to become self-regulated when they are prompted to do so, either directly (through instruction) or indirectly (through feedback or activity prompts). Research shows that periodic self-assessments that ask students to reflect on what they know or do not know about a topic (to overcome illusions of knowing), and their depth of knowledge about key points promotes regulation of learning. Research further suggests that metacognitive training is most effective during small group instruction (Hattie, 2009).

Return once more to your Starting Position routine *List, Write, Draw* and review your memory about an experience where you felt motivated or unmotivated. Can you explain using the research from this chapter why you felt motivated and unmotivated? If you could change something in your story, what would you change that might increase the support in that context for your motivation? Use the routine *List, Write, Draw* to gather notes as you read the next chapters.

ALL-ED Classroom Routine Directions: List, Write, Draw (Individual Routine)

Before an activity begins, teachers activate student prior knowledge and gather information about what students know and questions they have about the topic. *List, Write, Draw* is an individual routine designed to provide options for students to record their memories. The options make writing about memories easier so that the focus for students is thinking about the topic. Any options that are available and easily used by students in your setting could be used, such as *Type*, *Picture with Caption*, or *Collage* if you are using a computer. The goal is to facilitate all students making a quick visible recording of their thinking on the topic. This routine can be used as an introduction to a topic, a check for understanding in the middle of a lesson, or story being read aloud. It can also be used as a reflection at the end of the assignment reflecting on what the student will remember from completing the learning task and why that part is memorable.

Strengths of this routine:

- takes little time
- is fun—students like sharing because students choose different options
- shows key points that are on the minds of students.

Implementation Directions

Objective: Record your thinking with details.

Starting Positions (individually)

Individually: Ask students to think "in their head" about a question or a prompt. For example, "Think of a time when you (related to the topic—maybe how you learned _____ or when you were motivated ...)." You might ask the students to summarize a lesson using _List, Write, Draw_ capturing the most important points. Or to describe a part of a story or a character.

Criteria

- _Must Haves_: Answers the prompt, includes details.
- _Amazing_: Answer/response to the question uses vocabulary from the class word wall, includes how you felt.

Action Pattern

The teacher identifies in the directions:

- **Rules:** Must use the whole time to add to your response, so if you finish your drawing then add words or if you finish writing then add a sketch. When you think that you are finished, then reread what you have written or drawn and add two more details. Continue until time is called.
- **Time:** About two to four minutes.

1. Ask students to _List, Write, Draw_ to answer the prompt.
2. Remind students that when they think that they are finished to reread and add two more details.

Reflections

3. Ask students to reread what they have written and circle the most important part.

This routine can be followed by a table discussion and then _Domino Discover_ to gather the most important parts (circled) of the responses.

Applying Research to Classroom Practice

As Marvin, an exemplary science teacher, noted, "motivation fuels learning, whereas cognition puts the brakes on learning like a parachute on a drag racecar." When we are designing learning experiences, we want to both foster motivation and to pay attention to how cognitive limits may enhance or create constraints for effective learning. Although the acronyms facilitate your memory of ABC+M and WERMS, we have designed recommendations from this research into classroom routines to facilitate learning so that you can focus on implementing the routine. For example, you could begin with a simple habit of recording student responses at least once in every lesson. The student responses could be answers to any question that is asked that could have multiple answers or explanations. This teacher habit can be used with many different classroom routines and has many benefits. For students, it provides a means for them to reflect on how their thinking has changed because of learning in a lesson or unit. Teachers use the responses to adjust instruction by answering specific student questions or grouping students by similar or different answers. Recording student responses also draws the teacher's attention to the effectiveness of questions. The quality of a question is revealed in what is done with the answers. Recording student responses is a great place to begin agile teacher thinking.

There are many ways to record responses without adding too much time to a lesson. We organize the possibilities into three categories, **Share-Out, Gather and Group**, and **Around the Room**. The differences are important because the way responses are recorded makes a difference in how students receive feedback and how quickly teachers can use the responses to adjust instruction. For example, each table can summarize individual responses into a table response that is shared by a table reporter or written largely on a paper for the routine, *Show and Share*, without any speaking. Responses can be written by each table or group and posted on the board or typed into a digital document. *Show and Share* takes very little time; the teacher gathers responses at the group level, not from individuals. For feedback, groups generally can notice how their responses were similar or different than other groups.

There are at least three different ways to record responses. Each method results in a different collection of student responses. Remember that the teacher habit is to record student responses visibly at least once during every lesson. You will need a variety of methods for recording responses considering the time allowed in the lesson, length of student responses, feedback you would like students to receive, and organization of collected responses for adjusting instruction. Students may respond to questions in a variety of forms, such as: writing, drawing, speaking, moving, and building. The method of gathering student responses will need to fit for the form as well as the length of student responses.

Methods for Recording Student Responses

1. **Share-Out**—Purpose: Assess student responses so that students see how their ideas are similar or different from those of other students. Ideas should be shared from all members of the class. Avoid calling on hands as a first routine for gathering student responses. Begin with a group or individual routine and then call on hands for additional responses. Routines that use the *Share-Out* method are *Domino Discover* and *Show and Share.*

2. **Gather and Group**—Purpose: When you need student responses to be grouped into patterns to determine the next steps of the lesson or student groups, then *Gather and Group* should be used instead of *Share-Out*. The difference is that in *Gather and Group*, individual student responses are sorted into categories as part of the gathering process. This enables teachers to respond to the patterns during lessons rather than taking student responses home, sorting them, and then returning a day or two later to respond to student differences. In addition, because individual student responses are written down and saved, both teachers and students may return to original responses for reflection. The routine, *Rumors*, uses the *Gather and Group* method.

3. **Around the Room**—Purpose: When you need students to generate responses on a focused topic or question through discussion in small groups and students need written feedback on their responses, then *Around the Room* is the most efficient method. For *Around the Room*, you will post a topic, photograph, data table, question, map—any prompt that you would like students to discuss and record their responses. Students form small groups at each station, discuss, and document their responses on chart paper or a laptop. Then students rotate, reading the responses of other groups and contributing feedback to the original responses. This rotation continues "around the room" until students have participated in discussion on the needed topics. Together as a class, you and your students can look for patterns across student responses to the different prompts. This is a great way to introduce or review units, a time in the curriculum where you both want to activate student knowledge and get them remembering what they know and at the same time further student knowledge through peer discussions. The teacher benefits from the time to listen to student conversations around the room. The routine, *Idea Carousel*, uses the *Around the Room* method.

Domino Discover or *Show and Share* should be used first before calling on hands to collect responses from students. In these routines, every student shares their response in small groups, or representatives share responses from each group to the whole class. The opportunity to hear from each individual or individuals via a group representative sends a message to students that their ideas are valued in class. For students, *Domino Discover* and *Show and Share* build feelings of ABC+M through exchanging and building on the ideas of peers. Students know that the teacher is interested and values the responses of everyone because everyone is heard and the responses are recorded on paper, the board or in a digital document. Hands can be called on for additional responses following the routine. Teachers can only adjust instruction based on the student needs that they perceive. *Domino Discover* and *Show and Share* are essential routines because while furthering student learning, teachers listen and observe students to consider their strengths and needs for effective learning.

Gather and Group routines of *Rumors* and *Sort and Post (or Place)* usually take more time than the *Share-Out* routines, such as *Domino Discover* and *Show and Share*. However, students receive more oral practice and feedback, and teachers finish with student responses sorted into groups versus one big list. These routines can be used at any time in the lesson, beginning, middle, or end. Anytime you want to find out what students are thinking and then use the thinking to form groups, the *Gather and Group* routines are the most efficient routine.

ALL-ED Classroom Routine Directions: Rumors

Rumors is a group learning routine where students write their individual responses on a sticky note or paper, share their responses with another student, listen to the partner's response, and then exchange or swap responses. Students continue sharing and swapping with other students to listen for patterns among the responses for a designated amount of time or number of "response swaps." Students must read the response each time before exchanging. At the end, students generate labels or categories of patterns that they perceived from their exchanges. The responses are sorted into categories, ending with patterns among student responses and the ability to see individual student responses.

Strengths of this routine:

- gets students on their feet and moving
- everyone has to engage in conversation
- requires students to listen and repeat the ideas of others
- allows many students to talk at the same time, no waiting for a turn
- patterns or groupings may be used to further instruction.

Implementation Directions

**Objective:** Exchange ideas to find similarities and differences.

**Starting Positions:** Ask students to jot down an idea on a sticky note or piece of paper along with their name. Ideas include:

- note three questions, put a star next to the most urgent to get answered
- sum up how you are feeling in a word
- identify a next step for learning
- list one strategy used to review for a test.

Note: Use only one idea at a time for _Rumors_. Ask students to star the most important question or idea if they have written more than one. Students will share the one question or idea with a star during _Rumors_.

Criteria

- _Must Haves_: Uses the word "because," explains with detail, includes visual representation of ideas.
- _Amazing_: Makes connection to previous unit or word, uses vocabulary from word wall.

Action Pattern

Directions: The teacher identifies in the directions:

- **Roles:** Speaker, Listener
- **Turns:** Simultaneously, all students pair up, then take turns being the speaker and then the listener.
- **Rules:** Students must read what is written on the rumor (they cannot just exchange or swap rumors without sharing them)
- **Time:** Three minutes

1. Invite students to join you in an open space with their completed Starting Position on a sticky note or piece of paper.
2. Tell students there are a lot of rumors going around about _____ (whatever the topic was for the rumor). Ask students what they know about rumors (e.g., they spread quickly and people repeat what they heard from other people).
3. Tell students that we are going to spread our rumors by going up to someone, reading our rumor, listening to their rumor, and then exchanging rumors. Then each person goes

up to another student and does the same thing again. Give the directions for the action pattern Listen, Read, Exchange. Students can use the name written on the rumor when they tell a rumor—"I heard from Marvin that ...".

4. Allow students to exchange ideas with as many people as possible in three minutes.

5. Stop the rumors. Ask a student who is currently holding a rumor that they think is similar to other rumors to read the rumor out loud. Post the rumor on a whiteboard or chart paper and then ask other students to post their rumor next to it if it could be in a group with this one. Ask students to read their rumor out loud as they post them in a group.

6. Encourage students to give the group of similar rumors a name. Ask for a very different rumor—and start a second group. Invite others to post similar rumors to make a second group and brainstorm a name for the new group of rumors.

7. Continue adding groups until all rumors are collected.

Reflections

1. Discuss what our rumors may tell us about our learning, questions, and ourselves.

2. Adjust instruction based on results from *Rumors*. For example, group students by similar rumors for a discussion or save original rumors and then have students return to their rumor after several lessons to reflect on how their thinking has stayed the same and/or changed.

Around the room routine, *Idea Carousel*, is particularly useful when you feel many students may not have an answer to your question. The collaboration allows students to learn from their peers and generate ideas collaboratively. Usually following the *Idea Carousel*, all students will be able to individually answer the question. *Idea Carousel* is a great routine when introducing or reviewing a topic, because students don't form individual responses to begin. Usually, it makes sense to assign the groups or to ask students to move to the prompt that they are ready to answer—this pushes students to begin at a place where they feel the greatest confidence and are more likely to participate because they have an idea to share. Students have plenty of time to practice speaking during *Idea Carousel* and the teacher gains essential listening time. You will notice a pattern for the structure of the routine always beginning with an objective, then offering criteria to monitor the quality of responses, and ending with reflection. Review the Research Roots in this chapter and notice how the structure of these routines prompts self-regulated learning. The structure of the routines leverages the recommendations from this research. By building on basic principles of motivation and cognitive science, ALL-ED provides teachers with a decision-making framework that will transform the learning climate into one where *all* students feel motivated to learn, both on their own and with others, and achieve durable learning outcomes.

Try Classroom Routines:

Precise, Effective, Efficient Learning for All

Plan: Choose Questions and Record Student Responses

Examine an upcoming lesson plan. Identify at least one question that you will ask where you could use a routine to record student responses. You will want to choose a question where student responses matter. For example, you may want to know if all students remember five vocabulary words, realize the steps to solving a problem, can infer a response to an abstract question, or remember what was read the day before. Then, recording student responses enables you to gather that information. Select a question that has multiple answers and that student responses matter, in terms of the next part of the lesson.

Teach: Rumors or FQA

To embark on your journey toward agile teacher thinking, consider simply recording student responses at least once during a lesson. For example, you might ask a big question, such as, "How does the energy from the sun get into the food that we eat?" or, "What will you remember from today's lesson?" As students raise their hands and are called on, you, a co-teacher, or a student can record the responses. These recorded responses act as a Starting Position, and can be used to help students to recognize their own growth. Routine recording of student responses during every lesson provides students a point to return to for reflection. Visible, written student responses provide students with additional benefits. For example, students needing longer language processing time or support with working memory can use the written list to understand student responses. Students who are simply sitting where it is hard to hear their peers can now read the written responses. Recorded responses provide all students with a means to engage in thinking instead of being confused because they missed what was said in class. Most importantly, this routine also offers teachers an opportunity to check for student understanding while lessons are in progress.

Choose one of the five routines to record responses to implement once in every lesson, *Domino Discover* (Chapter 2), *Show and Share* (Chapter 5), *Rumors* (Chapter 1), *Sort and Post (or Place)* (Chapter 5), and *Idea Carousel* (Chapter 7). These routines have many benefits for students, including promoting reflection, goal setting, and accountability while giving value and importance to student responses. At the same time, this routine provides teachers with needed data to clarify perceptions and then adjust instruction. For example, before a mini-lesson the teacher makes students record one question about the topic from each table and then adjusts instruction during the mini-lesson to answer the questions. This routine requires no planning time or any additional materials and expands teacher perceptions of student Starting Positions (including their questions) to adjust the lesson to the students who are in the classroom at that moment.

Adjust Instruction: React to Student Responses

Use the student responses that you have recorded in some way during the lesson. For example, you might add to the list of responses new ideas that emerge during the lesson. You might ask students which ideas from the recorded responses were talked about in class. If questions are recorded, then you might ask students how the questions were answered in the mini-lesson. If students are using *Must Have*-required vocabulary words in their responses, then you can adjust instruction to review other words or words that stretch students. Recording responses will give you a signal as to possible adjustments to instruction to spend time more strategically and to maintain a written record summarizing student learning.

Checklist to Try Routines in Your Teaching

See https://www.routledge.com/9780815370819 for additional resources: *Domino Discover* Step by Step Directions.

Plan	Teach	Adjust Instruction
☐ Plan to record student responses to at least one of your questions in every lesson. Plan possible ways to use student responses in the lesson.	☐ Rumors, FQA, or Domino Discover	☐ React to student responses during the lesson.

Quality Criteria to Implement Classroom Routines	
Must Haves	**Amazing**
• Classroom routine is implemented on a regular basis, either daily, weekly, or is tied to a specific type of instruction, such as a mini-lesson, independent practice, or review. • Identify criteria for high quality work when assigning at least one task in every lesson (for example, the teacher might say before asking students to share their ideas with a partner, called an *Elbow Exchange, Must Haves* for high quality listening means that you can repeat what your partner said to you; *Amazing* listening means that you can repeat and build on or ask a question about your partner's idea).	• Look at student work or student responses before planning the next lesson. • Record what students said that surprised you during the routines every day for at least one week. • Return to recorded responses to notice growth with students. • Use recorded responses to tailor instruction by answering questions that were raised or assigning a task or question related to their responses.

Chapter Reflection

Chapter Summary

In this chapter we explored why classroom routines promote student engagement from a motivational standpoint and from a cognitive perspective. We described the genesis of the ALL-ED framework and roots in both classroom practice and research. We synthesized motivation research into autonomy, belonging, competence, and meaning (**ABC+M**) and cognitive science into working memory, elaboration, retrieval, metacognition, and self-regulated learning (**WERMS**) for teachers to use as tools to plan more effective instruction and understand how learning happens. We encouraged you to try out routines that are rooted in science, yet practical to implement on a daily basis, such as establishing a Starting Position, the elaboration routine, *FQA*, and Recording Student Responses.

Learning Journal: Record Important Takeaways

Create a *Learning Journal* to track your thinking about meeting the needs of diverse learners by recording in a notebook or computer file answers to the following four questions:

1. What was most interesting and useful for you in this chapter?
2. Why was this interesting and useful?
3. How does this connect to what you know about meeting the learning needs of all learners?
4. What research from this chapter could you use to explain or support decisions to adjust instruction?

Save these responses for reflection after reading more of this book and trying out ideas in your classroom. We will answer these same four questions at the end of every chapter.

Return to Your Starting Position

Return to your preliminary first draft answer to our chapter question, "Why do classroom routines promote learning?" Add new ideas or revise in another way. Circle the most important part and save to return to after Chapter 4: Step Two: Look and Listen and Chapter 6: Step Four: SHOp Adjustments to see how your thinking both stays the same and changes as you read and try routines in your classroom.

Note

1. You may be wondering what the difference is between working memory and short-term memory. It's essentially the same thing, if you conceptualize working memory as a memory system that involves the temporary storage of information. But, as its

name denotes, you often do more than simply store information in working memory. Often you are engaging in strategies to keep information in there so that you can do something with it later. For example, in the spelling activity, you have to keep the symbol–letter connection in your working memory in order to actually perform the spelling test. This is why cognitive scientists now prefer to use the term "working memory" over "short-term memory." There are other more complicated aspects of working memory (e.g., episodic buffer, phonological loop, visuospatial sketch-pad, central executive) that we did not review here that also distinguish it from short-term memory.

References

American Psychological Association, Coalition for Psychology in Schools and Education. (2015). *Top 20 principles from psychology for pre-K–12 teaching and learning.* Retrieved from http://www.apa.org/ed/schools/cpse/top-twenty-principles.pdf

Baddeley, A. (2004). *Your memory: A user's guide.* Buffalo, NY: Firefly Books.

Baddeley, A., Eysenck, M., & Anderson, M. (2014). *Memory.* New York, NY: Psychology Press.

Bandura, A. (1997). *Self-efficacy: The exercise of control.* New York, NY: Freeman.

Brown, P. C., Roedinger, H. L., & McDaniel, M. A. (2014). *Make it stick: The science of successful learning.* Cambridge, MA: Harvard University Press.

Dweck, C. S. (2006). *Mindset: The new psychology of success.* New York, NY: Ballantine Books.

Hattie, J. (2009). *Visible learning: A synthesis of over 800 meta-analyses relating to achievement.* New York, NY: Routledge.

Kahneman, D. (2011). *Thinking fast and slow.* New York, NY: Farrar, Straus, and Giroux.

Kaplan, A., Sinai, M., & Flum, H. (2014). Design-based interventions for promoting students' identity exploration within the school curriculum. In S. Karabenick & T. Urdan (Eds.), *Motivational interventions: Advances in motivation and achievement* (Vol. 18, pp. 243–291). Bingley, England: Emerald Group Publishing.

Lazowski, R., & Hulleman, C. (2016). Motivational interventions in education: A meta-analytic review. *Review of Educational Research, 86,* 602–640. doi:10.3102/0034654315617832

Linnenbrink-Garcia, L., & Patall, E. A. (2016). Motivation. In L. Corno & E. Anderman (Eds.), *Handbook of educational psychology* (3rd ed.) (pp. 91–103). New York, NY: Routledge.

Maehr, M. L., & Zusho, A. (2009). Achievement goal theory: The past, present, and future. In K. Wentzel & A. Wigfield (Eds.), *Handbook of motivation in school* (pp. 76–104). New York, NY: Routledge.

Mayer, R. E. (2011). *Applying the science of learning.* New York, NY: Pearson.

Pickering, S. J. (2006). *Working memory and education.* Burlington, MA: Academic Press.

Pintrich, P. R., & Zusho, A. (2007). Student motivation and self-regulated learning in the college classroom. In R. Perry & J. Smart (Eds.), *The scholarship of teaching and learning in higher education* (pp. 731–810). Dordrecht, The Netherlands: Springer.

Roseth, C. J., Johnson, D. W., & Johnson, R. T. (2008). Promoting early adolescents' achievement and peer relationships: The effects of cooperative, competitive, and individualistic goal structures. *Psychological Bulletin*, 134, 223–246. doi:10.1037/0033-2909.134.2.223

Ryan, R., & Deci, E. (2017). *Self-determination theory: Basic psychological needs in motivation, development, and wellness.* New York, NY: Guilford.

Turner, J. C. (2014). Theory-based interventions with middle-school teachers to support student motivation and engagement. In S. Karabenick & T. Urdan (Eds.), *Advances in motivation and achievement: Motivational interventions* (pp. 341–378). Bingley, UK: Emerald http://dx.doi.org/10.1108/S0749-742320140000018009

Wentzel, K. R. (2010). Students' relationships with teachers. In J. Meece & J. Eccles (Eds.), *Handbook of research on schools, schooling, and human development* (pp. 75–91). New York, NY: Routledge.

White, M. C., & DiBenedetto, M. K. (2015). *Self-regulation and the common core: Application to ELA standards.* New York, NY: Routledge.

Wigfield, A., & Eccles, J. S. (2000). Expectancy-value theory of achievement motivation. *Contemporary Educational Psychology*, 25, 68–81.

Zimmerman, B. J., (1990). Self-regulated learning and academic achievement: An overview. *Educational Psychologist*, 25, 3–17.

Zimmerman, B. J., & Schunk, D. H. (2011). *Handbook of self-regulation of learning and performance.* New York, NY: Routledge.

Reading 2.5

Peer Mediation

A Means of Differentiating Classroom Instruction

Douglas Fuchs, Lynn S. Fuchs

Vanderbilt University

Adina Shamir

Bar Ilan University (Israel)

Eric Dion

University of Quebec at Montreal

Laura M. Saenz

University of Texas—Pan American

Kristen L. McMaster

University of Minnesota

PICTURE THIS: 34 CHILDREN IN AN urban third-grade classroom, one third of whom live in poverty. Six live with grandparents, *and three are in foster care. Five come from homes in which a language other than English is spoken; two children do not speak English at all. Seven, six, five, three, two, and one are African American, Hispanic American, Korean, Russian, Haitian, and Chinese, respectively. Six are new to the school, and four will relocate to a different school next year. Only five of the 34 students are at or above grade level in reading; 10 are two or more grade levels below. There is a 5-grade spread in reading achievement. In addition, three students have been certified as learning disabled. One is severely mentally retarded, and another is deaf. According to the Department of Health and Human Services, the child with mental retardation and two other students in the class have been physically or sexually abused.*

The teacher of this imaginary but arguably representative (see Headden, 1995; Hodgkinson, 1991, 1995; Jenkins, Jewell, Leicester, Jenkins, & Troutner, 1990; Natriello, McDill, & Pallas, 1990; Puma, Jones, Rock, & Fernandez, 1993) urban class is Mr. Stasis, who believes it is his job to present information, his students' job to listen and learn. His stand-and-deliver approach reflects the view that teaching is a centralized and unidirectional phenomenon. Mr. Stasis uses the texts in reading, mathematics, social studies, and science that were adopted by his district's central office. And, on orders from this office, his students get these books regardless of their reading level and math skills.

We (Fuchs, Fuchs, Mathes, & Simmons, 1996) wrote this more than 10 years ago to describe the serious disconnect in many communities between students' diversity of languages, cultures, experiences, and readiness to learn and the uniformity of classroom instruction. Educators in school buildings, district offices, and universities recognize this disconnect as an important, if not primary, cause of hundreds of thousands of students' poor learning. Many would say that what Mr. Stasis's class needs first and foremost is *differentiated instruction.*

For more than a decade, differentiated instruction has been one of the "it" phrases in K–12 education. Teachers who differentiate their instruction have been described as leveraging knowledge about their students' varying experiences, interests, learning styles, and readiness levels; conveying information in multiple sensory modalities; grouping children flexibly; varying the pace of their instruction; and assessing student learning with varied and balanced measures and procedures (cf. Kapusnick & Hauslien, 2001; Tomlinson, 1999). Differentiated instruction has been advanced by some as a tested strategy for accelerating student learning and for celebrating their diversity (e.g., Carolan & Guinn, 2007)—promoted even as a biological imperative. In this last regard, Tomlinson and Kalbfleisch (1998) wrote, "the amassed understandings about how the brain works have added to our considerable research base on the importance of ... curriculum and instruction ... responsive to individual learning needs" (p. 53).

Enthusiasm for differentiated instruction notwithstanding, there is persuasive evidence that most classrooms are bereft of it, a fact undiminished by the occasional description of exemplary instructors (cf. Pressley, Allington, Wharton-McDonald, Block, & Morrow, 2001). Baker and Zigmond (1990), for example, conducted interviews and observations in reading and math classes in an elementary school to explore whether teachers implement routine adaptations (e.g., differentiating instruction by creating multiple reading groups to accommodate weak-to-strong readers at the start of the school year). The researchers found no evidence of routine adaptations. Rather, they reported that teachers typically taught to large groups, using lessons incorporating little or no differentiation based on student needs. McIntosh, Vaughn, Schumm, Haager, and Lee (1994) described similar results from their observations of 60 social studies and science classrooms across Grades 3 to 12.

L. Fuchs, Fuchs, and Bishop (1992) explored whether general and special educators used *specialized*, not routinized, adaptations (i.e., instruction deliberately customized in response to an individual student's difficulty). They administered a Teacher Planning Questionnaire to 25 general educators and 37 special educators whose responses reflected a view that individualized instruction and small-group instruction were not important to their students' academic success—a result also found by Baker and Zigmond (1990), D. Fuchs, Fuchs, and Fernstrom (1993), D. Fuchs, Roberts, Fuchs, and Bowers (1996), Peterson and Clark (1978), and Zigmond and Baker (1994). Others have expressed a different take on why educators often fail to differentiate instruction. This perspective sometimes begins with the fact, dramatized at the start of this chapter, that many classroom teachers, especially those in large urban school districts, are faced with a considerable diversity of languages and cultures and a broad range of academic performance. Peterson and Clark (1978), Brown and Saks (1981, 1987), and Gerber and Semmel (1984) have written that teachers typically react to this student heterogeneity by ignoring it; that is, by monitoring student performance in selective fashion, and by teaching to the more academically accomplished students.

According to Schumm and Vaughn and their colleagues, teachers in Grades 3 through 12, whom they interviewed in focus groups and observed in classrooms, are unresponsive to this student diversity because they believe themselves lacking in necessary knowledge and skills (e.g., Schumm & Vaughn, 1992; Schumm, Vaughn, Gordon, & Rothstein, 1994). Further, say their teachers, even if they were more knowledgeable and skillful, providing differentiated instruction would be nearly impossible because of inadequate resources for the necessary comprehensive and systematic monitoring of student performance.

More recently, Tomlinson and Allan (2003) struck the very same note by quoting Darling-Hammond: "After a decade of reform, we have finally learned in hindsight what should have been clear from the start: Most schools and teachers cannot produce the kind of learning demanded by the new reforms—not because they do not want to, but because they don't know how, and the systems in which they work do not support them in doing so" (p. 78; also see Leithwood, Leonard, & Sharratt,1998). Irrespective of why teachers typically do not provide differentiated instruction, its absence clearly contributes to the school failure of many at-risk children. Findings from numerous studies document that many low-achieving children, including those with special needs, not only fail to obtain differentiated instruction but receive less *undifferentiated* instruction and practice than their more accomplished classmates (e.g., Delquadri, Greenwood, Whorton, Carta, & Hall, 1986; Hall, Delquadri, Greenwood, & Thurston, 1982; Lesgold & Resnick, 1982; McDermott & Aron, 1978; O'Sullivan, Ysseldyke, Christenson, & Thurlow, 1990).

Helping teachers differentiate their instruction is surely one of the most important and difficult challenges facing public schools in the 21st century. There are various reasons for this. One is definitional, which is to say that "differentiated instruction" is often defined so broadly as to become ambiguous. Hall's (2002) conceptualization is typical: "To differentiate instruction is to recognize students [vary in] background knowledge, readiness, language, [modes of learning], [and] interests.... The intent of differentiating instruction is to maximize each student's growth ... by meeting each student where he or she is, and assisting in the learning process."

Whereas Hall (2002) and others identify or promote various components of differentiated instruction—components that address instructional content, processes, and products—there is no consensus on which components are necessary and sufficient. There is no agreed upon understanding of what exactly it is. Additionally, there is little evidence that anyone's proposed components—alone or in combination—positively effect students' academic achievement. Hall remarks, "Based on [my] review ... the 'package' itself [i.e., differentiated instruction] is lacking empirical validation. There is an acknowledged and decided gap in the literature in this area and future research is warranted. [Nevertheless] there [is] a generous number of testimonials and classroom examples. ..." Without a clear conception of the construct and an absence of research that connects specific and replicable implementations to student achievement, it is impossible to provide classroom teachers with meaningful professional development and support.

One promising approach is peer-mediated instruction, whereby children work together to support each others' learning. The connection between peer-mediation and differentiated instruction is that peer-mediation represents an important re-organization of the conventional classroom; an alternative to the "sage-on-stage" and "stand-and-deliver" approach to learning and teaching; a decentralized learning environment. This decentralization provides teachers (and students-as-teachers) with opportunities for customizing goals, activities, supports, and accountability that do not exist in more conventional classrooms. Below we discuss several research-backed peer-mediated programs for the elementary grades, emphasizing Peer-Assisted Learning Strategies (PALS; e.g., Fuchs, Fuchs, Mathes, & Sim-mons, 1997). Because most of these programs are explicit, they address the vagueness associated with many current approaches to differentiated instruction; because they are scripted (or partially scripted), they speak to teachers who complain they lack requisite knowledge; and because they are inexpensive, they connect to teachers' concerns that they don't have adequate resources.

Peer-Mediated Approaches to Instruction

Broadly speaking, there have been two groups developing peer-mediated approaches to teaching and learning: a socio-cultural group and cognitive-behavioral group. Many in the socio-cultural group base their R&D on Vygotsky's (1978) theorizing, which reflects a belief that mastery of complex skills and the development of underlying cognitive processes occur as a result of repeated inteactions between novice and expert. The expert initially compensates for the novices weaknesses by accomplishing parts of a task, but gradually pushes the novice toward more autonomous and mature performance through a series of scaffolded interactions. The cognitive-behavioral group, as the term implies, taps either cognitive theories (e.g., Palincsar & Brown, 1984) or Direct Instruction principles (e.g., Carnine, Silbert, Kameenui, & Tarver, 2004; Delquadri et al., 1986) or a combination of the two (e.g., Fuchs et al., 1997).

A Sociocultural Approach

The Peer Mediation with Young Children (PYMC; Shamir & Tzuriel, 2002, 2004) program is based on Vygotsky's (1929, 1962, 1978, 1981) sociocultural theory and Feuerstein's "mediated learning experience" (MLE) theory (Feuerstein, Rand, & Hoffman, 1979). According to Vygotsky, learning takes place through interactions between children and more competent persons, whether adults or peers. For Feuerstein, MLE helps children adapt previously learned principals and competencies to new circumstances and, in so doing, "children learn how to learn." Although Feuerstein characterized MLE in terms of 12 interaction-based criteria, only the first five have been proceduralized. They are: (a) focusing on the problem; (b) attaching meaning to the stimulus and its characteristics by labeling an object; (c) transcendence, or the application of acquired information to new knowledge domains by employing principles and procedures already learned; (d) regulation of behavior through attempts to control responses before, during, and after task performance or problem-solving; and (e) mediation of feelings of competence by providing positive feedback while explaining successful performance.

These criteria were used in the development of the PMYC program because they have been found in research to predict cognitive modifiability and self-regulation. In the PMYC program, the five MLE criteria were translated into a series of age- and capacity-adjusted statements and questions directed at children's learning experiences: Below is the transcript of a partial interaction between a mediator (M; or tutor) and learner (L; or tutee) concerning math computation. The mediator's (tutor's) use of MLE criteria are shown in parentheses.

Researcher: Which topic would you like to choose?
  (Focusing on the problem)
L: (Points at the screen.)
M: This is the 100 range (Meaning) Wow ... good for you! *(Mediation of feelings of competence)*
L: (Chooses a game.)
M: 42 divided by 7?
L: (Immediately states the answer and types it.)
M: Very good. *(Mediation of feelings of competence)*

M: Press the block 6 times 8?

L: That's hard.

M: Do it like this: 8 plus 8 plus 8 plus ... (*Transcendence*)

L: 8 plus 8 is 16.

M: Think again before answering ... 16 plus 16? (*Regulation of behaviour*)

L: That's hard....

M: Check, how much is 10 plus 10?

L: 20. Ah, the answer is 32.

M: Good, you checked and succeeded. (*Mediation of feelings of Competence*).

M: Now, 32 plus 16.

L: 45.

M: Think again. (*Regulation of behavior*)

L: 46. (Types the answer. The computer's response—think again).

M: Think about the rule. (*Regulation of behavior*)

L: 48. (Types the answer.)

M: Wow ... It's good you work according to the rules. (*Mediation of feelings of competence*)

M: Press the block. 7 times 7?

L: 49.

M: Good! You did it! (*Mediation of feelings of competence*)

M: 9 times 9?

L: 80 ... 1 ... (Types an answer.)

M: Good!. 7 times 9? That's like nine sevens. (*Transcendence*)

L: 7 times 9 is ... (L is about to press the wrong answer.)

M: No! You have to think again; think how we did it before. (*Regulation of behaviour*)

L: Oops. (Types an answer.)

M: Great! You solved it correctly. (*Mediation of feelings of competence*)

M: And 56 divided by 8?

The PMYC program is delivered in heterogeneous classrooms by means of cross-age tutoring; that is, involving an older child as tutor and younger child as tutee. The program is conducted for 3 weeks, and is divided into 7 lessons, each of which is constructed to include 3 basic components: (a) directly teaching MLE principles, (b) observing and discussing a film in which the principles are demonstrated, and (c) practicing peer mediation using multimedia and more conventional materials. The videotaped demonstrations are used to reinforce internalization of the peer-mediation principles. The multi-media and more conventional learning aids include special computer programs, games, posters, stickers with visual symbols of the principles, verbal slogans and work sheets. The tutor's experience with the MLE criteria is structured by a metacognitive training process (Brown, 1987; Flavell, 1979) embedded in the PMYC program. The training is consequently meant to nurture *metacognitive knowledge* about mental processes, task characteristics, and performance-oriented cognitive strategies; *metacognitive experience*, or self-awareness and monitoring of one's own mental processes; and *metacognitive control* of mental processes (self-regulation) directed at the construction and application of strategies appropriate for the completion of learning tasks. In the course of the program, these processes are gradually internalized as integrated cognitive mechanisms to be activated during learning.

The PMYC program, consequently, is designed to help tutors apply MLE criteria to their own learning experiences. They are expected to achieve this by exercising associated skills in a peer-mediated context. In other words, participation in the PMYC program and subsequent peer tutoring promotes a cognitive reconstruction of the child's meta-cognitive skills together with the MLE principles acquired during the PMYC program (for further details see Shamir & Lazerovitz, 2007). Research has indicated positive effects of the PMYC program on tutors' mediation style, cognitive modifiability and self-regulated learning in general domains (Shamir & Tzuriel, 2002, 2004; Shamir, Tzuriel, & Guy, 2007; Shamir & Van der Aalsvoort, 2004; Tzuriel & Shamir, 2007) as well as in specific domains such as math (Shamir, Tzuriel, & Rozen, 2006).

Recently, the PMYC program was implemented with children with LD (Shamir & Lazerovitz 2007). On the basis of previous studies, it was assumed that tutors with LD, once exposed to the program and later peer tutoring, would demonstrate improved self-regulation and performance. The tutors' self-regulated learning was measured by modifications in their mediation style (process of tutoring) and capacity to benefit from adult mediation for analogical thinking (outcomes of tutoring). The study involved 162 pupils, demonstrating considerable diversity of academic needs: 81 (tutors) from Grade 5 and 81 (tutees) from Grade 2. Tutors were chosen from classes of children with LD as defined by the National Joint Committee on Learning Disabilities and adopted by Israel's Ministry of Education (Margalit, 2000). Tutees were randomly selected from regular classes. Tutor and tutee pairs were assigned randomly to either an experimental (PMYC) or control (No PMYC) group. (Control children, however, practiced peer tutoring without experiencing the PMYC intervention.) During the final tutoring session, the children's interactions were videotaped and later assessed with the Observation of Mediation Instrument. The tutors also completed a Dynamic Assessment Analogies Test.

When compared to controls, tutors with LD in the PMYC group improved their mediation style, cognitive modifiability and self-regulated learning and performance, expressed in improved scores on an analogies test across the pre-intervention, adult mediation, and post-intervention phases of the study. Findings demonstrate the contribution peer tutoring can make when applied in academically-diverse general education classrooms. The fact that the tutors with LD successfully participated in active peer-assisted learning likewise lends support to the model's relevance for children with special needs.

Cognitive-Behavioral Approaches

Reciprocal Teaching

Palincsar and Brown's (1984) reciprocal teaching method is a small-group intervention designed to improve low achievers' reading comprehension. Students read a passage of expository material, paragraph by paragraph. While reading, they learn and practice how to generate questions, summarize, clarify word meanings and confusing text, and predict subsequent paragraphs. Vygotsky's influence may be seen equally clearly in Reciprocal Teaching as in the PMYC program. In the early stages of Reciprocal Teaching, the teacher models these strategies; then students practice them on the next section of text as the teacher tailors feedback through modeling, coaching, hints, and explanations. The teacher also invites students to react to peers' statements by elaborating or commenting, suggesting other questions, requesting clarifications, and helping to resolve misunderstandings. In the course of this guided practice, the teacher gradually shifts responsibility to the students for mediating discussions, as the teacher observes and helps as needed. At this point, sessions become dialogues among students as they support each other and alternate between prompting the use of a strategy, applying and verbalizing that strategy, and commenting on the application.

Palincsar and Brown (1986) have successfully popularized the notion that reading comprehension can and should be taught explicitly, and they have developed an imaginative and apparently effective means of doing so. At the same time, some concern has been expressed about Reciprocal Teaching's feasibility and usability. Its relatively complex and unfamiliar strategic comprehension strategies can be difficult for teachers and students to master (Pressley, 1997), with the result that many low-achieving students may be inconsistently involved (Hacker & Tenant, 2002). In addition, the program may be more appropriate for older than younger elementary age children, where its effects are less clear (e.g., Rosenshine & Meister, 1994).

Cooperative Integrated Reading and Composition (CIRC; e.g., Stevens, Madden, Slavin, & Farnish, 1987). Cooperative learning, according to Slavin (1994), relies on teamwork with group rewards that are dependent on a team score reflecting all members' achievement. The team whose members obtain the highest average on individual weekly quizzes is declared classroom "team of week." The idea is to encourage mutual helping among team-mates so that all learn. Student groups are deliberately heterogeneous with high- and low-achievers (including students with LD), distributed evenly among them. A well-researched example of cooperative learning programs is CIRC.

CIRC replaces all regular reading and composition activities of second- to sixth-grade elementary classrooms (Stevens et al., 1987). It comes with its own materials, as well as detailed lesson plans for teachers. Each new reading text is introduced to the class during a teacher-led activity, which is followed by peer-mediated activities, including oral story reading and answering of comprehension questions. For some of these activities, students work in pairs rather than in small groups. At the end of the cycle of activities, students take individual quizzes and teams are rewarded if they meet the criterion. Text composition is also taught by the teacher and practiced by students during a cycle of drafting and editing with feedback from peers. Students accumulate points for their team by being productive writers.

Several teams of investigators exploring the effectiveness of CIRC have demonstrated positive results for students with and without disabilities (Slavin, Madden, & Leavey, 1984; Stevens et al., 1987; Stevens, Slavin, & Farnish, 1991). Especially impressive are Stevens and Slavin's (1995) results. In this study, teachers mainstreamed students with LD and, with the help of their special education colleagues, implemented CIRC for two consecutive school years. At study's end, students with LD in CIRC classes outperformed students with LD in non-CIRC classes on reading comprehension, vocabulary, and basic writing skills. Similar results were obtained for non-disabled students.

There is more to the story, however, about cooperative learning and students with disabilities. McMaster and Fuchs (2002) searched for published studies between 1990 and 2000, inclusive, whose authors' examined effects of cooperative learning on the academic achievement of mainstreamed students with LD. Only studies that employed an experimental or quasi-experimental design were considered. Less than half of the studies meeting inclusion criteria reported statistically significant differences in favor of students with LD in cooperative learning classes. That is, in a majority of studies, cooperative learning did *not* promote the academic achievement of students with LD beyond what they would have achieved in business-as-usual classes.

One explanation of these outcomes has focused on the inconsistent involvement of low achievers, including students with LD, in team activities. Low achievers are sometimes inadvertently or purposefully excluded from these activities by other team members who ignore their contributions or give them answers without explanations (Jenkins & O'Connor, 2003). One way to circumvent this exclusion is to reduce group size to two members, creating a situation in which paired students have little choice but to work together.

Classwide Peer Tutoring (CWPT; e.g., Delquadri, Greenwood, Whorton, Carta, & Hall, 1986). Organizing students into same-age dyads is the instructional format adopted by those who have explored peer-tutoring activities. Delquadri and his colleagues have done much to validate this approach and generate interest in it—specifically, by their work on CWPT. They designed CWPT activities to facilitate rote learning (e.g., word spelling) by allowing students ample practice in a fast-paced, supportive context with immediate corrective feedback (e.g., Delquadri et al., 1986). At the beginning of each week, students in a given classroom are paired randomly with a new partner and given lists of spelling words, simple mathematical problems and reading assignments from their basal text. For a few minutes each day, partners alternate roles of tutor and tutee, asking each other questions and reading aloud. The pair earns points for correct answers, reading without errors, and correcting their mistakes. Each pair is assigned to one of two classroom teams and the points the pairs accumulate go to their team. A winner is declared each week. Points and teams are meant to serve only as motivation.

A majority of teachers and students conduct these activities well enough to bring about notable improvement in basic skills mastery (Greenwood, Terry, Arreaga-Mayer, & Finney, 1992). In the most ambitious study of the effectiveness of CWPT, Greenwood, Delquadri, and Hall (1989) randomly assigned first-grade classrooms to either experimental or control conditions. Experimental students participated in CWPT activities from first to fourth grade. At the end of their fourth-grade year, experimental students demonstrated superior reading, language, and mathematics scores on a standardized test. Furthermore, students in CWPT classes were less likely to have been given a high-incidence disability label (e.g., LD or behavioral disorders; Greenwood, Terry, Utley, Montagna, & Walker, 1993).

The effectiveness of CWPT for mainstreamed students with disabilities has also been examined in multiple case studies, with generally positive results (e.g., Sideridis et al., 1997). A drawback of CWPT seems to be its focus on basic skills. To be sure, repeated practice of basic skills with immediate corrective feedback is essential for many low achievers and students with disabilities (e.g., Torgesen et al., 1999). But such exclusive focus de-emphasizes higher-order skills (e.g., conceptual mathematical understanding), which may make CWPT seem somewhat non-aligned with current curriculum reform (Gersten & Baker, 1998).

Peer-Assisted Learning Strategies (PALS), to which we now turn, were developed with the goal of combining the supportive, engaging, and practical dyadic format of CWPT with some of the rich, challenging content of Reciprocal Teaching and CIRC. If we had to place PALS and the three cognitive-behavioral approaches just described on a continuum of "most opportunity" and "least opportunity" for differentiated instruction, we would locate Reciprocal Teaching towards "most"; PALS towards "least." This is because PALS is more strictly routinized; more directive in terms of permissible student action and language. And yet, PALS still affords participants opportunity for modifying instructional materials, activities, rewards, and expectations for performance. One dyad in a class of fourth graders, for example, may include a student reading on a second grade level and, because of this, she and her partner are reading text reflecting this skill level. Another pair in the same class, however, may be reading at a fifth grade level. Because the class is divided into multiple dyads, this variation in instructional material can be accommodated. Because of the opportunity for this kind of general flexibility and modification of tasks, teachers have been able to include virtually all their students in PALS.

PALS programs in reading have been developed and field-tested for preschool (D. Fuchs et al., 2004), kindergarten (D. Fuchs, Fuchs, Thompson, Al Otaiba, Yen, McMaster, et al., 2001; D. Fuchs, Fuchs, Thompson, Al Otaiba, Yen, Yang, et al., 2001; D. Fuchs et al., 2002), first grade (D. Fuchs, Fuchs, Svenson, et al., 2001; D. Fuchs, Fuchs, Yen, et al., 2001), second through sixth grade (D. Fuchs, Fuchs, Mathes, & Martinez, 2002; Fuchs et al., 1996; D. Fuchs et al. 1997), and high school (L. S. Fuchs, Fuchs, & Kazdan, 1999). Following is a description of two of these reading programs: Grade 2–6 PALS and First-Grade PALS.

Grade 2–6 PALS: Overall Program Effects

In a series of quasi-experimental studies, Fuchs and colleagues tested the contributions of various components of Grade 2–6 PALS. In one such study Simmons, Fuchs, Fuchs, Pate, & Mathes (1994) determined that a relatively complex set of peer-mediated activities supported greater student learning than did a set of simpler CWPT peer-mediated activities. In the same study, they also found that role reciprocity, where students of a pair serve as both tutor and tutee in each session, promoted greater reading gains than a more static arrangement whereby tutors and tutees did *not* exchange roles. Across several years, then, Fuchs and associates frequently added and subtracted components based on their relative effectiveness and feasibility, finally settling on a "package" they believed to boost reading performance and which was perceived by teachers as practical for classrooms use. Below, we describe this PALS program and two quasi-experimental investigations of its effectiveness. The first was conducted with children whose primary language was English (Fuchs et al., 1996); the second, with children with limited English proficiency (Saenz, Fuchs, & Fuchs, 2005).

The PALS Intervention

Each week, teachers conduct three 35-minute PALS sessions as part of their allocated reading time, implementing PALS with all children in their classes. Teachers begin the program by conducting seven lessons on how to implement PALS. Each of these training lessons lasts 45 to 60 minutes and incorporates teacher presentations, student recitation of information and application of principles, and teacher feedback on student implementation (see Fuchs, Fuchs, Mathes, & Simmons, 2008, for the teacher manual).

During PALS, like CWPT, every student in the class is paired; each pair includes a higher- and lower-performing student. The teacher determines pairs by first ranking students from strongest to weakest reader, then calculating a median split, and finally pairing the strongest reader from the top half of the rankings with the strongest reader from the bottom half and so on. Although tutoring roles are reciprocal, the higher-performing student reads first for each activity to serve as model for the lower-performing student. Both students read from material appropriate for the lower reader, which typically is literature selected by the teacher.

Pairs are assigned to one of two teams for which they earn points. Students give points to themselves for completing reading activities correctly and teachers award points to pairs who demonstrate good tutoring behavior. Each pair keeps track of points on a consecutively numbered score card, which represents joint effort and achievement. Each time a student earns a point, the tutor slashes the next number. At the end of the week, each pair reports the last number slashed as the pair's total; the teacher sums each team's points; and the class applauds the winning team. Every 4 weeks, the teacher creates new pairs and team assignments. Thus, like CIRC, the motivational system combines competitive (team vs. team) and cooperative (combined effort of the pair) structures.

The first activity in every PALS session is *Partner Reading*. Each student reads connected text aloud for 5 minutes, for a total of 10 minutes. The higher-performing student reads first; the lower-performing student rereads the same material. After both students read, the lower-performing student retells for 2 minutes the sequence of what occurred. Students earn 1 point for each correctly read sentence and 10 points for the retell.

The second PALS activity, *Paragraph Shrinking*, was inspired by Reciprocal Teaching. It is designed to develop comprehension through summarization and main idea identification. Students read orally one paragraph at a time, stopping to identify its main idea. Tutors guide the identification of the main idea by asking readers to identify who or what the paragraph is mainly about and the most important thing about the who or what. Readers put these two pieces of information together in 10 or fewer words. For each summary, students earn 1 point for correctly identifying who or what; 1 point for correctly stating the most important thing about the who or what; and 1 point for using no more than 10 words. Students continue to monitor and correct reading errors, but points no longer are awarded for reading sentences correctly. After 5 minutes, students switch roles.

The last activity is *Prediction Relay*. It extends Paragraph Shrinking to larger chunks of text and requires students to formulate and check predictions. Prediction Relay comprises five steps. The reader makes a prediction about what will be learned on the next half page; reads the half page aloud while the tutor corrects reading errors; confirms or disconfirms the prediction; and summarizes the main idea. Students earn 1 point for each correct prediction; 1 point for reading each half page; 1 point for accurately confirming each prediction; and 1 point for each summary component (identifying the who or what, what mainly happened, and making the main idea statement in 10 words or less). After 5 minutes, students switch roles.

Effects on English-Proficient Students at Various Levels of Achievement

To study the effects of Grade 2–6 PALS on English-proficient students at different achievement levels, Fuchs et al. (1997) assigned 12 schools, stratified on academic achievement and family income, to experimental (PALS) and control (No-PALS) groups. At Grades 2–6, 20 teachers implemented PALS; 20 did not. PALS teachers implemented the treatment class-wide, but only three students in each class were identified as study participants: one with LD in reading, one low achiever never referred for special education (LA), and one average achiever (AA). Each of these students was identified by the classroom teacher as either typical of the children with LD or representative of LA and AA students in her class. All selected students spoke English as their primary language. Each was tested with the Comprehensive Reading Assessment Battery (CRAB; Fuchs et al., 1997) before and after PALS implementation, which lasted 15 weeks. Fidelity data, collected 3 times during classroom observations, indicated strong teacher and student implementation. Teacher-completed instructional plan sheets revealed that PALS and No-PALS teachers allocated comparable time to reading instruction.

We analyzed student achievement data using treatment (PALS vs. No-PALS), trial (pre-treatment testing vs. post-treatment testing), and student type (LD vs. LA vs. AA) as factors. Treatment was a between-group factor and trial and student type were within-group factors. Classroom was the unit of analysis. We found statistically significant treatment by trial interactions on all CRAB scores. These interactions indicated that, compared to students in business-as-usual No-PALS classrooms, PALS students grew more on reading fluency, accuracy, and comprehension. Moreover, the 3-way interaction between treatment, trial, and student type was not statistically significant. So, PALS effects were not mediated by students' initial achievement status. Aggregated across the LD, LA, and AA students, effect sizes were 0.22, 0.55, and 0.56, respectively, on the CRAB words read correctly, CRAB questions answered correctly, and CRAB maze blanks restored correctly. These effects compare favorably with more comprehensive and complex cooperative learning programs. As reported by Slavin (1994), the median effect size for 52 studies of cooperative learning treatments that lasted more than 4 weeks was 0.32, a figure identical to the one reported by Rosenshine and Meister (1994) for Reciprocal Teaching.

Effects on Students with Limited English Proficiency (LEP) at Various Levels of Achievement

Saenz et al. (2005) conducted a study paralleling the Fuchs et al. (1997) investigation just described, with these important differences. First, participants were 12 teachers in South Texas, working in schools that served a mostly LEP population. From each class, Saenz et al. sampled only students ($n = 132$) who were native Spanish speaking and who were identified by their school district as LEP according to Texas eligibility criteria. Second, in contrast to Fuchs et al., Saenz et al. included high-achieving classmates (HA) from each participating classroom so that 11 children were pre- and post-tested from each class: 2 LD, 3 LA, 3 AA, and 3 HA. PALS was implemented in English for 15 weeks with strong fidelity.

As with Fuchs et al. (1997), CRAB data supported PALS effectiveness. On CRAB questions answered correctly, for example, PALS students outperformed No-PALS students, and the effect sizes were large: 1.06 for LD, 0.86 for LA, 0.60 for AA, and 1.02 for HA (across student types, 1.02). So, Saenz et al.'s findings extend those of prior work supporting PALS by including both LEP students and students who began their PALS participation reading better than their classmates (i.e., the HA students in PALS classrooms improved their reading comprehension in comparison to HA students in No-PALS classes). For those with interest in LEP children, also see McMaster, Kung, Han, and Cao (2008) for an evaluation of the Kindergarten PALS program involving LEP children in the Minneapolis Public Schools.

Across Both Efficacy Studies

Across the Fuchs et al. (1997) and Saenz et al. (2005) studies, results demonstrate the potential of PALS to enhance children's reading comprehension. The source, or "active ingredient," of the program's apparent effectiveness may reside both in its specific activities and in its overall organization. PALS-related activities—taken from or inspired by Reciprocal Teaching, CIRC, and CWPT—encourage students to practice research-based strategies, which have been shown to strengthen reading comprehension when implemented regularly on instructional-level text. With respect to organization, PALS organizes highly structured, reciprocal, one-to-one interaction, which (a) provides all students with frequent opportunity to respond, (b) facilitates immediate corrective feedback, (c) increases academic engaged time, and (d) offers social support and encouragement, with all students sharing the esteem associated with the tutoring role. Moreover, with the PALS score-card system, students work cooperatively with partners but compete in teams to earn points. We have often observed that this keeps students working in a focused, productive, and constructive manner.

Finally, PALS materials are concrete, specific, and user friendly—important criteria if practices are to be implemented (see McLaughlin cited in Gersten, Vaughn, Deshler, & Schiller, 1995). A comprehensive teacher manual guides implementation; there is no need for teachers to develop additional materials. Finally, PALS can complement most instructional approaches, including whole language as well as explicit phonics because it supplements, rather than substitutes for, teachers' ongoing reading practices. We know this because we have worked closely with many PALS teachers over the years, including strong advocates of implicit approaches and others preferring more explicit strategies.

First-Grade PALS

Over the past decade, Grade 2–6 PALS has been extended downward to address the development of reading and pre-reading skills at preschool, kindergarten, and first grade (see D. Fuchs & Fuchs, 2005, for a summary). First-Grade PALS parallels the organization of PALS at the higher grades, but its activities and content are different.

Overview of First-Grade PALS

All students in First-Grade PALS classrooms are divided into pairs based on their rapid letter naming performance. A higher- and lower-achieving student constitutes each pair. The higher-performing student is always the Coach (tutor) first. When the pair completes an activity, the students switch roles and repeat the activity. Partners change every 4 weeks. In contrast to PALS in higher grades, First-Grade PALS sessions begin by the teacher conducting 5 minutes of instruction: introducing new letter sounds and sight words and leading students in segmenting and blending activities. Then, students participate in pairs in Sounds & Words and Partner Reading.

The first Sounds & Words activity is *letter-sound correspondence*, lasting 3 minutes. The Coach points to a letter and prompts the Reader to say its sound. If the Reader makes a mistake or does not know the sound of a letter, the Coach uses a correction procedure. When the Reader has said all of the sounds, the Coach marks a happy face on a lesson sheet and five points on a point sheet. Partners then switch roles and repeat the activity.

The second Sounds & Words activity involves *segmenting and blending* the 8–10 words used during the teacher-directed instruction. The Coach prompts the Reader to sound out a word, and then directs the Reader to "Say it fast." The Reader responds by reading the word. If the Reader makes a mistake, the Coach uses a correction procedure. When the 8–10 words have been segmented and blended, the Coach marks a happy face on the lesson sheet and five points on the point sheet, and the partners switch roles and repeat the activity. This task lasts 5 minutes.

Sight word practice is the third Sounds & Words activity. The Coach points to each word and prompts the Reader to read it by saying, "What word." If the Reader says the wrong word, the Coach uses a correction procedure. The Coach marks a happy face and five points. Partners then switch roles and repeat the task. Sight word practice is conducted for 4 minutes.

In the fourth Sounds & Words activity, students read *decodable words* and sight words in First-Grade PALS short stories. Beforehand, the teacher introduces new "rocket words" and reviews old "rocket words." These words (e.g., "playground," "birthday party," and "office") were added to First-Grade PALS stories to increase interest value. The teacher reads the story as students follow on their lesson sheets. The teacher emphasizes the importance of reading quickly and correctly. Coaches then prompt their Readers to read. Coaches use a correction procedure for oral reading errors. When the story is completed, the Coach marks a happy face and five points. Partners switch roles and repeat the activity. The story activity lasts 5 minutes. Coaches and Readers mark a star on a chart if they have read the story the number of times the teacher designates (never to exceed three times in one session). When all the stars on the chart are marked, the student receives a bookmark and a new chart.

After students have implemented Sounds & Words activities independently for 4 weeks, 10 minutes of Partner Reading is added. In Partner Reading, students apply decoding skills and sight word knowledge to narrative text appropriate to their reading level. Teachers prepare students to participate in Partner Reading in two 20-minute sessions. The Coach reads the book's title, pointing to each word. Then the Reader reads the title, pointing to each word. The Coach reads a page of the book, again pointing to each word. The Reader then does the same on the same page. Partners proceed through the book in this manner, mark five points, and repeat the process, switching roles. Each book is read four times before the pair trades it for a new one. Partner Reading is conducted for 10 minutes per session.

PALS Effects on English- and French-Speaking Students of Varying Levels of Performance

Previous work has indicated that First-Grade PALS promotes stronger gains than business-as-usual reading instruction in decoding and word recognition for LA students with and without disabilities and average-achieving and high-achieving students in both high-poverty Title I and middle-class schools (see Fuchs & Fuchs, 2005, for a summary). More recently, Dion and colleagues (Dion, Borri-Anadon, Vanier, Potvin, & Roux, 2005) developed a French version of First-Grade PALS ("Apprendre a lire a deux"), and explored its importance for boosting reading achievement among children in several of Montreal's lowest-income schools.

Dion, Roux, Landry, Fuchs, and Wehby (2007) randomly assigned 58 first-grade classrooms to one of three study condition: controls, First-Grade PALS, or First-Grade PALS plus attention training. The attention training component was an adaptation of the Good Behavior Game, which teachers used every day during their reading instruction. Students in First-Grade PALS plus attention training classes were divided in two teams. Teachers reinforced attention and penalized disruptions by adding or subtracting points to team total. End-of-first-grade outcomes (i.e., performance on word recognition, decoding, and comprehension) were analyzed separately for low-achieving and average-achieving students identified prior to treatment implementation. Average-achieving students who participated in First-Grade PALS activities outperformed controls on all reading measures regardless of whether they also had the attention training; that is, attention training seemed to have little value for these students. It appeared to have greater value for low-achieving students. These students in the First-Grade PALS plus attention training group showed greater improvement in sight-word reading, decoding, and reading comprehension than their counterparts in the control group and First-Grade PALS only group. Thus, it appears attention training may be an important addition to First-Grade PALS activities for lower-performing young children in low-income schools.

What We Still Need to Know about Peer-Mediated Instruction

We have briefly described several approaches to peer-mediated instruction. The PMYC program was highlighted because we believe it is a viable alternative to perhaps better known cognitive-behavioral approaches. We discussed Reciprocal Teaching, CIRC, and CWPT because they are important and successful and, as mentioned, were a basis for the development of PALS. Despite the apparent effectiveness of these programs, peer mediation is an under-appreciated and still infrequently used approach to differentiate and strengthen learning and teaching. This is unfortunate for many obvious reasons, including that numerous approaches to differentiated instruction are unvalidated and peer mediation is inexpensive and virtually all schools should be able to afford it. Although we are obviously bullish on it, we recognize, too, that important R&D remains. We express two caveats about PALS to make this point.

First, the development of Grade 2–6 PALS in the 1990s shows that, despite statistically significant and practically important effects across low achievers with and without LD and average achievers, a small subset of children do not profit. In the D. Fuchs et al. (1997) study, for example, 4 of 20 of children with LD failed to make adequate growth. These 4 children were the poorest readers among the 20, and 3 of the 4 were also described by their teachers as often showing disruptive behavior. Clearly, some children require more intensive or different reading methods. This underscores the importance of monitoring at-risk students' reading progress throughout the school year to identify those who require program adjustments (L. Fuchs & Fuchs, 1998b). In this regard, we support the relatively new policy of Responsiveness-To-Instruction (RTI), which, in principal, redefines general education as multiple levels of increasingly intensive prevention (cf. D. Fuchs, Fuchs, & Vaughn, 2008; L. Fuchs & Fuchs, 1998). In addition, research is needed to examine the characteristics of these so-called treatment non-responders so that additional methods, PALS or otherwise, can be developed to address their educational needs (cf. Al Otaiba & Fuchs, 2003; Al Otaiba & Fuchs, 2006; Duff et al.,2008; Nelson, Benner, & Gonzalez, 2003).

Second, in all the PALS studies just described, teachers receive frequent on-site technical assistance, whereby research assistants observed teachers conduct PALS lessons and helped them solve implementation problems. This, of course, provides opportunities for research staff to quickly correct teachers' misconceptions and ensure proper implementation. Although study teachers consistently described PALS methods as practical, it remains unclear what level of technical support, if any, is required to guarantee accurate implementation. An independent replication of PALS conducted by Vadasy, Jenkins, Antil, Phillips, and Pool (1997) found that when teachers were given access to only a teacher's manual, few implemented it. And among those who did, fewer did so with fidelity. Other independent PALS implementations, however, suggest that a 1-day workshop together with minimal ongoing encouragement may be sufficient to ensure strong PALS implementation (e.g., Grimes, 1997; Raines, 1994). Several of us are currently funded by a grant from the Institute of Education Sciences to evaluate how much and what kind of technical assistance is required to scale up PALS in Nashville, South Texas, and Minneapolis-St. Paul (e.g., D. Fuchs, Saenz, McMaster, et al., 2008; Kearns, Fuchs, Meyers, et al., in preparation; Stein, Berends, Fuchs, et al., 2008).

References

Al Otaiba, S., & Fuchs, D. (2003). Characteristics of children who are unresponsive to early literacy instruction: A review of the literature. *Remedial and Special Education, 23*(5), 300–316.

Al Otaiba, S., & Fuchs, D. (2006). Who are the young children for whom best practices in reading are ineffective? An experimental and longitudinal study. *Journal of Learning Disabilities, 39*(5), 414–431.

Baker, J. M., & Zigmond, N. (1990). Are regular education classes equipped to accommodate students with learning disabilities? *Exceptional Children, 56,* 515–526.

Brown, A. L. (1987). Metacognition, executive control, self-regulation and other more mysterious mechanisms. In F. E. Weinert & R. H. Kluwe (Eds.), *Metacognition, motivation and understanding* (pp. 65–116). Hillsdale, NJ: Erlbaum.

Brown, B. W., & Saks, D. H. (1981). The microeconomics of schooling. In D. C. Berliner (Ed.), *Review of research in education* (Vol. 9, pp. 217–254). Washington, DC: American Educational Research Association.

Brown, B. W., & Saks, D. H. (1987). The microeconomics of the allocation of teachers' time and student learning. *Economics of Education Review, 6,* 319–332.

Carnine, D. W., Silbert, J., Kame'enui, E. J., & Tarver, S. G. (2004). *Direct instruction reading* (4th ed.). Upper Saddle River, NJ: Prentice Hall.

Carolan, J., & Guinn, A. (2007). Differentiation: Examining how master teachers weave differentiation into their daily practice can help reluctant teachers take the plunge. *Educational Leadership, 64*(5), 44–47.

Delquadri, J. C., Greenwood, C. R., Whorton, D., Carta, J. J., & Hall, R. V. (1986). Classwide peer tutoring. *Exceptional Children, 52*(6), 535–561.

Dion, E., Borri-Anadon, C., Vanier, N., Potvin, M.-C., & Roux, C. (2005). *Apprendre à lire à deux. Manuel de l'enseignante et matériel de lecture.* [Apprendre à Lire à Deux Teachers' Manual]. Unpublished manuscript, Université du Québec à Montréal, Montréal, Québec, Canada.

Dion, É., Roux, C., Landry, D., Fuchs, D., & Wehby, J. (2007, July). *Preventing reading disabilities among disadvantaged first-graders: A two-pronged approach.* Poster presented at the Fifteenth Annual Meeting of the Society for the Scientific Study of Reading, Prague, Czech Republic.

Duff, F. J., Fieldsend, E., Bowyer-Crane, C., Hulme, C., Smith, G., Gibbs, S., et al. (2008). *Reading and vocabulary intervention: Evaluation of an instruction for children with poor response to reading intervention.* Unpublished manuscript.

Feuerstein, R., Rand, Y., & Hoffman M. B. (1979). *The dynamic assessment of retarded performers: The learning potential assessment device, theory, instruments, and technique.* Baltimore, MD: University Park Press.

Flavell, J. H. (1979) Metacognition and cognitive monitoring: a new area of cognitive developmental inquiry. *American Psychologist, 34,* 906–911.

Fuchs, D., & Fuchs, L. S. (2005). Peer-Assisted Learning Strategies: Promoting word recognition, fluency, and reading comprehension in young children. *Journal of Special Education, 39*(1), 34–44.

Fuchs, D., Fuchs, L. S., Eaton, S., Young, T., Mock, D., & Dion, E. (2004). *Hearing sounds in words: preschoolers helping preschoolers in a downward extension of peer-assisted learning strategies.* Paper presented at the National Disabilities Association Annual Conference, Atlanta, GA.

Fuchs, D., Fuchs, L. S., & Fernstrom, P. (1993). A conservative approach to special education reform: Mainstreaming through transenvironmental programming and curriculum-based measurement. *American Educational Research Journal, 30,* 149–177.

Fuchs, D., Fuchs, L. S., Mathes, P. G., & Martinez, E. A. (2002). Preliminary evidence on the social standing of students with learning disabilities in PALS and NO-PALS classrooms. *Learning Disabilities Research & Practice, 17,* 205–215.

Fuchs. D., Fuchs, L. S., Mathes, P. G., & Simmons, D. C. (1996). *Peer-assisted learning strategies: Reading methods for grades 2–6.* Nashville, TN: Vanderbilt University.

Fuchs, D., Fuchs, L. S., Mathes, P. G., & Simmons, D. C. (1997). Peer-assisted learning strategies: Making classrooms more responsive to diversity. *American Educational Research Journal, 34,* 174–206.

Fuchs, D., Fuchs, L.S., Simmons, D. C., & Mathes, P. G. (2008). *Peer-assisted learning strategies: Reading methods for grades 2–6.* Nashville, TN: Vanderbilt University.

Fuchs, D., Fuchs, L. S., Svenson, E., Yen, L., Thompson, A., McMaster, K. L., et al. (2001). *Peer-assisted learning strategies: First grade reading.* Nashville, TN: Vanderbilt University.

Fuchs, D., Fuchs, L. S., Thompson, A., Al Otaiba, S., Yen, L., McMaster, K. L., et al. (2001). *Peer assisted learning strategies: Kindergarten reading.* Nashville, TN: Vanderbilt University.

Fuchs, D., Fuchs, L. S., Thompson, A., Al Otaiba, S., Yen, L., Yang, N. J., et al. (2001). Is reading important in reading-readiness programs? A randomized field trial with teachers as program implementers. *Journal of Educational Psychology, 93*, 251–267.

Fuchs, D., Fuchs, L. S., Thompson, A., Al Otaiba, S., Yen, L., Yang, N. J., et al. (2002). Exploring the importance of reading programs for kindergartners with disabilities in mainstream classrooms. *Exceptional Children, 55*, 295–311.

Fuchs, D., Fuchs, L. S., & Vaughn, S. (2008). *Response to intervention: A framework for reading educators.* Newark, DE: International Reading Association.

Fuchs, D., Fuchs, L. S., Yen, L., McMaster, K. L., Svenson, E., Yang, N. J., et al. (2001). Developing first-grade reading fluency through peer mediation. *Teaching Exceptional Children. 34*, 90–93.

Fuchs, D., Roberts, P. H., Fuchs, L. S., & Bowers, J. (1996). Reintegrating students with learning disabilities into the mainstream: A two-year study. *Learning Disabilities Research & Practice, 11*(4), 214–229.

Fuchs, D., Saenz, L., McMaster, K., Yen, L., Fuchs, L., Compton, D., et al. (2008). Scaling up an evidence-based reading program for kinder-gartners. In L. Fuchs (Chair), *Feasibility and effectiveness of early preventive reading interventions.* Symposium presented at the Society for the Scientific Study of Reading conference, Asheville, NC.

Fuchs, L. S., & Fuchs, D. (1998). Treatment validity: A unifying concept for reconceptualizing the identification of learning disabilities. *Learning Disabilities Research and Practice, 13*, 204–219.

Fuchs, L. S., Fuchs, D., & Bishop, N. (1992). Teacher planning for students with learning disabilities: Differences between general and special educators. *Learning Disabilities Research & Practice, 7*, 120–128.

Fuchs, L. S., Fuchs, D., & Kazdan, S. (1999). Effects of peer-assisted learning strategies on high-school students with serious reading problems. *Remedial and Special Education, 20*, 309–319.

Gerber, M. M., & Semmel, M. I. (1984). Teacher as imperfect test: Reconceptualizing the referral process. *Educational Psychologist, 19*(3), 137–148.

Gersten, R., & Baker, S. (1998). Real world use of scientific concepts: Integrating situated cognition with explicit instruction. *Exceptional Children, 65*, 23–35.

Gersten, R., Vaughn, S., Deshler, D., & Schiller, E. (1995). *What we know (and still don't know) about utilizing research findings to improve practice: Implications for special education.* Unpublished manuscript.

Greenwood, C. R., Delquadri, J. C., & Hall, R. V. (1989). Longitudinal effects of classwide peer tutoring. *Journal of Educational Psychology, 81*(3), 371–383.

Greenwood, C. R., Terry, B., Arreaga-Mayer, C., & Finney, R. (1992). The classwide peer tutoring program: Implementation factors moderating students' achievement. *Journal of Applied Behavior Analysis, 25*, 101–116.

Greenwood, C. R., Terry, B., Utley, C. A., Montagna, D., & Walker, D. (1993). Achievement, placement, and services: Middle school benefits of classwide peer tutoring used at the elementary school. *School Psychology Review, 22*, 497–516.

Grimes, J. (1997). *Implementing reading PALS in Iowa.* [Unpublished data]

Hacker, D. J., & Tenant, A. (2002). Implementing reciprocal teaching in the classroom: Overcoming obstacles and making modifications. *Journal of Educational Psychology, 94*(4), 699–718.

Hall, T. (2002). *Differentiated instruction.* Wakefield, MA: National Center on Accessing the General Curriculum. Retrieved January, 13, 2009, from http://www.cast.org/publications/ncac/ncac_diffinstruc.html

Hall, R. V., Delquadri, J. C., Greenwood, C. R., & Thurston, L. (1982). The importance of opportunity to respond in children's academic success. In E. Edgar, N. Haring, J. Jenkins, & C. Pious (Eds.), *Mentally handicapped children: Education and training* (pp. 107–140). Baltimore, MD: University Park Press.

Jenkins, J. R., & O'Connor, R. (2003). Cooperative learning for students with learning disabilities: Evidence from experiments, observations, and interviews. In L. Swanson, S. Graham, & K. Harris (Eds.), *Handbook of learning disabilities* (pp. 417–430). New York: Guilford.

Kapusnick, R. A., & Hauslein, C. M. (2001). The 'silver cup' of differentiation. *Kappa Delta Pi Record, 37*, 156–159.

Kearns, D., Fuchs, D., Meyers C. V., Berends, M., McMaster, K. L., Saenz, L., et al. (in preparation). *Factors contributing to teachers' sustained use of kindergarten peer-assisted learning strategies.*

Leithwood, K., Leonard, L., & Sharratt, L. (1998). Conditions fostering organizational learning in schools. *Education Administration Quarterly, 34*(2) 243–276.

Lesgold, A. M., & Resnick, L. (1982). How reading difficulties develop: Perspectives from a longitudinal study. In J. Das, R. Mulcahy & A. Wall (Eds.), *Theory and research in learning disabilities.* New York: Plenum.

Margalit, M. (2000). *Learning disabilities in the classroom: Educational dilemmas of the new reality* [in Hebrew]. Tel Aviv, Israel: The Mofet Institute.

McDermott, R. P., & Aron, J. (1978). Pirandello in the classroom: On the possibility of equal educational opportunity in American culture. In M. C. Reynolds (Ed.), *Futures of education for exceptional students* (pp. 41–64). Reston, VA: Council for Exceptional Children.

McIntosh, R., Vaughn, S., Schumm, J. S., Haager, D., & Lee, O. (1994). Observations of students with learning disabilities in general education classrooms. *Exceptional Children, 60*(3), 249–261.

McMaster, K. N., & Fuchs, D. (2002). Effects of cooperative learning on the academic achievement of students with learning disabilities: An update of Tateyama-Sniezek's review. *Learning Disabilities Research and Practice, 17*(2), 107–117.

McMaster, K. L., Kung, S. H., Han, I., & Cao, M. (2008). Peer-Assisted Learning Strategies: A "tier 1" approach to promoting English learners' response to intervention. *Exceptional Children, 74*, 194–214.

Nelson, R. J., Benner, G. J., & Gonzalez, J. (2003). Learner characteristics that influence the treatment effectiveness of early literacy interventions: A meta-analytic review. *Learning Disabilities Research and Practice, 18*, 255–267.

O'Sullivan, P. J., Ysseldyke, J. E., Christenson, S. L., & Thurlow, M. L. (1990). Mildly handicapped elementary students' opportunity to learn during reading instruction in mainstream and special education settings. *Reading Research Quarterly, 25,* 131–146.

Palincsar, A. S., & Brown, A. L. (1984). Reciprocal teaching of comprehension-fostering and comprehension-monitoring activities. *Cognition and Instruction, 1,* 117–175.

Palincsar, A. S, & Brown, A. L. (1986). Interactive teaching to promote independent learning from text. *Reading Teacher, 39,* 771–777.

Peterson, P. L., & Clark, C. M. (1978). Teachers' reports of their cognitive process during teaching. *American Educational Research Journal, 15,* 555–565.

Pressley, M. (1997). *Remarks on reading comprehension.* Notes prepared for the Chesapeake Institute, Washington, DC.

Pressley, M., Allington, R. L., Wharton-McDonald, R., Block, C. C., & Morrow, L. (2001). *Learning to read: Lessons from exemplary first-grade classrooms.* New York: Guilford.

Raines, R. (1994). *Implementing reading PALS in Bakersfield, CA.* [Unpublished data]

Rosenshine, B., & Meister, C. (1994). Reciprocal teaching: A review of research. *Review of Educational Research, 64,* 479–530.

Saenz, L. M., Fuchs, L. S., & Fuchs, D. (2005). Effects of peer-assisted learning strategies on English language learners with learning disabilities: A randomized controlled study. *Exceptional Children, 71,* 231–247.

Schumm, J. S., & Vaughn, S. (1992). Planning for mainstreamed special education students: Perceptions of general classroom teachers. *Exceptionality, 3*(2), 81–98.

Schumm, J. S., Vaughn, S., Gordon, J., & Rothstein, L. (1994). General education teachers' beliefs, skills, and practices in planning for mainstreamed students with learning disabilities. *Teacher Education and Special Education, 17,* 22–37.

Shamir, A., & Lazerovitz, T. (2007). A peer mediation intervention for scaffolding self-regulated learning among children with learning disabilities. *European Journal of Special Needs Education.*

Shamir, A., & Silvern, S. (2005). Effects of peer mediation with young children on autonomous behavior. *Journal of Cognitive Education and Psychology, 5*(2), 199–215.

Shamir, A., & Tzuriel, D. (2002). Peer mediation: A novel model for development of mediation skills and cognitive modifiability of young children. In W. Resing, W. Ruijssenaars, & D. Aalsvoort (Eds.), *Learning potential assessment and cognitive training: Actual research perspectives in theory building and methodology* (pp. 363–373). New York: JAI Press/Elsevier.

Shamir, A., & Tzuriel, D. (2004). Characteristics of children's mediational teaching style as a function of intervention for cross-age peer mediation with computers. *School Psychology International, 25*(1), 59–78.

Shamir, A., Tzuriel, D., & Guy, R. (2007) Computer-supported collaborative learning: cognitive effects of intervention for peer mediation tutoring. Peer-assisted learning: state of the art as we turn towards the future [Special issue]. *Journal of Cognitive Educational Psychology, 6,* 433–455.

Shamir, A., Tzuriel, D., & Rozen, M (2006). Peer mediation: The effects of program intervention, math level, and verbal ability on mediation style and improvement in math problem solving. *School Psychology International, 27*(2), 209–231.

Shamir, A., & Van der Aalsvoort, G. (2004). Children's mediational teaching style and cognitive modifiability: A comparison between first and third graders in Holland and Israel. *Educational Practice and Theory, 26*(2), 61–85.

Sideridis, G. D., Utley. C. A., Greenwood, C. R., Delquadri, J., Dawson, H., Palmer, P., et al. (1997). Classwide peer tutoring: Effects on the spelling performance and social interactions of students with mild disabilities and their typical peers in an integrated instructional setting. *Journal of Behavioral Education, 7,* 435–462.

Simmons, D. C., Fuchs, D., Fuchs, L. S., Hodge, J. P., & Mathes, P. G. (1994). Importance of instructional complexity and role reciprocity to classwide peer tutoring. *Learning Disabilities Research & Practice, 9,* 203–212.

Slavin, R. E. (1994). *Cooperative learning: Theory, research, & practice* (2nd ed.). Boston: Allyn & Bacon.

Slavin, R. E., Leavey, M. B., & Madden, N., A. (1984). Combining learning and individualized instruction: Effects on student mathematics achievement, attitudes, and behaviors. *Elementary School Journal, 84,* 409–422.

Slavin, R. E., Madden, N. A., & Leavey, M. B. (1984). Effects of team assisted individualization on the mathematics achievement of academically handicapped and nonhandicapped students. *Journal of Educational Psychology, 76,* 813–819.

Stein, M. L., Berends, M., Fuchs, D., McMaster, K., Saenz, L., Yen. L., et al. (2008). Scaling up an early reading program: Relationships among teacher support, fidelity of implementation, and student performance across different sites and years. *Educational Evaluation and Policy Analysis, 30*(4), 368–388.

Stevens, R. J., Madden, N. A., Slavin, R. E., & Farnish, A. M. (1987). Cooperative integrated reading and composition: Two field experiments. *Reading Research Quarterly, 22,* 433–454.

Stevens, R., & Slavin, R. (1995). The cooperative elementary school effects on students' achievement, attitudes, and social relations. *American Educational Research Journal, 32*(2), 321–351.

Stevens, R. J., Slavin, R. E., & Farnish, A. M. (1991). The effects of cooperative learning and direct instruction in reading comprehension strategies on main idea identification. *Journal of Educational Psychology, 83,* 8–16.

Tomlinson, C. (1999). Mapping a route toward differentiated instruction. *Educational Leadership, 57*(1), 12–16.

Tomlinson, C., & Allan, S. D. (2003). *Leadership for differentiating schools and classrooms*. Alexandria, VA: Association for Supervision and Curriculum Development.

Tomlinson, C. A., & Kalbfleisch, M. L. (1998). Teach me, teach my brain: A call for differentiated classrooms. *Educational Leadership, 56*(3), 52–55.

Torgesen, J. K., Wagner, R. K., Rashotte, C. A., Lindamood, P., Rose, E., Conway, T., et al. (1999). Preventing reading failure in young children with phonological processing disabilities: Group and individual responses to instruction. *Journal of Educational Psychology, 91*, 579–593.

Tzuriel, D., & Shamir, A. (2007). The effects of peer mediation with young children (PMYC) on children's cognitive modifiability. *British Journal of Educational Psychology.*

Vadasy, P. F., Jenkins, J. R., Antil, L. R., Phillips, N. B., & Pool, K. (1997). The research to practice ball game: Classwide peer tutoring and teacher interest, implementation, and modifications. *Remedial and Special Education, 18*, 143–156.

Vygotsky, L. S. (1929). The problem of the cultural development of the child. *Journal of Genetic Psychology, 36*, 415–434.

Vygotsky, L. S. (1962). *Thought and language*. Cambridge, MA: MIT Press.

Vygotsky, L. S. (1978). *Mind in society: The development of higher psychological process*. Cambridge, MA: Harvard University Press.

Vygotsky, L. S. (1981). The genesis of higher mental functions. In J. V. Wertsch (Ed.). *The concept of activity in Soviet psychology* (pp. 144–188). Armonk, NY: Sharpe.

Zigmond, N., & Baker, J. (1994). Is the mainstream a more appropriate educational setting for Randy? A case study of one student with learning disabilities. *Learning Disabilities Research & Practice, 9*(2), 108–117.

Reading 2.6

The Changing Extremes in Our Classrooms

Rhonda Bondie and Akane Zusho

Overview

Objective:

Why do we need to adjust or differentiate instruction?

Think: Circle the most __important__ word in the Objective.

Criteria:

Use the following criteria to increase the quality of your answer to the chapter question. Try to "Take It Up a Notch" or expand your answer by reading the chapter to add these details.

- Identify ways students vary, which create opportunities and obstacles to student engagement in your subject area.

- Explain research that describes the ways that students vary.

- Try Classroom Routines:

    - Plan—*Traction Planner.*

    - Teach—*Domino Discover.*

    - Adjust Instruction—*Inclusive Directions.*

Starting Position: Jot Notes—Perceptions of the Extremes

Begin by reflecting on your students within the context of your subject area. Identify a specific task used in lessons such as independent reading and surround the task with a brainstorm of ways that students vary that impact learning. Think about all of the things that students have and bring to the task as well as things that they might need to learn:

- Consider their interests that relate to this task.

- Surround the task with student strengths.

- Break the task down and consider all of the things that students would need to learn or have before even beginning this task.

Use this exercise to begin to examine the many variations and dimensions of student characteristics (experiences, strengths, needs, interests, understandings) that impact learning in your subject area (see Figure 2.6.1).

Reread your networks of student variations. To learn more about this approach to making our own perceptions about student variability visible in relation to our curriculum, try the *Traction Planner* routine. Consider how the extremes of your network begin to answer our chapter question, "Why do we need differentiated instruction?" Take a moment to jot down your draft answer. We will return to this question at the end of this chapter and at the end of this book to reflect on how your thinking has been confirmed, challenged, or changed.

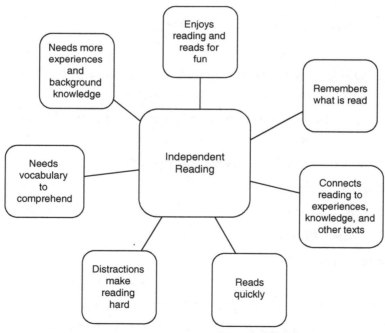

FIGURE 2.6.1   Independent Reading Brainstorm of Student Variability.

From the Classroom: *What Are the Extremes?*

Near the end of the school year, one of Ms. Ford's favorite annual activities is to play a video from the first day of school where her sixth-grade students individually state their names and what they hope to learn. The initial goals recorded on this video serve as a starting position to help students reflect on their learning over the year. The students scream with laughter as they recognize how much they have changed in just eight months. Of course, the physical changes are dramatic from the beginning to the end of each school year. Students have grown, their voices have changed, and often their hair or dress styles are new. After spending a year together, they also now recognize the myriad ways in which they are different and unique in their knowledge, language, interests, childhood experience, family, culture, and special skills.

This story of the sixth-grade video illustrates just how much students are constantly changing in a variety of ways, and at differing rates. When we aim to adjust instruction to meet the academic needs of all learners, we must remember that students are continuously changing, and that, along with differences, students share common experiences. The amount of time we have at school for learning is set, as is much of the curriculum. The varying starting positions and rates of change among students, along with a fixed amount of class time and required learning standards, create a tension for teachers. How do you provide instruction that is appropriate for each individual student within time and curriculum constraints? We find that impactful teachers have their fingers on the pulse of the class. They monitor student learning by considering the interactions among students and themselves during lessons, and the relationships between students and the curriculum. This perception is vital because it is the beginning—the impetus for why adjustments are made to instruction.

Rooted in Research: *Identifying the Extremes*
Diversity in Our Classrooms

Research generally confirms teachers' perceptions about shifts in the overall diversity of the K–12 student population. When it comes to ethnic diversity, according to a recent report released by the U.S. Department of Education (2014), the percentage of public school K–12 students who identified as White fell to under 50%, whereas the percentage of Hispanic and Asian students increased (Musu-Gillette et al., 2016). The percentage of public school students who were non-native speakers of English was higher in 2014–2015 than a decade ago, making up roughly 9% of the student population. Not surprisingly, the percentage of English as a New Language learners varies by state—West Virginia has the fewest number (only 1%), whereas almost a quarter of the student population in California are English as a

New Language learners. In 2014, about 14% of the English as a New Language student population were identified as having learning disabilities.

In terms of the overall population of students receiving special education services, approximately 13% (or 6.6 million) of the public school population received services in 2014–2015, with more male students receiving special education services under the Individuals with Disabilities Education Act (IDEA) than female students, and more American Indian and Black students receiving services than White students. An overwhelming majority of students receiving special education services (95%) were enrolled in regular schools. Moreover, there was a dramatic increase in the percentage of students who spent most of their time in general education classes, from 33% in 1990 to 62% in 2014/2015—an increase of 29 percentage points. There is limited recent data available on students considered to be gifted and talented, although in 2006, approximately 6% of the overall public-school population in the United States was identified as gifted (Snyder & Dillow, 2015).

The National Assessment of Educational Progress (NAEP, 2015), more commonly referred to as the Nation's Report Card, is useful in providing an overall picture of U.S. students' academic achievement. NAEP assessments are administered periodically to a nationally representative sample of fourth, eighth, and 12th-grade students in nine different subject areas. Examining the 2015 achievement results for the core subjects of reading and mathematics helps us understand variability in achievement within and across grades.

First, in terms of reading, 36% of fourth-grade students, 34% of eighth-grade students, and 37% of 12th-grade students performed at or above the proficient level on the reading assessment in 2015, indicating solid academic performance. By contrast, 31% of fourth-grade, 24% of eighth-grade, and 28% of 12th-grade students performed below "basic" levels (NAEP, 2015). As for mathematics, 40% of fourth-grade, 33% of eighth-grade, and 25% of 12th-grade students performed at or above the proficient level, whereas 18% of fourth-grade, 29% of eighth-grade, and 38% of 12th-grade students performed below the basic level. When the data is disaggregated by specific groups, students receiving special education services and English as a New Language learners generally perform below the basic level of proficiency across all grades in both reading and mathematics.

These results suggest a trend toward increasing academic diversity in U.S. schools. The NAEP assessments attest that there is a substantial percentage of elementary, middle, and high school students who are not meeting grade-level standards of mathematics and reading proficiency. These data confirm that not all students are learning in school every day. It is important to note that these trends are not unique to the U.S. context. Results of large-scale international assessments like the Programme for International Student Assessment (PISA), which focuses on issues of equity, also speak to variability in achievement scores. In reporting the results of the 2015 assessments, the Organisation for Economic Co-operation and Development (OECD) who oversees PISA made the following conclusion: "Clearly all countries and economies have excellent students, but few have enabled all students to excel" (p. 6). Indeed, they reported that only a handful of countries were able to get four out of five 15-year-olds to achieve basic levels of proficiency in science, reading, and mathematics. These included Canada, Estonia, Finland, Hong Kong (China), Japan, Macao (China), and Singapore (OECD, 2016).

Danger of Perceiving General Extremes

To achieve our goal of engaging the extremes, it is important to understand the nature of the extremes and especially the extent of variability that exists in academic proficiency in our nation's schools. As the statistics above demonstrate, teachers are confronted by considerable academic diversity, which speaks to the urgent need for differentiated education (Fuchs, 2006). However, research also suggests that differentiated instruction is relatively uncommon in most classrooms, particularly in large urban school districts that face considerable linguistic, cultural, and academic diversity. In the face of such a challenge, most teachers opt for a one-size-fits-all instructional approach, only selectively attending to student differences, or focusing more on academically competent students. Findings from numerous studies indicate that children who perform at lower levels of achievement receive less differentiated instruction than students who perform at higher levels, which may increase achievement gaps between the extremes (Fuchs, 2006).

It is in this context that we interpret the statistics presented in the previous section. Although the NAEP data clearly show specific achievement patterns with certain groups outperforming others, we fundamentally believe that a major contributing factor is lack of targeted instruction and not that certain students are more capable than others. Proponents of universal learning design (UDL) support this belief:

> Advances in neuroscience and education research over the past 40 years have reshaped our understanding of the learning brain. One of the clearest and most important revelations stemming from brain research is that there is no such thing as a "regular student." Instead, learning is as unique to individuals as their fingerprints or DNA. The notion of broad categories of learners—"smart– not smart," "disabled–not disabled," "regular–not regular"—is a gross oversimplification that does not reflect reality. By categorizing students in this way, we miss many subtle and important qualities and strengths. Science shows that individual qualities or abilities are not static or fixed; rather they are continually shifting, and they exist in relationship to the environment.
>
> (Hall, Meyer, & Rose, 2012, p. 2)

It is important to keep in mind that the extremes of achievement differences are not enduring, stable characteristics of an individual or groups of students, and that targeted instruction can go a long way in closing achievement gaps. A recent study found that 71% of the variability in student engagement could be attributed to classroom rather than student variables (Cooper, 2014), underscoring the importance of looking beyond student traits when it comes to understanding academic engagement.

Although statistics are useful in allowing us to better understand the range in academic ability that exists in our schools, they do not tell us anything about specific students, and there is an inherent danger in extrapolating these results to individuals. As the research on UDL would attest, variability or heterogeneity within groups of students is the norm; an "average" score cannot adequately capture the profiles of every member of that group. Just because students are English as a New Language learners, or are identified as having a disability, does not necessarily mean that they will struggle with *all* academic tasks; similarly, this does not mean that gifted students do not have their own share of challenges, even academic ones. We all have our strengths and weaknesses, and these attributes are likely to change depending upon the context. This is why we advise implementing frequent individualized assessments for *all* students in a learning community, not just those who are struggling.

Teacher Perception and Thinking

With this in mind, consider what Carol Dweck (2006) would call a growth mindset—thinking not about what certain students or groups *cannot* do but rather to think about what *all* students *can* do, and what changes you need to make in your curriculum and your practices to achieve this goal. Can you think of the educational system, the curriculum or the lessons, rather than students, as having "disabilities"? (Hall et al., 2012). Researchers of UDL suggest that traditional curricula are "disabled" in the sense that a curriculum only works for certain kinds of students who can decode print-based text or physically turn pages. Some would argue that the educational system, too, is currently set up to advantage certain learners over others. Research on culturally relevant pedagogy (Ladson-Billings, 1995), for example, suggests many minority students do not perceive school and schooling as validating, liberating, or emancipatory (Kumar et al., submitted). What changes do you need to make to your instructional practice to ensure fair and equal access so that all students achieve at the proficient level? Can you shift your thinking from teachers to teaching (Hiebert & Stigler, 2017) and from students to learning?

Teacher Expectations

Among the major contributions of the last century of psychological research on learning is the research on teacher expectations. *Teacher expectations matter.* In the first study on teacher effects—now aptly referred to as the Pygmalion experiment (Rosenthal & Jacobson, 1968)—teachers who were simply told that their students were likely to "bloom" expected more of these students, and these bloomers, consequently, were found to achieve at higher levels. Building on this initial study, researchers have since examined how teacher expectations affect teacher behavior.

There is empirical evidence to suggest that teachers generally interact less with and provide less wait time and praise for low-expectation students (Brophy, 1985), ultimately undermining their motivation and subsequent achievement. In contrast, teachers with high expectations for their students are more likely to engage in motivationally supportive practices intended to promote a warm classroom climate (Rubie-Davies, Peterson, Sibley, & Rosenthal, 2015). They are more likely to believe in and employ non-ability grouping practices (flexible grouping), promote self-regulated learning (i.e., goal-setting and support in monitoring progress toward goals), and provide choice and autonomy to all students (Rubie-Davies et al., 2015). These are all practices emphasized by ALL-ED.

We are all biased in some way, shape, or form,[1] and we do not mean to suggest that some teachers are more biased than others. Even the most successful, well-intentioned educators are capable of falling prey to teacher expectation effects. The good news is that teacher expectations, like academic ability, are not fixed. Interventions for teacher expectations demonstrate not only that these beliefs are malleable, but training teachers in the practices of high expectations can promote student achievement. For example, Rubie-Davies et al. (2015) trained a subset of New Zealand teachers in flexible grouping, student choice, and goal-setting and found that these teachers' students obtained higher mathematics scores than teachers who did not receive this training. In a similar way, our approach to differentiated instruction supports teachers in establishing high expectations for all students.

Teacher Decision-Making Framework—ALL-ED

Now that you have some background about the extremes, let's return to your starting position at the beginning of the chapter to consider again: what are the extremes that we are aiming to engage? Students do not fall into clear levels such as high, medium, and low because there are too many variables involved in learning activities, and students vary on more than one critical dimension. For example, during a reading activity, students may vary on their current reading level, creating extremes related to access and rigor for students engaged in the same task. Factors such as lack of regular attendance and cultural background knowledge also impact student understanding of the text regardless of their independent reading level. The ways that students vary have connections or dimensions that matter for learning. During the course of the year as students grow, the ways in which they vary are constantly changing. Teacher effort to perceive student variability must therefore be a continuous process where teachers learn about students with some depth and make connections among students and the teacher. In addition to learning from students, teachers need to revise their understanding of students to reflect changes in students.

When we think of engaging everyone in our diverse classes, we imagine a three-dimensional network, with new connections lighting up continuously. Academic diversity is a dynamic network of strengths, needs, and interests that both facilitate and sometimes block or challenge learning within different contexts. These student characteristics are situational, related to the individual learning task, and not fixed attributes of a learner. Strong causal conversation skills with friends might facilitate project work in small groups, but might pose a challenge for students responding to academic questions spontaneously during a structured literature discussion or when giving a speech for an audience. Being adept at academic writing in Spanish might present both a strength and a challenge when writing in English because of the different cultural expectations for the structure of a written text.

Student characteristics on the extremes are specific to the task and the topic being taught. Because the extremes are related to each learning task, teachers are in a continuous cycle of perceiving student strengths that facilitate learning and eliminating or avoiding challenges to effective and efficient learning. Classroom routines enable teachers to find time during daily lessons to listen and observe students as they learn, continuously perceiving student strengths and needs, and recognizing the ever-changing student extremes within the context of specific learning tasks. This ability to listen and look is vital to ensuring all learners are learning every day, because teachers can only respond to what they perceive in the classroom. Learning from students is a foundational teacher habit essential to differentiating or adjusting instruction. All adjustments to instruction are based on teacher perception of student learning needs, so routine efforts to notice, expand, and revise our perceptions of students are necessary before we begin to make instructional decisions.

The Classroom Routines highlighted in this chapter, *Jot Notes*, *Traction Planner*, and several routines to support the daily teaching habit of recording student responses all increase our awareness of our knowledge of students and invite us to draw on student strengths in our lesson plans. For example, you might revise one activity or question each week to learn more about your students. The activity could be a question on an exit card, an opportunity to draw a picture, or a three-minute individual conference where students share something they enjoy outside of school. Students could be asked to place a stamp or a sticker on their work to show a skill that they used, such as thinking, listening, or focusing. Another way to learn from students is to ask students to teach you or the class a game that they know or how to say something in a language that they speak. Finally, by saving records of student responses, you, as well as students, can notice patterns in their thinking, language, and understanding. The responses provide a means to learn more about students and precisely adjust instruction to meet learning needs.

Classroom Routines provide necessary observation and listening time to help teachers expand their perceptions of students in every unit throughout the year. This is a shift from getting to know students in the first unit of the year and then jumping into the curriculum, to an intentional, planned effort to continuously learn from and about students to strategically build new learning onto the foundations that are present. Our perceptions inform our expectations, so making our perceptions visible to ourselves and pursuing learning with and from our students is fundamental in providing precise, effective, and efficient differentiated instruction.

Try Classroom Routines
Precise, Effective, Efficient Learning for All
Plan: Traction Planner

In planning, the *Traction Planner* prepares our thinking prior to unit and lesson planning to recognize our own and student characteristics that can strengthen or challenge learning. The traction planner asks teachers to jot down the objectives for a unit or topic of study in the center of the circle. Then the teacher brainstorms student strengths that connect to the objectives. The attention is focused on passions of both the teacher and the students, listing all the things that might be interesting, valuable, useful, and meaningful about these objectives.

ALL-ED Classroom Routine Directions: Traction Planner—Teacher Planning

This planner is designed to focus our attention on the strengths that **students and teachers** bring to a unit of study. The *Traction Planner* helps teachers envision practical, concrete ways to increase the relevance of a unit of study. (See Figure 2.6.2.)

Strengths of this routine:

- reflects teacher perceptions
- sets frame or lens for planning
- can be adapted and completed by students.

Implementation Directions

Objective: Root the new learning of a unit in strengths (planning like an environmentally conscious land developer).

Starting Position: Complete the *Jot Notes* activity (Starting Position for this chapter).

Criteria

- *Must Haves*: Connections to Objectives are reasonable.
- *Amazing*: Connections include a wide variety of skills, strengths, and interests shared by individuals as well as groups of students.

Action Pattern

The teacher follows these directions in planning:

1. Identify the goals for the unit of study: the core understanding, knowledge, and skills that students will learn.
2. Build new learning from a base of student strengths and student and teacher passions related to the goals of the unit of study.
3. Consider connections from the goals of the unit to student everyday life and the importance of this topic for both now and the future.
4. Identify student needs and learning the hardest part of the unit. Use the information from two and three to support student needs and learning the hardest part of the unit.

Reflections

1. Share your *Traction Planner* with a colleague asking them to add at least two ideas to your planner of additional strengths, skills, and interests of your students and yourself that connect to your topic.
2. Connect these ideas and possibly revise to strengthen connections, the major assessments, or activities in the unit.

It is important to consider strengths and passions with a wide scope. Some characteristics may be less valued during lessons, such as texting or talking with friends, but include those and any other ideas that relate to the objectives in this brainstorm. Literally, you are rooting the objectives in the strengths and passions that you and your students bring to the classroom to help you see how learning will build on previous learning and offers traction to launch new understanding.

Unit Title _____

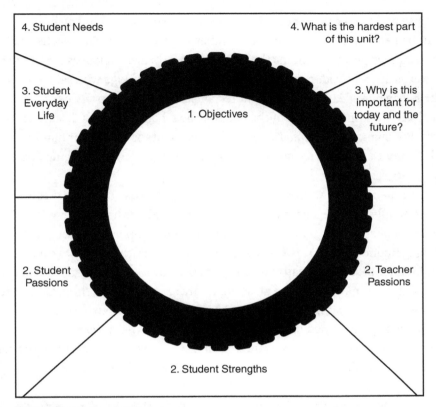

4. Student Needs

4. What is the hardest part of this unit?

3. Student Everyday Life

3. Why is this important for today and the future?

1. Objectives

2. Student Passions

2. Teacher Passions

2. Student Strengths

FIGURE 2.6.2   Traction Planner.

After rooting the objectives for a unit of study in teacher and student strengths, then you will make connections between the objectives and student everyday life and predict how mastering these objectives may be useful for the students' futures. Finally, you will identify the hardest part of the unit and learning needs for accomplishing these objectives that you can already predict using what you already know about your students. This *Traction Planner* supports teachers in building on strengths, leveraging previous learning to gain new learning, and identifying from the onset where time will be needed to meet student learning needs.

Teach: Domino Discover Before Calling on Raised Hands

After asking a question and providing time for students to discuss their responses at a table or in a small group, tell students that they will hear a response from each table from one reporter. As reporters speak, everyone else will be a listener, listening for a teacher-identified goal for listening, such as patterns, vocabulary words, text evidence, or other teacher-tailored instruction. Each person in the group prepares to be the reporter, perhaps by jotting down one response and two backup ideas. The reporter's responses should be brief so that each group can be heard and listeners can remember what was said. The teacher calls on one reporter from each group, enforcing the "Add or Repeat" rule; responses can confirm something that was already said, but the reporter has to acknowledge who said it, or responses can contribute a new idea. Record student responses as each group shares on a list visible to all students. Reminding students of the listening goal helps students discuss and organize responses. Following the *Domino Discover*, allow students to raise their hands to add additional ideas. Invite students to offer compliments to groups by referencing posted criteria for high quality responses.

Why use *Domino Discover* before calling on raised hands? *Domino Discover* promotes inclusive equitable engagement in classrooms where students have diverse learning needs, because teachers ensure that all students have an equal opportunity for their voice to be heard. Engagement increases as every student knows that they will have a turn to share their thinking, or that their ideas will be represented by a group reporter. As engagement increases so does thinking, because all students are accountable to think about a response to questions. This gives students more opportunities in class to purposefully use academic vocabulary and to gain immediate feedback on their ideas. Finally, *Domino Discover* provides an efficient means to collect and organize formative assessment data from the class that teachers can use to tailor instruction to better meet the needs of students.

ALL-ED Classroom Routine Directions: Domino Discover

Domino Discover equitably gathers responses from all members of a class or group. In *Domino Discover*, representatives from each group (Table or Group reporters) share out a response while the teacher records answers on chart paper, chalk/whiteboard, or projected slide or document. Additional responses are gathered from individual students following the representatives.

Strengths of this routine:

- equity in gathering student responses
- students practice using oral language, vocabulary, and listening
- students learn from many students in the class
- students are up, moving, and having fun
- students have a reason to listen.

Implementation Directions

Objective: To find patterns and surprises among student responses.

Starting Positions: Individuals consider a response to a question. You may use the _List, Draw, Write_ routine.

Criteria

- _Must Haves:_ Uses the word "because," explains with detail, includes visual representation of ideas.
- _Amazing:_ Makes connection to previous unit or current events, uses vocabulary from word wall.

Action Pattern

Directions: The teacher identifies in the directions:

- **Roles:** Speaker and Listeners
- **Turns:** Teacher selects students who will go first and second in each group, establishing the direction for each member of the group to take turns sharing their response one at a time.
- **Rules:** "Add or repeat"—students can add new ideas or repeat another student. This supports the speaker—when someone is the speaker and they need a response to share (for example, if a student was absent or late and doesn't have the Starting Position to share out) then someone in the group can let the group member use their response—this rule ensures that all students practice speaking on the topic.
- **Time:** Each student speaks for a set amount of time (ranging anywhere from ten seconds to two minutes, depending on the length of the response and class time).

1. State a reason for listening or an Objective.
2. Decide who will share first in the group (individuals sharing at a table or reporters sharing a response to represent their group).
3. Point to the person that will go second, establishing the direction for each person to share one after another.
4. Take turns completing the task until everyone has gone, one after the other, like dominoes falling.
5. Ask each person in the group to share their response (usually the Starting Position).
6. Record student responses (capture responses on the board/chart/computer).

1. Take a few minutes to notice patterns and surprises that learners noticed as well as pose questions.
2. Ask students to generate compliments to reporters using specific criteria.
3. Ask students for feedback about the process, suggestions, adjustment, or new rules for the next _Domino Discover._
4. Adjust instruction based on student responses.

Adjust Instruction: Inclusive Directions

Use _Inclusive Directions_ to adjust group learning routines to fit learner needs in addition to structuring the routine with OSCAR. There are four parts to _Inclusive Directions_: roles, turns, rules, and time. We refer to this as _Inclusive Directions_ when each of these parts are identified, because being specific with students increases clarity of the outcome and behaviors expected. In addition, these parts can be adjusted to fit learning needs. For example, you can assign students who were absent to take the last turn in sharing a response with their small group. You might also state a rule of "Add or Repeat," meaning that students could repeat a response spoken by another student or add a new idea. In this way, all students can meaningfully participate in the group discussion, whether absent or present the day before. The more specific you are with roles, turns, rules, and time, the greater the possibilities for challenging and engaging all learners. As discussed above in the research section, roles involve designating who will be the listener and the speaker. A recorder and/or a reporter or group representative may be added to share the results of the group's collaboration with the class. Managerial roles, such as materials gatherer or clean-up, should be used before or after a group learning routine but not during. During group learning routines, the roles should be essential to furthering discussion. There always needs to be a reason to listen to a speaker or students will not know what to listen for and remember.

"Turns" means to simply identify who is going first as the speaker in each group. This resolves problems with social loafing and wasted time, as students negotiate who is going to go first. The turns should always be assigned by the teacher to reach an instructional goal. For example, there may be times when you would want to assign a student with a question to begin. There may also be times when you want a student with a correct and complete answer to begin. By assigning a student to start the group conversation for a particular reason, teachers can move group discussions efficiently toward the instructional goal.

Rules are made to ensure rigor and access for all students. For example, a rule of "Point and Repeat" enables students who are still forming a response and those who are new to speaking in English to simply point to a student to have that student repeat what they said.

In this way, every student can engage in the group's discussion. As the year progresses, rules can change to ensure the routine maintains rigor for students. So, our rule of "Point and Repeat" might shift to "Point, Repeat, Repeat" or "Point, Repeat, Add or Repeat" to ensure that all students are using academic oral language in the group discussion.

Finally, time is always designated to ensure equity in opportunities, to share ideas in the class, and to protect time to think about responses before being required to reply. Time may be kept by the teacher using a watch, or a timer may be used. Time should always be designated and kept for each individual to share and for all group members to think about what was heard before moving on to more sharing. There should also be free discussion time during every group learning routine. Keeping time enables a teacher to shorten time when students are just developing their responses, so that students can give a partial response and be successful. It also enables a teacher to extend time to foster longer explanations from students. Another advantage to keeping time is that group learning routines never run over the time allotted in a lesson, because time is kept for each part of the routine.

Teachers use the four parts of *Inclusive Directions*—roles, rules, turns, and time—to ensure equity and engagement for all learners during small group discussions. There are sample dilemmas in Chapter 8 where you can practice adjusting roles, turns, rules, and time to eliminate challenges and increase rigor and student learning from the group routine.

Checklist to Try Routines in Your Teaching

See https://www.routledge.com/9780815370819 for additional resources: *Domino Discover* Step by Step Directions, Knowing Your Students, and Printable *Traction Planner*.

Plan	Teach	Adjust Instruction
☐ *Traction Planner*	☐ *Domino Discover*	☐ *Inclusive Directions*

Quality Criteria to Implement Classroom Routines	
Must Haves	**Amazing**
• Notice student strengths in planning and in the classroom. • Increase time spent reflecting in planning and in the classroom. • Share the results of these routines with a friend and discuss your observations about student responses. • Shift task structure on a daily or weekly basis, or tie a specific structure to a type of instruction, such as a mini-lesson, independent practice, or review.	• Implement an activity or question aimed at learning from and about students in every lesson. • Stretch your thinking and perceptions about students. • Stretch student perceptions about themselves. • Encourage student ownership by asking students to assist in recording responses or managing the collection.

Chapter Reflection

Chapter Summary

In this chapter we answered the question, "Why do we need to adjust or differentiate instruction?" To accomplish this objective, we identified our starting positions with the *Jot Notes* routine to consider teacher perceptions of student characteristics that vary widely, creating extremes that are challenging to engage within time and curriculum constraints. We examined statistics that speak to the increasing range of student ethnic and academic diversity, which confirms teacher perception of the wide range and diversity of student strengths and needs that impact effective learning in every lesson. We provided classroom routines to launch daily differentiated instruction. For planning instruction, we highlighted how the *Traction Planner* routine can build our awareness of the relationships between student characteristics that we perceive and the required curriculum. We also described how shifting structures allows teachers to listen to and observe students, while students receive feedback on their thinking from peers. By using shifting structures, you began to develop agile teacher responses to student needs as learning occurred during lessons. We encouraged you to adjust instruction by planning to learn from your students in every lesson before you began teaching. Finally, we asked you to return to your starting position of how your perceptions of students reflect on learning and plan the next steps toward ensuring all learners are learning every day.

Learning Journal: Record Important Takeaways

In your *Learning Journal*, track your thinking about meeting the needs of diverse learners by answering the same four questions we presented in Chapter 1:

1. What was most interesting and useful for you in this chapter?
2. Why was this interesting and useful?
3. How does this connect to what you know about meeting the learning needs of all learners?
4. What research from this chapter could you use to explain or support decisions to adjust instruction?

Save these responses for reflection after reading more of this book and trying out ideas in your classroom.

Return to Your Starting Position

Return to your chart of student characteristics that impact learning in your subject area. Add and adjust characteristics that may be important when planning instruction. Consider how these characteristics might change and how you along with the students will notice the changes throughout the school year. Consider ways to document student characteristics through student work, photos of learning, and video to facilitate noticing changes in a way similar to our opening story.

Now, go all the way back to our chapter question, "Why do we need differentiated instruction?" Reread your preliminary first draft answer to our chapter question. Consider how your answer has been confirmed, changed, or challenged after reading this chapter and trying out the classroom routines in your planning and practice with students. Add new ideas to your answer or revise it in another way. Circle the most important part and save it to return to after Chapter 8. Now that we know why we need differentiated instruction, let us turn our attention to our next chapter, step one of our framework, **Identify OSCAR**.

Note

1. For those of you who are interested in further exploring your biases, we would recommend looking into the implicit association test. https://implicit.harvard.edu

References

Brophy, J. E. (1985). Teacher–student interaction. In J. B. Dusek (Ed.), *Teacher expectancies* (pp. 303–328). Hillsdale, NJ: Lawrence Erlbaum.

Cooper, K. S. (2014). Eliciting engagement in the high school classroom: A mixed methods examination of teaching practices. *American Educational Research Journal*, 51, 363–402. doi:10.3102/0002831213507973

Dweck, C. S. (2006). *Mindset: The new psychology of success*. New York, NY: Ballantine Books.

Fuchs, D. (2006). Cognitive profiling of children with genetic disorders and the search for a scientific basis of differentiated education. In P. Alexander & P. Winne (Eds.), *Handbook of educational psychology* (pp. 187–208). Mahwah, NJ: Erlbaum.

Hall, T. E., Meyer, A., & Rose, D. H. (2012). *Universal design for learning in the classroom: Practical applications*. New York, NY: Guilford.

Hiebert, J., & Stigler, J. W. (2017). Teaching versus teachers as a lever for change: Comparing a Japanese and U.S. perspective on improving instruction. *Educational Researcher*, 46, 169–176. doi:10.3102/0013189X17711899

Ladson-Billings, G. (1995). Toward a theory of culturally relevant pedagogy. *American Educational Research Journal*, 32(3), 465–491.

Musu-Gillette, L., Robinson, J., McFarland, J., KewalRamani, A., Zhang, A., & Wilkinson-Flicker, S. (2016). *Status and trends in the education of racial and ethnic groups 2016* (NCES Report No. 2016-007). Washington, DC: U.S. Department of Education, National Center for Education Statistics. Retrieved from http://nces.ed.gov/pubsearch

NAEP (2015). U.S. Department of Education, Institute of Education Sciences, National Center for Education Statistics, National Assessment of Educational Progress (NAEP), various years, 1992–2015 Mathematics Assessments. https://www.nationsreportcard.gov/reading_math_2015/#reading?grade=4; https://www.nationsreportcard.gov/reading_math_2015/#mathematics?grade=4

OECD (2016). *PISA 2015 Results (Volume 1): Excellence and Equity in Education.* Paris, France, OECD Publishing. http://dx.doi.org/10.1787/9789264266490-en

Rosenthal, R., & Jacobson, L. (1968). Pygmalion in the classroom. *The Urban Review*, 3(1), 16–20. doi:10.1007/BF02322211

Rubie-Davies, C. M., Peterson, E. R., Sibley, C. G., & Rosenthal, R. (2015). A teacher expectation intervention: Modeling the practices of high expectation teachers. *Contemporary Educational Psychology*, 40, 72–85. doi:10.1016/j.cedpsych.2014.03.303

Snyder, T. D., & Dillow, S. A. (2015). *Digest of Education Statistics 2013* (NCES Report No. 2015-011). Washington, DC: U.S. Department of Education, Institute of Education Sciences, National Center for Education Statistics.

Reading 2.7

Differentiated Instruction

John P. W. Hudson

If it were admitted that the great object is to read and enjoy a language ...
all might in their own way arrive there, and rejoice in its flowers.
—Harriet Beecher Stowe

E VERY LEARNER APPROACHES NEW ENCOUNTERS WITH unique ideas, lived experiences, and habits of learning. Differentiated learning teaching strategies enable all learners to engage with a topic from these unique perspectives and ability levels at the same time by having many openings for inquiry. Differentiated instruction is teaching that matches the learning profile of every learner like a key in a lock, allowing all students to open the lock no matter which key they have.

Inductive and Deductive Thinking: The First Building Blocks of Differentiated Instruction

It is important to understand that making meaning, or drawing conclusions, based upon combining what we know with what we experience, is fundamentally *inductive* thinking. Inductive thinking is a rational construct that involves discovering the principles of an experience and applying existing knowledge to come up with an entirely new hypothesis. A good example is to understand a scientific principle, combine it with a known idea to create a new invention.

Deductive reasoning, on the other hand, is like Skinner's reductionist model: a simpler process of taking an existing rule and creating a prediction about a future event: *if* I make change X, I *then* predict outcome Y. Both processes, inductive and deductive, are potent and useful in educational settings because they closely match how the brain makes sense. The skillful teacher can evoke either to their advantage. Yin and Yang. Different, but complimentary. Both are needed in education.

Skillful Learning—Intelligence: The Second Building Block of Differentiated Instruction

We have complex gifts of character, emotion, size, shape, and gender, and we occupy every region on the planet living widely different lives, so the *ways* we learn are diverse. We have many things in common despite our vast differences, but one universal is learning. I believe that the learning of intelligence is a process of learning how to learn skillfully, like the musician who can improvise and harmonize beautifully over music never before heard. Learning how to *learn* skillfully is part of the process of learning how to *live* skillfully. However, when we can apply our life's and school's lessons skillfully and independently, we demonstrate intelligence.

Multiple Senses and Emotions: The Third and Fourth Building Blocks of Differentiated Instruction

Learning, therefore, is not just about information we need to know; it is inseparable from life and living, because it is the basic function of the brain as we experience the ever-unfolding present. We perceive the world through our five (or more) senses, we are moved to respond by the strength of our emotions, and we gain insight, sophistication, and wisdom as we become more experienced.

It is therefore important to combine as many of the five senses, our emotions, and the multiple ways of knowing as possible into every learning activity. Want to help students remember a poem? Set it to music and sing it. Want to help remember sequence? Use a dance move. Want to promote respect for a biome? Visit it. Because we know that learning happens in the learner's head, constantly, it is the teacher's duty to learn how to make intended learning happen there. Creating learning experiences that involve many senses, emotions, and movement is a good start. Here is what Karen Olsen (1995) describes:

> In order to create the rich environment needed to stimulate powerful learning for all students, current research shows that all 19 senses need to be stimulated. YES, 19 Senses (*not 5*): sight, hearing, touch, taste, smell, balance, vestibular, pain, eidetic imagery (vivid mental imagery), temperature, magnetic, ultraviolet, infrared, ionic, vomeronasal, proximal, electrical, geogravimetric, barometric.

SENSES	KIND OF INPUT
sight	visible light
hearing	vibrations in the air
touch	tactile contact
taste	chemical molecular
smell	olfactory molecular
balance	kinesthetic geotropic
vestibular	repetitious movement
temperature	molecular motion
pain	nociception
eidetic imagery	neuro-electrical image retention
magnetic	ferromagnetic orientation
infrared	long electromagnetic waves
ultraviolet	short electromagnetic waves
ionic	airborne ionic charge
vomeronasal	heromonic sensing
proximal	physical closeness
electrical	surface electrical charge; static
barometric	atmospheric pressure
geogravimetric	sensing mass differences

Whether or not one believes Olsen's assertions about senses, the point is that the fewer of the senses involved, the more difficult it is for the brain to learn. Conversely, the greater the number of senses involved, and the more intense the emotions, the easier it is for the brain to learn. Students therefore need to learn in complex and authentic (real) settings, or as close to that as possible. Some call it "'authentic," "hands-on," or "in the field." However you describe it, the greater the number of connections, the stronger the memory of the learning event.

Memory: The Fifth Building Block of Differentiated Instruction

Our understanding of memory has changed. Notions of how memory worked once revolved around discrete locations in the brain for each episode of our lives, with new experiences, things we learn, facts, figures, names, places, and so on each occupying an area of its own. This is not the case. Each memory we have is constructed from a set of neurons whose task does not change. Take for example, a memory of a glass of red wine: the brain will construct a memory by employing a group of neurons dedicated to the color red, another set for fluid, another for scent, still another set for glass, the concept of round, the sound of clinking glass, the taste of the wine, the feel of the glass, the ambient temperature, one's feelings, the scent of the flowers; the list is long. When these cells and connections (neurons and synapses) are visited often as a group, the brain's ability to reconstruct the experience strengthens. The more complex the experience, the more pathways the brain has to find the group and reconstruct it. This is the basic building block of recognition.

Although brain research is still very much in its infancy, it is certain that complexity is the environment the brain thrives in. Again, the more pathways to the memory set, the easier it will be for the brain to construct the memory. The relevance, significance, emotional intensity, consequences of the event, the complexity of the context, and the number of senses and emotions involved together will determine the strength and longevity of the memory. The more complex and intense the event, the greater the impact on the learner. Take for example, the memory of a serious car accident. The multitude of details, right down to the millisecond, often last a lifetime. Please refer to the References section for a link to a Web site for more insight into brain research by Ron Brandt (1997).

Multiple Intelligence Theory: The Sixth Learning Block of Differentiated Instruction

The theory of multiple intelligences was put forward in 1983 by Dr. Howard Gardner, professor of education at Harvard University, in response to limitations of intelligence tests. Intelligence was thought to be one-dimensional. Instead, he suggests that there are eight categories of intelligence observable across populations. Whether or not one believes this theory literally, it helps us to design learning experiences that access learning from eight different approaches, providing multiple pathways for differentiated learning.

- Linguistic intelligence: the degree of ability to use language
- Logical/mathematical intelligence: the degree of ability to manipulate and apply mathematical ideas
- Spatial intelligence: the degree of ability to use visual sense: design, art, photography
- Body/kinesthetic intelligence: ability in sports, dance, carving, all things one does physically
- Musical intelligence: an ability to appreciate, compose, or perform music; to hear exquisitely
- Interpersonal intelligence: social intelligence; an ability to read body language; to say the right thing

- Intrapersonal intelligence: understand and respond to one's own physical and spiritual needs
- Naturalist intelligence: an ability to exist successfully in natural settings, understanding many things from weather to plants and animals, wild and domesticated

Students' Teachable Learning Tools: The Seventh Building Block of Differentiated Instruction

Learners are also diverse because their lived experiences are diverse: region, family, culture, life experiences, interests, gender, tendencies, and emotions all play a role in the development of their individual learning style. In addition to Gardner's multiple intelligences, I believe there are multiple tendencies, approaches, and attitudes to learning, which are part of the learner's acquired learning habits.

Tendencies, Approaches, and Attitudes

Tendencies, approaches, and attitudes means the habits of learning and emotional response a student develops over time. These are changeable. For example, a common habit is to stop thinking about a problem if another student puts up their hand and answers the question. I have witnessed this for many years, but I had a clear example recently. Alan (not his real name) was selected to answer a question, which he did. He then stopped thinking about the question and resumed daydreaming as others responded to the same question. I quickly returned to him to ask a more sophisticated question that he could have answered if he had been listening to the contributions of the other students. He could not answer. By understanding this habit, Alan has learned to improve his listening attitudes and skill.

Another troublesome habit is to select the first correct answer on a multiple choice question without reading the remaining choices. Correcting this habit increased many students' scores. Another is learned helplessness. Students who are slower to process information may become dependent on others to provide them with clues or answers whenever they are asked to respond. They cultivate the art of losing their work, creative blaming, and shirking of responsibility, and may remain helpless as long as the adults and other students in their lives accept it. This might start from the very first days of school and may determine their self-concept throughout life. In adulthood, the individual who has learned helplessness could possibly transform into the learned victim. Although extinguishing learned helplessness takes much caring and persistence, a measure of confidence and determination can return to these individuals.

Sam

Sam was a student whose shoulders hung low, who rarely looked up, and whose work was deliberately messy, if it was not already lost. He always looked in high anxiety when asked questions, and rarely spoke. His scores in English were below the pass level. One day, I explained to him that he was on the same path as all the others, but that he was just at the start of his learning journey. I helped him understand some test-writing skills that increased his mark above the pass line on the next test. The day following the test, when we analyzed our learning deficits and celebrated our successes, the class listened intently as I began to describe an unnamed student who had increased his score by 10%! Everyone thought I was talking about one of our top students, but when I said Sam's name, the room was silent at first, then, as everyone looked at Sam and started to applaud. Sam's face went from believing I was talking about someone else, to realizing I had been talking about him! His face lit up like sunrise! It was a life-changing moment for him. His marks at the end of the year were still the lowest in the class, but no matter: he celebrated getting 80% on the final English exam.

Supporting Diverse Learners

Supporting diverse learners is not about teaching in different ways for each learner. Rather, it is placing students in situations where they can make sense of what they experience, compare it with what they know, reach a new understanding, and have an opportunity to express their understanding in original, unique ways. The kinds of lessons that serve diverse learners well have many entry points, or opportunities for open-ended questions. Of the six basic questions: *who, what, where, when, why,* and *how,* activities that engage *why* and *how* questions should achieve the "thickest" ideas and the greatest number of pathways to deeper understanding.

Performance-driven, outcomes-based teaching strategies are at the heart of student-centered learning. The central consideration in selecting a strategy is its effectiveness in attaining engagement and achieving the learning outcome. Keep in mind too, that the strategy needs to allow the learning to happen in students' heads and provide ample opportunity for useful, formative assessment.

Student-centered, performance-driven education is challenging at first. It can be interesting, especially if one's students have no experience with group learning. I understand too, how especially difficult it is to break away from your familiar teaching methods when the demands of examinations and prescribed textbooks rule your classroom. It can be done. It has been done, and in time, you can do it too. The key is to use emotion to motivate them and find a way to get them eager to engage.

Reluctant Learners

Learners who are used to sitting quietly in rows without speaking during instruction may find the transition to learner-centered strategies confusing at first, because they are used to silence, right answers only, and direct instruction. In some instances, students in traditional classes may not share responses so others cannot beat them on future tests. To overcome this, explain before starting exactly what will happen and what your expectations are about their learning. Students may need direct instruction and lots of practice to know when to speak freely and when to be respectful listeners. Be sure to make your first experiences very short; extended time is difficult to manage with inexperienced participants.

Thinking and Reflection

Reflection gives learners time to connect what they have learned with what they experience. Truly great minds in history like Socrates, Einstein, Newton, Nietzsche, Beethoven, Bach, and Galileo were all common people who achieved uncommon greatness. One could attribute their wisdom to genius, but a common thread among all these people is that they had time to reflect over many years. Their greatest accomplishments were not achieved in their youth; rather, their greatest ideas came after long, long years of reflection. Inspiration is not an idea arriving afresh at the lucky one's doorstep; rather, it is the moment—a beautiful moment—when the final link between the last two dangling questions lets new light flood in.

This chapter is intended to be a useful starting place for one to explore teaching for diverse learners. It is not at all complete! There is a forest of books that very capably present all these methods in much greater detail than is practical here. Often, by putting the teaching strategy in your favorite search engine, one will find a wealth of information and suggestions for implementation.

Untying the Knot

As we lead ourselves, so must we lead others. As we construct thoughts out of experiences, so must we allow others to do the same. Try not to give away understanding. Rather, engage curiosity and wonder, for it may be years later for the sown seeds of wonder to sprout, and more time yet to emerge from fertile soil as a plant of deep understanding. A lifetime of wonder may be needed for a seed to flower and bear fruit, and we cannot know, looking at our common young learners, who may bear uncommon fruit. We might not live long enough to find out, but plant the seeds we must, water well, and wait.

References

Brandt, R. (1997). *Brain research and effective teaching.* Reported by David Ruenzel. San Francisco: Posit Science. Retrieved 2008 from http://community.freechal.com/ComService/Activity/PDS/CsPDSContent.asp?GrpId=1072865&ObjSeq=8&PageNo=1&DocId=11050070

Gardner, H. (1983). *Frames of mind: The theory of multiple intelligences.* New York: Basic Books.

Olsen, K. (1995). *Synergy: Transforming America's high schools through integrated thematic instruction 2–9 to 2–11.* Federal Way, WA: Susan Kovalik & Associates.

Reading 2.8

Selections from Using Differentiated Classroom Assessment to Enhance Student Learning

Tonya R. Moon, Catherine M. Brighton, and Carol A. Tomlinson

Why Differentiated Classroom Assessment? Why Now?

Consider these classroom scenarios:

1. Miss Apple works with and designs lessons for 30 or more students who differ in age, ranging from 5 to 17 (grades 1–8) but who otherwise are very similar in terms of race, ethnicity, and English language proficiency. Rather than organizing the students by grade level, she identifies the needs of students in specific areas (reading, writing, arithmetic, history, and geography) and they work together to learn and complete necessary tasks. In front of the teacher's desk is a bench where groups of students are called to read aloud to the teacher or solve specific problems to evidence their developing understandings. From this, she noted students' progress.

2. Mr. Barnes is assigned to work with groups of students organized into grade levels by age, and the lessons are characterized by lectures delivered to the entire group at once. Most students share common racial and cultural backgrounds, although there are some recent immigrants who have joined the class. Students complete examinations to demonstrate their progress with the expectation that all students will move together to the next grade-level assignment upon completion of the year's lessons.

3. Ms. Conner teaches fifth grade in a class of 25 students ranging from 9 to 11 years old. The class is diverse with students identifying as Caucasian, African American, Latinx, and multi-racial. Several students who are English Language Learners (ELLs) receive English as Second Language (ESL) services, and others have designated support needs noted in 504 Plans and individual education plans (IEPs). One student has a documented physical disability that can present challenges in certain classroom activities. Several

students participate in the federal free and reduced lunch program. The 25 students not only vary in terms of cultural and language characteristics, but also in terms of their interests both within and outside of school, their readiness to learn, as well as their individual preferences for interacting with academic materials. Ms. Conner's principal expects her to use data to inform her classroom instruction in ways that acknowledge, value, and support students with a broad array of learning preferences and needs.

The descriptions of the classrooms above provide a brief glimpse into the shifting characteristics of American education. The first, from a one-room schoolhouse, embodies a multi-age, multilevel classroom where addressing student variance was a given and the teacher planned instruction based on students' current points of entry into a topic or skill-set. Students collaborated in a variety of teacher-guided learning groups designed to help all students progress from their current points of development while the teacher instructed individuals and small groups of students with the same goal in mind. Assessment at the recitation bench was an organic part of Miss Apple's classroom, helping her determine when students were ready to progress to the next set of skills and topics. In this classroom, and others like it across the United States, there was no illusion that students of the same age would fare well by doing the same work, at the same time, with the same support. What we now call differentiation was simply how teachers planned and how students learned.

The second scenario is typical of 19th-century American classrooms, and it reflects the influence of America's rapidly changing economy, the shift from agriculture to industry, and an increasing number of immigrants joining the new workforce. Schools were changing to prepare young people for the new world of work they would enter and to which they would need to contribute. Perceived efficiency was the order of the day, and classrooms now contained students of the same age. The assumption was that all six-year olds, for example, could successfully pursue learning in a lockstep progression. Also during this time, single examinations determined whether students progressed to the next grade level, and there was scant, if any, provision for students who were outliers. In many ways, schools mirrored the factories for which their students were being prepared.

The third scenario reflects typical classrooms across the United States today. An obvious marker of today's classroom is the rise of diversity in many forms. School systems around the nation are experiencing rapid growth in the number of culturally and linguistically diverse students, while about 13% of school-age students receive special education services (https://nces.ed.gov/programs/coe/indicator_cgg.asp) for identified exceptionalities. About 6% of students are identified as academically gifted (https://www.nea.org/assets/docs/twice-exceptional.pdf); about 1 in 59 students are identified with autism spectrum disorder (ASD; https://www.cdc.gov/ncbddd/autism/data.html); and parents' reports of approximately

64% of children aged 2–17 having a mental, emotional, or behavioral disorder at some point during their school careers (https://www.cdc.gov/ncbddd/autism/data.html). Some students, of course, have learning issues that cross multiple categories and may be English language learners as well. Further, there are students who come to school from both privileged and economically disadvantaged environments, and they manifest diversity in less evident ways as well (for example, different levels of motivation to do school, varied world views, a great range of personal interests). It is also the case that students come to the classroom with a wide array of experiences, both inside and outside of school, a variety of ways in which they approach learning, and varying social identities. All of these sources of learner variance, of course, have considerable bearing on learning success. This sweeping range of diversity, perhaps more than any other characteristic, defines 21st-century classrooms. Challenging as it is to effectively teach each learner in classrooms typified by such a degree of diversity, these classrooms also provide a considerable opportunity to prepare young people for life in a 21st-century world in which the ability to appreciate and work harmoniously and productively with people from many different cultures and exceptionalities whose perspectives, proclivities, and talents are sculpted, at least in part, by those exceptionalities and cultures.

The challenge of teaching in academically diverse classrooms is amplified by the nearly two-decade, single-minded emphasis on high-stakes testing—a second core reality in U.S. public school classrooms. A baseline assumption of high-stakes testing is that all students should be ready to succeed on the prescribed tests at the same time in the school year, with accommodations available only in documented need instances. Building administrators and teachers are held accountable for student outcomes on the tests, without regard to student language, economic status, adult support, and life experiences—and sometimes even without regard to learner exceptionality. The resulting pressure to prepare all students to master an over-abundance of content by a specified date causes many teachers to feel they have no choice but to steamroll through their curricula so they will have "covered" massive amounts of rigid and prescriptive content prior to the test date. This inclination is reinforced and amplified by pacing guides and/or required lesson plans that must be carried out in a specific sequence according to a rigid timeline.

This kind of accountability policy is paradoxical in at least two ways. First, it encourages teachers largely to ignore the student variance they continually observe in their classes, and results in one-size-fits-all instruction at the very point in our history when individual student-focused instruction is most needed. Second, the policies that were intended to yield primary benefit for students from low-income and minority groups appear to serve these students particularly poorly (though the policies appear to serve few students well). Since the implementation of high-stakes accountability testing in public schools was mandated by *No Child Left Behind* (2001), a great deal was documented about the unintended consequences of such legislation. Although the law's intent was to reduce on-going achievement gaps, there exists little to no evidence that there has been any closing of the gaps (Nichols & Harris, 2016). Rather, evidence of high-stakes testing practices indicates that teachers' instructional and assessment practices follow a narrow curriculum where students are not exposed to non-tested content and, instead, engage in a steady diet of test preparation activities (e.g., Herman, 2004; Koretz, 2017; Moon, Brighton, & Callahan, 2003; Moon, Callahan, & Tomlinson, 2003).

While the testing accountability policies' intent is to increase student learning, according to recent government reports (https://www.nationsreportcard.gov/), only about one-third of U.S. fourth- and eighth-grade students read at a proficient level as measured by the National Assessment of Educational Progress (NAEP). Many scholars and policymakers point to the combination of demographic shifts in U.S. classrooms and annual testing policies as root causes of the stagnation. For students leaving the K-12 educational system, national rates of remediation in post-secondary institutions indicate that many students are underprepared to engage in college-level work, with 40%–60% of students entering the first year requiring remediation in English, mathematics, or both (http://www.highereducation.org/reports/college_readiness/CollegeReadiness.pdf). The problem is more acute for low-income students and students of color, with 56% of African American students and 45% of Latinx students enrolling in remedial post-secondary courses nationwide, compared to 35% of white students. The renewed emphasis on accountability policies found in the *Every Student Succeeds Act* (ESSA, 2015) does little to lessen teachers' conclusion that "one-size-fits-all" teaching and assessment is their only instructional option.

Re-creating the Classroom: A Different Approach to Instruction and Assessment

Excellent teaching is both an art and a science. Our two-decadelong experiment with achievement via test-driven pedagogy, rigid, often de-contextualized and low-relevance curriculum, and classrooms in which young human beings take a back seat to test scores, is clearly anything but artful. That approach is also inconsistent with our best knowledge about the science of teaching—as we will see in Chapter 2. Further, we have ample evidence that in one-size-fits-all classrooms few, if any, students have their needs met.

Differentiated instruction (Sousa & Tomlinson, 2018; Tomlinson, 2014, 2017; Tomlinson & Imbeau, 2010; Tomlinson & Moon, 2013) provides a framework for re-designing classrooms to place individual students in the center of learning, uses curriculum that enlivens learning, provides instruction that reflects both the art and science of teaching, and creates learning environments that enhance the development of both students and teachers. Central to

Tomlinson's (2001) original model of differentiation is the role of formative/on-going assessment as a vehicle for advancing learning. In this book, we will expand the original model to include focusing on the critical role of differentiated assessment, including both formative and summative, in understanding students' varied learning needs, guiding instructional planning, and developing student agency in learning.

Before we begin exploring the purpose, practice, and promise of assessment in differentiated classrooms, it is helpful to provide a brief overview of the broader model of differentiation. The purpose here is not to explore the model in depth, but rather to establish the context in which we envision assessment—and to provide readers with a "refresher" on the model.

Differentiation

Differentiation is rooted in a philosophy that is guided by five principles, and enacted through the use of several key practices. All of these aspects inform and shape the nature and use of assessment in differentiated classrooms. The three tables that follow capture these aspects (Tables 2.8.1, 2.8.2, and 2.8.3).

The philosophy, principles, and practices of differentiation are all "cut from the same cloth"—that is, they stem from the same bodies of research on teaching and learning and work together to create classrooms designed to encourage and support maximum development of the potential of each learner in the classroom—and of the teacher as well. The philosophy, principles, and practices are highly interdependent. For instance, the nature of the learning environment will either encourage or discourage student motivation to learn, which, in turn, will accordingly influence the impact of instruction on student learning. The way in which a teacher envisions and implements assessment practices will make the environment less, or more, invitational for students (Tomlinson & Moon, 2011, 2014). Flat curriculum that has little relevance for learners will necessarily diminish the impact

TABLE 2.8.1 Assumptions of Differentiation

Key Assumptions	Brief Explanation of the Assumption
Diversity is normal and valuable.	Inclusion honors the contributions of all individuals. Segregation and isolation are diminishing.
Seeing every student's capacity to learn and contribute is essential to inclusion.	Teachers who believe in both the hidden and evident abilities of their students make room for those abilities to grow in the classroom.
The role of the teacher is to maximize the growth of each learner.	Teachers who accept responsibility for maximizing the growth of each learner plan and teach to realize that goal.
It is the responsibility of schools to ensure that all students consistently have equity of access to excellent learning opportunities.	Teachers and other school leaders have the responsibility to remove barriers that deny many students equal access to excellence.

TABLE 2.8.2 Some Key Principles of Differentiation

Principles	Key Indicators of the Principle	Brief Explanation
Quality teaching said learning stem from an invitational learning environment	Teacher with a growth mindset Strong teacher/student connections Strong sense of "team" or "community" in the classroom	Students need to feel safe, valued, appreciated, challenged, and supported in order to learn well
Quality curriculum is foundational to student success	Clear learning targets (KUDs) Emphasis on student understanding Plan for engaging learners	The brain needs "sense" (understanding) and "meaning" (relevance) to learn
Assessment information informs teaching and learning	Strongly aligned with learning targets (KUDs) Emphasizes understanding Used to guide teacher and student planning	Tight alignment of assessment with learning targets focuses assessment appropriately. Information gleaned from assessment is the compass of daily planning
Instruction responds to student variance	Tightly aligned with learning targets (KUDs) Based on assessment information Responsive to student readiness, interest, and approach to learning Proactively planned	Tight alignment of instruction with learning targets focuses teaching and learning effectively. Attention to varied learning needs provides each student with a pathway to grow
Classroom routines should balance flexibility and stability	Students understand and participate in developing a differentiated classroom The teacher leads students and then works with them to manage routines	Developing a differentiated classroom is a team effort that seeks the contributions of everyone in the class to support the success of each learner

of instruction and the "draw" of the environment, just as highly engaging curriculum will enliven both instruction and the environment in which it takes place.

Together, the core philosophy, principles, and practices of differentiation guide teachers in effectively differentiating content (what students learn or how they access what they learn), process (how students make sense of and come to "own" the content), products (how students show what they know, understand, and can do), and affect/learning environment (both the physical nature and feelings-related nature of the classroom and interactions in it; Callahan, Moon, Oh, Azano, & Hailey, 2015). Content, process, product, and affect/learning environment are differentiated in response to student readiness (current point of entry into content), interests (student passion for or curiosity about an idea or topic), or learning

TABLE 2.8.3 Some Key Practices of Differentiation

The Practice	Description	Rationale
"Teaching up"	Teachers plan first for their advanced students, then differentiate by scaffolding other students to work with the challenging assignments	This approach opens the way for all students to have equity of access to excellent learning opportunities. Differentiate by "teaching up," not by "dumbing down"
Respectful tasks	Every student's work looks equally important, equally appealing, and equally engaging	This respects the dignity of each student and signals the expectation that each student will do meaningful work
Flexible grouping	Students work regularly in a variety of groupings with students who have both similar and different points of readiness, interests, and approaches to learning	This builds community, avoids stereotyping, and extends student awareness of strengths of all members of the class

preferences (ways of engaging with learning at a given time in the learning process). The primary intent of all aspects of differentiation is to facilitate student proficiency with the targets for any segment of learning, and, whenever possible, to guide the learning in moving beyond those targets (Bondie, Dahnka, & Zusho, 2019).

The Role of Assessment in Effective Differentiation

For purposes of this book, six key ideas or components of differentiation will be emphasized:

- The classroom functions as a *Community of Learning* where all students feel safe, supported, respected, and are willing to take the risk of learning.

- *High-Quality Curriculum* engages students with relevant and important knowledge, ideas, and skills that enable them to lead productive and meaningful lives.

- *Respectful Tasks* ensure that work and working conditions for all learners are equally important, equally appealing, and equally engaging, enabling every learner to see him or herself and every other learner as held in high regard by the teacher, expected to do important work, and capable of doing that work. Respectful tasks also take into account student entry point, strengths, interests, and approaches to learning so that success is just within the reach of the learner.

- *Flexible Grouping* allows students to work in a variety of grouping arrangements based on interests, current readiness levels, and/or learning preferences. Groupings are sometimes heterogeneous and sometimes homogeneous in nature and may be selected by students or assigned by the teacher based on the nature of the work and the needs of the learners.

- *Teaching Up* sets a high ceiling of student expectations and scaffolds the process of moving toward those expectations so that each learner regularly finds the balance of academic challenge and support necessary to extend his or her current levels of proficiency with important content.

- *Continual Assessment* allows teachers to understand students' learning trajectories, both individually and collectively, and to establish and maintain an effectively differentiated classroom. This element is the chief focus of this book. However, it is important to understand that continual, effective differentiated assessment intersects with the other five elements as well.

Building on a foundation of clear and meaningful learning goals, teaching in a differentiated classroom adopts classroom assessment practices that allow you to determine students' progress toward expected milestones and to use current evidence to inform instructional planning. Information derived from differentiated formative assessment guides you in creating purposeful instructional *groupings*, determining the *pace of instruction*, making sound choices about *materials and other resources*, and determining how to *support and extend learning* for students in a given instructional moment. Information derived from differentiated summative assessment guides you in evaluating student learning at the end of an instructional segment whether it be at the end of a series of lessons (e.g., quiz) or at the completion of a unit of study (e.g., performance assessment or exam). In addition, differentiated summative assessments can also be used formatively to guide decisions in subsequent instructional units.

Too often, however, classroom assessment practices follow the one-size-fits-all model, using the same assessments and assessment processes for all students. The resulting data then lead to ill-informed instructional decisions that overlook students' varied learning needs. If the purpose of classroom assessment is to generate insights about students that are as accurate as possible in order to support student-focused decision-making, then using assessment practices that overlook the diversity of students' academic needs suggests a lack of understanding of what constitutes appropriate assessment practice (Marzano, 2000). In classrooms where teachers aspire to reach each student, assessments themselves will often be differentiated to help the teacher understand and address the range of student needs throughout learning cycles as well as increase student agency and involvement in the assessment process.

Classroom Assessments during Formative Assessment

While many definitions exist for formative assessment, the Chief Council of State School Officers (CCSSO, 2008, p. 2), define it as "a planned, ongoing process used by all students and teachers during learning and teaching to elicit and use evidence of student learning to improve student understanding of intended disciplinary learning outcomes and support students to become self-directed learners." Said a bit differently, formative assessment is a process through which a teacher formally or informally collects data on student proficiency with targeted content and analyzes the data to understand patterns of student development in that content, in order to make better decisions about next steps in teaching and learning and to help students plan effectively for continued learning. Appropriate use of formative assessment results in a teacher changing teaching and learning plans with the goal of more positive student outcomes than had the data not been available.

In this book, we will often separate "formative assessment" into two stages—*pre-assessment*, which, as noted above, occurs prior to the start of a unit of study to understand students' points of entry into upcoming unit, and *on-going assessment*, which occurs regularly throughout a unit of study to maintain awareness of students' degrees of progress as the unit unfolds. Both pre- and on-going assessments are types of formative assessment. The distinction simply clarifies the time during which the assessment occurs. We will always use the term pre-assessment to refer to classroom diagnostic assessment that takes place before formal study of a unit begins. We will use the terms formative assessment and on-going assessment interchangeably to refer to assessments that occur throughout a unit of study to inform teaching and learning.

The Differentiated Assessment Cycle: What, When, and Why?

When thinking about differentiated classroom assessment (DCA) and the data that are generated from such assessments, it is helpful to have an understanding of *when* to assess, *what* to assess, and *why* assessment matters. Answering these questions informs the three phases of the assessment cycle within an instructional setting—pre-assessment, on-going/formative assessment, and summative assessment. It is important to note that assessments in any of the three phases can, and often should, be differentiated (Figure 2.8.1).

Phase I of the Assessment Cycle: Pre-assessment

In effectively differentiated classrooms, teachers gather data at the individual student level prior to the start of a new unit of study or topic because students enter the space with a wide range of pre-existing knowledge, skills, beliefs, attitudes, motivations, and understandings, all of which influence how they will process and integrate new information. This in turn affects how students will think, apply, and create new knowledge, skills, and understandings.

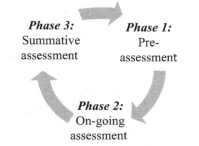

FIGURE 2.8.1 Phases of the assessment cycle.

Intentionally deciding to gather these data prior to a new unit of study and make sense of the collected data for instructional planning, signals that the teacher intends to align the delivery of instructional content with students' needs thereby avoiding pitching the content either beyond or beneath the appropriate place for the students. Pre-assessment data allow you and the student to work with the new content in efficient and productive ways. While teachers often pre-assess student status with upcoming learning targets (KUDs) a day or two before a new unit begins, there is obvious benefit to giving pre-assessments several days before the start of a new unit. Giving pre-assessments several days in advance allows sufficient time in a busy schedule for you to study the pre-assessment result in some depth to identify patterns of student need revealed in the pre-assessment data and to adjust instructional plans accordingly.

Pre-assessments should never be graded. It is important to remember that grades are used to answer the question "How well did a student learn and achieve the identified learning targets?" Grading pre-assessments completely ignores the fact that some students have more knowledge or skills than others before instruction ever begins, thus often penalizing those with less knowledge or skills at the outset. The sole purpose of pre-assessment is to identify where students are relative to identified learning targets prior to instruction in order to know how to target early instruction to learners' varied entry points. You will be most successful in your instructional efforts if all students have at least a basic level of knowledge once the lesson(s) is taught.

Phase II of the Assessment Cycle: On-going Assessment

Fundamental to a differentiated classroom is persistent collection of data to support the teacher's instructional planning and the student's plans for learning as well. This phase of the assessment cycle also supports teacher reflection on the effectiveness of the instructional choices you make in support of student learning to the current point in a unit or sequence of study. Data collected via on-going assessment can be formal or planned assessments (for example, quizzes, exit cards, short answer responses) or informal data (for example, observing student work in process and making notes on the observations, conversations with students about their work, asking students to indicate with a hand signal or colored card their confidence level with an idea or skill). Some of these informal assessments are at the individual student level (e.g., concept map or a student check-in with you). Others are at the whole-class level (e.g., on-the-fly assessment through student finger signals to show degree of mastery).

The importance of the on-going phase of the assessment cycle is that it provides an opportunity for both yourself and your students to focus on what is required next to reach the targeted learning goals. It provides information useful in planning student groupings, differentiating upcoming tasks, and planning next steps for whole class or small group instruction. For the students, on-going assessment provides information about progress to date in a unit and opportunity to regulate or plan for their continued learning. When using on-going assessment information to teach more effectively, the assessment is sometimes referred to as assessment *for* learning, which is not a different idea from formative assessment but rather emphasizes why we do this in our teaching process. When a student uses on-going assessment to better understand their current learning and to plan more proactively for continued growth, the assessment is sometimes referred to as assessment *as* learning. Ideally, many formative (i.e., on-going) assessments serve the dual purpose of assessment *for* and assessment *as* learning (e.g., Earl, 2013). By that, we mean the actual process of engaging with the formative assessment itself serves as a source of learning for the students. Assessment *as* learning places students in the position of self-regulating their own learning through which they make decisions about how they will use feedback in order to move toward mastery of the targeted learning goals. Again, on-going assessments should rarely, if ever, be graded. They take place during the part of the learning cycle when students need practice to master content. When teachers assign grades prematurely during practice, student willingness to continue practicing and risk making mistakes that are necessary for learning diminishes. The goal for formative assessment is providing meaningful, actionable, differentiated feedback that helps a student move forward in learning, not judging or grading students.

Phase III of the Assessment Cycle: Summative Assessment

The third phase of the assessment cycle is summative assessment, sometimes referred to as assessment *of* learning. This phase plays an important role in the instructional planning process because it provides information regarding the degree to which a student has mastered (or exceeded) the pre-determined learning goals (KUDs). Unlike pre- and on-going assessments, summative assessment is generally graded. The summative phase occurs only after students have had the opportunity to engage with and practice the content, allowing sense-making to occur so they are in a good position to demonstrate their level of under-standing of the content and skills with some success.

It is important to note that summative assessment can occur both at the end of a series of lessons (i.e., quiz) and at the end of a completed unit of study (e.g., exam). In the former instance, students demonstrate at the end of a discrete segment of learning within a unit of study that they have (or do not have) foundational knowledge upon which subsequent lessons in the unit will build. Examples of this type of summative assessment include short assignments, tests, and quizzes. At the end of a unit, of course, students demonstrate their level of mastery of the larger or complete segment of learning. While both examples are types of summative assessment, those that occur at the end of the unit may be more encom-passing (cumulative) than the type that occurs after a series of lessons within the unit. The difference occurs in the level of interpretation and types of decisions that can be made ear-lier versus later in the summative phase of the cycle. Both types of summative assessment are typically graded. However, the end-of-cycle summative assessment should likely carry more weight in determining reported grades, particularly in instances where the end-of-cycle assessment is cumulative.

This book primarily focuses on how to gather and use data from DCAs (pre-assessments, on-going/formative, summative) to promote learning for all students, with the goal of hon-oring and serving effectively the full range of academically diverse students in today's classrooms. We also believe it is important to also provide some guidance on how to differ-entiate classroom assessments themselves. For complete details on this process, you can refer to Tomlinson and Moon (2013).

A (Brief) Guide to Differentiating Classroom Assessment

Inherent in the key practices of differentiation outlined in Table 2.8.3 is that effective dif-ferentiation occurs through one or more mechanisms (Tomlinson, 2017):

1. Differentiation of the content to be taught to different groups of students;
2. Differentiation of the process by which you use different instructional strategies tar-geted to different groups of students and/or different sense-making strategies that students engage with the content for the purposes of learning; and/or
3. Differentiation of the "product" whereby students demonstrate their learning.

These avenues for differentiation occur in response to learners' interests that may have rel-evance to the new content to learn, readiness to learn the new content, and/or through the ways in which best set students up for success in learning the content. Undergirding all of this is that the learning goals remain the same (KUDs) regardless of the type of differentiation employed unless noted in special cases (e.g., special education modifications). From a differentiated assessment framework, these same avenues for differentiating the assessment still hold. When the learning targets and the content *remain the same* for all students, the assessment can be differentiated through the ways in which students engage with the assessment content, and/or by the final product students produce in response to assessment requirements. When the learning standards *are not tied to specific content* and thus can be different across students, the assessment's content may be differentiated. For example, in a high school Life Science class, students are studying the interdependence of relationships in ecosystems. One of the learning standards from the Next Generation Science Standards is that students are to test solutions to a proposed problem related to threatened or endangered species (HS-LS4.6, www.nextgenscience.org). In this example, the proposed problem that students tackle may be different (i.e., different content), but the purpose of the assessment remains the same: measuring the HS-LS4.6 standard. The ways that students engage with the assessment task (i.e., process) or the final product may, or may not, be differentiated. It is an important note that not all assessments can or should be differentiated. For example, certain types of assessments (e.g., closed-ended tests—multiple choice, true/false, matching) should only be differentiated by the ways in which students *have access to the assessment* (e.g., paper-and-pencil versus being audio-recorded) or *the way in which they respond* (e.g., paper-and-pencil versus computer or verbally) or the *conditions around their complexity*, such as extended time allowed or completion of the items in a different location. Additional details are provided for consideration of differentiating assessments in upcoming chapters (i.e., Chapters 3 and 4).

The emphasis of the book is on the element of *differentiated assessment* within the context of a differentiated classroom and on how to *interpret* and *use* data that stems from such assessments to make instructional decisions that are appropriate for students' varied academic needs. While instruction is surely a central component of the learning cycle, this text will concentrate primarily on DCA, with emphasis on how data obtained from both formal and informal forms of DCA (formative and summative) help you provide learning experiences that are a good fit for your students.

Figure 2.8.2 depicts the frequency of administration of classroom assessment relative to the full spectrum of educational assessments given in today's schools. From this figure, it is easy to see that classroom assessments—both formative and summative—are the types of assessments best situated to have a consistent, direct, and positive impact on day-to-day teaching, and therefore on student learning.

Four key assumptions undergird this book's focus on DCA:

1. Students differ—they differ in readiness to learn new knowledge and skills, in interests and their ability to engage in the learning process, and in preferences at a given time for taking in, making sense of, and expressing information.

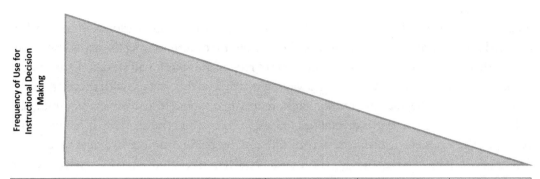

Frequency of Use for Instructional Decision Making

	CLASSROOM ASSESSMENTS		GRADE LEVEL ASSESSMENTS	ACCOUNTABILITY ASSESSMENTS	OTHER ASSESSMENTS
PRIOR:	Pre-assessment (Formative)		Common Formative Assessments	End-of-Course Assessments	PSAT
DURING:	"On-the-Fly"/Minute-by-Minute		Tests		SAT
	• Hand Signals (e.g., thumbs-up/down; windshield)		PBAs	End-of-Year	
	• 1-minute Response		Running Records	Assessments	ACT
	• 1-sentence Summary		Interim Assessments		NAEP
	• Etc.				
			Benchmark		PISA
	Day-by Day (Formative)		Assessments		
	• Exit Tickets				Special Assessments (e.g., gifted program, language proficiency)
	• Journal Entry		ETC.		
	• Teacher Conferencing				
	• Concept Map				
	• Teacher Observation				ETC.
	• Quick Checks				
	• Running Records				
	• Etc.				
AFTER:	End-of-Series of Lessons or Unit (Summative)				
	• Tests				
	• Performance-based Assessment				
	• Projects				
	• Portfolios				
	• Etc.				

FIGURE 2.8.2 The continuum and frequency of educational assessments.

2. Quality teaching requires responding to students' academic needs based on information derived from both formal and informal classroom assessments.

3. Clearly defined learning goals (KUDs) guide effective teaching and establish tight linkages between those curricular goals, assessments, and instruction. Classroom assessment is a crucial resource for ensuring coherence between high-quality curriculum, learning goals embedded in the curriculum, and the process of high-quality teaching.

4. Learning goals:

   a. can be domain-specific (focused on the core ideas and practices of a particular discipline);

b. can be domain-general (knowledge, understandings, and skills useful across a range of disciplines—e.g. problem-solving, self-regulation, making connections); and

c. can differ in time span required for student competence—from years (Lehrer & Schauble, 2011) to weeks, days, or even minutes (Siegler, 1995).

These assumptions play out in what Pellegrino, Chudowsky, and Glaser (2001) termed the *Assessment Triangle*, which proposes that there are three areas that underlie all assessment situations—including classroom assessment: cognition, observation, and interpretation. Cognition is the starting point for all teaching and assessment, embodying the core learning targets (knowledge, understandings, skills) on which teachers and students will focus. Observation refers to the methods and analytic tools through which a teacher determines the degree to which students are meeting the intended learning targets. Finally, interpretation represents the process of eliciting evidence from the assessments to inform instructional decisions. The premise is represented by an inverted triangle where the base represents the cognition component, which highlights the importance of having clarity about learning targets. In instances where there is a misalignment between the KUDs and the methods and analytic tools used to assess intended learning targets, the resulting data are not useful for making instructional inferences about students' learning. If, however, the KUDs are too narrow or broad, then the methods employed to gather evidence of student learning do not lend themselves to differentiation. In either case, high-quality data are not obtained, which results in teachers making ill-informed instructional decisions.

We will focus on applying this conceptual framework to the process of facilitating learning based on DCA and data resulting from such assessment.

Looking Back and Ahead

This chapter highlights the current diversity of today's classrooms and the inevitability of diversity in classrooms for the foreseeable future. It provides a digest of the elements of differentiation from which the practice of DCA derives. It also establishes a case for using classroom assessment data to enhance student learning in differentiated classrooms.

In the next chapter, we provide a digest of theoretical and empirical literatures that frame the model for DCA. There is strong scientific evidence for DCA and for using data from these assessments to better position students for mastering essential learning goals.

Chapter 3 examines the role of pre- and on-going assessment data in instructional planning and how to make sense of that formative assessment evidence in a way that leads teachers to make meaningful decisions. Chapter 4 parallels Chapter 3 by looking at the same questions as Chapter 3, but in regard to summative rather than formative assessment data. Chapter 4 places particular emphasis on differentiated performance assessments.

The final chapter brings the ideas explored in the earlier chapters together by providing a process for using data from DCA to plan instruction. It provides readers with recommendations and useful tips to inform data-use work in this aspect of successful teaching. We hope you will find the ideas accessible, the tools practical, and the "cases in point" relatable.

References

Bondie, R. S., Dahnka, C., & Zusho, A. (2019). How does changing "one-size-fits-all" to differentiated instruction affect teaching? *Review of Educational Research, 43,* 336–362. doi: 10.3102/0091732X18821120.

Callahan, C. M., Moon, T. R., Oh, S., Azano, A. P., & Hailey, E. P. (2015). What works in gifted education: Documenting effects of an integrated curricular/instructional model. *American Educational Research Journal, 52,* 1–31. doi: 10.3102/0002831214549448.

Council of Chief State School Officers. (2008). *Revising the definition of formative assessment.* Author.

Earl, L. (2013). *Assessment as learning: Using classroom assessment to maximize student learning.* Thousand Oaks, CA: Corwin.

Every Child Succeeds Act (ESSA) of 2015, Public Law No. 114–195, S.1177, 114th Cong. (2015). Retrieved from https://www.congress. gov/114/plaws/publ95/PLAW-114publ95.pdf.

Herman, J. L. (2004). The effects of testing on instruction. In S. H. Fuhrman & R. F. Elmore (Eds.). *Redesigning accountability systems for education* (pp. 141–166). New York, NY: Teachers College Press.

Koretz, D. (2017). *The testing charade: Pretending to make schools better.* Chicago, IL: University of Chicago Press.

Lehrer, R., & Schauble, L. (2011). Designing to support long-term growth and development. In T. Koschmann (Ed.), *Theories of learning and studies of instructional practice* (pp. 19–38). New York, NY: Springer.

Marzano, R. (2000). *Transforming classroom grading.* Alexandria, VA: ASCD.

Moon, T. R., Brighton, C. M., & Callahan, C. M. (2003). The influences of state testing programs on elementary teachers and students. *The Roeper Review, 25*(2), 49–60.

Moon, T. R., Callahan, C.M., & Tomlinson, C.A. (2003). Effects of state testing programs on elementary schools with high concentrations of student poverty—Good news or bad news? *Current Issues in Education* [On-line], *6*(8). Retrieved from https://cie.asu.edu/ojs/index.php/cieatasu/article/view/1683.

Nichols, S. L., & Harris, L. R. (2016). Accountability assessment's effects on teachers and schools. In G. T. L. Brown & L. R. Harris (Eds.), *Handbook of human and social conditions in assessment* (pp. 40–56). New York, NY: Routledge. doi: 10.4324/9781315749136.ch3

Pellegrino, J. W., Chudowsky, N., & Glaser, R. (2001). *Knowing what students know: The science and design of educational assessment.* Committee on the Foundations of Assessment, Board on Testing and Assessment, Center for Education, National Research Council. Washington, DC: National Academies Press.

Siegler, R. S. (1995). How does change occur: A microgenetic study of number conservation. *Cognitive Psychology, 25,* 225–273.

Sousa, D., & Tomlinson, C. (2018). *Differentiation and the brain: How neuroscience supports the learner-friendly classroom* (2nd Ed.). Bloomington, IN: Solution Tree.

Tomlinson, C. (2001). *How to differentiate instruction in mixed-ability classrooms* (2nd Ed.). Alexandria, VA: ASCD.

Tomlinson, C. (2014). *The differentiated classroom: Responding to the needs of all learners* (2nd Ed.). Alexandria, VA: ASCD.

Tomlinson, C. (2017). *How to differentiate instruction in academically diverse classrooms* (3rd Ed.). Alexandria, VA: ASCD.

Tomlinson, C., & Imbeau, M. (2010). *Leading and managing a differentiated classroom.* Alexandria, VA: ASCD.

Tomlinson, C. A., & Moon, T. R. (2011). The relationship between assessment and differentiation. *Better: Evidence-Based Education, 3*(3), 3–4.

Tomlinson, C. A., & Moon, T. R. (2013). *Assessment and student success in a differentiated classroom.* Alexandria, VA: ASCD.

Tomlinson, C. A., & Moon, T. R. (2014). The relationship between assessment and differentiation. In R. E. Slavin (Ed.), *Proven practices in education: Classroom management and assessment* (pp. 1–5). Thousand Oaks, CA: Corwin.

The Science behind Differentiated Classroom Assessment

For centuries, beliefs about student learning were based on the premise that a person was born with "tabula rasa"—a blank slate that would be written upon by experiences and perceptions, or a mind like an empty vessel waiting to be filled with information. While we still see evidence of those ancient philosophies in the ways we "do school," we now have a better sense of how the brain is structured at birth, and how those structures support learning. We know, for example, that the brain is organized at birth to help humans make meaning of the world around them, to learn from social interaction (Darling-Hammond, Flook, Cook-Harvey, Barron, & Osher, 2019), and to arrange and store information in ways that support meaning and efficient retrieval of that information (e.g., Lenroot & Giedd, 2007). We have evidence from research in psychology and neuroscience that the process of learning involves complex interactions (Zelazo, Blair, & Willoughby, 2017), such as reconciling new information with prior knowledge (Darling-Hammond, et al., 2019), monitoring the physical and social context where learning may occur, and cultivating positive relationships among the teacher, student, peers, and new content. It is helpful as we explore the principles and practices of differentiated assessment to briefly examine five research-supported pillars that have direct relevance to those principles and practices.

- Growth mindset is foundational to the nature and purpose of assessment;
- New knowledge builds on and extends a learner's prior knowledge and experiences;
- People learn when challenges are in their Zone of Proximal Development (ZPD)—when the challenges are a bit beyond their reach and they have the support necessary to extend their reach;
- Learning progressions provide a roadmap for assessment and instructional planning based on information gleaned from that assessment; and
- A social classroom environment supports learning through co-construction of knowledge, understanding, and skills.

Growth Mindset as Foundation for Differentiated Classroom Assessment

Consider the following scenario:

> Seventh-grade students Carlos and Tomas share the same physical education class. As part of the curriculum called Active Bodies-Healthy Lives, students complete short mini-courses, each focused on a different sporting activity

and its benefits for healthy living. The current session is focused on golfing. During each class, local golf enthusiasts guide students as they learn new golf techniques. Following each lesson, students practice the new skill. During the last week of the course, Mr. Jones, the golf pro from a local recreation league, watches each of the students swing the clubs and drive balls into the field so he can provide feedback to help each student improve their skills.

Later, the boys discussed the last golf session as they changed classes.

Carlos—I learned so much from Mr. Jones! I never thought about golf before this class but now I'm excited to keep practicing my swing and all the things we talked about.

Tomas—Not me! All he ever told me was what I did wrong. I stink at golf, and I'll never play again!

All classroom exchanges communicate tacit beliefs and assumptions, but perhaps none more powerfully than the messages we communicate through the ways we handle assessments, the ways we interpret success or failure based on assessments, the decisions we make as a result of students' performances on assessments, and how we share information from assessments with learners and other relevant stakeholders. In teaching, it is easy over time to forget the power assessments hold in students' minds (McMillan, 2016). McMillan's review of the literature on student perceptions regarding assessment suggests that there are factors that affect students' performances and their reactions to their performances prior to an assessment event, during an assessment event, and after an assessment event. Understanding these factors and their implications for teaching is an important aspect of student learning. What we might consider to be a minor exchange about a student's progress sends messages to those students about themselves as learners and our beliefs about the likelihood that they can be successful in their endeavors well beyond the sphere of the assessment. In the end, our assessment practices influence students' beliefs about learning, their purpose as learners, and even their worth as human beings. Therefore, it is helpful to start our discussion of the science of learning with the importance of expectations and motivation as those elements relate to assessment.

Assessments should be tools for educators and students to gauge a student's progress toward developing expertise in a given area. Assessments should serve as a source of student and teacher reflection that motivates both of them to persist. However, assessments often become obstacles rather than springboards to success when students equate struggle with lack of capacity, and interpret assessment results that show opportunities for growth to be tantamount to failure. In the example of golf class, Carlos approached the feedback he received as guidance that enabled him to continue improving his skills. In contrast, Tomas interpreted the feedback he received as an indictment of poor performance and inadequate ability. Through that lens, his decision to walk away from the sport entirely seemed the best way to avoid further discomfort and erosion of self-concept. At this point, Carlos reflected a "growth mindset" and Tomas a "fixed mindset." Teachers who want to ensure that their students grow as learners and see learning as key to building promising lives understand the importance of helping each learner develop a growth mindset. Because of the weight educators and schools place on measuring student growth, the way a teacher thinks about, uses, and communicates to students about assessment will likely be instrumental in shaping a student's mindset in ways that will undergird or undercut learning for a considerable period of time.

The psychological theory of mindset has emerged over the past three decades (for example, Dweck, 2006). It proposes intrinsic theories of intelligence, or mindsets, along a continuum from *fixed* (ability is in-born and cannot be markedly changed) to *growth* (ability can be developed throughout life). Psychologists David Yeager and Carol Dweck define mindset as "core assumptions about the malleability of personal qualities" (Yeager & Dweck, 2012, p. 303). A large body of research across a variety of settings and conditions indicates that academic mindsets can be quite influential in student motivation to learn, as well as in learning itself. A growth mindset can increase student motivation (e.g., Ng, 2018), contribute to student sense of belonging in an academic setting (e.g., Rattan, Good, & Dweck, 2012; Walton & Cohen, 2011), reduce achievement gaps across racial, social class, and gender groups (e.g., Blackwell, Trzensniewski, & Dweck, 2007; Claro, Paunesku, & Dweck, 2016; Degol, Wang, Zhang, & Allerton, 2018; Walton & Cohen, 2011), and build resilience in the face of difficulty (Blackwell et al., 2007). Research findings on mindset indicate that mindset can be shaped by expectations of self and others (e.g., Siegle, McCoach, & Roberts, 2017), through feedback (Smith, Brumskill, Johnson, & Zimmer, 2018), and through explicit teaching about mindset (Aronson, Fried, & Good, 2002).

Within educational settings, mindset manifests in goal orientations that greatly impact a student's approach to learning and learning outcomes. Students who have a *learning goal orientation* believe that mastery develops over time with practice and persistence. These students tend to find learning both challenging and satisfying and therefore learn for the sake of learning. By contrast, students with a *performance goal orientation* believe their abilities come from innate talent and that practice and persistence cannot significantly change that reality. Rather than valuing learning for its own sake, these students generally learn for the sake of rewards—or to avoid some sort of punishment. Too often schools further reinforce this performance-focused orientation. In the golf example, Carlos exhibited a learning goal orientation while Tomas evidenced a performance goal orientation. Students who learn because learning is satisfying are much more likely to continue to pursue learning over a lifetime than are students with performance orientations. Individuals who are motivated by rewards most often lose their motivation to learn when the rewards cease.

Mindset theory is especially important to consider in the context of differentiated assessment because in order to optimize students' academic achievement, both teachers and students must view the process of assessing, providing feedback, and responding productively to feedback as opportunities to learn and to enhance deeper understanding and skills. In other words, assessment must be envisioned, implemented, and presented in ways that reinforce a growth mindset, a learning orientation, for both students and teachers. It is important that both teachers and students view the opportunity to gather and act on information about progress toward learning goals as key to student success. When differentiated classroom assessment is implemented by a teacher with a growth mindset, with the intent to help students develop a growth mindset, it increases the chances that a student's experience with the assessment is an encouragement—an invitation to learn—rather than causing the student to feel discouraged about the likelihood that his or her participation in learning will lead to growth and success. Differentiated classroom assessment should be an invitation to students to be partners in and ultimately agents of their own learning. Likewise, teachers who approach differentiated assessment with a growth mindset are more likely to develop a deeper belief in the capacity of each student to succeed, and to develop a greater sense of their own agency as a teacher, as they come to understand the positive impact of assessment-informed instructional planning on the growth of their academically diverse students.

Building on Prior Knowledge to Gain New Knowledge

A second key principle to guide a consideration of differentiated classroom assessment is the importance of building upon students' prior knowledge. Phases I and II of the assessment cycle discussed in Chapter 1 outline not only the rationale for building on prior knowledge but also offer suggestions on how to build on students' prior knowledge. Each student comes to a classroom with educational and personal experiences that shape how they respond to teaching and learning—and, in fact, each student likely brings different constellations of backgrounds and perspectives. Students' brains are active seekers and processors of information. They attend to environmental elements (e.g., the teacher's mood, peers, instruction), encode the information to be learned, relate the new information to knowledge already in memory, store the new knowledge in memory, and retrieve it as needed (Schunk, 2016). From an instructional perspective, this provides support for differentiated instruction and assessment because with differentiation, both instruction and assessment are designed to build upon a student's prior knowledge and to enable each student to make connections between what she/he already knows and what she/he is about to learn.

Given that students come to classrooms all along the continuum of experiences, knowledge, and skills, and presuming that instruction is built around these differences (i.e., differentiated instruction), the same rationale applies to using differentiated classroom assessments. That is, by gathering data about students' knowledge, understandings, and skills related to a new topic of study through a pre-assessment and on-going assessment, you can use the resulting data to develop an instructional roadmap. That map prepares you to understand and build on students' prior knowledge as you plan instruction. It also enables you to be aware of and directly target any misconceptions students may hold. Simply said, to help a student continue to grow in any content sequence, you need to know where the student is at a given time in a learning progression.

Returning to the earlier golf example, a pre-assessment might reveal that while Carlos has never played golf before, he has had experiences with baseball, and his familiarity with batting prepared him for shifting the plane of his swing in golf. Tomas, we might learn, has had no prior experience in either sport and so the biomechanics of swinging at balls is completely new to him. Had the teacher merely surveyed the students about their general familiarity with golf before the unit began, neither boy would have indicated that they had prior knowledge or experience. Rather, having a more nuanced approach to identifying prior knowledge might provide a more insightful picture.

One way to obtain more precise insights is to differentiate the pre-assessment—providing multiple ways to show readiness and experiences related to golf ranging from an interview with the teacher about a student's background experiences in sports; asking students to analyze a short video showing a golfer swing a club; or asking students to swing a bat or club to hit a variety of balls. Through each pathway the student would likely provide a different type of information related to the sport and give the teacher a clearer pathway forward for each student.

The following scenario sets the stage for another example of how gathering data to help make better instructional decisions might look:

> Ms. Willis knew that in the upcoming weeks, her high school English class would be studying Shakespeare. Based on her previous experience with teaching Shakespearean literature, she knew her students would likely come to the unit with all kinds of experiences, knowledge, interests, and attitudes about Shakespeare. As class was ending a few days prior to the start of the Shakespeare unit, Ms. Willis asked students to jot down what they knew about Shakespeare and what experiences they had had with his work. She reminded them that if they didn't know anything about Shakespeare, that was okay—and that their responses would help her know how to plan the unit more effectively. When

Ms. Willis looked at the students' responses, she saw a great deal of variation. Some responses to the first question were accurate (for example, the time during which he was born, names of plays he had written, and that he acted in many of his plays). A few responses went beyond baseline information (for example, that his themes applied to people in all times and places, that he had a deep understanding of human nature and human emotions, and that his plays were adapted for various cultures, times, and media). Other responses were inaccurate (e.g., he wrote novels, he lived about 100 years ago), revealed student apprehension (his plays were too hard to understand or didn't connect with modern people). As Ms. Willis read their responses to the second question, she saw that some students had seen live performances of Shakespeare—some even at the Globe Theater, that some knew West Side Story was an adaptation of Romeo and Juliet, and that a few students knew about Shakespearian adaptations in countries from which they had emigrated to the U.S. Some students turned in blank pages. Using the students' responses from this pre-assessment and her growing knowledge about them as individuals, Ms. Willis began to envision ways she might plan the unit to connect with students' varied experiences, entry points, cultures, interests, and concerns so each student could grow in understanding and appreciation of Shakespeare's enduring legacy.

Part of Ms. Willis' considerations for her instruction after reviewing her students' exit tickets is to decide how she will support students during instruction so that each has the full opportunity to master the upcoming unit's learning goals. Ms. Willis should note her students' variation related to prior knowledge with Shakespeare with the range of insights about his work from none to shallow to emerging insights. From this conclusion, she proactively plans for ways to provide instructional experiences—recognizing these will be different for different students. Understanding the concept of ZPD (1978) developed by the Soviet psychologist, Lev Vygotsky, is helpful in planning how to address both the cognitive and affective variation that Ms. Willis finds in the exit tickets.

Zone of Proximal Development as Central to Learning Growth

Vygotsky's (1978) ZPD has, in large measure, shaped our current understanding that a student learns by building on his or her own prior knowledge. Vygotsky's defined ZPD as "the distance between the actual development level as determined by independent problem solving and the level of potential development as determined through problem solving under adult guidance or in collaboration with more capable peer" (p. 86). The ZPD can be characterized

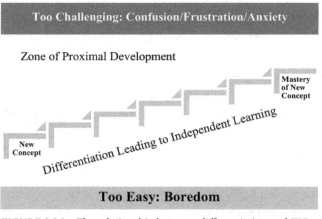

FIGURE 2.8.3   The relationship between differentiation and ZPD.

from both a cognitive and affective perspective. From the cognitive perspective you want to ensure that the content that students engage with is neither too difficult nor easy. From the affective perspective, having content too difficult or easy results in boredom or being confused and frustrated, which lead to student distraction or lack of motivation to engage. Importantly to note as well is that the optimal conditions for learning differ for each student and can differ for the same students in different contexts. Figure 2.8.3 displays visually the relationship between the concept of ZPD and differentiation.

Increasing Task Difficulty

Vygotsky (1978) theorized that a learner grows in knowledge, understanding, and skills by working with tasks at his or her current level of development (ZPD), as well as with scaffolding and support necessary to progress to a next level of learning. Similarly, Roosevelt (2008) proposed that students work in their ZPD with learning activities that are interesting and culturally meaningful to them, that are slightly more difficult than they can accomplish alone, and with peer/adult collaboration or scaffolding would enable them to close the gap between the manageable and the slightly out-of-reach. The premise is that after a student successfully completes a learning activity with a competent peer or adult support, or other appropriate scaffolding, he or she is then able to complete the task individually in the next encounter. By continuing this process, the student is able to learn progressively more difficult material. More recently, neuroscientists have shared the physiology behind the psychologists' observations. People learn, neuroscientists say, when the work we ask them to do is moderately challenging. When work is too demanding, the brain is over-taxed and unable to process the new information or skill. When work is too easy, no learning occurs because there is nothing new for the brain to make sense of (Sousa & Tomlinson, 2018; Willis, 2010). The concept of moderate challenge is individual-specific, not class-specific.

Using an example familiar to many, Judy Willis (2010), both a neuroscientist and an educator, explains how teaching students just beyond their current levels of challenge in a continually escalating cycle benefits learning:

> The compelling nature of computer games is an excellent example of differentiating instruction to the students' ZPD…The most popular computer games take players through increasingly challenging levels. As skill improves, the next challenge motivates practice and persistence because the player feels challenge is achievable. Similar incremental, achievable challenges in the classroom, at the appropriate level for students' (current) abilities, are motivating and build mastery by lowering the barrier, not the bar.
>
> (pp. 44–46)

The ideas of ZPD and moderate challenge should inform classroom assessment in the same. In other words, an assessment, just as a lesson, should ask a student to stretch just a bit—and should support the student in doing so. Assessments that are completely out of reach for a student are highly likely to be unproductive and negative for that student. It is unlikely that they will act as catalysts for further growth. Similarly, assessments that only asks student to repeat what has long been familiar to the student are a waste of that student's time—a lost learning opportunity. Thus, pre-assessments and on-going assessments that make room for the entry points of a range of learners will be more effective in helping a teacher target students' ZPDs for instructional planning than pre-assessments and formative assessments that do not make room for student variance. One mechanism that can help teachers plan effectively to address a range of student readiness through pre-assessment, formative assessment, and instruction is the use learning progressions.

Learning Progressions as Tools for Differentiating Assessments and Instruction

Learning progressions are pathways that students might take to reach the end goal contained in the content standards or other learning targets. A learning progression is "a carefully sequenced set of building blocks that students must master en route to mastering a more distant curricular aim" (Popham, 2007). In other words, learning progressions provide the building blocks to standards. That is, they outline the movement toward understanding, although the movement in most instances is not a lock-step sequence of steps (Hess, 2008). Instruction is the process by which students move along the pathway and assessment allows the teacher to know where students are at a specific point in time, a sociocognitive approach to teaching and assessing students' understandings as they develop proficiency with the content (Penuel & Shepard, 2016). What is important is that you use content learning progressions that map onto the curricular program of study. In most cases, this defaults to the state standards as a proxy for the curriculum, but as we noted in Chapter 1, standards are not synonymous with curriculum.

Learning progressions are also helpful when mapping learning targets in other programs such as Advanced Placement (AP) and International Baccalaureate (IB) courses, as well as more "open" curriculum such as Montessori. A mathematics learning progression developed around the Common Core is not the same as a learning standard developed around the Virginia Standards of Learning or the Texas Essential Knowledge and Skills Standards (TEKS). Common to all learning progressions is that they span across ages or grade levels and clearly articulate what students should know and be able to do at specified points in their K-12 educational experiences. The progressions are organized by content areas (e.g., mathematics, science) and provide a roadmap for more complex, challenging, and sophisticated content. These detailed progressions provide guideposts for teachers to address a wider range of academic readiness around a given topic.

Learning progressions answer questions such as "In what order should I teach these skills?" "Which skills develop earlier and which later during a given grade or age group?" "Where might I focus students when they are lagging behind at a particular point—or when they are ahead of most of their peers?" An example of the relevancy of learning progressions for instructional and assessment planning is demonstrated by the following primary mathematics scenario:

> In Mr. Hawkins' primary classroom, one of the units that his students will be learning is about money. Mr. Hawkins knows that coming to understand money can be a difficult concept for students because while decimals are involved, money is not a true decimal. Rather money is based on a face value system (i.e., the value of coins and dollars). In order to help him plan for both instruction and assessment appropriate for the unit, Mr. Hawkins identifies a learning progression in primary numeracy involving money[1]:
>
> LP#1: Students are able to match similar coins or dollars in a pile of coins or dollars.
> LP#2: Students are able to recognize different coins based on their face value (e.g., 1 cent (penny), 5 cents (nickel), 10 cents (dime), etc.).
> LP3#: Students are able to sort and count the number of coins with the same face value.

LP#4: Students are able to count the value of 10 coins of the same value.

LP#5: Students are able to count the value of $5 using coins of the same value.

LP#6: Students are able to the value of $5 using different combination of coins with different values.

LP#7: Students are able to correctly give change using complementary addition between two amounts.

In the case of Mr. Hawkins' money unit, he can adjust students' starting places in the unit based upon pre-assessment data and in accordance with the learning progression sequence.

In designing pre-assessments and on-going assessments that enable a range of learners to show what they currently know, understand, and can do, it is quite helpful for teachers to design questions or prompts that reflect a progression from past to future expectations for student learning. Doing so gives most, if not all, students a chance to reflect on what they comfortably know and to stretch a bit to illustrate their current upper limits of knowledge. In other words, if the assessment samples knowledge along a continuum of development, results from the assessment are likely to help the teacher place students on that continuum more accurately. In turn, the teacher can create instructional sequences designed to meet students at their varied entry points as the unit begins.

The Social Environment as a Catalyst for Learning

A century or more of research in the cognitive sciences confirms that students learn best and make more significant learning gains in a social classroom environment (e.g., Chaiklin, 2003; John-Steiner & Mahn, 1996; National Research Council, 2000). This suggests that students fare best when there is a variety of interactions that allow learners to engage in active learning that leads to understanding. These interactions include meaningful teacher-to-student, student-to-student, small groups, and whole class interactions taking place consistently, over time.

Revisiting the Shakespeare scenario, Ms. Willis uses a variety of grouping configurations to engage her students. These configurations range from whole class discussions to small group work that includes such strategies as a Tea Party, Turn and Talks, Think-Pair-Square-Share, learning stations designed around data she collected through the pre-assessment, concept mapping, peer review, and jigsaw groups. Designed effectively, these strategies create social moments when students engage in conversation and explore varied perspectives on the content they are learning as they navigate toward mastery of designated learning goals.

Additionally, research suggests that the more socially relevant a classroom environment is, the more motivated students are to engage with activities, thus increasing the probability of their learning (e.g., Ryan & Patrick, 2001). Socially relevance within an environment is evident in several distinct, dimensions: student belief that the teacher cares and supports them, interaction among classmates, a general atmosphere created by the teacher that promotes mutual respect and social harmony, and de-emphasis on competition among students—that is, de-emphasis on a performance focus (e.g., Butler, 1995). This sociocultural perspective of student learning is viewed as an interaction between the student and the social environment where the student both shapes and is shaped by the environment (i.e., community of practice; James, 2006). Because students learn through interactions with others while engaged in relevant instructional activities, the focus of assessment becomes about gathering data in order to adapt instruction to improve future learning rather than measuring past performance (Penuel & Shepard, 2016).

Feedback and the Socially Relevant Classroom

In the socially relevant classroom environment, emphasis has been placed on creating instructional opportunities that actively engage students with both the teacher and their peers. However, the socially relevant classroom environment also includes active engagement of both teacher and students in the feedback process. Teachers provide feedback for students, and discuss the feedback with students as needed, to guide their particular next steps in learning. Students review and plan the action they will take based on the written and conversational feedback. Students also review one another's work based on clear guidelines and criteria, incorporating that feedback as appropriate in their own learning plans. (For more information on using peer feedback for learning, see Topping, 2018.) Teachers guide, observe, and coach the peer feedback process, leading the teacher to expand his or her understanding of how students think about, understand, and act on feedback. Research on feedback has also identified several key ways in which feedback can (and should) serve as a tool to further student learning (e.g., Hattie, 2009; Hattie & Timperley, 2007):

1. Feedback allows students the opportunity to understand the intent of identified learning goals which gives students a greater opportunity to reach the goals.
2. Descriptive feedback provides quality information to students about their current learning and identifies what the student needs to do to continue to move along the targeted learning trajectory.
3. Peer feedback enables students to develop metacognitive thinking, which has a positive impact on the student's own work as well as on the work of peers with whom that student interacts.
4. Feedback provides opportunities to close the gap between current and desired performance.

5. Feedback provides information to teachers to shape instruction for students of differing readiness levels as opposed to planning one-size-fits-all instruction.

Looking Back and Ahead

Teaching is both an art and a science. The more fully teachers understand the principles of both those facets, the more positively they can impact student learning in their present as well as future lives. This chapter has explored five conclusions from education science that help us teach more students more effectively—and that help more students learn more fully. Understanding the importance of growth mindset, building new knowledge on past knowledge, ZPD and moderate challenge, learning progressions, and social classroom environments provides teachers with clear guidance for creating classrooms that respond effectively to students' diverse learning needs through differentiating both instruction and assessment to capitalize on students' current knowledge and to move them ahead in a trajectory of learning efficiently and effectively and with enhanced motivation to learn.

Note

1. Based on a Numeracy Progression from the Australian Curriculum, Assessment, and Reporting Authority (ACARA).

References

Aronson, J., Fried, C. B., & Good, C. (2002). Reducing the effects of stereotype threat on African American college students by shaping theories of intelligence. *Journal of Experimental Social Psychology, 38*, 113–125. doi: 10.1006/jesp.2001.1491.

Blackwell, L. S., Trzensniewski, K. H., & Dweck, C. S. (2007). Implicit theories of intelligence predict achievement across an adolescent transition: A longitudinal study and an intervention. *Child Development, 78*, 246–263.

Butler, R. (1995). Motivational informational functions and consequences of children's attention to peers' work. *Journal of Educational Psychology, 87*, 347–360.

Chaiklin, S. (2003). The zone of proximal development in Vygotsky's theory of learning and school instruction. In A. Kozulin, B. Gindis, V. S. Ageyev, & S. M. Miller (Eds.), *Vygotsky's educational theory in cultural context* (pp. 39–64). Cambridge, UK: Cambridge University Press.

Claro, S., Paunesku, D., & Dweck, C. S. (2016). Growth mindset tempers the effects of poverty on academic achievement. *Proceedings of the National Academy of Sciences, 113*, 8664–8668. doi: 10.1073/pnas.1608207113.

Darling-Hammond, L., Flook, L., Cook-Harvey, C., Barron, B., & Osher, D. (2019). Implications for educational practice of the science of learning and development. *Applied Developmental Science*. doi: 10.1080/10888691.2018.1537791.

Degol, J. L., Wang, M. T., Zhang, Y., & Allerton, J. (2018). Do growth mindsets in math benefit females? Identifying pathways between gender, mindset, and motivation. *Journal of Youth and Adolescence, 47*, 976–990. doi:10.1007/s10964-017-0739-8.

Dweck, C. S. (2006). *Mindset: The new psychology of success.* New York, NY: Random House.

Hattie, J. (2009). *Visible learning: A synthesis of over 800 meta-analyses relating to achievement.* New York, NY: Routledge.

Hattie, J., & Timperley, H. (2007). The power of feedback. *Review of Educational Research, 77*, 81–112. doi:10.3102%2F003465430298487.

Hess, K. (2008). *Developing and using learning progressions as a schema for measuring progress.* Dover, NH: National Center for Assessment. Retrieved from https://www.nciea.org/publications/CCSSO2_KH08.pdf.

James, M. (2006). Assessment, teaching, and theories of learning. In J. Gardner (Ed.), *Assessment and learning* (pp. 47–60). London, UK: Sage Publications.

John-Steiner, V., & Mahn, H. (1996). Sociocultural approaches to learning and development: A Vygotskian framework. *Educational Psychologist, 31*, 191–206.

Lenroot, R. K., & Giedd, J. N. (2007). The structural development of the human brain as measured longitudinally with magnetic resonance imaging. In D. Coch, K. W. Fischer, & Dawson, G. (Eds.), *Human behavior, learning, and the developing brain. Typical development* (pp. 50–73). New York, NY: Guilford Press.

McMillan, J. H. (2016). Section discussion: Student perceptions of assessment. In G. T. L. Brown & L. R. Harris (Eds.), *Handbook of human and social conditions in assessment* (pp. 221–243). New York, NY: Routledge.

National Research Council. (2000). *How people learn: Brain, mind, experience, and school: Expanded edition.* Washington, DC: The National Academies Press. doi: 10.17226/9853.

Ng, B. (2018). The neuroscience of growth mindset and intrinsic motivation. *Brain Sciences, 8*(2). doi: 10.3390/brainsci8020020. Retrieved from https://www.ncbi.nlm.nih.gov/pmc/articles/PMC5836039/.

Penuel, W. R., & Shepard, L. A. (2016). Assessment and teaching. In D. H. Gitomer & C. A. Bell (Eds.), *Handbook of research on teaching* (pp. 787–850). Washington, DC: AERA.

Popham, W. J. (2007). All about accountability/The lowdown on learning progressions. *Educational Leadership, 64*, 83–84.

Rattan, A., Good, C., & Dweck, C. S. (2012). "It's ok—not everyone can be good at math": Instructors with an entity theory comfort (and demotivate) students. *Journal of Experimental Social Psychology, 48*, 731–737. doi: 10.1016/j.jesp.2011.12.012.

Roosevelt, F. D. (2008). Zone of proximal development. In N. J. Salkind (Ed.), *Encyclopedia of Educational Psychology* (pp. 1017–1022). Thousand, Oaks, CA: SAGE. doi: 10.4135/9781412963848.0282. Retrieved from https://sk.sagepub.com/reference/educational psychology/n282.xml.

Ryan, A., & Patrick, H. (2001). The classroom social environment and changes in adolescents' motivation and engagement during middle school. *American Educational Research Journal, 38,* 437–460. doi: 10.3102%2F00028312038002437.

Schunk, D. H. (2016). *Learning theories: An educational perspective* (7th Ed.). London, UK: Pearson.

Siegle, D., McCoach, D. B., & Roberts, A. (2017). Why I believe I achieve determines whether I achieve. *High Ability Studies, 28,* 59–72. doi: 10.1080/13598139.2017.1302873.

Smith, T., Brumskill, R., Johnson, A., & Zimmer, T. (2018). The impact of teacher language on students' mindsets and statistics performance. *Social Psychology of Education, 21,* 775–786. doi: 10.1007/s11218-018-9444-z.

Sousa, D., & Tomlinson, C. (2018). *Differentiation and the brain: How neuroscience supports the learner-friendly classroom* (2nd Ed.). Bloomington, IN: Solution Tree.

Topping, K. (2018). *Using peer assessment to inspire reflection and learning.* New York, NY: Routledge.

Vygotsky, L. S. (1978). *Mind in society: The development of higher psychological processes.* Cambridge, MA: Harvard University Press.

Walton, G. M., & Cohen, G. L. (2011). A brief social-belonging intervention improves academic and health outcomes of minority students. *Science, 6023,* 1447–1451. doi: 10.1126/science.1198364.

Willis, J. (2010). The current impact of neuroscience on teaching and learning. In D. Sousa (Ed.), *Mind brain, and education* (47–67). Bloomington, IN: Solution Tree.

Yeager, D. S., & Dweck, C. S. (2012). Mindsets that promote resilience: When students believe that personal characteristics can be developed. *Educational Psychologist, 47,* 302–314. doi: 10.1080/00461520.2012.722805.

ZelaZo, P. D., Blair, C. B., & Willoughby, M. T. (2017). *Executive function: Implications for education* (NCER 2017-2000). Washington, DC: National Center for Education Research, Institute of Education Sciences, U.S. Department of Education. Retrieved from http://ies.ed.gov.

Part II   Differentiated Instruction

Topics for Further Discussion

1. How do you view DI as a means of teaching all students? How do you feel as a teacher who will have to differentiate to make sure all students are learning?
2. How do you see technology as a tool for DI? Do you think it plays a role in supporting and assisting students with disabilities?
3. What is the relationship between self-regulated strategies and schoolwide positive behavioral support? What activities can we include when differentiating instruction for these students?
4. How can role-playing be used in developing lessons for students with disabilities? How do you see this as a tool for instruction?
5. How would you develop a tiered model for teaching students with disabilities? How would you incorporate a program of DI into this model?

Part III

Universal Design for Learning

Universal Design for Learning (UDL) began as a concept in the business world, particularly in architecture. UDL has a philosophy that all children will learn and that accommodations to make this happen will occur in all classrooms. Although similar to DI, UDL expects that the way to teach all children will be discovered and that more traditional methods will not be used. There are seven different stages of UDL that you will learn about, and you will be able to see ways to modify the curriculum to meet the needs of all students. UDL is a concept that is widely used in schools today and is an approach that makes learning fun and meaningful.

UDL requires that you develop and implement lessons for every student. Your goal is to ensure student success, and modifying the curricular approaches enhances this possibility. You become the leader of learning as you engage students in mastering the material. While it might sound like a lot of work, getting to know your students and how they learn plays a large part in their success. As you modify the subject matter and lessons, you will be able to identify students' strengths that you might have previously overlooked. UDL provides you the opportunity to become part of each student's success.

Guided Questions

1. How does UDL impact the quality of teaching for all students?
2. How do you see UDL as a tool for meeting the individual needs of students?
3. What factors go into the development of goals and objectives when teaching impacts all students but is based upon their individual needs?
4. How can you ensure that students are successful when you implement UDL in the curriculum?
5. How can you evaluate the learning outcomes of students when you use UDL as a learning tool?

Reading 3.1

Expert Classroom Instruction for Students with Reading Disabilities

Explicit, Intense, Targeted ... and Flexible

Ruth Wharton-McDonald

University of New Hampshire

C HILDREN WITH LEARNING DISABILITIES represent about half of the students currently identified for special education (Denton, Vaughn, & Fletcher, 2003). The Presidents' Commission on Excellence in Special Education (2002) has estimated that two out of five children in special education are there because of difficulties in reading. Elsewhere in this volume, authors have described the characteristics of these students and specialized intervention programs developed to target their specific needs. In this chapter, I focus on the teaching and the learning environments created within heterogeneous classrooms—by regular education teachers—to support the growth and development of students with reading difficulties.

Until recently, it was widely believed that children who struggled to read in the primary grades were destined to continue their struggle as they progressed—trapped by their learning profiles, by the challenges posed by early reading development, and by instruction that failed to overcome those challenges. Juel's now classic (1988) study—in which the probability that a poor reader in first grade would be a poor reader in fourth grade was 0.88—was cited in nearly every examination of the effects of schooling on reading development. The findings from several recent studies, however, indicate that when struggling readers are matched with highly effective classroom teachers, their developmental trajectory *can* be altered (e.g., Bembry, Jordan, Gomez, Anderson & Mendro, 1998; Ferguson & Ladd, 1996; Foorman, Fletcher, Francis, Schatschneider, & Mehta, 1998; Juel & Minden-Cupp, 2000; O'Connor et al., 2002; Pressley, Allington, Wharton-McDonald, Block, & Morrow, 2001; Taylor, Pearson, Clark, & Walpole, 2000). Three different expert panels (the National Commission on Teaching and America's Future, 1997; the National Reading Panel, 2000; Snow, Burns, & Griffin, 1998) have concluded that the most powerful intervention tool that schools have to offer students who struggle to read is the classroom teacher. The expert practice of the teacher can overcome the failing trajectory of the young struggling reader, substantially reducing the numbers of children who experience reading and other learning disabilities.

In a national study of first-grade classrooms, Pressley and his colleagues (Pressley et al., 2000) reported that the lowest-achieving students in classrooms with exemplary teachers achieved at the same level as the average students in classrooms with more typical teachers. Under the guidance of exemplary teachers, students not only performed better on a standardized test at the end of the year, they spent more time engaged in instruction, read a variety of texts at grade level, and wrote more coherently than students in classrooms with typical teachers. In a longitudinal study, Bembry et al. (1998) found that after 3 years, students enrolled in classrooms with high-quality instruction achieved standardized reading scores that were approximately 40 percentile ranks higher than students enrolled in classrooms with lower quality instruction. Studies such as these—and the others cited above—emphasize the role of the classroom teacher. Indeed, Snow and her colleagues at the National Research Council have concluded that high-quality classroom instruction in the early grades is "the single best weapon against reading failure" (Snow, Burns & Griffin, 1998, p. 343). Thus, despite a current emphasis on programs, materials, and assessment tools, it is the *teacher*—and the instruction she or he provides in the classroom—that matters most to the development of successful readers.

Distinguishing Instructional Needs for Disabled and Non-Disabled Readers

Students with reading disabilities are more like their non-disabled peers than they are different from them. All learners need high-quality instruction in the components of reading (concepts of print, phonological awareness, phonics, fluency, vocabulary, comprehension, and writing) matched to their current understandings and abilities; they all need instruction that motivates them to engage in the learning process; they all need access to texts they can—and want to—read, and adequate time to read them. In *Preventing Reading Disabilities*, Snow and her colleagues (Snow, Burns & Griffin, 1998, p. 159) suggest that "there is little evidence to support the notion that struggling readers, even those with identified disabilities, need dramatically different reading instruction from students who learn to read more easily."

Students with reading disabilities, of course, are not all alike; nor do they all benefit from a single type of instruction. They do, however, share some learning characteristics. What students with reading disabilities need is instruction that is more *explicit*, more *intense*, and provides more *support* than instruction suited to their typically developing peers (Foorman & Torgesen, 2001; Jenkins et al., 1994).

Thus, despite some common misconceptions about best practices, effective classroom teachers do not provide dramatically different instruction for students with disabilities. The key to these teachers' expertise lies in their ability to identify the struggling readers in their classrooms and to know how to modify the nature and the intensity of high-quality instruction to meet the needs of those students (Fuchs, Fuchs, & Hamlett, 1998).

What Students with Reading Disabilities Need

Explicitness

As they learn to read, students with reading disabilities are less likely than their peers to notice and generalize patterns in the sounds and spellings of the language on their own (Atkinson, Wilhite, Frey, & Williams, 2002; Foorman et al., 1998). They are less likely to infer strategies required for comprehension (Atkinson et al., 2002; Jenkins et al., 1994). Students at risk for reading difficulties often do not discover what teachers leave unsaid about the use of strategies for reading; therefore effective instruction for these students includes an explicit sharing of knowledge needed to read—at the word level, for fluency, and for the use of comprehension strategies and metacognition (Foorman & Torgesen, 2001). Atkinson and her colleagues propose that "a never assume" approach often works well for students with learning disabilities (Atkinson et al., 2002, p. 160).

Explicit instruction means that teachers teach skills and strategies clearly and directly. They model their use, and deliberately guide students' application of learning in text. The instruction and scaffolding provided by teachers through explicit instruction reduces students' reliance on inference to figure out how written language works (Denton et al., 2003). In describing the explicitness required by these learners, Foorman and Torgesen (2001) suggest that they need two types of scaffolding. The first is a careful sequencing of skills so that concepts and skills build gradually upon a strong, coherent foundation. The second is an on-going teacher-student dialogue that demonstrates directly to the child the kind of processing or thinking that must be done in order to accomplish a particular task successfully.

In a study by Foorman and her colleagues (1998), teachers provided one of three types of word level instruction to first and second graders receiving Title I services. Students in the *direct* code group received direct instruction in letter-sound correspondences practiced in decodable text. The lessons introduced the 42 phonic rules using sound-spelling cards, alliterative stories and text with controlled vocabulary matched to the most recent instruction. Those in the *embedded* code group received less direct instruction in systematic sound-spelling patterns embedded in connected text. The emphasis in this group was on phonemic awareness and spelling patterns, taught using predictable books. And students in the <u>implicit</u> code group received either the district standard curriculum, emphasizing the importance of a print-rich environment with teacher as facilitator, or a similar intervention grounded in an established definition of whole language instruction. Students in this group received implicit instruction in the alphabetic code while reading connected text. All of the interventions took place in the context of a literature-rich classroom environment. Over the course of the year-long intervention, children in the direct code group improved in word reading at a faster rate and had higher word recognition skills than those receiving the implicit code instruction. Moreover, children who began with low scores in phonological processing showed more growth in word reading than children with low phonological processing scores in the other instructional groups. The positive effects were limited to growth in decoding and did not extend to differences in passage comprehension. However, this finding is hardly surprising, given that the instruction did not address comprehension; one might hypothesize that the same students who benefited from explicit instruction in word recognition skills would also benefit from explicit instruction in comprehension strategies.

Many studies have supported the explicit instruction of comprehension strategies for all children (National Reading Panel, 2000; Block & Pressley, 2002). A review of the research on the teaching of comprehension strategies to students with learning disabilities in particular confirms that this type of instruction may be especially valuable for these students (Gersten, Fuchs, Williams, & Baker, 2001). Joanna Williams, one of the review's authors, argues that while a constructivist approach in which students learn to be metacognitive, reflecting on their own thinking while they read, has been effective at the middle and high school levels (e.g., Allington, Guice, Michelson, Baker & Li, 1996), it is not adequate for struggling and at-risk students at the elementary level (Williams, 2005). Williams conducted a series of studies with at-risk second and third graders that assessed the effectiveness of explicit instruction in narrative and expository text structures. Compared with groups of students who received content instruction but not explicit comprehension instruction, the students with explicit instruction group demonstrated superior comprehension of themes taught—in both instructional materials and on near-transfer tasks involving the same themes.

Intensity

Students who struggle with reading not only need explicit instruction, they need more of it (Foorman & Torgesen, 2001; Torgesen, 2000). Kvale has described instruction for these learners as necessarily more "intense" and more "relentless" than effective instruction for other students (1988, p. 335). Generally speaking, there are two related ways to increase instructional intensity: (a) by increasing the amount of time children spend in instruction, and/or (b) by reducing the size of the group in which students learn.

Increasing Instructional Time

Traditionally, it has been the case that students placed in groups for struggling readers have spent less time receiving instruction (Hunter, cited in Barr & Dreeben, 1991; McDermott, 1976), have spent less of that instructional time on task (Gambrell, 1984); and read less material (Allington, 1984; Barr & Dreeben, 1983). This is in direct opposition to their needs, which are for more instruction, more time on task, and more opportunities to read.

Daily lessons and support are more likely to impact learning than lessons scheduled less frequently (Allington, 2006). The strong history of Reading Recovery (Clay, 1993; Forbes & Briggs, 2003; Lyons, 2003), in which poor first-grade readers receive 20 (or more) weeks of daily, individual reading instruction is evidence of the effectiveness of directed, frequent instruction. In a study of early intervention based loosely on the Reading Recovery model, Vellutino and his colleagues (Vellutino & Scanlon, 2002; Vellutino et al., 1996) also provided 30-minute sessions of daily tutoring to poor readers in the first grade. The model matched the intensity of Reading Recovery, differing in part, in the amount of professional development provided for teachers (Vellutino's study required significantly less teacher training than that demanded by Reading Recovery). Vellutino's tutors—all of whom were certified teachers—addressed letter identification, phoneme awareness, word reading skills, and practice in reading connected text. After one or two semesters (depending on student progress), the majority of these children became average readers.

Despite the recognized value of daily instruction for struggling readers, it is rarely possible for a student to meet with the reading specialist every day. It is the classroom teacher who necessarily sees every student every day, who can ensure such frequent instructional opportunities for the students who need them. Evidence indicates that effective classroom teachers spend more time teaching—and their students spend more time engaged in instruction—in on-task behavior (Bohn, Roehrig, & Pressley, 2004; Pressley et al., 2001; Wharton-McDonald, Pressley, & Motretta, 199). This is especially important as it relates to students' need for instructional intensity.

Decreasing Group Size

The most practical method for increasing instructional intensity for students with reading disabilities is to provide instruction in small groups created to provide targeted instruction to particular groups of learners (Foorman & Torgesen, 2001). In fact, grouping students for reading is almost a universal practice (Barr & Dreeben, 1991; Hiebert, 1983; Jenkins et al., 1994). Unfortunately, students with reading disabilities are often pulled out of their classrooms and provided with instruction in groups designed to meet the indications of overall reading levels—and scheduling demands. Thus, the groups tend to be relatively large (4–7 students) and relatively undifferentiated with respect to specific literacy needs (Allington,

2002; Elbaum, Vaughn, Hughes & Moody, 2000; Vaughn et al., 2002). Moreover, such groups have been criticized in the past for dooming low achieving students to a lifetime in low groups (Anderson, Hiebert, Scott & Wilkinson, 1985; Barr & Dreeban, 1991; Gamoran, 1992; Hiebert, 1983; Oakes, 1985) and for providing consistently lower quality, less engaging instruction (Allington, 1983; Hiebert, 1983). Such grouping practices clearly result in instruction that fails to meet the needs of individual children.

Despite the evidence against traditional intervention groups, expert classroom teachers regularly utilize small groups and one-on-one instruction to meet the needs of individual children. The available evidence indicates that this form of intensive instruction and support is significantly more effective than whole class or large group instruction—particularly for students who struggle in reading (Pressley et al., 2001; Schumm, Moody & Vaughn, 2000; Taylor, Pearson, Clark & Walpole, 2000). In a review of 18 studies of early interventions with struggling readers, Wanzek and Vaughn (2007) reported the largest effects for individual interventions and the smallest effects for interventions with the largest group sizes. Clearly, students with reading disabilities benefit from more individualized time with an effective teacher.

The work of the CIERA School Change project (e.g., Taylor et al., 2000) confirms these findings. In studying schools and classrooms that beat the odds—where students learn to read and write at high levels in the face of overwhelming odds against it—Taylor and her colleagues found that the most accomplished teachers and the teachers in the most effective schools consistently relied on small groups to teach and support important literacy skills and understandings.

The critical difference between traditional small groups, in which students have received low-quality instruction and failed to improve, and those where student achievement has been accelerated appears to lie in the expertise of the teacher—and some have argued—in the location of the group itself. Allington and others have argued vehemently against instructional practices that remove students from the classroom and place them in remedial groups in an alternative location (e.g., the resource room). A great deal of instructional time can be lost in the transition from classroom to intervention space. When students spend time engaged in effective instruction as opposed to packing up their materials and transitioning down the hall to the resource room, they learn more.

While instructional time lost to transitions is likely a factor in student learning (or lack thereof), the most important factor in determining learning is undoubtedly the teacher. In fact, attempts to keep students in regular classrooms by having Title I or special education aides work with students in classroom groups have been no more effective than similar instruction provided in groups pulled out of the classroom (Archambault, 1989; Puma, Jones, Rock, & Fernandez, 1993). Expert teachers who use small groups in the classroom adapt both instruction and group membership to meet the immediate needs of the students in ways that less expert teachers are not able to do. They use ongoing formative assessments to determine the specific needs of individual students and to ensure that students are neither overwhelmed by instruction that is too difficult or bored by instruction that is no longer needed.

In summarizing the research on group size and intervention effects, Allington (2006) concludes that "as the size of the instructional group decreases, the likelihood of acceleration increases. Thus, the most effective designs employ the most expert teachers and have them tutoring or working with very small (2–3) instructional groups" (p. 152). Indeed, in a meta-analysis examining the effects of grouping practices, Elbaum and associates (2006) found consistently positive effects of grouping practices that increased instructional intensity.

What Expert Teachers Provide

> Teaching is more than a technical process; it is a complex human process in which the teacher's knowledge of reading and learning processes intersects with his or her knowledge of the needs, interests, and individual characteristics of the learners. (Farstrup, 2002, pp. 1–2)

Expert teachers have substantial knowledge of literacy processes, of pedagogy, of books and other teaching materials, and of their students (e.g., Allington & Johnston, 2002; Pressley et al., 2001; Taylor & Pearson, 2002). Their ability to apply their knowledge in providing learning experiences for their students is what makes them so effective. It is what enables students with reading disabilities to develop the skills, strategies, and dispositions of successful readers. Expert teachers provide instruction that targets the particular skills needed by individual learners. They provide explicit and intense instruction, accompanied by ongoing scaffolding to ensure student success. They provide lessons and materials at an appropriate level of challenge, so that learners are engaged and moving forward. And they do it in an environment that nurtures motivation and sustains engagement.

Instruction Matched to Individual Skills, Understandings, and Needs

> You should design the program around your students, not the students around a program ... We have students of all different abilities. We should look at each of their individual abilities and work with them and find something that will work for each of them at different levels. (a highly effective teacher, cited in Achinstein & Ogawa, 2006, p. 48)

Teaching is not a generic enterprise. For any instruction to be effective, it must target the learning needs and characteristics of a particular student or group of students. This is true for both disabled and non-disabled literacy learners: "Effective instruction is characterized by adaptation of the standard form of instruction in ways that better meet the needs of individual students" (Allington, 2006, p. 149). The profiles of learners with reading disabilities are found on the same continua as learners without reading disabilities. Since all students vary in their development, it is reasonable to speculate that all students will differ with respect to the aspects of reading instruction that will be most critical for their success at a particular time. It is crucial that the teacher matches the instruction to the specific needs of the learner (Atkinson et al., 2002). Despite this well recognized finding, a summary of observational studies conducted with students with learning disabilities indicates that all too often, these students are provided with generic reading instruction that is *not* directly linked to their specific needs (Denton et al., 2003; Vaughn, Levy, Coleman, & Bos, 2002).

To target support to individual students, teachers must have detailed knowledge about literacy processes and their development; they must be familiar with a wide range of reading materials and the pedagogy required to use them effectively; and they must know their students extremely well. Expert teachers are astute observers of their students. They are familiar with students' cognitive abilities, their learning histories and characteristics, their preferences, their temperaments, their cultural influences, and their goals (Allington & Johnston, 2002; Berliner, 1992; Clay, 1993; Louden et al., 2005; Mazzoli & Gambrell, 2003; Pressley et al., 2001). Expert teachers combine their knowledge of literacy development and their knowledge of students as learners to individualize the instruction they provide. Not all students with reading disabilities share the same set of difficulties. While this point seems obvious, it is too often the case that they all receive the same intervention nevertheless. If the special education teacher has been trained in the LiPS program (see www.lindamoodbell.com), then all of the students in grades 1–4 with reading disabilities receive the same sequence of lessons from the LiPS manual. If the teacher has been trained in Wilson Reading (see www. wilsonlanguage.com), then everyone receives that program instead. There are undoubtedly students for whom these programs (both of which meet the criteria of explicit and intensive) are useful. What differentiates the expert teacher from a less effective colleague is the ability to match the intervention to the individual student. The expert's planning is not based on a set program or what is written in a teacher's manual; rather it is based on what an individual student needs at a given time (Thomas & Barksdale-Ladd, 1995; Pressley et al., 2001; Allington & Johnston, 2002). Thus, each learner receives the instruction and scaffolding needed to move him or her forward on a given day. While this is important for all learners, Juel (1996) concludes that the ability to offer individualized, targeted support in the form of scaffolding while children are developing reading skills may actually have increasing significance as the severity of a child's learning disability increases.

Scaffolding

Exemplary teachers are expert at scaffolding students' learning (Allington & Johnston, 2002; Pressley, 2006; Loudon et al., 2005; Taylor & Pearson, 2002; Wharton-McDonald et al., 1998). Scaffolding in this context refers to the support provided by a teacher or a peer that enables the student to solve a problem on his or her own that he or she would not otherwise be able to solve independently. Scaffolding may take the form of a question or a hint (sometimes a question that is a hint), or a reminder to pay attention to a particular feature or strategy that the student is not using (for example, "What do you know about words that end with an 'e'?" or "Is there a strategy you could use to figure that out?"). By definition, scaffolding is individualized and cannot be scripted in advance. Scaffolding provides immediate support to a reader so that she will stay engaged and learning. It demands a high level of knowledge of both the student and the instructional task in which he is engaged.

Appropriate Level of Challenge

A great deal of research confirms the significant positive effect of matching a student with the appropriate instructional materials. To maximize learning, learners must be moderately challenged by instructional tasks and texts, without being overwhelmed. The Beginning Teacher Evaluation study (Denham & Lieberman, 1980) was among the first of many to find that students learn best when they experience high rates of success on the tasks in which they are engaged. They have the lowest rates of learning when they are expected to complete tasks which are too difficult and on which they make numerous errors. In confirming these findings, others have noted that students who experience high rates of success not only learn more, but they also have better attitudes toward learning and are more motivated to pursue other, similar tasks (e.g., Berliner, 1992; Brophy, 1987; Guthrie & Wigfield, 2000).

With respect to reading, these findings emphasize the importance of providing students with texts that are not only appealing, but also accessible. Allington (2005) refers to the matching of pupils and texts as one of the "pillars of effective reading instruction" (p. 347). All too often, students with reading disabilities (and others who struggle) are expected to read texts that are well beyond the moderate level of challenge that research supports. This is especially true at the intermediate and secondary levels, where teachers can be driven to "cover curriculum" rather than acknowledge students where they are and move them forward. O'Connor and her colleagues (2002) reported that when struggling middle school readers were asked to read grade-level texts as opposed to texts matched to their actual reading abilities, their reading development was adversely affected. According to Allington (2002), any classroom in which all students are expected to read the same book "will fail to successfully develop reading proficiencies in all students" (p. 276).

Motivational Learning Environments

Students can only learn from engaging with texts they can read. Thus, matching the difficulty of a text to the instructional level of the student is critical from the perspective of skills development. Moreover, when students experience success with a text, they are more likely to be motivated to sustain their effort and engagement (Brophy, 1987; Guthrie & Wigfield, 2000). Expert teachers do many things to motivate children with disabilities to engage in classroom learning opportunities. They construct interesting lessons; they connect reading and writing to content area learning; they provide students with moderately challenging tasks and a variety of interesting book selections; and they use positive redirection to manage behavior (Bohn et al., 2004; Pressley et al., 2001). The research on reading development and instruction includes many references to the importance of motivation. Many of them (e.g., the National Reading Panel Report) note the need for further research. Every section in the National Reading Panel Report (2000) mentions motivation as a potentially significant variable, but one on which there are still scant data. Expert teachers, however, create classrooms where students are already motivated and engaged. Consequently, students in these classrooms spend more time on task, more time reading, and more time learning.

Informed Flexibility

It is now well recognized that there is not—and cannot be—one best way to teach children to read (Allington, 2002; Allington & Walmsley, 2007; Duffy & Hoffman, 2002; Farstrup, 2002; International Reading Association, 2000; Mathes et al., 2005; Mazzoli & Gambrell, 2003; Taylor & Pearson, 2002). The nature of human development means that, even within the context of a single, grade-level classroom, individual students will enter with different understandings and backgrounds, learn in different ways, at different rates, and in the context of different social environments. The most effective teachers use their complex knowledge of literacy, pedagogy, and student characteristics flexibly, to provide uniquely responsive instruction for their students (Wharton-McDonald, 2008).

In contrast to the frequently documented one-size-fits-all approach to students with reading disabilities (e.g., teach them all explicit phonics, or group them for instruction according to a particular available program), the expert teacher eschews a single, static approach in favor of a flexible, dynamic one. Expert teachers have extensive knowledge in literacy development, in the range of instructional materials, in children's literature, in child development, and in the learning profiles of their students. Using this depth of knowledge, the teacher can sit with two fourth graders, both identified with reading disabilities, both reading at a level J (mid-second grade), and determine that Anna needs instruction that builds English vocabulary, background knowledge in the content areas, and fluency, whereas Mohammed has significant difficulties with phonemic awareness and has not yet mastered decoding of multi-syllabic words. Moreover, having made an individualized analysis of their needs, the expert teacher is familiar with a range of strategies and materials she can use to support each student's growth.

The teacher described above begins with a great deal of knowledge. But just knowing about students, strategies, and materials is only part of what makes her effective. It is the flexibility to shift methods and materials to meet the dynamic needs of the students that characterizes the most effective teachers (Wharton-McDonald, 2008). It has been a frequent critique of special education that once students are identified and coded, they remain in the system for life (Mueller, 2001). In too many cases, these students continue to receive more of the same instruction that hasn't worked in the past; neither the system nor their teachers have had the informed flexibility to recognize what is working (and what isn't) and make ongoing changes to ensure growth. The special education placement in these cases tends to stabilize students' reading growth rather than accelerating it (Denton et al., 2003). After all, even if the instruction is effective and the student is making progress, then his needs are not the same as they were when the intervention began; almost by definition, the student will require a new combination of instructional variables in order to continue to move forward. More of the same is rarely the best combination for long. "In the final analysis, effective teaching and learning rests on the shoulders of the teacher who makes informed decisions about the instructional approaches and practices that are most appropriate for [individual students]" (Mazzoli & Gambrell, 2003, p. 11). The flexibility to make these decisions in an always changing context is central to the success of effective teachers.

The Role of Classroom Context

Beyond the significant role of the teacher in supporting the development of children with reading disabilities, the classroom context itself (the students) appears to play a role in students' success. The 1997 reauthorization of the Individuals with Disabilities Education Act Amendment (IDEA) specifically identified the general education setting as the most appropriate placement for all students (IDEA ref; Schmidt, Rozendal, & Greenman, 2002). Being in a general education setting provides students with access to the same high-quality instruction offered to their typically achieving peers. It also provides struggling students with ongoing interactions—social and academic—with those peers. Foorman, York, Santi, and Francis (2008) reported that when beginning readers were placed in classrooms with higher average fluency scores, they demonstrated greater achievement gains than similar students who were placed in classrooms with lower fluency scores.

In the study cited, the *combination* of student pretest score (in fluency) and the mean pretest score for a classroom was a better predictor of student achievement than the student pretest score alone. Examining first- and second-grade data from 210 randomly selected schools in Texas, Foorman and her colleagues found that students with low fluency scores in first grade who happened to be placed in classrooms with higher mean fluency scores achieved higher fluency scores in second grade. The authors hypothesize that gains in fluency were not influenced by repeated reading (conducted in all first-grade classrooms) alone, but that "repeated readings in the context of faster reading models, in this case faster reading peers in the classroom" accounted for the difference in achievement gains (p. 391). Findings such as these related to classroom context have implications not only for inclusion practices (in which students with disabilities are educated in regular classrooms), but for grouping practices within the classroom. Foorman et al. (2008) conclude that for slower readers, simply being in a classroom of faster reading peers "seems to be an intervention all by itself" (p. 391). These recent findings suggest the need to further investigate the role of the student-generated classroom environment in other areas of literacy learning as well.

Students and Teachers: Understanding Students' Needs and Addressing Them in the Classroom Context

Students with reading disabilities have much in common with their typically developing peers. They demand high-quality reading instruction that supports development across the essential components of literacy; they need access to materials they can—and want to—read; they need opportunities to read and discuss books with others; they need motivating learning environments that support ongoing engagement in learning. And they need instruction that flexibly adapts to their changing needs. From an instructional perspective, what distinguishes students with reading disabilities is their need for particularly explicit instruction, provided with greater intensity than that which characterizes typical reading instruction. Expert teachers understand the needs of their students and are able to provide a great deal of informed, targeted instruction in the context of a motivating environment. Moreover, they flexibly adapt their instruction in response to student successes, struggles, and interests in order to sustain maximum student growth. The critical role of the teacher in developing and sustaining student learning is recognized by a growing number of researchers and educational organizations. Students with reading disabilities *can* make accelerated growth and develop the literacy behaviors and dispositions demonstrated by their typically achieving peers. They need to spend less time in static, ineffective learning environments, and more time in the company of expert classroom teachers and successful peers.

References

Achinstein, B., & Ogawa, R. (2006). (In)fidelity: What the resistance of new teachers reveals about professional principles and prescriptive educational policies. *Harvard Educational Review, 76*(1), 30–63.

Allington, R. L. (1984). Content coverage and contextual reading in reading groups. *Journal of Reading Behavior, 16,* 85–96.

Allington, R. L. (2002). Research on reading/learning disability interventions. In A. E. Farstrup & S. J. Samels (Eds.). *What research has to say about reading instruction* (3rd ed., pp. 261–290). Newark, DE: International Reading Association.

Allington, R. L. (2005, June/July). The other five "pillars" of effective reading instruction. *Reading Today, 22*(6), 3.

Allington, R. L. (2006). *What really matters for struggling readers: Designing research-based programs* (2nd ed.). Boston: Pearson Education.

Allington, R. L., Guice, S., Michlson, N., Baker, K., & Li, S. (1996). Literature-based curricula in high poverty schools. In M. F. Graves, P. van den Broek, & B. M. Taylor (Eds.), *The first R: Every child's right to read* (pp. 73–96). New York: Teachers College Press.

Allington, R. L., & Johnston, P. H. (2002). *Reading to learn: Lessons from exemplary fourth-grade classrooms.* New York: Guilford.

Allington, R. L., & Walmsley, S. (Eds.). (2007). *No quick fix, the RTI edition: Rethinking literacy programs in America's elementary schools.* New York: Teachers College Press.

Anderson, R. C., Hiebert, E. H., Scott, J. A., & Wilkinson, I. A. (1985). *Becoming a nation of readers.* Washington, DC: National Institute of Education.

Archambault, M. X. (1989). Instructional setting and other design features of compensatory education programs. In R. E. Slavin, N. Karweit, & N. Madden (Eds.), *Effective programs for students at risk* (pp. 220–263). Boston: Allyn-Bacon.

Atkinson, T. S., Wilhite, K. L., Frey, L. M., & Williams, S. C. (2002). Reading instruction for the struggling reader: Implications for teachers of students with learning disabilities or emotional/behavioral disorders. *Preventing School Failure, 46*(4), 158–162.

Barr, R., & Dreeben, R. (1983). *How schools work.* Chicago: University of Chicago Press.

Barr, R., & Dreeben, R. (1991). Grouping students for reading instruction. In D. P. Pearson (Ed.), *Handbook of reading research* (Vol. II, pp. 885–912). New York: Longmire.

Bembry, K. L., Jordan, H. R., Gomez, E., Anderson, M., & Mendro, R. L. (1998, April). *Policy implications of long-term teacher effects on student achievement.* Paper presented at the American Educational Research Association.

Berliner, D. (1992). Exemplary performances: Studies of expertise in teaching. *Collected speeches.* National Art Education Association Convention, Milwaukee, WI.

Block, C. C., & Pressley, M. (2002). *Comprehension instruction: Research-based best practices.* New York: Guilford.

Bohn, C. M., Roehrig, A. D., & Pressley, G. (2004). The first days of school in the classrooms of two more effective and four less effective primary-grades teachers. *The Elementary School Journal, 104,* 269–287.

Brophy, J. (1987). On motivating students. In D. Berliner & B. Rosenshine (Eds.), *Talks to teachers* (pp. 201–245). New York: Random House.

Clay, M. (1993). *Reading recovery: A guidebook for teachers in training.* Portsmouth, NH: Heinemann.

Denton, C. A., Vaughn, S., & Fletcher, J. M. (2003). Bringing research-based practice in reading intervention to scale. *Learning Disabilities Research & Practice, 18,* 201–211.

Duffy, G., & Hoffman, J. (2002). Beating the odds in literacy education: Not "betting on" but the "bettering of" schools and teachers. In B. Taylor & P. D. Pearson (Eds.), *Teaching reading: Effective schools, accomplished teachers* (pp. 375–387). Mahway, NJ: Erlbaum.

Elbaum, B., Vaughn, S., Hughes, M. T., & Moody, S. W. (2000). How effective are one-to-one tutoring programs in reading for elementary students at risk for reading failure? A meta-analysis of the intervention research. *Journal of Educational Psychology, 92,* 605–619.

Farstrup, A. E. (2002). There is more to effective reading instruction than research. In E. Farstrup & S. J. Samuels (Eds.), *What research has to say about reading instruction* (3rd ed., pp. 1–7). Newark, DE: International Reading Association.

Ferguson, R. F., & Ladd, H. F. (1996). How and why money matters: An analysis of Alabama schools. In H. Ladd (Ed.) *Holding schools accountable: Performance-based reform in education* (pp. 265–298). Washington, DC: Brookings Institution.

Foorman, B. R., Fletcher, J. M., Francis, D. J., Schatschneider, C., & Mehta, P. (1998). The role of instruction in learning to read: Preventing reading failure in at-risk children. *Journal of Educational Psychology, 90,* 37–55.

Foorman, B. R., & Torgesen, J. (2001). Critical elements of classroom and small-group instruction promote reading success in all children. *Learning Disabilities Research & Practice, 16,* 203–212.

Foorman, B. R., York, M., Santi, K. L., & Francis, D. (2008). Contextual effects on predicting risk for reading difficulties in first and second grade. *Reading and Writing, 21,* 371–394.

Fuchs, L. S., Fuchs, D., & Hamlett, C. (1989). Effects of instructional use of curriculum-based measurement to enhance instructional programs. *Remedial and Special Education, 10,* 43–52.

Gambrell, L. (1984). How much time do children spend reading during teacher-directed reading instruction? In J. Niles & L. Harris (Eds.), *Changing perspectives on research in reading/language processing and instruction. Thirty-Third Yearbook of the National Reading Conference* (pp. 193–198). Rochester, NY: National Reading Conference.

Gamoran, A. (1992). Is ability grouping equitable? *Educational Leadership, 50*(2), 11–17.

Gersten, R., Fuchs, L. S., Williams, J. P., & Baker, S. (2001). Teaching reading comprehension strategies to students with learning disabilities: A review of the research. *Review of Educational Research, 71*, 279–320.

Guthrie, J. T., & Wigfield, A. (2000). Engagement and motivation in reading. In M. Kamil, P. B. Mosenthal, P. D. Pearson, & R. Barr (Eds.), *Handbook of reading research* (Vol. 3, pp. 403–422). Mahwah, NJ: Erlbaum.

Hiebert, E. H. (1983). An examination of ability grouping for reading instruction. *Reading Research Quarterly, 8*, 231–255.

Individuals with Disabilities Education Act Amendments of 1997 (IDEA), Publ. L. No. 105–17, 20 U.S.C. 1400 et seq.

International Reading Association. (2000). *Making a difference means making it different: Honoring children's rights to excellent reading instruction.* Position statement of the International Reading Association. Newark, DE: International Reading Association.

Jenkins, J. R., Jewell, M., Leicester, N., O'Connor, R. E., Jenkins, L. M., & Troutner, N. M. (1994). Accommodations for individual differences without classroom ability groups: An experiment in school restructuring. *Exceptional Children, 60*, 344–358.

Juel, C. (1988). Learning to read and write: A longitudinal study of 54 children from first to fourth grades. *Journal of Educational Psychology, 80*, 437–447.

Juel, C. (1996). What makes literacy tutoring effective? *Reading Research Quarterly, 31*, 268–289.

Juel, C., & Minden-Cupp, J. (2000). Learning to read words: Linguistic units and instructional strategies. *Reading Research Quarterly, 35*, 458–492.

Kvale (1988). The long-term consequences of learning disabilities. In M. C. Wang, H. J. Walberg, & M. C. Reynolds (Eds.), *The handbook of special education: Research and practice* (pp. 303–344). New York: Pergamon.

Loudon, W., Rohl, M., Barratt-Pugh, C., Brown, C., Cairney, T., Elderfield, J., et al. (2005). In teachers' hands: Effective literacy teaching practices in the early years of schooling. [Special issue]. *Australian Journal of Language and Literacy, 27*(3).

Mathes, P. G., Denton, C. A., Fletcher, J. M., Anthony, J. L., Francis, D. J., & Schatschneider, C. (2005). The effects of theoretically different instruction and student characteristics on the skills of struggling readers. *Reading Research Quarterly, 40*, 148–182.

Mazzoli, S., & Gambrell, L. B. (2003). Principles of best practice: Finding the common ground. In L. M. Morrow, L. B. Gambrell, & M. Pressley (Eds.), *Best practices in literacy instruction* (2nd ed., pp. 9–21). New York: Guilford.

McDermott, R. (1976). *Kids make sense: An ethnographic account of the interactional management of success and failure in one first-grade classroom.* (Unpublished doctoral dissertation). Stanford University, Palo Alto, California.

Mueller, P. (2001). *Lifers: Learning from at-risk adolescent readers.* Portsmouth, NH: Heinemann.

National Reading Panel. (2000). *Teaching children to read: An evidence-based assessment of the scientific research literature on reading and its implications for reading instruction*. Washington, DC: National Institute of Child Health and Human Development and U.S. Department of Education.

Oakes, J. (1985). *Keeping track: How schools structure inequality*. New Haven, CT: Yale University Press.

O'Connor, R., Bell, K., Harty, K., Larkin, L., Sackor, S., & Zigmond, N. (2002). Teaching reading to poor readers in the intermediate grades: A comparison of text difficulty. *Journal of Educational Psychology, 94,* 474–485.

President's Commission on Excellence in Special Education. (2002). *A new era: Revitalizing special education for children and their families*. Retrieved from http://www.ed.gov/inits/commissionsboards

Pressley, M., Allington, R. L., Wharton-McDonald, R., Block, C. C., & Morrow, L. (2001). *Learning to read: Lessons from exemplary first-grade classrooms*. New York: Guilford.

Pressley, M., Wharton-McDonald, R., Allington, R. L., Block, C. C., Morrow, L., Tracey, D., et al. (2000). A study of effective first-grade reading instruction. *Scientific Studies of Reading, 5,* 35–58.

Puma, M. J., Jones, C. C., Rock, D., & Fernandez, R. (1993). *Prospects: The congressionally mandated study of educational growth and opportunity—the interim report*. (No. GPO 1993 0-354-886 QL3). Washington, DC: U. S. Department of Education, Office of Planning and Evaluation Services.

Samuels, C. A. (2007, September 10). Experts eye solutions to the 4th grade slump. *Education Week,* 1–4. Retrieved from http://www.edweek.org/ew/articles/

Schmidt, R. J., Rozendal, M. S., & Greenman, G. G. (2002). Reading instruction in the inclusion classroom: Research-based practices. *Remedial and Special Education, 23*(3), 130–140.

Schumm, J. S., Moody, S. W., & Vaughn, S. (2000). Grouping for reading instruction: Does one size fit all? *Journal of Learning Disabilities, 33,* 477–488.

Snow, C. E., Burns, M. S., & Griffin, P. (Eds.). (1998). *Preventing reading difficulties in young children*. Washington, DC: National Academy Press.

Taylor, B., & Pearson, P. D. (2002). *Teaching reading: Effective schools, accomplished teachers*. Mahwah, NJ: Erlbaum.

Taylor, B., Pearson, P. D., Clark, K., & Walpole, S. (2000). Effective schools and accomplished teachers: Lessons from primary grade reading instruction in low-income schools. *The Elementary School Journal, 101,* 121–165.

Thomas, K. F., & Barksdale-Ladd, M. A. (1995). Effective literacy classrooms: Teachers and students exploring literacy together. In C. K. Kinzer, K. A. Hinchman, & D. J. Leu (Eds.), *Inquiries into literacy theory and practice: Forty-sixth yearbook of the National Reading Conference* (pp. 37–53). Chicago: National Reading Conference.

Torgesen, J. K. (2000). Individual differences in response to early interventions in reading: The lingering problem of treatment resisters. *Learning Disabilities Research & Practice, 15,* 55–64.

Vaughn, S., Levy, S., Coleman, M., & Bos, C. S. (2002). Reading instruction for students with LD and EBD: A synthesis of observation studies. *Journal of Special Education, 36*(1), 2–13.

Velluntino, F. R., & Scanlon, D. M. (2002). The interactive strategies approach to reading intervention. *Contemporary Educational Psychology, 27,* 573–635.

Vellutino, F. R., Scanlon, D. M., Sipay, E., Small, S., Pratt, A., et al. (1996). Cognitive profiles of difficult-to-remediate and readily remediated poor readers: Early intervention as a vehicle for distinguishing between cognitive and experiential deficits as basic causes of specific reading disability. *Journal of Educational Psychology, 88,* 601–638.

Wanzek, J., & Vaughn, S. (2007).Research-based implications from extensive early reading interventions. *School Psychology Review, 36,* 541–561.

Wharton-McDonald, R. (2008). The dynamics of flexibility in effective literacy teaching. In K. B. Cartwright (Ed.), *Literacy processes: Cognitive flexibility in learning and teaching* (pp. 342–357). New York: Guilford.

Williams, J. P. (2005). Instruction in reading comprehension for primary-grade students: A focus on text structure. *The Journal of Special Education, 39*(1), 6–18.

Reading 3.2

The Three-Block Model of Universal Design for Learning (UDL)

Engaging Students in Inclusive Education

Jennifer Katz

Inclusive Education (Inclusion)

Inclusive education, or inclusion, has been globally recognized as a goal for educational systems around the world (Curcic, 2009; Katz, 2012b). Inclusion can be divided into two sub-types; academic inclusion, defined by full and equal participation in interaction with typical peers in academic activities and curriculum within a regular classroom (Katz, 2012a), and social inclusion, defined by the opportunity to interact with peers in a regular classroom, and having a sense of belonging and acceptance within the learning community (Koster, Nakken, Pijl, & van Houten, 2009; Specht & Young, 2010). Social inclusion is vital to student development, because social and emotional well-being is directly related to resiliency, citizenship, and mental health (Wotherspoon, 2002; Zins & Elias, 2006), and increases academic motivation and aspirations, and achievement (Brock, Nishida, Chiong, Grimm, & Rimm-Kaufamn, 2008; Zins, Bloodworth, Weissberg, & Walberg, 2004). Inclusion, however, is not just about social and emotional well-being, or even social justice. Students come to school to learn—all students, including those with disabilities. Inclusive education must set high standards for all students, and support students to achieve them.

Comparisons of the literacy and numeracy skills, standardized tests, college entrance, and other academic scores of typical and gifted students in classrooms with and without students with disabilities are identical, including classrooms with students demonstrating significant behavioral challenges (Bru, 2009; Cole, Waldron, & Majd, 2004; Crisman, 2008; Kalambouka, Farrell, Dyson, & Kaplan, 2007; Timmons & Wagner, 2008). This research has been replicated over decades and across countries (Curcic, 2009). It is now clear that the presence of students with disabilities does not negatively impact the learning of other students. In fact, research shows that typical students in classrooms that include students with disabilities develop stronger communication and leadership skills, have more positive attitudes toward diversity, and may also demonstrate superior reading and math skills to those in classrooms that do not include students with disabilities (Bunch & Valeo, 2004; Cole & Waldron, 2002; Kalambouka, Farrell, Dyson, & Kaplan, 2007).

Globally, students with disabilities demonstrate improved academic outcomes, including literacy, numeracy, general knowledge, and higher order thinking when placed in inclusive settings as compared to peers matched for level of disability in segregated classrooms (Ruijs & Peetsma, 2009). Students with disabilities also outperformed their peers in segregated classrooms in adaptive/life skills, vocational and academic competence (Kurth & Mastergeorge, 2010; Myklebust, 2006). Clearly, inclusive education benefits students with and without disabilities, both socially and academically. Despite this, many students with disabilities in Canada continue to be excluded and placed in segregated classrooms (Canadian Council on Learning, 2007).

Inclusive education means just that—an educational system that creates learning communities inclusive of all students. Exploration of student engagement and research pointing to high levels of disengagement, particularly in secondary school, have raised concerns about educational systems and pedagogies that do not create social and academic engagement and inclusion for diverse learners (Dunleavy & Milton, 2008). According to Willms, Friesen, & Milton (2009):

> Across Canada, many students have told CEA (Canadian Education Association) that classrooms and learning as they are currently organized are not working. They are not working for students who can keep up with the pace set by the lectures, textbooks and tests, and they are not working for those who cannot (p. 5).

Perhaps as a result, the field of inclusive education is now focusing on the practical application of inclusive pedagogy—that is, what are the best instructional paradigms to facilitate social and academic inclusion and engagement for ALL students? The active engagement of students in their learning is predictive of educational achievement, positive attitudes to learning, and student self-efficacy (Skinner, Kindermann, & Furrer, 2009). One promising instructional framework for inclusive education appears to provide the opportunity for social and academic inclusion of all students, while improving student engagement: Universal Design for Learning (McGuire, Scott, & Shaw, 2006).

Universal Design for Learning (UDL)

The concept of Universal Design comes from the field of architecture and is driven by the goal of accessibility (Mace, Story, & Mueller, 1998). Inclusive education similarly seeks access to the social and academic life of the classroom for all learners (Katz, Porath, Bendu, & Epp, 2012).

Drawing on new research in neuroscience, and principles from universal design, Universal Design for Learning (UDL) is an approach to instruction that promotes access, participation, and progress in the general education curriculum for all learners (CAST, 2012). UDL recognizes the need to create opportunities for the inclusion of diverse learners through providing curricula and instructional activities that allow for multiple means of representation, expression, and engagement (King-Sears, 2008). In its early years, the focus of UDL was on the use of technology to facilitate accessibility. More recent development of the theory and practice of UDL recognizes many instructional pedagogies that facilitate accessibility for diverse learners (Burgstahler, 2009). UDL has been shown to support access, participation and progress for all learners (Jimenez, Graf, & Rose, 2007; King-Sears, 2009; Kortering, 2008; Meo, 2012; Rose & Meyer, 2002). However, few have provided a comprehensive framework to put the pieces together, in a practical, research grounded, K-12, efficient manner.

The "Three-Block Model" of UDL

The Three-Block Model of UDL (Katz, 2012c) provides teachers with a method for creating inclusive environments and improving student engagement. To help teachers manage the process of implementation, the model is broken into three blocks (see Appendix A). The first block examines *Social and Emotional Learning*, and involves building compassionate learning communities, utilizing the Respecting Diversity (RD) program and democratic classroom management with class meetings (Katz, 2012a; Katz & Porath, 2011). Results show profound impact in terms of social inclusion and engagement for both students and teachers when this program is put into place (Katz & Porath, 2011; Katz, 2012c).

In the second block of this model, called *Inclusive Instructional Practice*, a step-by-step planning and instructional framework is outlined (Katz, 2012a). First, physical and instructional environments are designed so that students have access to differentiated learning opportunities in order to address their varied learning modes. Second, teachers are taught a method of year and unit planning that incorporates evidence based practices such as Understanding by Design (Brown, 2004; Wiggins & McTighe, 2005), Differentiated Instruction (Beecher & Sweeny, 2008; Tomlinson, 2010), Curriculum Integration (Drake & Burns, 2004), Inquiry (Brusca-Vega, Brown, & Yasutake, 2011; Wilhelm, 2007), and Assessment for Learning (William, Lee, Harrison, & Black, 2004). Essential understandings within curricula are identified, and inquiry activities that promote higher order thinking are planned. Expectations for success and challenging lessons influence student academic engagement and achievement, social engagement, and health and wellness (Willms et al., 2009). Thus the model seeks to emphasize mastery of complex concepts, with scaffolding through team work and differentiated processes. As part of this practice, teachers build rubrics using Bloom's Taxonomy

(Kuhn, 2008) that reflect multiple developmental levels of understanding, and can be used to assess multi-modal expressions of understandings. Regular feedback and assessment is ongoing so that teachers can assess for learning, and when needed, conduct assessment/ evaluation of learning, including grading (Katz, 2012). Finally, student autonomy is emphasized, as it has been shown to increase student engagement and achievement, and develop higher order, deeper thinkers (Hafen et al., 2012; You & Sharkey, 2009). Similar instructional interpretations of UDL have recently been shown to improve mathematics and reading comprehension scores (Friesen, 2010; Meo, 2012); however, no investigation of engagement and overall achievement was delineated.

Student Engagement

Children's academic engagement predicts their achievement in and completion of school (Skinner et al., 2009). Students who are highly engaged at school learn more, get higher grades, and more often pursue higher education (Park, Holloway, Arendtsz, Bempechat, & Li, 2012). However, engagement levels often decrease as students move through the educational system (Fredricks, Blumenfeld, & Paris, 2004; Shernoff, Csikszentmihalyi, Schneider, & Shernoff, 2003). It is vital, therefore, that instructional pedagogies be developed that facilitate students' social and academic engagement in diverse, inclusive classrooms from K-12.

The Link Between Inclusive Education and Student Engagement

Engagement can be related to inclusion. As Willms et al. (2009) state:

> Disengagement from school—whether a student leaves or struggles through to graduation—is also a significant source of inequity in Canadian society, not only because it places a large number of students at a disadvantage as they move into adult roles, but because disengagement is disproportionately experienced by students living in poverty, students with disabilities, and students from ethnic minority and Aboriginal communities. (p. 7)

Thus, the same students who are most often excluded, are those who become disengaged (Canadian Council on Learning, 2009). For a student to be socially engaged, they must experience a sense of belonging, interact with peers, and be involved in extracurricular and social activities within the school (Archambault, Janosz, Morizot, & Pagani, 2009). This resembles definitions of social inclusion, in which all students experience a sense of belonging and are a part of the social life of their school and classroom (Katz & Porath, 2011; Wotherspoon, 2002). Thus, students who are highly socially engaged can be said to be socially included.

The relationship between academic engagement and inclusion is slightly more complicated. Academic engagement involves the active participation of students in their learning (Skinner et al., 2009). Students are said to be academically engaged when they demonstrate engaged behaviors, such as on task activity, and express an interest in their learning (Park et al., 2011). Students who are academically included are a part of the learning activities of the regular classroom. It is possible, therefore, for a student to be academically engaged, but not academically included (i.e., engaged in a separate task than others). However, the ideals of academic inclusion would presume academic engagement, because in order to be an active part of the learning in a classroom, a student would need to be engaged. Thus, if academic and social engagement were assessed in the context of the regular classroom when all students are working on the same tasks, student engagement could be used as a measure of social and academic inclusion, and potentially be predictive of achievement.

Measuring Social and Academic Engagement and Inclusion

There are many definitions of student engagement (Dunleavy & Milton, 2008). On a theoretical level, most researchers would agree that a student who is socially engaged interacts positively with their peers and teachers, feels a sense of belonging, and has a positive social self-concept. However, the measures of these constructs are significantly different. Social interactions are observable, but belonging and self-concept require self-report, either through interview or survey. Academic engagement is now frequently defined by both participation in academic tasks, and cognitive investment in those tasks (Dunleavy & Milton, 2008; Willms et al., 2009). Similar to the measurement of social engagement, in measuring academic engagement, on task behavior is observable, but enjoyment of learning, academic self-efficacy, and beliefs about learning require self-report.

Purpose of the Study

Research has demonstrated positive outcomes of many of the practices included in the Three-Block Model of UDL individually, for instance, differentiating instruction, inquiry, and assessment for learning (George, 2005; Scigliano & Hipsky, 2010; Summerlee & Murray, 2010). However, no research has been completed to determine academic outcomes of the implementation of these strategies in combination through a universally designed curriculum and pedagogy. The current study therefore explored the outcomes of implementing the Three Block Model in terms of student social and academic engagement in inclusive classrooms from K-12. The following research questions were addressed:

1. Is the social and academic inclusion of diverse students in inclusive classrooms from K-12 facilitated by the implementation of an instructional pedagogy based on the Three Block Model of Universal Design for Learning?

   Specifically:

   a. Is there a significant difference in students' academic engagement following the implementation of an instructional pedagogy based on the Three Block Model of Universal Design for Learning?

   b. Is there a significant difference in students' social engagement following the implementation of an instructional pedagogy based on the Three Block Model of Universal Design for Learning?

Methods

The methodology for this study parallels common practice in the field of program evaluation (e.g., Greenberg, Kusche, Cook, & Quamma, 1995). This involves pre intervention/program delivery and post/during intervention measurement processes using both qualitative and quantitative measures. A quasi-experimental control group pretest-posttest design was used. This article reports the quantitative results related to student outcomes of the study. Future articles will report quantitative and qualitative data regarding teacher perceptions of student outcomes, and outcomes for teachers related to job satisfaction, instructional practice, and attitudes to inclusion and UDL.

Participants

Participants were drawn from five school divisions in Manitoba, Canada. Two of these divisions were rural, and three were urban. These divisions support an inclusive model for all students. In this definition of inclusion, students attended their neighborhood school, and were enrolled in age appropriate regular education classrooms. Services were for the most part delivered in class through the use of educational assistants, and co-teaching between resource teachers, ESL teachers, and classroom teachers. Some pull-out, short term support (e.g., a 30 minute block three times a week) took place for such services as speech and language, physiotherapy, and occasionally, literacy intervention. Students in the schools speak more than 60 languages, and on average, 20% of the student population is learning English as a second language (ESL).

TABLE 3.2.1 School Demographics

Division	School	Population	Grades	Treatment/ Control
Urban	A	120	K–4	T
	B	130	5–8	T
Urban	C	220	K–8	T
	D	250	K–8	C
Urban	E	800	K–12	C
Rural	F	200	K–8	T
	G	90	K–8	C
	H	150	K–12	C
	I	90	K–4	T
Rural	J	250	7–12	T

Ten schools volunteered to participate in the study. All schools had determined that universal design for learning was a professional development and school goal. All staff within these schools were given an initial one-day workshop on the Three Block Model of Universal Design for Learning. Subsequently, purposive sampling was used to identify teachers who were interested in pursuing further professional development in this area and implementing the model in their classrooms. These teachers were drawn from six schools, and were enrolled as the treatment group. Three half days of further professional development were provided. Teachers who were not interested in pursuing further professional development or implementing the model were enrolled as control classes, and were drawn from four of the ten schools. Purposive sampling was chosen to increase the likelihood of program implementation, and is commonly used for educational program evaluation (Harlacher & Merrell, 2010). Teachers in the control group had received a one day workshop on the model, thus some contamination is possible. However, this would increase the likelihood of NOT getting significant differences between the two groups (since some teaching practices would be shared), and reduced the possibility of getting type one error (or a false positive), thus making findings of this research conservative, and significant differences more powerful.

Student participation in the classrooms involved was 82%. Treatment group classes and control group classes were located in separate schools, to avoid further transference of program materials/ideas, and allow treatment group teachers to support and collaborate with each other. No intervention was made in control classrooms between pre and post testing.

Fifty-eight educators, including classroom teachers, resource teachers, and school administrators were involved in the study. They ranged in experience, from 3 to 36 years. Fourteen

TABLE 3.2.2 Student Demographics

		Treatment	Control
Grade	Elementary (1–6)	225 (61%)	185 (71%)
	Secondary (7–12)	146 (39%)	75 (29%)
Gender	Male	197 (53%)	130 (50%)
	Female	174 (47%)	130 (50%)
First Language	English	328 (88%)	226 (87%)
	Other	43 (12%)	34 (13%)
Time in Canada	Born in Canada	328 (88%)	225 (87%)
	Immigrated to Canada	43 (12%)	35 (13%)

educators were male, the rest female. Six hundred and thirty-one students from grades one to twelve took part in the study.

Chi square analyses were used to investigate any group differences. Significant differences were found for teacher years of experience, $(X^2 [2, N=58]=109.6, p < .001)$, with the control group having significantly more teachers in the 11+ years category, and higher teacher education, $(X^2 [5, N=58]=24.5, p < .001)$, thus YOE and education were used as covariates in all subsequent tests. There were no significant differences between groups in student grade, gender, first language, or place of birth.

Students who had severe cognitive disabilities, or who had not developed sufficient proficiency in the English language to take part in the programs' activities and complete measurement scales and interviews were excluded from participating in the survey aspects of the study. However, they were included in observational data.

The Intervention
Program Procedures

Teachers were asked to implement the Three Block model of Universal Design for Learning framework for planning and instruction within their classrooms. This required them to co-plan an integrated unit with grade level peers, determine essential understandings for the unit, create inquiry based projects and multiple intelligences activities that differentiated the complexity and modality of activities, and develop rubrics that allowed for differentiated assessment (For more information, see Katz, 2012a). In a secondary/high school, single subject setting, the science teacher will then teach the science of the unit, the Social Studies teacher their curriculum, and so on but all can refer to what students are learning in other classes and help students see the connections. For some time, educators in an inclusive model have used parallel tasks for students with disabilities or learning English. Developmentally, parallel play is immature in contrast to interactive play. Similarly, parallel learning (Johnny does math when we do math, but a different math, with "his" EA), is not a mature form of inclusion, as it does not provide exposure to the general curriculum or differing points of view that may develop critical thought. In the Three Block Model of UDL ALL students work together in heterogeneous groupings/"teams", at all age and grade levels, to master curriculum through differentiated inquiry activities.

Training Procedures

Without measures of implementation, it would be unclear to what extent effect sizes were mitigated by the degree to which the program was actually carried out. What might appear to be an ineffective program could actually be an ineffectively implemented program. Thus it is essential that implementation be both supported and measured. To promote program implementation, intervention teachers attended three half day follow-up sessions facilitated by the author that included viewing of classroom videos, planning of a unit through the Three Block Model of Universal Design for Learning, development of rubrics for assessment, and the opportunity to pose questions and have any concerns addressed. Subsequent consultation and observation meetings were held on an individual basis at teachers requests. At times these meetings were one to one after school and, at other times, took place in the classroom with students present, during program implementation. At these times, the author co-taught lessons, gave feedback to the teachers, or clarified ideas for students when requested to do so. Observations/data collection did not take place during these times.

Several measures were used to assess implementation. First, personal visits allowed the author to determine level of understanding and implementation. Second, observations in the class recorded types of tasks and grouping structures. Given that differentiated tasks and small group centre/station work is integral to the model, this data allowed for an implementation check. Finally, teachers were asked to provide feedback after the intervention was completed regarding their perceptions, experiences, and implementation.

Data Collection

Data were gathered through both observations and self-report measures (surveys), prior to intervention, and during implementation of the intervention.

Observations

There is evidence that observed behavioral engagement is strongly related to academic success in much the same way as student reported engagement (Hafen et al., 2012). Academic engagement can be further broken down into active engagement, in which students are actively involved in a learning task such as writing, drawing, speaking, or constructing (Iovanne, Dunlap, Huber, & Kincaid, 2003), and passive engagement, in which students are passively on task—such as listening to a teacher's lecture or viewing a film (Katz, Mirenda, & Auerbach, 2002). Active engagement in learning is highly predictive of academic achievement (Dunleavy & Milton, 2008).

Observations were conducted for two half hour periods on separate days and subjects/activities per student twice (pre and during), using a one-minute time sampling procedure. Observations took place only during core academic curriculum instruction (math, language arts, science, or social studies), to avoid bias in engaged behavior for elective tasks. Observers naïve to the purposes of the study were first trained using an instructional video, until reliability with the trainer at 90% was achieved. Subsequently, the trainer and observer visited a classroom, and reliability tests were conducted. All observers achieved 90% reliability with the trainer.

Two students, one male and one female from each classroom were randomly selected, for a total of 94 students, or approximately 14% of the larger participant sample. Administrators pointed out the chosen students to observers as students entered the school, so that neither teachers nor students were aware of who was being observed. On each one-minute interval, observers recorded a code for type of task (traditional paper and pencil, or differentiated/other media), instructional grouping (independent, partner/small group, or whole class), engaged behavior (student was actively, passively, or not engaged), and interactive behavior (interacting with peer, adult, or no one). (See Appendix B for operational definitions of codes.)

Surveys

Surveys were conducted twice, pre and during intervention. Grade one students did not complete surveys, as they were unable to read/comprehend at a level required to complete this task—thus observations only were conducted for them. Items were read aloud, but students still needed to be able to track the line they were on, and comprehend the item.

Many of the scales used were created/utilized by the Child Development Project (CDP) (http://www.devstu.org/cdp/). To measure social and academic inclusion/exclusion, the *Global Portrait of Social and Moral Health for Youth* (GPSMHY) (Davidson & Kmelkov, 2006) and *Acceptance of Outgroups* scale (CDP) were used to assess students' attitudes and behaviors relating to valuing diversity, and the extent of shared vision and goals present in their classroom. Two subscales of the Marsh Self-Description Questionnaire (SDQ) (Marsh, 1992) were used to assess self-concept. To explore school and classroom climate and sense of belonging, the CDP classroom supportiveness and safety subscales of the *sense of school as a classroom community* instrument were used. Student autonomy was measured using the CDP *Student Autonomy and Influence in the Classroom* scale.

Results & Discussion

Student data were examined using a process recommended by Hair, Anderson, Tatham, and Black (1998). This process begins by recoding negative items. Reliability was then computed for each scale; all scales had reliability (coefficient alpha) greater than .7 (range .72 to .94). It should be noted that students completed multiple multi-question scales. One skipped question/item on one scale rendered the entire student's data as *missing*. Thus almost 25% of data were lost if only complete cases were used. For this reason, imputed means were used for survey data.

A MANOVA was then computed to check for pretest differences in observed behaviors/variables (engagement, task assigned, grouping structure, and interactive behavior). Significant differences were found for engaged behavior (Wilk's Lambda, $F(13,86) = 8.96$, $p < .001$), type of task (Wilk's Lambda, $F(13,86) = 8.18$, $p < .001$), and grouping structures (Wilk's Lambda, $F(13,86) = 8.69$, $p < .001$). However, the differences were in the opposite

TABLE 3.2.3 Mean Behaviors by Group and Grade

Variable	Group	Mean (Pre)/ 60 mins.	SD	Mean (Post)/ 60 mins.	SD	N
Overall Engaged Behavior	Treatment	41.54	10.23	54.52	4.00	56
	Elementary	42.97	8.96	53.97	4.22	31
	Secondary	39.76	11.55	55.20	3.69	25
	Control	50.18	7.98	43.64	9.27	44
	Elementary	50.11	7.39	45.59	9.22	27
	Secondary	50.29	9.08	40.53	8.72	17
Active Engagement	Treatment	20.75	9.42	43.80	8.35	56
	Elementary	23.45	8.46	43.87	8.14	31
	Secondary	17.40	9.64	43.72	8.78	25
	Control	34.39	10.85	19.36	11.64	44
	Elementary	31.56	10.44	21.74	11.20	27
	Secondary	38.88	10.23	15.59	11.66	17
Passive Engagement	Treatment	20.79	11.57	10.71	6.88	56
	Elementary	19.52	10.59	10.10	5.97	31
	Secondary	22.36	12.72	11.48	7.92	25
	Control	15.80	8.64	24.27	9.96	44
	Elementary	18.56	8.54	23.85	10.55	27
	Secondary	11.41	6.99	24.94	9.20	17

Variable	Group	Mean (Pre)/ 60 mins.	SD	Mean (Post)/ 60 mins.	SD	N
Non-Engagement	Treatment	18.43	10.24	5.48	4.00	56
	Elementary	16.97	8.98	6.03	4.22	31
	Secondary	20.24	11.55	4.80	3.69	25
	Control	9.82	7.98	16.36	9.27	44
	Elementary	9.89	7.39	14.41	9.22	27
	Secondary	9.71	9.08	19.47	8.72	17
Interacting with Adult	Treatment	4.20	3.39	4.34	2.96	56
	Elementary	4.16	3.77	4.87	3.21	31
	Secondary	4.24	2.92	3.68	2.51	25
	Control	4.07	3.54	4.95	4.28	44
	Elementary	5.04	4.05	5.00	4.23	27
	Secondary	2.53	1.70	4.88	4.48	17
Interacting with a peer	Treatment	10.95	7.68	25.52	10.79	56
	Elementary	12.06	7.92	26.55	11.95	31
	Secondary	9.56	7.29	24.24	9.23	25
	Control	9.52	7.84	8.89	8.51	44
	Elementary	7.44	5.32	8.44	7.37	27
	Secondary	12.82	10.02	9.59	10.27	17
Not Interacting	Treatment	44.82	7.83	30.07	10.64	56
	Elementary	43.71	7.96	28.48	11.29	31
	Secondary	46.20	7.59	32.04	9.64	25
	Control	45.73	9.93	44.80	11.43	44
	Elementary	47.51	7.64	44.33	11.51	27
	Secondary	42.88	12.50	45.53	11.62	17

direction from post-test results. That is, the control group began with higher levels of overall engaged behavior, and active engagement, and lower levels of passive and non-engagement. These means then reversed after intervention.

The same pattern held true for task and grouping structure as for engagement—that is, the control group pretest had higher levels of differentiated tasks and lower levels of pencil and paper and transition times. They also had higher levels of small group and independent structures, and lower levels of whole class instruction. Since differentiated tasks and small group work are core practices of UDL, one might have expected a self-selected treatment group to be implementing more of these than the control group. However, this was not the case, but once again, all of these means reversed after intervention. There were no significant differences pre-intervention in interactive behavior. This pattern of association between

TABLE 3.2.4   Mean Instructional Practices by Group

Variable	Group	Mean (Pre/ 60 mins)	SD	Mean (Post/ 60 min.)	SD	N
Pencil & Paper Task	Treatment	38.00	20.45	23.98	20.63	56
	Control	18.27	20.26	22.45	23.43	44
Other Media (Differentiated) Task	Treatment	19.05	20.07	35.77	20.57	56
	Control	38.66	20.69	36.89	23.88	44
No Task	Treatment	2.95	4.10	.25	.67	56
	Control	2.39	3.46	.66	1.40	44
Whole Class Grouping	Treatment	34.61	15.97	4.95	6.87	56
	Control	15.95	14.98	15.25	14.90	44
Small Group/ Partner Grouping	Treatment	11.30	10.73	41.55	14.22	56
	Control	14.82	15.41	20.18	19.71	44
Independent	Treatment	14.09	12.41	13.50	11.46	56
	Control	29.20	17.58	24.57	19.36	44

higher levels of differentiated tasks and small group work and increased engagement fits with past research (Baker, Clark, Maier, & Viger, 2008; Fredricks et al., 2004).

The obvious question is why the pregroup differences? As noted above, one might have thought that given that teachers self-selected, it would be teachers who were inclined to use differentiation and small group work that would be interested in UDL. However, this intervention was presented as an instructional framework that would support teachers in increasing their students' engagement. It may be, therefore, that teachers who were struggling to get or keep their students engaged chose to participate, while those who felt they were already doing a good job of this did not feel the need to explore the program.

A MANOVA was then computed to check for pretest differences in survey/social and emotional variables (inclusion/exclusion, classroom climate, school climate, and student autonomy). Significant results were found for classroom climate ($F(4,624) = 18.44, p < .001$), and school climate ($F(4,624) = 8.90, p < .003$). Once again, control classes scored higher on classroom climate, and school climate, with these means reversing post intervention. There was no significant difference in levels of inclusivity or student autonomy, and no significant interaction effects for gender, first language, place of birth, or grade.

A MANCOVA was then computed to explore treatment outcomes post intervention, controlling for teacher years of experience and education, with treatment group, gender, and grade, language, and place of birth and interactions examined.

TABLE 3.2.5 Means for Social Variables by Group

Variable	Group	Mean (Pre)	SD	Mean (Post)	SD	N
Inclusivity/Exclusivity (higher score = greater inclusiveness)	Treatment	2.33	.43	2.56	.38	373
	Control	2.38	.38	2.31	.44	257
Student Autonomy	Treatment	2.76	.71	2.99	.73	373
	Control	2.76	.70	2.73	1.38	257
Classroom Climate	Treatment	3.32	.83	3.30	.69	373
	Control	3.60	.72	3.40	.65	257
School Climate	Treatment	3.68	.76	3.69	.65	373
	Control	3.85	.66	3.62	.69	257

Academic Inclusion and Engagement

Overall engaged behavior was significantly different between the treatment and control groups post intervention. Students in the treatment classes were significantly more engaged than students in control classes, with treatment group students' scores increasing overall, and control group students' scores decreasing. This pattern of decreasing scores for control groups (i.e., students who have had no intervention) is commonly found in the literature (Katz & Porath, 2011; Park et al., 2012). In particular, students in treatment classes were significantly more actively engaged, while student in control classes were significantly more passively engaged, and spent significantly more time not engaged. In fact, means were almost doubled in both directions—with the treatment group spending twice as much time actively engaged, while control groups spent twice as much time passively or not engaged (see table 3.2.3). Neither gender, first language, nor place of birth significantly impacted engagement. However, student grade levels did impact engaged behavior, $F(2,85) = 10.977, p < .001$, such that students in higher grades spent more time passively engaged (see Table 3.2.3 for means).

TABLE 3.2.6 Mancova Results for Observed Engaged Behavior

Variable	Df	F	partial η
Overall Engaged Behavior	9,68	92.421*	.549
Active Engagement	1,68	105.699*	.582
Passive Engagement	1,68	48.694*	.391
Non-Engagement	1,68	38.413*	.336

* = p < .001

TABLE 3.2.7 Mancova Results for Observed Engaged Behavior by Grade

Variable	Age/Grade	Df	F	partial η
Overall Engaged Behavior	Elementary	9,48	62.564*	.528
	Secondary	9,32	89.584*	.691
Active Engagement	Elementary	1,48	75.464*	.574
	Secondary	1,32	79.542*	.665
Passive Engagement	Elementary	1,48	38.571*	.408
	Secondary	1,32	25.634	.391
Non-Engagement	Elementary	1,48	20.632*	.269
	Secondary	1,32	56.486*	.585

$^* = p < .001$

Sample size for secondary students was smaller, which may have mitigated some results. However, results show that post intervention, in both grade groupings, overall engaged behavior, and active engagement, was significantly higher in treatment classes. Examination of means for these groups indicated that in elementary school, students in treatment classes spent an average of 44/60 minutes actively engaged, while those in control classes averaged 19/60 minutes actively engaged. In secondary classes, differences were even more pronounced. High school students in UDL classes spent 44/60 minutes actively engaged, while those in control classes spent 16/60 minutes actively engaged. Passive engagement and non-engagement were also significantly different post intervention, with students in control classes spending significantly more time passively and not engaged. However, the differences were greater in terms of non-engagement than in passive engagement. Since passive engagement involves listening to teacher lecture or viewing of a demonstration or film, it appears these types of tasks are similar in both types of classes (ie teachers giving lectures or instructions). However, when tasks are assigned, students in secondary UDL classes become actively engaged in their learning, while students in control classes spent significantly more time disengaging, a problem reported often in the literature about the engagement of students in secondary schools (Hafen et al., 2012; Park et al., 2012).

Factors Influencing Student Engagement

Past research exploring underlying factors influencing student engagement has identified relationships between type of task and grouping structures and engaged behavior (Baker et al., 2008).

TABLE 3.2.8   Mancova Results for Type of Task

Variable	Df	F	partial η
Task	9,68	4.415*	.139
Paper & Pen	1,68	.386	.005
Other Media	1,68	.253	.003
No Task/Transition	1,68	5.889**	.072

* = p < .001 ** = p = .02

Type of Task

Fredricks et al. (2004), summarized findings related to student engagement. In their article, they outline how tasks that allow students to create products, and are application, real life problem based, improve student engagement. In this study, types of task did not differ significantly, with the exception of a significantly greater amount of time with no task/in transition in control classes. Examination of group means indicates almost identical amounts of paper and pencil tasks, but a slightly higher mean (though not significant) of other media tasks in treatment classes, counterbalancing the time with no task (see table 3.2.4). Although teachers reported high levels of implementation, the lack of significant difference in paper and pencil and other media tasks raises some questions. It is possible control group teachers were also differentiating instruction (they had received the professional development as well), or it is possible that treatment group teachers continued to emphasize paper and pencil tasks beyond what the model suggests. Examination of the means reveals that over half of the observed time in both types of classes was spent in differentiated tasks—good news, and perhaps, explanatory of the lack of significant difference!

The Three Block Model of UDL promotes longer blocks of time spent in integrated instruction, as opposed to having the day's schedule broken up into separate subjects. Even in subject specific settings (such as high school), students are involved in ongoing, long-term investigations as opposed to short, question and answer type activities. As a result, UDL classes may have less transition time involving students putting away materials and gathering materials for the next subject/activity, perhaps explaining the "no task" time difference. The numbers here were small and interpretations therefore must be cautious, however, over weeks and months this time would add up.

Effective learning time influences student academic engagement and achievement, social engagement, and health and wellness (Willms et al., 2009). As we seek to improve student outcomes, using integrated curriculum and longer blocks of teaching time becomes an important factor.

TABLE 3.2.9   Mancova Results for Grouping Structures

Variable	Df	F	partial η
Overall	9,68	11.434*	.289
Whole Class	1,68	15.925*	.173
Small Group	1,68	29.678*	.281
Independent	1,68	7.814*	.093

* = $p < .001$

Flexible Groupings

Grouping structures have also been shown to influence student engagement, such that small group and partner work leads to higher levels of active engagement, as compared to whole class and independent grouping structures (Baker et al., 2008). In this study, control classes spent significantly more time in whole class and independent structures post intervention (see table 3.2.4), while treatment classes spent significantly more time working in small groups, thus perhaps influencing active engagement.

Student Autonomy

Research has shown that classrooms in which students have high level of autonomy promote engagement and achievement (Hafen et al., 2012). Student autonomy involves youth in making choices, taking responsibility for their learning, and empowering youth to believe in their own capacity to learn and grow. As students develop a sense of autonomy, emotional well-being is improved (Ryan & Deci, 2000). Given that emotional well-being influences academic engagement and achievement, it is not surprising that studies have shown student autonomy influences student engagement. In fact, Hafen et al. (2012) reported that "the strongest predictor of change in both observed and student-reported engagement was adolescents' perceptions about autonomy within the classroom" (p. 251). Students in treatment classes reported significantly higher levels of student autonomy than did students in control classes (see tables 3.2.5 & 3.2.11), perhaps contributing to group differences in engaged behavior.

Social Inclusion & Engagement

Student engagement has been shown to decrease over time—both within a school year and over the years from elementary to secondary school (Archambault et al., 2009). Providing a positive classroom climate in which students value self and diverse others, have opportunities to learn with, engage in dialogue with, and interact socially with others, and feel

TABLE 3.2.10 Mancova Results for Interactions

Variable	Df	F	partial η
Overall	9, 68	34.893*	.511
Interact with Adult	1, 68	10.497*	.121
Interact with Peer	1, 68	24.305*	.242
No Interaction	1, 68	94.179*	.553

$*$ = p < .001

empowered to make choices, set goals, and take risks increases student well-being, engagement, and achievement (Katz & Porath, 2011; Willms et al., 2009).

In order to be socially included and engaged, students need to feel accepted by teachers and peers, and have opportunities to interact with both. Students in treatment classrooms implementing the Three Block Model of UDL were observed to more frequently interact with adults and peers and reported higher levels of student autonomy, while students in control classrooms spent more time not interacting. Thus despite running a more child-centered program in which students spent more time interacting in co-operative groups, students continued to be supported and scaffolded in their learning through interactions with teachers.

In the first block of the Three Block Model of UDL, social inclusion and the development of self-concept and emotional resiliency is promoted. The Respecting Diversity (RD) program, and classroom meetings are used to create a positive classroom climate at the beginning of the year (Katz, 2012). This program has been shown to improve student self-concept, emotional resiliency, valuing of diverse others, inclusiveness, and prosocial behaviors, while reducing levels of aggression (Katz & Porath, 2011).

In the present study, teachers were not asked to implement the RD program or classroom meetings. The research was intended to determine the outcomes of Block 2, instructional practices inherent in the model only. For that reason, significant outcomes for social

TABLE 3.2.11 Mancova Results for Social Variables

Variable	Df	F	partial η
Overall	4,620	21.947*	.124
Inclusion/Exclusion	1,620	57.537*	.085
Student Autonomy	1,620	32.418*	.049
Classroom Climate/Belonging	1,620	3.003 (Not significant)	.005
School Climate	1,620	1.511 (Not Significant)	.002

$*$ = p < .001

variables other than interactions were not expected. However, levels of inclusion/exclusion, student autonomy (because of its dual effects on both academic engagement and emotional well-being), and classroom climate/sense of belonging to a supportive community were assessed to determine if instructional practices in themselves influenced these variables.

Students in treatment classes reported significantly higher levels of social and academic inclusiveness and autonomy (see table 3.2.5). Sense of belonging and classroom climate were not significantly different, however, this is an indicator of growth for treatment classes as there were pretest differences favoring control classes. Effect sizes were very small, thus it appears there is need to invest the time to specifically create a sense of belonging and community through interventions such as the Respecting Diversity program if we wish to have significant impact on social and emotional variables (Katz & Porath, 2011; Katz, 2012a).

Conclusion

There has been limited research regarding the outcomes of Universal Design for Learning, despite its adoption into policies across Canada and the United States (Edyburn, 2010). McGuire (2006) challenged researchers to develop models of UDL and conduct research that determines effective methods for implementation and outcomes for both students and teachers.

Students were randomly selected for observation regarding engaged behavior. While students with severe disabilities were excluded from the survey aspects of the study, students with mild to moderate disabilities were included, and all students were included in observational data. Thus the sample and results reflect the engagement of diverse learners, including students learning English as a second language, students with disabilities, gifted students, and typical students alike. Students with disabilities were not singled out in this study, precisely because our philosophy, and our question—was education for all. Subsequent studies may choose to look at differential effects of the Three Block model of UDL for specific populations. In the big picture of UNIVERSAL design for learning, however, it appears that students in treatment classes were significantly more academically engaged in UDL classrooms than in typical inclusive classrooms. Effect sizes were moderate, but in educational programming, relatively high. An effect size of .5 for student engagement is clinically very significant, and raises hope that indeed significant change can happen when inclusive pedagogy is implemented. Given that this was teachers' first experience with UDL, and first unit created in this way, results are promising.

The stated goal of the Three Block Model of UDL is to promote social and academic inclusion, while improving achievement for diverse learners (Katz, 2012a,b). Previous research indicated the model had positive impacts on student self-concept and social inclusion (Katz & Porath, 2011). The current study demonstrates that the instructional framework promoted in the model improves student academic and social engagement.

Limitations of the Study/Future Directions

Purposive sampling was used in this study to select teachers and classrooms to insure implementation and thereby truly assess outcomes of the model. However, if the model is to be used as a tool for inclusive education as it is broadly implemented, future research will need to determine whether teachers less motivated to implement the model can effectively be involved in its implementation, and what training methods would be required under such circumstances. It is possible more intensive supports would be required under these conditions, as teacher self-efficacy and attitude is related to implementation (Ransford, Greenberg, Domitrovich, Small, & Jacobson, 2009).

Engagement has previously been shown to be related to academic achievement, however this study did not assess specific academic achievement outcomes. Future studies will need to determine the model's effects on specific academic achievement indicators, and determine whether the combined implementation of both the first and second block of the model has differential outcomes for students.

References

Archambault, I., Janosz, M., Morizot, J., & Pagani, L. (2009). Adolescent behavioral, affective, and cognitive engagement in school: Relationship to dropout. *Journal of School Health, 79*(9), 408–415.

Baker, J. A., Clark, T. P., Maier, K. S, Viger, S. (2008). The differential influence of instructional context on the academic engagement of students with behavior problems. *Teaching and Teacher Education, 24*(7), 1876–1883.

Beecher, M., & Sweeny, S. M. (2008). Closing the achievement gap with curriculum enrichment and differentiation: One school's story. *Journal of Advanced Academics, 19*(3), 502–530.

Brock, L. L., Nishida, T. K., Chiong, C., Grimm, K. J., & Rimm-Kaufman, S. E. (2008). Children's perceptions of the classroom environment and social and academic performance: A longitudinal analysis of the contribution of the Responsive Classroom approach. *Journal of School Psychology, 46*, 129–149.

Brown, J. L. (2004). *Making the Most of Understanding by Design*. Association for Supervision and Curriculum Development (ASCD): Alexandria, VA.

Bru, E. (2009). Academic outcomes in school classes with markedly disruptive pupils. *Social Psychology of Education: An International Journal, 12*(4), 461–479.

Brusca-Vega, R., Brown, K., & Yasutake, D. (2011). Science achievement of students in co-taught, inquiry-based classrooms. *Learning Disabilities: A Multidisciplinary Journal, 17*(1), 23–31.

Bunch, G. & Valeo, A. (2004). Student attitudes toward peers with disabilities in inclusive and special education schools. *Disability & Society, 19*(1), 61–77. doi: 10.1080/0968759032000155640

Burgstahler, S. (2008). Universal Design in education: Process, principles and applications. Retrieved Nov. 18/08 from http://www.washington.edu/doit/Brochures/Programs/ud.html

CAST. (2012). Retrieved from http://www.cast.org/udl/

Canadian Council on Learning. (2007). *Equality in the classroom: The educational placement of children with disabilities*. Retrieved from http://www.cclcca.ca/CCL/Reports/LessonsInLearning/LinL20070502_Disability_Provincial_differences.html

Cole, C. M., & Waldron, N. (2002). The academic progress of students across inclusive and traditional settings. *ISEAS Cable, 23*(4), 1–6.

Cole, C. M., Waldron, N., & Majd, M. (2004). Academic progress of students across inclusive and traditional settings. *Mental Retardation: A Journal of Practices, Policy and Perspectives, 42*, 136–144.

Crisman, B. W. (2008). Inclusive programming for students with autism. *Principal, 88*, 28–32.

Curcic, S. (2009). Inclusion in PK-12: An international perspective. *International Journal of Inclusive Education, 13*(5), 517–538.

Davidson, M. L., & Kmelkov, V. T. (2006). *A Global Portrait of Social and Moral Health for Youth*. Retrieved from http://www.cortland.edu/character/instruments.asp

Drake, S. & Burns, R. (2004). *Meeting Standards Through Integrated Curriculum*. Association for Supervision and Curriculum Development (ASCD): Alexandria, VA.

Dunleavy, J., & Milton, P. (2008). Student engagement for effective teaching and deep learning. *Education Canada, 48*(5), 4–8.

Edyburn, D. (2010). Would you recognize universal design for learning if you saw it? Ten propositions for new directions for the second decade of UDL. Learning Disability Quarterly, 33, 33–41.

Fredricks, J. A., Blumenfeld, P.C., & Paris, A. H. (2004). School engagement: Potential of the concept, state of the evidence. *Review of Educational Research, 74*(1), 59–109.

Friesen, S. (2010). Raising the floor and lifting the ceiling: Math for all. *Education Canada, 48*(5), 50–54.

George, P. S. (2005). A rationale for differentiating instruction in the regular classroom. *Theory Into Practice, 44*(3), 185–193. http://dx.doi.org/10.1207/s15430421tip4403_2

Greenberg, M. T., Kusche, C. A., Cook, E. T., & Quamma, J. P. (1995). Promoting emotional competence in school-aged children: The effects of the PATHS curriculum. *Development and Psychopathology, 7*, 117–136.

Hafen, C. A., Allen, J. P., Mikami, A. Y., Gregory, A., Hamre, B. & Pianta, R. C. (2012). The pivotal role of adolescent autonomy in secondary school classrooms. *Journal of Youth and Adolescence, 41*(3), 245–255.

Hair, J. F., Anderson, R. E., Tatham, R. L., & Black, W. C. (1998). *Multivariate Data Analysis* (5th ed.). New Jersey: Prentice Hall.

Harlacher, J. E., & Merrell, K, W. (2010). Social and emotional learning as a universal level of student support: Evaluating the follow-up effect of strong kids on social and emotional outcomes. *Journal of Applied School Psychology, 26*(3), 212–229. http://dx.doi.org/10.1080/15377903.2010.495903

Iovanne, R., Dunlap, G., Huber, H., & Kincaid, D. (2003). Effective educational practices for students with autism spectrum disorders. *Focus on Autism and Other Developmental Disabilities, 18*, 150–165.

Jimenez, T. C., Graf, V. L., & Rose, E. (2007). Gaining access to general education: The promise of universal design for learning. *Issues in Teacher Education, 16*(2), 41–54.

Kambouka, A., Farrell, P., Dyson, A. & Kaplan, I. (2007). The impact of placing pupils with special educational needs in mainstream schools on the achievement of their peers. *Educational Research 49*, 365–382.

Katz, J. (2012a). *Teaching to Diversity: The Three-Block Model of Universal Design for Learning.* Winnipeg, MB: Portage & Main Press.

Katz, J. (2012b). Reimagining Inclusion. *Canadian Association of Principals Journal. Summer,* 22–26.

Katz, J. (2012c). Making imagination real: Inclusive education and the Three Block Model of Universal Design for Learning. *Canadian Association of Principals Journal. Summer,* 30–34.

Katz, J., Mirenda, P., & Auerbach, S. (2002). Instructional Strategies and Educational Outcomes for Students with Developmental Disabilities in Inclusive "Multiple Intelligences" and Typical Inclusive Classrooms. *Research & Practice for Persons with Severe Disabilities, 27*(4), 227. Retrieved from EBSCO*host.*

Katz, J., & Porath, M. (2011). Teaching to diversity: Creating compassionate learning communities for diverse elementary school communities. *International Journal of Special Education, 26*(2), 1–13.

Katz, J., Porath, M., Bendu, C., & Epp, B. (2012). Diverse Voices: Middle years students insights into life in inclusive classrooms. *Exceptionality Education International, 22*(1), 2–16.

King-Sears, M. (2009). Universal design for learning: Technology and pedagogy. *Learning Disabilities Quarterly, 32*, 199–201.

Kortering, L. J., McLannon, T. W., Braziel, P. M. (2008). Universal design for learning: A look at what algebra and biology students with and without high incidence conditions are saying. *Remedial and Special Education, 29*(6), 352–363. doi: 10.1177/0741932507314020

Koster, M., Nakken, H., Pijl, S. J., & van Houten, E. (2009). Being part of the peer group: A Literature study focusing on the social dimension of inclusion in education. *International Journal of Inclusive Education, 13*(2), 117–140.

Kuhn, M. (2008). Connecting depth and balance in class. *Learning & Leading with Technology, 36*(1), 18–21.

Kurth, J., & Mastergeorge, A. M. (2010). Individual education plan goals and services for adolescents with autism: Impact of age and educational setting. *Journal of Special Education, 44*(3), 146–160.

Mace, R. L., Story, M. F., & Mueller, J. L. (1998). A Brief History of Universal Design. In *The universal design file: Designing for people of all ages and abilities.* North Carolina: The Center for Universal Design. Retrieved June 18, 2006 from http://www.design.ncsu.edu/cud/publications/udfiletoc. html.

Marsh, H. W. (1992). Content specificity of relations between academic achievement and academic self-concept. *Journal of Educational Psychology, 84,* 35–42.

McGuire, J. M., Scott, S. S., & Shaw, S. F. (2006). Universal design and its application in educational environments. *Remedial and Special Education,' 27*(3), 166–175.

Meo, G. (2012). Curriculum planning for all learners: Applying Universal design for Learning (UDL) to a high school reading comprehension program. Preventing School Failure: Alternative Education for Children and Youth, 52(2), 21–30. http://dx.doi.org/10.3200/PSFL.52.2.21-30

Myklebust, J. (2006). Class placement and competence attainment among students with special educational needs. *British Journal of Special Education, 33*(2), 76–81.

Park, S. Holloway, S. D., Arendtsz, A., Bempechat, J., & Li, J. (2012). What makes students engaged in learning? A time-use study of within- and between-individual predictors of emotional engagement in low-performing high schools. *Journal of Youth and Adolescence, 41,* 390–401. DOI 10.1007/ s10964-011-9738-3

Ransford, C. R., Greenberg, M. T., Domitrovich, C. E., Small, M., & Jacobson, L. (2009). The Role of teachers' psychological experiences and perceptions of curriculum supports on the implementation of a social and emotional learning curriculum. *School Psychology review, 38*(4), 510–532.

Rose, D. & Meyer, A. (2002). *Teaching Every Student in the Digital Age.* ASCD.

Ruijs, N. M., & Peetsma, T. D. (2009). Effects of inclusion on students with and without special educational needs reviewed. *Educational Research Review, 4*(2), 67–79.

Ryan, R. M., & Deci, E. L. (2000). Self-determination theory and the facilitation of intrinsic motivation, social development, and wellbeing. *American Psychologist, 55,* 68–78.

Scigliano, D., & Hipsky, S. (2010). Three ring circus of differentiated instruction. *Kappa Delta Pi Record, 46*(2), 82–86.

Shernoff, D. J., Csikszentmihalyi, M., Schneider, B. & Shernoff, E. S. (2003). Student engagement in high school classrooms from the perspective of flow theory. *School Psychology Quarterly, 18*(2), 158–176.

Skinner, E.A., Kindermann, T. A., & Furrer, C. J. (2009). A motivational perspective on engagement and disaffection: Conceptualization and assessment of children's behavioral and emotional participation in academic activities in the classroom. *Educational and Psychological Measurement, 69*(3), 493–525. doi: 10.1177/0013164408323233

Specht, J.A., & Young, G. (2010). How administrators build schools as inclusive communities. In A. Edmunds and R. Macmillan (Eds) *Leadership for inclusion: A practical guide* (pp. 65–72). Rotterdam, the Netherlands. Sense Publishers.

Summerlee, A., & Murray, J. (2010). The impact of enquiry-based learning on academic performance and student engagement. *Canadian Journal of Higher Education, 40*(2), 78–94.

Timmons, V. & Wagner, M. (2008). *Inclusive Education Knowledge Exchange Initiative: An Analysis of the Statistics Canada Participation and Activity Limitation Survey*. Retrieved from Canadian Council on Learning website: http://www.cclcca.ca/CCL/Research/FundedResearch/201009TimmonsInclusiveEdu cation.html

Tomlinson, C. A., & Imbeau, M. B. (2010). *Leading and Managing a Differentiated Classroom*. Association for Supervision and Curriculum Development (ASCD): Alexandria, VA.

Wiggins, J., & McTighe, J. (2005). *Understanding by Design*. Prentice Hall.

William, D., Lee, C., Harrison, C., & Black, P. (2004). Teachers developing assessment for learning: Impact on student achievement. *Assessment in Education Principles Policy and Practice, 11*(1), 49–65.

Willms, J. F., Friesen, S., & Milton, P. (2009). *What did you do in school today? Transforming classrooms through social, academic, and intellectual engagement*. (First National Report) Toronto: Canadian Education Association.

Wotherspoon, T. (2002). *Dynamics of Social Inclusion: Public Education and Aboriginal People in Canada*. Retrieved from http://www.laidlawfdn.org/working-paper-series-social-inclusion.

You, S., & Sharkey, J. (2009). Testing a developmental–ecological model of student engagement: a multilevel latent growth curve analysis. Educational Psychology, 29(6), 659–684.

Zins, J. E., Bloodworth, M. R., Weissberg, R. P., & Walberg, H. J. (2004). The scientific base linking social and emotional learning to school success. In J. E. Zins, R. P. Weissberg, M. C. Wang, & H. J. Walberg (Eds.), *Building academic success on social and emotional learning* (pp. 23–39). New York: Teachers College Press.

Zins, J. E., & Elias, M. E. (2006). Social and emotional learning. In G. G. Bear & K. M. Minke (eds.), *Children's Needs III*, (p. 1–13). National Association of School Psychologists.

APPENDIX A

THE THREE-BLOCK MODEL OF UDL

System & Structures	Inclusive Instructional Practice

• Inclusive Policy—No "Except!"
• Hiring of administrators with expertise/vision
• Distributed Leadership
• Professional Development
• Staffing to support collaborative practice
   o Team planning time, scheduling in cohorts/teams
   o Resource/EA allocations to classrooms/cohorts, not individual children
   o Co-planning, co-teaching, co-assessing
   o Consistent, authentic assessment across classes—rubrics
• Budgeting
   o Changed from segregated practices/funding allocations
   o Assistive technology
   o Multi-leveled resources
	• Integrated Curriculum
	• Student Choice
	• Flexible Groupings/Co-operative Learning
	• Differentiated Instruction
	• Differentiated Assessment
	• Assessment for learning/Class Profiles/Strategic Teaching
	• Technology
	• Discipline Based Inquiry
	• Meta-Cognition—Assessment as learning
	• Understanding by Design/Essential Understandings
	• Social & Academic Inclusion of Students with Exceptionalities

Social and Emotional Learning—Developing Compassionate Learning Communities

- Respecting Diversity (RD) Program
  - Developing Self-Concept
  - Awareness of and pride in strengths and challenges
  - Sense of belonging
  - Goal setting and planning—building a vision for the future, self-efficacy, hope
  - Leadership skills/opportunities

- Valuing Diversity
  - Awareness of the strengths and challenges of others
  - Valuing of diverse contributions to community
  - Sense of collective responsibility for well-being, achievement of all
  - Empathy, Perspective taking, Compassion

- Democratic Classroom Management
  - Collective problem solving, recognition of rights and responsibilities
  - Promotion of Independent learning, student choice & empowerment, leadership
  - Increase in student engagement, ownership

APPENDIX B

Engaged Behavior

To simplify both the coding and statistical analysis of engaged behavior, we used 3 composite codes that indicated active, passive, and non-engaged behavior.

1. Active engagement—operationally define active engagement as "the active participation (e.g. involving a motor or verbal response) of target students in classroom activities." This definition included behaviors such as writing, reading, talking, raising a hand, manipulating materials (e.g. math manipulatives, playing a board game), etc.
2. Passive engagement—operationally define passive engagement as "the passive participation of target students in classroom activities through listening or observing silently." This definition required that students demonstrate attention by looking at the speaker or object (such as an overhead, film, etc.) being presented.
3. Non-engagement—operationally define non-engagement as "the non-participation or the demonstration of competing responses (i.e. off-task behavior) of target students in classroom activities." This definition included competing responses such as looking around, disruptive/aggressive behavior, talking inappropriately, playing with objects inappropriately, self-stimulatory behavior and self-abuse, etc.

Social Interactions

To simplify both the coding and statistical analysis of social interactions, we used 2 composite codes that indicate interactive and non-interactive behavior.

4. Interactive behavior—operationally defined a social interaction as "attempts by the target student to initiate, attend to, or respond to verbal or nonverbal communications with other students or adults in their classrooms." This definition included asking/answering questions, discussing, listening, reading with/to, playing with, singing, etc. *Listening within a one to one or small group discussion was coded as an interaction, however, listening to a teacher lecture was not considered a social interaction.*
5. Non-interactive behavior—operationally defined non-interactive behavior as "intervals in which target students were not attempting to initiate, attend to, or respond to verbal or nonverbal communications to/from other students or adults in their classrooms."

Interactive Partner

The Interactive Partner category was used to identify with whom the target child was interacting. Adult interactants included teacher, paraprofessional, etc. Peers were defined as "a peer with or without disabilities with whom the target student interacts." When students were not interacting, the code "none" was used to indicate that the target student was not interacting with anyone at that time.

Type of Activity

The "task" category was used to identify the type of activity in which target students engaged.

1. Rote paper-and-pencil tasks were coded using the "PAPER&PEN" code, defined as "tasks that involve traditional lecture, literacy, and/or paper-and-pencil response activities. These tasks are based primarily on verbal/linguistic and logical/mathematical intelligences." This definition includes the use of readers, textbooks, workbooks/worksheets, copying notes, handwriting/printing practice, math drill, listening to a lecture, etc.

2. Multiple intelligences activities (multisensory, multiple response options, hands-on, an/or co-operative activities) were coded using the "OTHMEDIA" code, defined as "activities which use/allow multiple methods of instruction or responding. These activities involve a variety of intelligences other than just verbal/linguistic or logical/mathematical intelligences, including body/kinesthetic (hands-on), musical, visual/spatial (e.g. artistic/constructive), interpersonal (social/co-operative), etc."

3. When no academic activity was taking place, the code "NOTASK" will be used, defined as "intervals in which target students are not assigned to an activity."

Instructional Groupings

1. "WHOLECLSS"—whole class instruction was recorded when the target student was receiving the same instruction as all other students. Examples included all students listening to the teacher lecture (same task) or the teacher calling out spelling words for a spelling test that involved the entire class.

2. "SMALLGRP"—small group instruction was recorded when the target student was receiving the same instruction or assigned the same task as at least one other student but not all students in the class. This included cooperative tasks, where students were working together to create a common product, or when students were working with a partner or small group in which they discussed the activity, but each created their own product. Examples of small group instruction include reading groups or when groups are located at work or interest stations in the room, each of which is devoted to a different activity, with different tasks, and different instructions about what to do.

3. "INDEPENDENT"—independent instruction was recorded when the target subject was engaged in an activity and task which was self-determined and self-managed. This is often described as independent seatwork.

Reading 3.3

Addressing Learner Variability on Campus Through Universal Design for Learning

Shannon Haley-Mize

U NIVERSAL DESIGN (UD) IS A TERM used to describe the process of planning with intentional consideration of usability, accessibility, and inclusion for a wide range of users with variable skills and characteristics (Burgstahler 2015a). Initially used in the field of architecture to describe structure and space that is designed to be accessible to those with a range of physical capacity, UD has translated into several theoretical models that are applicable to education. These include Universal Instructional Design (UID; see Chickering and Gamson 1987), Universal Design for Instruction (UDI; see Burgstahler 2015a), and Universal Design for Learning (UDL; see Meyer, Rose, and Gordon 2014). Despite many features shared among the three models and similarities in the recommended instructional practices, some distinctions exist between them (see Burgstahler 2015c). Each of these frameworks can assist institutions in moving closer to the goal of equitable access and full inclusion in higher education.

The primary focus of this chapter is on UDL because the recommendations for implementation draw on research and strategies that align with this model; however, the chapter also includes some review of research and projects that use either one of the other models or the broader term UD. After a review of UDL theory and its relationship to diversity, this chapter examines the research on UD in higher education, application of UDL to various elements of course design, and briefly considers UDL's application to online learning environments and appropriate supports for college students with mental health issues. The chapter concludes with suggestions for implementation.

Overview of UDL

Universal Design for Learning (UDL), developed by the Center for Applied Special Technology (CAST), is a framework for learning experiences and programs that are intentionally designed to meet the widest range of individual needs to allow universal access (Meyer et al. 2014). The UDL model is composed of the three principles of representation, action and expression, and engagement, and it espouses the notion that enhancing access for one group of individuals will ultimately benefit all. Each of the three principles, based on research in cognition and neuroscience, is associated with an area of the brain and align with what we know about how individuals learn. For each principle, CAST provided checkpoints that provide further detail on specific teaching and design approaches that support the three principles. These checkpoints can be invaluable tools for evaluating and improving current practice. CAST (2011) defines the UDL principles as follows:

1. *Representation*—The principle of representation is associated with the recognition network of the brain and is the "what" of learning. It includes how learners gather and categorize information perceived by the senses. To support recognition, instructors should present content in a variety of ways to facilitate learning. This includes multiple options for perception through different modalities (e.g., vision, hearing, or touch); options for language, mathematical expressions, and symbols to avoid inequalities in how students perceive content and support comprehension; and options for comprehension that include any scaffold necessary to ensure all learners have access to knowledge.

2. *Action and expression*—Action and expression is the domain of the strategic network of the brain and encompasses the "how" of learning. The principle of action and expression considers how learners organize and express ideas to plan and perform tasks. This domain incorporates options for physical action as well as expression and communication. Action and expression encompasses assessment of learning and includes providing options for students to demonstrate their knowledge, use of multiple media for communication, and support of executive functions such as goal setting.

3. *Engagement*—The principle of engagement is aligned with the affective networks of the brain and includes the "why" of learning. This principle examines why certain learners become engaged and are able to sustain motivation during the learning process. To achieve learner engagement, instructors should consider options for recruiting interest, sustaining effort and persistence, and self-regulation. Options that support engagement include optimizing choice and fostering collaboration, among other considerations.

UDL and Diversity

UDL is a potentially powerful tool to address equity and access issues that are presented by the growing diversity in the student body at institutions of higher education. UDL fills a void in research-based practice on equitable access for postsecondary students with disabilities. In contrast to the lack of research on students with disabilities in higher education, there is a growing body of work that deals with the impact of a racially and ethnically diverse educational community, and this research helps to guide campus supports. Disability is examined less frequently (McCune 2001), prompting some scholars to point out that even in conversations about inclusion, disability is marginalized (Higbee, Katz, and Schultz 2010).

UDL has the potential to impact all learners, but given the dearth of research on appropriate access for students with disabilities and the numbers of individuals with disabilities, it is imperative to eradicate barriers for this population specifically. Approximately 11 percent of college students report having a disability (NCES 2016). One study that examined types of disabilities reported approximately 31 percent of these students indicated a learning disability, 18 percent reported attention deficit, and 15 percent cited mental health conditions (NCES 1999). A variety of other disabilities such as autism were reported less frequently. There is a significant difference in achievement for this group when compared to peers who do not have a disability or other at-risk status. For example, college students with disabilities are far less likely to graduate when compared to peers without disabilities. About 38 percent of students with disabilities who begin attending will finish, compared to 51 percent of students who do not have a disability (Sanford et al. 2011). Both individual and institutional factors influence these poorer outcomes (Burgstahler 2015b). One example of an individual factor is self-determination skills, such as the ability to advocate for accommodations that remove barriers to access of facilities, services, and content. Institutional factors that impact these outcomes include accessibility of services and courses (Burgstahler and Cory 2008).

Many individuals with disabilities who go on to postsecondary institutions face barriers that contribute to the lower rates of retention and graduation. There is evidence that many students with disabilities do not enroll in campus disability services and, thus, do not request accommodations and modifications (Getzel 2008). The large number of students who do not access these services is likely partially attributable to the stigma surrounding disability as a construct. The model of requiring students to self-identify as having a disability and to request accommodation perpetuates the idea that the individual has a deficit and, thus, needs a "fix" to be able to participate. In contrast, UDL is aligned with the social model of disability that "posits that it is not an individual's impairment or adjustment but the socially imposed barriers—the inaccessible buildings, the limited modes of transportation and communication, the prejudicial attitudes—that construct disability as a subordinate social status and devalued life experience" (Berger and Lorenz 2015:1). Advocates for a UDL approach to course and service design recognize that addressing accessibility and inclusion during the planning process communicates that difference, or learner variability, is the expectation—the rule rather than the exception. As Burgstahler (2015b) intimates:

> focusing on difference rather than deficit supports the social model of disability and other integrated approaches within the field of disability studies that consider variations—such as those with respect to gender, size, socio-economic status, race, ethnicity, and ability—a normal part of the human experience. Thus, disability is viewed simply as one aspect of a spectrum of human variations. (P. 7)

UDL theory also exemplifies a social justice perspective because it ideally results in "full and equal participation of all groups in a society that is mutually shaped to meet their needs" (Adams, Bell, and Griffin 2007:1). This perspective makes UDL especially relevant to the teaching across disciplines that demonstrate a "long disciplinary history of engagement with social issues" (Petray and Halbert 2013:441) and allows faculty and support staff at institutions of higher education to assume and model the role of change agents. Additionally, UDL encourages examination of both environmental and individual characteristics employing sociological imagination to contextualize experience in terms of social structures to avoid confinement in the individual experience (Mills 2000). This inspires a transformative mind-set. This view insists that the environment is the source of the disability and, thus, should be the focus of interventions (Evans 2008).

Accommodations vs. UDL

The American with Disabilities Education Act (1990) defines a reasonable accommodation as one that renders existing facilitates accessible and useable by individuals with disabilities. This includes modifications to equipment, examinations, and content materials. It also includes provision of accessible documents and qualified readers or interpreters. Providing accommodations for individual students in a reactive fashion has disadvantages beyond perpetuating the idea that the disability is a problem or individual deficit and requires a solution. Institutions only provide accommodations to students that self-identify as having a disability and articulate that the course or service is inaccessible. This is a problem because, as previously noted, research shows that most college students with disabilities do not reach out to disability service offices, which makes them ineligible for supports (Wagner et al. 2005). Securing accommodations requires that the student make an extra effort that is not necessary for other students. This process of seeking out accommodations to access course materials and other campus services marginalizes students with disabilities. Accessible documents and materials may not be readily available and require time to produce, which may result in the student not having access to content in the same time frame as other students. In addition, providing accommodations to individual students does not have the potential to benefit all students.

In contrast, UDL is a proactive approach that involves designing courses and other student services in a manner that deliberately analyzes and removes barriers that may be present for a wide variety of learners. The UDL process prompts faculty and staff to think like designers and to create content, experiences, services, and environments that are more likely to be accessible to all. This represents a paradigm shift from a narrow focus on a "normal" user to instead consider a wide range of human characteristics and variability (Myers, Lindburg, and Nied 2013).

Research

As Edyburn (2010) articulated, there is a lack of empirical research on the application of UDL in learning environments. The existing, relatively small foundation of empirical research is more robust if the examination includes the broader term of UD as search criteria. Most of the work examined in the published reviews and in additional studies cited in this section is qualitative, including action research. This section includes a few examples of quasi-experimental studies (e.g., Davies, Schelly, and Spooner 2013) and one experimental study (Spooner et al. 2007).

A review of current research on UD in educational settings conducted by Rao, Ok, and Bryant (2014) identified only 13 journal articles that empirically evaluated application of UD to the teaching and learning process. A review by Roberts et al. (2015) included 19 articles, with five studies overlapping between the two reviews. Overall, results indicated that studies reported gains in specific academic outcomes, improved access for students with reading difficulties, increased student engagement, fostered formation of community, and increased interaction in college courses. Rao et al. (2014) warn that "the evidence should be interpreted with caution as a set of preliminary positive results based on varied methods of analysis" (p. 162).

A recent study by Black, Weinberg, and Brodwin (2015), not included in either of the aforementioned reviews, examined the perspectives of college students with disabilities on teaching methods and pedagogy that they perceived as being supportive of their learning. The researchers then determined if the strategies identified by the students as beneficial were aligned with UDL. Students reported that they experienced barriers to learning and that UDL practices were helpful. One interesting theme that emerged was the students' belief that faculty and staff would benefit from basic awareness training and professional development on how to work with students with disabilities. In a similar vein, students reported that some accommodations were not appropriately executed.

Some evidence exists that faculty professional development (PD) is effective in improving application of UD to course design and instruction. For example, a study by Zhang (2005) found that sustained and targeted PD was effective in improving participants' growth and use of technology. Faculty identified UDL as a high-need training topic, and web-based, self-paced PD increased participants' self-efficacy in meeting the needs of students with a wide variety of needs (Izzo, Murray, and Novak 2008). Davies et al. (2013) also reported that students perceived UDL professional development had significant positive effect on teaching methods employed by faculty.

The research investigating UD application to online course development demonstrates a positive impact on a variety of student factors and perceptions of learning. Ye He (2014) found that student self-efficacy in teaching and learning online improved after participation in a course using UD principles. Participants reported that pacing and flexibility were the most impactful elements in the course.

Application

UDL is a powerful academic design tool when employed in higher education. Consideration of several components of course construction using a UDL lens is advantageous, and resources for instructors are readily available. The following recommendations were compiled using resources available at CAST's UDL on Campus site (www.udloncampus.cast.org) and the DO-IT program housed at the University of Washington (http://www.washington.edu/doit).

Syllabus

The syllabus serves as a roadmap for the course and shapes the students' initial impressions of the type of learning environment that the instructor will establish in the classroom. Therefore, at a minimum, the syllabus should be an accessible document. Because UDL is best integrated during the design of the course, the syllabus is the perfect starting point for constructing a UDL course. The course instructor can use the syllabus to set the climate of the course, to articulate expectations, and to give information about options and accessibility. There are several modifications that can be made to syllabus design to support a broader range of individuals and improve access. For example, the course calendar can list the readings and media in all formats available and give guidance on how to access the content. The syllabus also usually outlines how learning will be assessed and allows another opportunity to articulate the UDL options embedded in the course by highlighting options for action and expression.

The syllabus should serve as a personal introduction of the instructor. A section in the syllabus should be dedicated to introducing the instructor, and this section can be used to engage students through use of a photo and video. This type of enhanced introduction allows students to get to know the instructor, the expectations, and the structure of the course. Several methods of communication and options for obtaining answers to questions should be provided such as email, phone, text, discussion boards dedicated to course questions, and links to any instructor, professional social media accounts.

The course syllabus should include the statement on accommodations, a description of the course, and course objectives. Instructors can apply UDL considerations to each of these syllabus components. First, consider putting the disability statement and available supports at the beginning of the syllabus rather than at the end. This ensures that students see the information, and it communicates that the instructor prioritizes their success in the course. Second, the course description should identify clear goals for the course and establish relevance to the students. Third, carefully articulate the objectives and connect them directly to the assignments. This makes the purpose of each assignment in the course explicit. To clarify the course material, divide objectives by topic. Utilizing a graphic organizer helps to display how course objectives relate.

Course Materials

During course design, instructors can also assemble course materials using the UDL approach. A UDL course designer considers a wide variety of materials beyond printed text. Content can be provided in different formats such as digital versions of class presentations. Videotaping the course sessions and making the videos available on the online course platform ensures multiple pathways to the content. Designers can also make any materials such as handouts, videos, and PowerPoint presentations accessible online. These alternatives allow for multiple sources of representation of the same content and increase engagement. Designers can invite students to contribute to a collection of materials related to the course content to encourage shared ownership. These materials might include online resources such as streaming video, related social media accounts, or links to pertinent professional agencies that extend the course content. As materials are amassed, the instructor should ensure that included material is accessible to all learners. For example, videos should have closed captioning, documents should be compatible with screen reader technology, and images should have captions.

Assignments and Assessments

Course assignments and assessments are under the purview of the UDL principle of action and expression. This principle prompts course designers to consider choices for physical actions, expression and communication, and executive functions. Potential barriers, including construct-irrelevant factors, should be identified. Instructors must differentiate the actual content that they want to test, from construct-irrelevant factors that potentially act as barriers. For example, if the purpose of an assessment is to analyze the student's content knowledge on a specific topic, it may be that requiring an essay response on an assessment includes factors that are irrelevant to the learning objective but are nonetheless required for the response. If part of the learning objective is to assess the student's ability to synthesize information, then an essay response may be appropriate, but perhaps spelling ability or the speed at which the student completes the response are construct irrelevant, so the designer could eliminate those potential barriers by allowing access to a dictionary and unlimited time for completion.

A course that incorporates dependable routines and expectations assists students with planning and prioritizing. Instructors should explicitly state assignment deadlines in the course schedule and incorporate feedback into a predictable routine. These routines can be outlined in the syllabus with weekly content and connections with the course objectives. A well-designed, UDL course also allows numerous opportunities for the instructor to detail expectations for learners. Instructors can articulate these expectations in the introductory video and revisit them frequently at different intervals over the length of the semester.

Course Delivery

Course delivery is a vital consideration from a ULD perspective. There are some general recommendations in this realm. For face-to-face classes, provide a digital space for collecting accessible artifacts and materials and to extend the discussion. Artifacts and materials include captioned photos of products created during class, digital versions of notes and presentations, and links to streaming or other videos used during class. Opportunities to extend the dialogue in the online course space might include discussion boards, designed boards for questions about the course content, or links to online platforms that include forums. For online courses, offer at least one opportunity for a meeting in person. The students may not take advantage of it or may not be able to meet due to factors such as distance, but it is a consideration when feasible.

Considerations for Online Learning

In order to meet the requirements of federal law and to provide equitable access, UDL should also be applied to online learning experiences (Case and Davidson 2011). There are some affordances of online learning for students with disabilities. In general, digital text is more flexible and malleable than printed material. Digital spaces can support multiple media and hyperlinked text that allow options for representation of content and scaffolding. Digital content can be varied in order to facilitate and support student engagement. Many digital platforms also support collaboration, allowing for options for action and expression.

To realize the potential of these affordances, instructors should create accessible materials and documents. The Web Content Accessibility Guidelines (WCAG 2.0 2016) provide guidance in the form of four principles to consider when creating accessible, web-based content.

In addition to the WCAG 2.0 guidance, data from studies conducted with students with disabilities identify priorities for UDL-designed, online learning experiences. For example, Catalano (2014) collected interview data from students with disabilities who were participants in a course using a UD design. The common themes that emerged from this examination included the need for clear expectations, frequent interaction with the professor, audio accompaniment for tutorials and presentations, and feedback on assignments. The students also highlighted a video introduction of the instructor, an invitation to meet in person, and timely answers to emails as essential components.

These student recommendations are consistent with CAST's suggestions on how to design effective online courses for a wide variety of learners. CAST also emphasizes the need for executive functioning support in an online environment. Executive functioning includes setting appropriate goals, planning and organizing, developing steps to achieve a goal, and using strategies for problem solving. Other executive functions are prioritizing, self-discipline, and monitoring progress (Huizinga, Dolan, and van der Molen 2006). Executive functioning is essential for success in all learning experiences, but becomes especially critical in an online environment. Designers can provide the necessary supports by incorporating clear, interactive course headings and icons; grouping content into small, logical modules; incorporating checklists for monitoring progress; and providing self-check quizzes and activities with immediate feedback. Students also benefit from options to create notes in various ways, annotate material, and organize resources.

Students with Mental Health Needs

Although it is difficult to discern exact statistics due to reliance on self-disclosure, evidence does exist that the number of college students with mental health issues is increasing, and these learners often experience educational challenges (Rickerson, Souma, and Burgstahler 2012). One estimate indicates that despite this growth in enrollment, as many as 86 percent of students with psychiatric disabilities withdraw before completing their degrees (Collins and Mowbray 2005). Teaching strategies consistent with UD can address various characteristics of this type of "invisible disability." Application of UD principles is especially important for these students because studies have found that as few as 10 percent access accommodations, which is likely due to the stigma associated with mental illness (Koch, Mamiseishvili, and Higgins 2014). Another contributing factor may be the lack of awareness of services.

Several components of the traditional college classroom may present barriers for these students. They may struggle with paying attention to the lecture and class discussion while simultaneously taking adequate notes. Pacing of courses may require that students grasp concepts quickly and that students navigate complex interactions with the instructor and their peers—especially if the instructor employs a variety of pedagogical strategies and uses flexible grouping.

Applying UDL to course design to reduce barriers for students with mental health issues also means that instructors should give consideration to testing and class assignments. These students may struggle with heightened test anxiety, which may impact performance. Poor time management and limited ability to organize multiple assignments can further negatively impact performance. Because of these factors, instructors must consider a variety of alternative assessment strategies that encourage students to express their knowledge in a variety of ways. Examples include portfolios, presentations, research assignments, peer and self-evaluations, and creative projects that align with the learning objectives. Digital tools provide a wealth of options for multiple means of expression from digital storyboards to comic strips. Class assignments can also include multiple means of expressing and gaining knowledge. These alternatives can incorporate activities such as debates, case studies, and discussion. Other tools include brainstorming sessions and cooperative projects. Students might also benefit from scaffolding for more complex assignments and frequent due dates for smaller portions of a large project.

Implementation

Institutional Level

Professional development (PD) to raise awareness for faculty and staff across campus has been demonstrated to be effective in establishing a foundation for greater accessibility and inclusion of students with disabilities in higher education (Lombardi and Murray 2011; Murray, Lombardi, and Wren 2011). To support faculty in making meaningful changes in course design and teaching practices, PD should include specific action steps (Edyburn 2010). Assessment tools are available to evaluate inclusive teaching practices (Lombardi, Murray, and Gerdes 2011) and guide PD topics.

Change Process at a Course Level

Nelson (2014) suggests the following steps to integrate UDL into instruction:

1. Reflect on the needs of students. Ask yourself, "What are my students struggling with?"
2. Identify a principle or a specific checkpoint that addresses the student need identified. Ask, "How might I use this checkpoint to meet the needs of learners?"

3. Investigate and create new pedagogical methods or strategies. Pose the question, "What brings this principle or checkpoint to life?"
4. Teach a lesson with the new method/strategy. Prompt yourself to think about "What does this principle or checkpoint look like in my teaching environment?"
5. Assess the method/strategy by asking, "In what ways did my students demonstrate knowledge or skills?"
6. Reflect on how the new method/strategy worked by considering, "How did the principle or checkpoint enhance student outcomes?"

Conclusion

The impetus for using the UDL framework is multifaceted and grounded in the social model of disability that conceptualizes learner variability as the expectation, rather than a problem to be rectified. UDL shifts the traditional deficit-based view of disability to a critical analysis of the curriculum as a source of potential barriers and provides guidance on ways to ameliorate those barriers. UDL has the potential to benefit all learners and is applicable to online learning environments. UDL also provides solutions for faculty and staff struggling to meet the needs of the growing population of students with mental health needs. Campuses can build capacity for the use of UDL across academic and student services by providing professional development and supporting a gradual implementation that includes incremental changes and reflection.

References

Adams, Maurianne, Lee Anne Bell, and Pat Griffin. 2007. *Teaching for Diversity and Social Justice.* New York: Routledge.

Americans with Disabilities Act of 1990, Public Law 101–336, 104 U. S. Statutes at Large 328 (1990).

Berger, Ronald J., and Laura S. Lorenz. 2015. *Disability and Qualitative Inquiry: Methods for Rethinking an Ableist World.* New York: Routledge.

Black, Robert D., Lois A. Weinberg, and Martin G. Brodwin. 2015. "Universal Design for Learning and Instruction: Perspectives of Students with Disabilities in Higher Education." *Exceptionality Education International* 25(2):1–16.

Burgstahler, Sheryl E. 2015a. *Equal Access: Universal Design of Instruction.* Seattle: University of Washington.

Burgstahler, Sheryl E. 2015b. "Universal Design in Higher Education." Pp. 3–28 in *Universal Design in Higher Education: From Principles to Practice,* edited by S. E. Burgstahler. Cambridge, MA: Harvard Education Press.

Burgstahler, Sheryl E. 2015c. "Universal Design of Instruction: From Principles to Practice." Pp. 3–28 in *Universal Design in Higher Education: From Principles to Practice,* edited by S. E. Burgstahler. Cambridge, MA: Harvard Education Press.

Burgstahler, Sheryl E., and Rebecca C. Cory. 2008. *Universal Design in Higher Education: From Principles to Practice.* Cambridge, MA: Harvard Education Press.

Case, D. Elizabeth, and Roseanna C. Davidson. 2011. "Accessible Online Learning." Pp. 47–58 in *Fostering the Increased Integration of Students with Disabilities: New Directions for Student Services,* edited by M. Huger. San Francisco: Jossey-Bass.

Center for Applied Special Technology (CAST). N.d. *UDL on Campus.* Retrieved January 20, 2017 (http://udloncampus.cast.org/home#.WHZvx7GZPU0).

Center for Applied Special Technology (CAST). 2011. *Universal Design for Learning Guidelines version 2.0.* Retrieved January 20, 2017 (http://www.udlcenter.org/aboutudl/udlguidelines /principle1).

Catalano, Amy. 2014. "Improving Distance Education for Students with Special Needs: A Qualitative Study of Students' Experiences with an Online Library Research Course." *Journal of Library and Information Services in Distance Learning* 8(1):17–31.

Chickering, Arthur W., and Zelda F. Gamson. 1987. "Seven Principles for Good Practice in Undergraduate Education." *AAHE Bulletin* 39(7):3–7.

Collins, Mary Elizabeth, and Carol T. Mowbray. 2005. "Higher Education and Psychiatric Disabilities: National Survey of Campus Disability Services." *American Journal of Orthopsychiatry* 75(2):304–15.

Davies, Patricia L., Catherine L. Schelly, and Craig L. Spooner. 2013. "Measuring the Effectiveness of Universal Design for Learning Intervention in Postsecondary Education." *Journal of Postsecondary Education and Disability* 26(3):195–220.

Edyburn, Dave L. 2010. "Would You Recognize Universal Design for Learning if You Saw It? Ten Propositions for the Second Decade of UDL." *Learning Disability Quarterly* 33(1):1–41.

Evans, Nancy. 2008. "Theoretical Foundations of Universal Instructional Design." Pp. 11–24 in *Pedagogy and Student Services for Institutional Transformation: Implementing Universal Design in Higher Education,* edited by J. L. Higbee and E. Goff. Minneapolis: Regents of the University of Minnesota, Center for Research on Developmental Education and Urban Literacy, College of Education and Human Development. Retrieved January 25, 2017 (http://www.cehd.umn.edu/ passit/docs/PASS-IT-Book.pdf).

Getzel, Elizabeth E. 2008. "Addressing the Persistence and Retention of Students with Disabilities in Higher Education: Incorporating Key Strategies and Supports on Campus." *Exceptionality* 16(4):207–19.

He, Ye. 2014. "Universal Design for Learning in an Online Teacher Education Course: Enhancing Learners Confidence to Teach Online." *MERLOT Journal of Online and Teaching* 10(2):283–98.

Higbee, Jeanne L., Rachel E. Katz, and Jennifer L. Schultz. 2010. "Disability in Higher Education: Redefining Mainstreaming." *Journal of Diversity Management* 5(2):7–16.

Huizinga, Mariette, Conor V. Dolan, and M. W. Maurits van der Molen. 2006. "Age-Related Change in Executive Function: Developmental Trends and a Latent Variable Analysis." *Neuropsychologia* 44(11):2017–36.

Izzo, Margaretha V., Alexa Murray, and Jeanne Novak. 2008. "The Faculty Perspective on Universal Design for Learning." *Journal of Postsecondary Education and Disability* 21(2):60–72.

Koch, Lynn C., Ketevan Mamiseishvili, and Kirstin Higgins. 2014. "Persistence to Degree Completion: A Profile of Students with Psychiatric Disabilities in Higher Education." *Journal of Vocational Rehabilitation* 40(1):73–82.

Lombardi, Allison R., and Christopher Murray. 2011. "Measuring University Faculty Attitudes Toward Disability: Willingness to Accommodate and Adopt Universal Design Principles." *Journal of Vocational Rehabilitation* 34(1):43–56.

Lombardi, Allison R., Christopher Murray, and Hilary Gerdes. 2011. "College Faculty and Inclusive Instruction: Self-Reported Attitudes and Actions Pertaining to Universal Design." *Journal of Diversity in Higher Education* 4(4):250–61.

McCune, Pat. 2001. "What Do Disabilities Have to Do with Diversity?" *About Campus* 6(2):5–12.

Meyer, Anne, Derek H. Rose, and David Gordon. 2014. *Universal Design for Learning: Theory and Practice.* Wakefield, MA: CAST Professional.

Mills, C. Wright. [1959] 2000. *The Sociological Imagination.* Oxford: Oxford University Press.

Murray, Christopher, Allison Lombardi, and Carol T. Wren. 2011. "The Effects of Disability-Focused Training on the Attitudes and Perceptions of University Staff." *Remedial and Special Education* 32(4):290–300.

Myers, Karen A., Jaci J. Lindburg, and Danielle M. Nied. 2013. *Allies for Inclusion: Disability and Equity in Higher Education.* Hoboken, NJ: Wiley Periodicals.

NCES (National Center for Educational Statistics). 1999. "An Institutional Perspective on Students with Disabilities in Postsecondary Education." *Postsecondary Education Quick Information System.* U. S. Department of Education. Retrieved September 8, 2017 (https://cms.hutchcc.edu/uploaded Files/StudentServices/DisabilityServices/instpers.pdf).

NCES (National Center for Education Statistics). 2016. *Digest of Education Statistics 2014* (2016–006). U. S. Department of Education. Retrieved January 21, 2017 (https://nces.ed.gov/fastfacts/display. asp?id = 60).

Nelson, Loui L. 2014. *Design and Deliver: Planning and Teaching Using Universal Design for Learning.* Baltimore, MD: Brookes.

Petray, Theresa, and Kelsey Halbert. 2013. "Teaching Engagement: Reflections on Sociological Praxis." *Journal of Sociology* 49(4):441–55.

Rao, Kavita, Min Wook Ok, and Brian R. Bryant. 2014. "A Review of Research on Universal Design Educational Models." *Remedial and Special Education* 35(3):153–66.

Rickerson, Nancy, Alfred Souma, and Sheryl Burgstahler 2012. *Psychiatric Disabilities in Postsecondary Education: Universal Design, Accommodations, and Supported Education.* Seattle: DO-IT, University of Washington.

Roberts, Kelly, Hye Jin Park, Steven Brown, and Bryan Cook. 2015. "Universal Design for Instruction in Postsecondary Education: A Systematic Review of Empirically Based Articles." *Journal of Postsecondary Education and Disability* 24(1):5–15.

Sanford, Christopher, Lynn Newman, Mary Wagner, Renée Cameto, Anne Marie Knokey, and Debra Shaver. 2011. *The Post–High School Outcomes of Young Adults with Disabilities Up to 6 Years after High School: Key Findings from the National Longitudinal Transition Study-2 (NLTS2)* (NCSER 2011–3004). Menlo Park, CA: SRI International. Retrieved January 26, 2017 (https://ies.ed.gov/ncser/pubs/20113004/pdf/20113004.pdf).

Spooner, Fred, Joshua N. Baker, Amber A. Harris, Lynn Ahlgrim-Delzell, and Diane M. Browder. 2007. "Effects of Training in Universal Design for Learning on Lesson Plan Development." *Remedial and Special Education* 28(2):108–16.

Wagner, Mary, Lynn Newman, Renée Cameto, Nicolle Garza, and Phyllis Levine. 2005. *After High School: A First Look at the Postschool Experiences of Youth with Disabilities. A Report from the National Longitudinal Transition Study-2 (NLTS2).* Menlo Park, CA: SRI International. Retrieved January 29, 2017 (http://www.nlts2.org/reports/2005_04/nlts2_report_2005_04_complete.pdf).

Web Accessibility Initiative. 2016. "How to Meet WCAG 2.0." Retrieved January 20, 2017 (https://www.w3.org/WAI/WCAG20/quickref/.).

Wisbey, Martha E., and Karen S. Kalivoda. 2011. "College Students with Disabilities." Pp. 347–370 in *Multiculturalism on Campus,* edited by M. J. Cuyjet, M. F. Howard-Hamilton, and D. L. Cooper. Sterling, VA: Stylus.

Zhang, Yixin. 2005. "A Collaborative Professional Development Model: Focusing on Universal Design for Technology Utilization." *ERS Spectrum* 23(3):32–33.

Reading 3.4

Developing Literacy in English Language Learners

Findings from a Review of the Experimental Research

Diane August

American Institutes for Research

Peggy McCardle

Peggy McCardle Consulting, LLC

Timothy Shanahan

University of Illinois at Chicago

O VER THE PAST DECADE, A SPAN during which total student enrollment grew by only 4.9%, the proportion of schoolchildren in the United States who were English language learners (ELLs) grew by an astonishing 32%. Now English learners make up 9% of the student population (U.S. Department of Education, National Center for Education Statistics, Common Core of Data, 2014). Given this growth and the specific educational challenges ELLs face (Lee, Grigg, & Donahue, 2007), there is a need to determine what constitutes effective reading instruction for them. Toward this end, this commentary makes use of research findings on the effectiveness of instructional interventions aimed at developing literacy in ELLs to suggest directions for school psychologists, who are in an ideal position to guide teachers and administrators in providing the best possible instructional supports for ELLs.

The report of the National Reading Panel (NRP; National Institute of Child Health and Human Development, 2000) provided an analysis of research on the teaching of reading. This report examined research into enhanced instructional efforts aimed at teaching component skills of reading (phonemic awareness, phonics, oral reading fluency, reading comprehension, vocabulary). To limit the scope of the effort, studies of ELLs were excluded. However, an approach that works well with English speakers may not work as well with those in the process of acquiring English (Gutiérrez, Zepeda, & Castro, 2010), so the Institute of Education Sciences convened the

National Literacy Panel on Language-Minority Children and Youth (August & Shanahan, 2006, 2008). This panel conducted a comprehensive synthesis of the literature on literacy learning in ELLs and attempted to answer questions about instructional effectiveness (Francis, Lesaux, & August, 2006; Shanahan & Beck, 2006).

This commentary is based on the findings of research studies included in the systematic National Literacy Panel reviews, augmented by studies published since that time. Not all studies reviewed are cited directly in this commentary; some are cited to make specific points about literacy development in ELLs. The purpose of this commentary is to provide school psychologists a summary of empirical evidence on which to base their professional actions.

The studies discussed here were experimental in nature because such studies allow for a sound evaluation of the effectiveness of educational approaches. Most of the studies were based on the learning of Spanish speakers in U.S. schools, but students from other language backgrounds and countries were also included. The researchers rarely reported the English language proficiency levels of the students in these studies, but when they did, the levels varied. Most of the studies took place in general education classrooms, but some focused on students with learning disabilities (e.g., Denton, Wexler, Vaughn, & Bryan, 2008). Collectively, these studies provide valuable insights into what might make a difference in the instruction of ELLs.

Teaching ELLs the Components of Literacy

Since the NRP report, there has been a heightened emphasis on the teaching of the component skills of reading. The research reviewed for this commentary shows similar benefits from this approach for ELL populations. Second language learners benefit from explicit instruction in phonological awareness, phonics, vocabulary, oral reading fluency, reading comprehension, and writing. Although these instructional routines benefit ELLs, they may vary in their degree of effectiveness and may require some adaptation to meet the special needs of ELLs. In the next sections we report on studies by literacy component.

Decoding

Reading most obviously differs from oral language in its reliance on printed, rather than spoken, words. The NRP analyses of phonological awareness and phonics instruction showed clear benefits for children's reading development as determined by a wide range of outcome measures (National Institute of Child Health and Human Development, 2000). What about teaching decoding to English learners?

Overall, the studies showed that instruction could boost the word reading skills of ELLs. The explicit teaching of phonological awareness and phonics benefited ELLs, much as it had native English speakers. However, unlike the research on native English speaking students, studies of ELLs (Elley, 1991; Tharp, 1982) showed that increased exposure to English text also had positive effects on the word reading of young ELLs. This is probably because ELLs are relatively less familiar with English text when they enter school, so extended experience with such text would be advantageous.

Many of the same instructional programs found to work with native speakers were also found to be effective with ELLs (e.g., Reading Mastery, Early Interventions in Reading, Corrective Reading, Jolly Phonics, Peer-Assisted Learning Strategies, Reading Rescue, Fast ForWord Language, and Orton Gillingham). However, there were particularly strong outcomes for ELLs when the instruction was tailored to their language differences by doing things like devoting more time to those English sounds not in the students' home language (Giambo & McKinney, 2004; Kramer, Schell, & Rubison, 1983). Other instructional approaches well suited to the decoding needs of ELLs included grouping of students according to their instructional needs, mastery learning with frequent teacher modeling, opportunities for practice, and cumulative review (Gunn, Biglan, Smolkowski, & Ary, 2000; Kamps et al., 2007; Lovett et al., 2008). Peer-assisted tutoring, in which higher performing readers are paired with lower performing readers, was also effective (Calhoon, Al Otaiba, Cihak, King, & Avalos, 2007; McMaster, Kung, Han, & Cao, 2008). These aspects of instruction are particularly important because ELLs are a heterogeneous group with different degrees of English proficiency and with language backgrounds that vary in their degree of correspondence with English.

Oral Reading Fluency

Oral reading fluency refers to the ability to read text accurately, with sufficient speed to allow sentences to cohere and with appropriate prosody (e.g., pausing in the right places). Oral reading fluency is not a pure skill but depends on the reader's automaticity in recognizing or decoding words and on his or her ability to comprehend. The NRP considered two basic approaches to teaching fluency: independent reading practice and guided oral reading with repetition (oral rereading) (National Institute of Child Health and Human Development, 2000). The NRP found too few studies, many badly flawed, to draw strong conclusions about the value of independent reading on fluency, but the panel did conclude that guided repeated oral reading procedures helped native English speakers improve fluency to an extent that improved reading comprehension.

Our review found that various instructional procedures were effective in developing ELLs' oral reading fluency. Most of these studies examined the fluency effects of explicit decoding instruction or of more comprehensive programs of explicit teaching that included decoding and fluency. Only one of these studies focused primarily on guided repeated oral reading, the instructional approach found effective with native speakers of English (VanWagenen, Williams, & McLaughlin, 1994); it was also effective with ELLs. Six studies found positive fluency outcomes for ELLs taught in small groups or one-on-one settings with tutors (Denton et al., 2008; Gunn et al., 2000; Gunn, Smolkowski, Biglan, & Black, 2002; Gunn, Smolkowski, Biglan, Black, & Blair, 2005; Kamps et al., 2007; VanWagenen, Williams, & McLaughlin, 1994). An additional study used fluency activities that were facilitated by teachers but were largely student led (Calhoon et al., 2007). Some features of the interventions may have made them particularly beneficial for ELLs, such as making particular efforts to ensure that students understood the stories they were reading (VanWagenen et al., 1994).

Vocabulary

Vocabulary is an obvious area in which to focus instruction for ELLs because it emphasizes teaching the meanings of words and their structural components (prefixes and suffixes). Even in a first language, increasing vocabulary knowledge increases the number of texts students will be able to understand (National Institute of Child Health and Human Development, 2000). Explicit vocabulary instruction improves the reading comprehension of native English speakers, and students also develop significant amounts of vocabulary learning incidentally through storybook reading, which is an avenue that may be less effective for ELLs, who would presumably know a smaller proportion of vocabulary on which to build.

The vocabulary studies with ELLs examined various approaches to teaching both general and domain-specific vocabulary, such as directly teaching individual words, immersing students in language-rich environments, and teaching word learning strategies (August, Branum-Martin, Cardenas-Hagan, & Francis, 2009; Biemiller & Boote, 2006; Carlo et al., 2004; Lesaux, Kieffer, Faller, & Kelley, 2010; Lesaux, Kieffer, Kelley, & Harris, 2014; Roberts & Neal, 2004; Silverman, 2007; Vaughn et al., 2009). Many of the ELL studies addressed teaching techniques similar to those considered by the NRP (National Institute of Child Health and Human Development, 2000); the one exception was a study that considered the vocabulary outcomes of enhanced decoding instruction (Giambo & McKinney, 2004). This study found a small, positive impact on vocabulary learning, probably because it introduced students to some new words. At especially early stages of language acquisition, any high quality English interactions may be effective.

Some studies are notable because they used the students' first language as the basis for English vocabulary development (August et al., 2009; Carlo et al., 2004; Perozzi, 1985; Roberts, 2008; Ulanoff & Pucci, 1999). Other approaches that were tailored to ELLs explicitly addressed concepts in the texts seen as potentially confusing to second language learners

(Pérez, 1981) and used visual aids and motor activities to reinforce word meaning (Roberts & Neal, 2004; Silverman, 2007; Silverman & Hines, 2009).

Reading Comprehension

Reading comprehension is the essence and goal of reading. It depends on decoding, vocabulary knowledge, and general language ability, including listening comprehension. The NRP found that comprehension could be facilitated with explicit teaching in comprehension itself (National Institute of Child Health and Human Development, 2000). In other words, students benefited from instruction in combinations of reading comprehension strategies in which students intentionally try to make sense of and remember the text information by summarizing, questioning, monitoring, visualizing, and performing other similar actions. However, success with these strategies would depend on English proficiency, something that ELLs by definition have not attained.

The studies of approaches to improving comprehension varied quite a bit for ELL students. Some studies emphasized instructional techniques that emphasized meaning and language development, including enriched book environments within the school day (Elley, 1991; Koskinen et al., 2000; Roberts & Neal, 2004) or in after school programs (Tudor & Hafiz, 1989), enhanced discussion emphases (Saunders & Goldenberg, 1999; Tharp, 1982), or intensive word meaning study (Perez, 1981). The instruction examined in other studies included strong doses of phonics. Generally, meaning-oriented instruction had a greater impact on reading comprehension than decoding-oriented interventions, although these also worked, highlighting the need for comprehensive approaches to instruction for ELLs.

Other techniques shown to be effective for ELLs included building background knowledge by previewing key vocabulary through definitions and context-rich sentences, providing brief story introductions that included details from the story (Liang, Peterson, & Graves, 2005), questioning students throughout the reading to help connect new text with the students' experiences and to clarify students' understanding of the meaning of the passages (Saunders & Goldenberg, 1999; Tharp, 1982), and showing students video clips that helped contextualize the story to be read (Roberts & Neal, 2004).

Writing

Writing has been a neglected part of literacy. Recent studies and a renewed emphasis on writing within school educational standards have led to a renewed interest in writing instruction (Miller, McCardle, & Long, 2014). Recent meta-analyses have revealed the most effective approaches to teaching writing to native English speakers (Graham & Perin, 2007), as well as the value of writing activity in developing student reading comprehension (Graham &

Hebert, 2010). As with the other literacy components, there have been far fewer studies of ELLs. Those studies that have been carried out have considered the effectiveness of encouraging after school reading and writing (Tudor & Hafiz, 1989), the Sheltered Instruction Observation Protocol model (Echevarria, Short, & Powers, 2006), word processing (Silver & Repa, 1993), collaborative writing (Prater & Bermudez, 1993), and structured writing (Gómez, Parker, Lara-Alecio, & Gómez, 1996). Most of these writing studies focused on older students (Grade 4 and higher); only one was carried out in the primary grades, and these students were followed from Grade 2 through Grade 5 (Saunders & Goldenberg, 1999).

Two studies demonstrated that ELLs' writing can be improved by explicit instruction on how to revise (Prater & Bermudez, 1993; Sengupta, 2000). A study of word processing (Silver & Repa, 1993) found that using a computer to complete writing assignments improved the quality of beginning ELLs' writing in comparison with their peers who used a pencil and paper.

There were several studies in which students wrote collaboratively; these had mixed results, suggesting that such collaboration may be more effective when combined with explicit teacher-directed instruction, including providing models of effective writing and targeted feedback to support writing revision (Franken & Haslett, 1999; Gómez et al., 1996; Prater & Bermudez, 1993).

Three studies evaluated comprehensive models designed to promote both reading and writing development among ELLs. Although these models may have included some of the elements of effective writing instruction emphasized by Graham and Perin (2007), they also included special design elements aimed at the needs of ELLs. The first indicated that the Sheltered Instruction Observation Protocol model, a model that emphasizes strategies and techniques to make new information comprehensible to ELLs, can improve students' writing (Echevarria et al., 2006). The second showed that the Pathway Project, which focuses on using a cognitive-strategies approach to reinforce the reading–writing connection, encourages the writing development of ELLs (Olson & Land, 2007). Finally, as reported earlier, Saunders and Goldenberg (1999) showed that ELLs' writing improved when they participated in a multiyear transitional bilingual program with enhanced literacy instruction, although some of this assessment was conducted in Spanish.

Other Aspects of Instruction

It is evident that curricula should support explicit instruction in key components of literacy. Teaching phonological awareness, phonics, vocabulary, oral reading fluency, comprehension, and writing can all reap benefits for ELLs. In addition, we identified some important cross-cutting themes that emerged from this review. Repetition and reinforcement, scaffolding, and capitalizing on first language strengths are all techniques that have been shown to be helpful in instructing EEL students.

Differentiating Instruction

It is important to keep in mind the many different factors that influence ELL students' development of literacy: age of arrival in a new country, educational history, socioeconomic status, and cognitive capacity (August & Shanahan, 2006). This point is highlighted by the differential effects of instruction on students of different ages with differing degrees of English proficiency (Neuman & Koskinen, 1992) and with varied abilities to read (Koskinen et al., 2000). There is little research that provides guidance about how to accommodate the diverse needs of students within a single classroom or school, but some of the studies provided clues as to how to successfully differentiate instruction for ELLs: building on first language proficiency and literacy (e.g., Carlo et al., 2004); considering levels of English proficiency (Neuman & Koskinen, 1992; Saunders & Goldenberg, 1999); accommodating the needs of older, recently arrived learners (Swanson, Hodson, & Schommer-Aikins, 2005); and taking into account individual differences in learning ability and rates (Slavin & Madden, 1999). The most effective instruction of ELLs will depend on sound information on the basis of which to vary the degree and type of instructional support that is provided. Teachers should have a way to find out a student's level of English proficiency and current first and second language reading skills (including skills in the various components already discussed). It would also be beneficial if the teacher had access to information about the similarities and differences between the student's first language and English.

Repetition and Reinforcement

Reinforcement of learned material with repeated exposures to words, concepts, and skills is known to effectively strengthen learning. In the research on ELLs, this reinforcement often consisted of revisiting material in ways that differed from the initial encounter. Some examples are reinforcing new word meaning through realia, drama and art activities, or a picture sequencing activity (Roberts & Neal, 2004); having students respond to questions using words from the story (Tharp, 1982); using choral repetition of target words (Silverman, 2007); and repeated reading that includes the target words (Biemiller & Boote, 2006). Carlo et al. (2004) reinforced word knowledge with a variety of postreading activities with target vocabulary, including cloze tasks that drew students' attention to the multiple meanings of some words, word association tasks, synonym–antonym tasks, and semantic feature analyses. To further reinforce learning, they also recycled learned words in later lessons. Surely, the amount of guided and varied repetition was a key part of why these instructional efforts were helpful to ELLs; repetition need not be boring and clearly can aid learning.

Literacy learning requires a deep immersion in written language, and many native English speaking students gain access to this through the combination of their home and school experiences. However, ELLs are less likely to have such access to English language materials and experiences away from school, so increasing the amount of repetition and review provides them with more equal access to literacy experience.

Scaffolding

Scaffolding refers to the support teachers provide that allows students to succeed in tasks that are beyond their independent abilities. With this teacher guidance and support, students can increase or extend their skills. Examples of successful scaffolding techniques include creating opportunities for children to act out meanings of words and using visual aids to illustrate the meanings of words in contexts beyond those in which the words were introduced (Silverman, 2007); using pictures to build students' early phonological awareness skills (Gerber et al., 2004); aligning reading materials to children's levels of reading proficiency with supports before and during reading, creating opportunities for teacher–student interaction around books to make them comprehensible during reading (Koskinen et al., 2000); providing a model of a process, task, or assignment before requiring students to undertake it; previewing material before questioning students; and using graphic organizers (Echevarria, Vogt, & Short, 2004).

Capitalizing on First Language Strengths

The most obvious difference between ELLs and their monolingual counterparts is that in addition to working through the school curriculum, ELLs have to learn another language, English, at the same time, and their school curriculum is in that other language. It is important, though, to remember that these students do have language skills in their home languages. Research confirms the value of approaches that use students' first language to help them become literate in the second language (Francis et al., 2006), and evidence suggests that there is a relationship between many literacy skills in the second language and knowledge acquired in children's first language (Dressler & Kamil, 2006).

In our review of research on ELLs' language and literacy, there were instructional routines that, though focused on the teaching of English, made effective use of the students' native languages. Examples of these instructional routines include previewing and reviewing storybook reading in students' first language (Liang et al., 2005; Ulanoff & Pucci, 1999), conducting instructional conversations that permit some interpretation to take place in the home language (Saunders & Goldenberg, 1999), using bilingual glossaries for the targeted vocabulary (Carlo et al., 2004), and providing instruction on the transfer of cognate knowledge from a first language to a second (Carlo et al., 2004).

Conclusions and Implications for School Psychologists

It is clear that there are many things that can be done to enhance the literacy learning of ELL students. Some are specific actions for this population, such as using the home language as the basis of instruction or providing ELLs with feedback on grammatical errors that result from their limited English proficiency. There are also many things that can be done that are not specialized at all but are just good teaching practices with greater intensity of effort, such as providing sufficient repetition and reinforcement, differentiating individual and small group teaching, and offering adequate scaffolding.

School psychologists are often the first allied health or education professionals consulted when a student's performance is lagging behind expectations or when placement is considered for new students. They are key professionals in the assessment process and in the diagnosis of learning or behavioral problems students may be experiencing. Moreover, school psychologists can consult with teachers to help with problem solving by suggesting interventions that might support ELLs who are in need of additional help. Finally, they should serve as consultants to school principals and other professionals, both regarding instruction and intervention and in policy development, implementation, and interpretation. In all of these roles, the school psychologist can help ensure that student assessments are fair; that students are assessed in both their home language and in English; that efforts are made to provide an adequate learning environment while ELL students are learning English; and that teachers understand students' needs for additional scaffolding, the value of repetition and reinforcement, and how important it is to know something about the student's first language and home culture.

References

August, D., Branum-Martin, L., Cardenas-Hagan, E., & Francis, D. (2009). The impact of an instructional intervention on the science and language learning of middle grades English language learners. *Journal of Research on Educational Effectiveness, 2,* 345–376.

August, D., & Shanahan, T. (2006). *Developing literacy in second-language learners: Report of the National Literacy Panel on language-minority children and youth.* Mahwah, NJ: Lawrence Erlbaum Associates.

August, D., & Shanahan, T. (2008). *Developing reading and writing in second-language learners.* New York, NY: Routledge.

Biemiller, A., & Boote, A. (2006). An effective method for building meaning vocabulary in primary grades. *Journal of Educational Psychology, 98*, 44–62.

Calhoon, M. B., Al Otaiba, S., Cihak, D., King, A., & Avalos, A. (2007). Effects of peer-mediated program on reading skill acquisition for two-way bilingual first-grade classrooms. *Learning Disability Quarterly, 30*, 169–184.

Carlo, M. S., August, D., McLaughlin, B., Snow, C. E., Dressler, C., Lippman, D., ... White, C. (2004). Closing the gap: Addressing the vocabulary needs of English language learners in bilingual and mainstream classrooms. *Reading Research Quarterly, 39*, 188–215.

Denton, C. A., Wexler, J., Vaughn, S., & Bryan, D. (2008). Intervention provided to linguistically divest middle school students with severe reading difficulties. *Learning Disabilities Research & Practice, 23*, 79–89.

Dressler, C., & Kamil, M. (2006). First- and second-language literacy. In D. August & T. Shanahan (Eds.), *Developing literacy in second-language learners: Report of the National Literacy Panel on Language-Minority Children and Youth* (pp. 197–238). Mahwah, NJ: Lawrence Erlbaum Associates.

Echevarria, J., Short, D., & Powers, K. (2006). School reform and standards-based education: A model for English language learners. *Journal of Educational Research, 99*(4), 195–211.

Echevarria, J., Vogt, M. E., & Short, D. (2004). *Making content comprehensible to English learners: The SIOP model.* Boston, MA: Allyn & Bacon.

Elley, W. B. (1991). Acquiring literacy in a second language: The effect of book-based programs. *Language Learning, 41*, 375–411.

Francis, D., Lesaux, N., & August, D. (2006). Language of Instruction. In D. August & T. Shanahan (Eds.), *Developing literacy in second-language learners* (pp. 365–414). Mahwah, NJ: Lawrence Erlbaum Associates.

Franken, M., & Haslett, S. J. (1999). Quantifying the effect of peer interaction on second language students' written argument texts. *New Zealand Journal of Educational Studies, 34*(2), 281–293.

Gerber, J., Jimenez, T., Leafstedt, J., Villaruz, J., Richards, C., & English, J. (2004). English reading effects of small-group intensive intervention in Spanish for K–1 English learners. *Learning Disabilities Research & Practice, 19*, 239–251.

Giambo, D. A., & McKinney, J. D. (2004). The effects of a phonological awareness intervention on the oral English proficiency of Spanish-speaking kindergarten children. *TESOL Quarterly, 38*(1), 95–117.

Gómez, R., Jr., Parker, R., Lara-Alecio, R., & Gómez, L. (1996). Process versus product writing with limited English proficient students. *Bilingual Research Journal, 20*, 209–233.

Graham, S., & Hebert, M. (2010). *Writing to read: Evidence for how writing can improve reading.* New York, NY: Carnegie.

Graham, S., & Perin, D. (2007). A meta-analysis of writing instruction for adolescent students. *Journal of Educational Psychology, 99*, 445–476.

Gunn, B., Biglan, A., Smolkowski, K., & Ary, D. (2000). The efficacy of supplemental instruction in decoding skills for Hispanic and non-Hispanic students in early elementary school. *Journal of Special Education, 34,* 90–103.

Gunn, B., Smolkowski, K., Biglan, A., & Black, C. (2002). Supplemental instruction in decoding skills for Hispanic and non-Hispanic students in early elementary school: A follow-up. *Journal of Special Education, 36,* 69–79.

Gunn, B., Smolkowski, K., Biglan, A., Black, C., & Blair, J. (2005). Fostering the development of reading skill through supplemental instruction: Results for Hispanic and non-Hispanic students. *Journal of Special Education, 39,* 66–85.

Gutiérrez, K. D., Zepeda, M., & Castro, D. C. (2010). Advancing early literacy learning for all children: Implications of the NELP report for dual-language learners. *Educational Researcher, 39,* 334–339.

Kamps, D., Abbott, M., Greenwood, C., Arreaga-Mayer, C., Wills, H., Lonstaff, J., … Walton, C. (2007). Use of evidence-based, small-group reading instruction for English language learners in elementary grades: Secondary-tier intervention. *Learning Disability Quarterly, 30,* 153–168.

Koskinen, P. S., Blum, I. H., Bisson, S. A., Phillips, S. M., Creamer, T. S., & Baker, T. K. (2000). Book access, shared reading, and audio models: The effects of supporting the literacy learning of linguistically diverse students in school and at home. *Journal of Educational Psychology, 92,* 23–36.

Kramer, V. R., Schell, L. M., & Rubison, R. M. (1983). Auditory discrimination training in English of Spanish-speaking children. *Reading Improvement, 20,* 162–168.

Lee, J., Grigg, W., & Donahue, P. (2007). *The nation's report card: Reading 2007* (NCES 2007–496). Washington, DC: National Center for Education Statistics, Institute of Education Sciences, U.S. Department of Education.

Lesaux, N. K., Kieffer, M. J., Faller, S. E., & Kelley, J. G. (2010). The effectiveness and ease of implementation of an academic vocabulary intervention for linguistically diverse students in urban middle schools. *Reading Research Quarterly, 45,* 196–228.

Lesaux, N. K., Kieffer, M. J., Kelley, J. G., & Harris, R. J. (2014). Effects of academic vocabulary instruction for linguistically diverse adolescents: Evidence from a randomized field trial. *American Educational Research Journal.* Retrieved from http://aer.sagepub.com/content/early/2014/04/25/0002831214532165.abstract?rss=1

Liang, L. A., Peterson, C. A., & Graves, M. F. (2005). Investigating two approaches to fostering children's comprehension of literature. *Reading Psychology, 26,* 387–400.

Lovett, M. W., De Palma, M., Frijters, J., Steinbach, K., Temple, M., Benson, N., & Lacerenza, L. (2008). Interventions for reading difficulties: A comparison of response to intervention by ELL and EFL struggling readers. *Journal of Learning Disabilities, 41,* 333–352.

McMaster, K. L., Kung, S., Han, I., & Cao, M. (2008). Peer-assisted learning strategies: A "Tier 1" approach to promoting English learners' response to intervention. *Exceptional Children, 74,* 194–214.

Miller, B., McCardle, P., & Long, R. (2014). *Teaching reading and writing.* Baltimore, MD: Brookes.

National Institute of Child Health and Human Development. (2000). Report of the National Reading Panel. *Teaching children to read: An evidence-based assessment of the scientific research literature on reading and its implications for reading instruction: Reports of the subgroups* (NIH Publication No. 00-4754). Retrieved from http://www.nichd.nih.gov/publications/nrp/report.htm

Neuman, S. B., & Koskinen, P. (1992). Captioned television as comprehensible input: Effects of incidental word learning from context for language minority students. *Reading Research Quarterly, 27,* 94–106.

Olson, C. B., & Land, R. (2007). A cognitive strategies approach to reading and writing instruction for English language learners in secondary school. *Research in the Teaching of English, 41,* 269–303.

Pérez, E. (1981). Oral language competence improves reading skills of Mexican American third graders. *The Reading Teacher, 35*(1), 24–27.

Perozzi, J. A. (1985). A pilot study of language facilitation for bilingual, language-handicapped children: Theoretical and approach implications. *Journal of Speech & Hearing Disorders, 50,* 403–406.

Prater, D. L., & Bermudez, A. B. (1993). Using peer response groups with limited English proficient writers. *Bilingual Research Journal, 17,* 99–116.

Roberts, T. (2008). Home storybook reading in primary or second language with preschool children: Evidence of equal effectiveness for second-language vocabulary acquisition. *Reading Research Quarterly, 43,* 103–130.

Roberts, T., & Neal, H. (2004). Relationships among preschool English language learners' oral proficiency in English, instructional experience and literacy development. *Contemporary Educational Psychology, 29,* 283–311.

Saunders, W. M., & Goldenberg, C. (1999). Effects of instructional conversations and literature logs on limited- and fluent-English proficient students' story comprehension and thematic understanding. *Elementary School Journal, 99,* 277–301.

Sengupta, S. (2000). An investigation into the effects of revision strategy instruction on L2 secondary school learners. *System, 28*(1), 97–113.

Shanahan, T., & Beck, I. L. (2006). Effective literacy teaching for English language learners. In D. August & T. Shanahan (Eds.), *Developing literacy in second-language learners: Report of the National Literacy Panel on Language-Minority Children and Youth* (pp. 415–488). Mahwah, NJ: Erlbaum.

Silver, N. W., & Repa, J. T. (1993). The effect of word processing on the quality of writing and self-esteem of secondary school English-as-a-second-language students: Writing without censure. *Journal of Educational Computing Research, 9,* 265–283.

Silverman, R. D. (2007). Vocabulary development of English-language and English-only learners in kindergarten. *Elementary School Journal, 107,* 365–383.

Silverman, R., & Hines, S. (2009). The effects of multimedia-enhanced instruction on the vocabulary of English-language learners and non-English-language learners in pre-kindergarten through second grade. *Journal of Educational Psychology, 101,* 305–314.

Slavin, R. E., & Madden, N. (1999). Effects of bilingual and English as a second language adaptations of success for all on the reading achievement of students acquiring English. *Journal of Education for Students Placed at Risk, 4,* 393–416.

Swanson, T. J., Hodson, B. W., & Schommer-Aikins, M. (2005). An examination of phonological awareness treatment outcomes for seventh-grade poor readers from a bilingual community. *Language, Speech, and Hearing Services in Schools, 36,* 336–345.

Tharp, R. G. (1982). The effective instruction of comprehension: Results and descriptions of the Kamehameha Early Education Program. *Reading Research Quarterly, 17,* 503–527.

Tudor, I., & Hafiz, F. (1989). Extensive reading as a means of input to L2 learning. *Journal of Research in Reading, 12,* 164–178.

Ulanoff, S. H., & Pucci, S. L. (1999). Learning words from books: The effects of read-aloud on second language vocabulary acquisition. *Bilingual Research Journal, 23,* 409–422.

U.S. Department of Education, National Center for Education Statistics, Common Core of Data. (2014). *ElSitableGenerator: Selected years, 2000 through 2012.* Retrieved from http://nces.ed.gov/ccd/elsi/tableGenerator.aspx

VanWagenen, M. A., Williams, R. L., & McLaughlin, T. F. (1994). Use of assisted reading to improve reading rate, word accuracy, and comprehension with ESL Spanish-speaking students. *Perceptual and Motor Skills, 79,* 227–230.

Vaughn, S., Martinez, L. R., Linan-Thompson, S., Reutebuch, C. K., Carlson, C. D., & Francis, D. J. (2009). Enhancing social studies vocabulary and comprehension for seventh-grade English language learners: Findings from two experimental studies. *Journal of Research on Educational Effectiveness, 2,* 297–324.

Part III   Universal Design for Learning

Topics for Further Discussion

1. How would you implement DI for engaging students with disabilities? What would you incorporate into the lessons when considering UDL as a strategy?
2. How do you view the three-tiered model of UDL? How would you use UDL to engage students with disabilities in inclusive classrooms?
3. How would you apply variations in learning to UDL? What strategies would you include, and how would you make decisions about teaching students with disabilities?
4. As a beginning teacher, how would you engage elementary students with disabilities in each of the core subjects? How would you develop strategies for school success?
5. In what ways do you think students with disabilities can benefit from UDL? How would you develop successful lessons for these individuals, who have a wide range of abilities?

In Closing

Now that you have completed the readings for the course, I hope you have learned a great deal about working with children with special needs. You should be able to understand how to accommodate these individuals and how to modify instruction for them in order to enable their success in your class. You should have learned how to make the classroom material more rewarding for this population, and you should have observed their successes.

Chances are that as you begin your student teaching—and, more importantly, as you teach in your own classrooms—you will find a student with an IEP who needs your help. Hopefully, what you learned in this class will better prepare you for those opportunities and will help you take ownership of making sure all children learn. As you get ready to teach, think about your students and about what motivates them to learn. Be willing to reach out, and to learn all you can about pedagogy and apply this in your classroom, to ensure student success.

Topics for Further Discussion

1. Why do you think it is important to develop literacy in English Language Learners? What suggestions do you have for differentiating the curriculum and incorporating UDL into the curriculum?
2. What similarities and differences do you see between DI and UDL? How do these play into teaching the child with special needs?
3. How do you think we can implement theory and practice in developing lessons using DI and UDL? How would you create lessons for students with disabilities, so they have the opportunity to learn?
4. How would you use DI and UDL for teaching English Language Learners? How would you develop lessons that are appropriate, especially for those students with disabilities?
5. What do you see as your role in teaching students with disabilities in the inclusive classroom? How would you meet the needs of these students, and how would you make decisions about teaching these individuals?